Memory and Society

Memory and Society explores the social factors which influence human memory and our conceptualisation of memory. It examines the relationships between memory, society and culture and considers the relevance of theories of memory to real world issues.

The opening part deals with the topic of autobiographical memory. It looks at the role of the self; how the self is shaped by society but also how it is the self which encodes and constructs memories. The reconstructive nature of episodic memory is considered and how the present acts as the basis for remembering the past, with the rememberer's beliefs, desires and interpretations playing a central role.

The middle part looks at the influence of the social environment on learning. It debates the relevance of the application of basic principles gained in laboratory settings to learning and memory in social settings. These principles are used to throw light on topics such as e-learning, eyewitness testimonies and optimal treatment and thinking. Moreover, these real world scenarios are themselves used to throw light on basic principles and how they can be improved.

The final part looks at the social consequences and costs of memory deficits, covering normal ageing and pathological changes in old age, memory deficits related to dyslexia, working memory problems in everyday cognition, problems in executive functions in chronic alcoholics, and Korsakoff amnesics. It also examines methods of rehabilitation for everyday life.

Incorporating contributions from leading international authorities in memory research, as well as new data and ideas for the direction of future research, this book will be invaluable to psychologists working in the fields of memory and society.

Lars-Göran Nilsson is the Olof Eneroth Professor of Psychology at Stockholm University, Sweden.

Nobuo Ohta is Professor in the Institute of Psychology at the University of Tsukuba, Japan.

Memory and Society
Psychological perspectives

Edited by
Lars-Göran Nilsson and Nobuo Ohta

Psychology Press
Taylor & Francis Group
HOVE AND NEW YORK

First published 2006 by Psychology Press
27 Church Road, Hove, East Sussex BN3 2FA

Simultaneously published in the USA and Canada
by Psychology Press
270 Madison Avenue, New York NY 10016

Psychology Press is a part of the Taylor & Francis Group

© 2006 Psychology Press

Typeset in Times by RefineCatch Limited, Bungay, Suffolk
Printed and bound in Great Britain by MPG Books Ltd, Bodmin,
Cornwall
Cover design by Hannah Armstrong

This publication has been produced with paper manufactured to strict
environmental standards and with pulp derived from sustainable
forests.

British Library Cataloguing in Publication Data
A catalogue record for this book is available from the British Library

Library of Congress Cataloging in Publication Data
Memory and society : psychological perspectives / [edited by]
Lars-Göran Nilsson and Nobuo Ohta.
  p. cm.
  Includes bibliographical references and index.
  ISBN 1–84169–614–5 (hardcover)
  1. Memory—Social aspects.   I. Nilsson, Lars-Göran, 1944–   II.
  Ohta, Nobuo.
BF378.S65M47 2005
153.1′2—dc22

                                    2005017193

ISBN 10: 1–84169–614–5
ISBN 13: 9–78–184169–614–5

Contents

Contributors

Dietrich Albert, Cognitive Science Section, Department of Psychology, University of Graz, Universitätsplatz 2/III, A-8010 Graz, Austria.

Elizabeth L. Bjork, Department of Psychology, University of California, Los Angeles CA 90095–1563, USA.

Robert A. Bjork, Department of Psychology, University of California, Los Angeles CA 90095–1563, USA.

Martin A. Conway, Department of Psychology, University of Durham, Science Site, South Road, Durham DH1 3LE, UK.

Fergus I. M. Craik, Rotman Research Institute of Baycrest Centre, 3560 Bathurst Street, Toronto, Ontario, Canada M6A 2E1.

Sergio Della Sala, Human Cognitive Neuroscience, University of Edinburgh, Scotland, UK.

Steve Fiore, Department of Psychology, University of Pittsburgh, Pittsburgh, PA 15260, Virginia, USA.

Michael M. Gruneberg, Psychology Department, University of Wales at Swansea, Singleton Park, Swansea SA2 8PP, UK.

Kazunori Hanyu, Department of Psychology, College of Humanities and Sciences, Nihon University, 3–25–40 Sakurajosui, Setagaya-ku 156–8550, Japan.

Satoshi Hara, Faculty of Contemporary Cultures, Department of Psychology, Surugadai University, 98 Azu, Hanno-shi, Saitama 357–8555 Japan.

Douglas J. Herrmann, Psychology Department, Root Hall, Indiana State University, Terre Haute, IN 47809, USA.

Cord Hockemeyer, Cognitive Science Section, Department of Psychology, University of Graz, Universitätsplatz 2/III, A-8010 Graz, Austria.

Yuji Itoh, Department of Psychology, Keio University, 2–15–45 Mita, Minato-ku Tokyo, 108 Japan.

Yukio Itsukushima, Department of Psychology, College of Humanities and Sciences, Nihon University, 3–35–40 Sakurajosui, Setagaya-ku 156–8550, Japan.

Susan Joslyn, Department of Psychology, University of Washington, Box 351525, Seattle, WA 98195, USA.

D. Stephen Lindsay, Department of Psychology, University of Victoria, PO Box 3050 STN CSC, Victoria, British Columbia, Canada V8W 3P5.

Robert L. Logie, Human Cognitive Neuroscience, University of Edinburgh, Scotland, UK.

Ingvar Lundberg, Psykologiska Institutionen, Göteborgs Universitet, Box 500, 405 30 Göteborg, Sweden.

Malcom D. MacLeod, School of Psychology, University of St Andrews, St Mary's College, South Street, St Andrews, Fife KY16 9JP, UK.

Masaru Mimura, Department of Neuropsychiatry, Showa University School of Medicine, 1–5–8 Hatanodai, Shinagawa-ku, Tokyo 142–8666, Japan.

Toshiaki Mori, Department of Learning Science, Graduate School of Education, Hiroshima University, Japan.

Makiko Naka, Graduate School of Letters, Hokkaido University, Japan.

Lars-Göran Nilsson, Department of Psychology, Stockholm University, 106 91 Stockholm, Sweden.

Nobuo Ohta, Institute of Psychology, University of Tsukuba, Tsukuba, 305–8572, Japan.

Yasunari Okabe, Research Institute of Science and Technology: Social Psychology Research Group, Japan.

Kathy Pezdek, Department of Psychology, Claremont Graduate University, 123 East State Street, Claremont, CA 91711–6175, USA.

J. Don Read, Simon Fraser University, 8888 University Drive, Burnaby, British Columbia, Canada, V5A 1S6.

Jonathan W. Schooler, 518 Learning Research and Development Center, 3939 O'Hara Street, University of Pittsburgh, Pittsburgh, PA 15260, USA.

Rebecca Torres, Psychology Department, Root Hall, Indiana State University, Terre Haute, IN 47809, USA.

Qi Wang, Department of Human Development, Cornell University, EB14 Martha Van Rensselaer Hall, Ithaca, NY 14853–4401, USA.

Barbara A. Wilson, MRC Cognition and Brain Sciences Unit, Box 58, Addenbrookes Hospital, Cambridge CB2 2QQ, UK.

Introduction: Harmony between principle-seeking and problem-solving research

Nobuo Ohta

Scientific research of human memory began with Herman Ebbinghaus' (1885) experimental studies of learning, forgetting and re-learning of information. Through rigorous experimentations with nonsense syllables, Ebbinghaus was the first to discover some of the basic principles of learning and forgetting and to describe the forgetting curve – the time course of forgetting. Whereas philosophers before Ebbinghaus discussed and speculated about memory, Ebbinghaus experimentally elucidated various aspects of learning and forgetting and communicated his findings to others in precise terms including figures and graphs.

Ebbinghaus started a new era: the era of scientific memory research that enabled researchers to communicate precisely their research methods, findings and, importantly, the conclusions based on those findings. This shift from introspection to rigorous scientific investigative methods fostered communication among researchers and fuelled expansion of new ideas and approaches to memory research.

The history of memory research reveals three major developments: (1) the proliferation and dominance of cognitive approaches; (2) the increased focus on everyday research and on real-life applications of research findings; and (3) the cross-fertilization of ideas and research methods with closely related fields including brain sciences, computer sciences, and linguistics. The cognitive approaches to memory research were pioneered by Sir Frederick Bartlett (1932) who is best known for his development of a mental schema concept. However, the cognitive revolution commenced in earnest with the first information processing models (e.g., Broadbent, 1958) inspired by concurrent developments in computational science and the advent of the first computers. The later milestones in cognitive approaches to memory research include research on the organization of semantic memory (Collins & Quillian, 1969), the development of the concept of working memory (Baddeley & Hitch, 1974), and the distinction between implicit and explicit memory (Schacter & Graf, 1986). Through observable behaviour, the cognitive researchers seek to study mental processes and inner mind.

The second major historical development in memory research is the increased focus and interest on everyday memory research – the study of memory as it occurs in real life – and on applications of research findings to real-life problems. Initially, memory was investigated primarily in laboratory settings using artificial materials and tasks. Some of the earliest studies focusing on remembering in everyday life were conducted by Bartlett (1932) who investigated memory for folk stories. Bartlett emphasized the notion of effort after meaning and argued that we try to make sense of events and remember their interpreted meaning rather than literal representations. From Bartlett's perspective, Ebbinghaus' investigations of how people remember nonsense syllables seemed irrelevant to how they remember folk stories told in everyday life. However, the major turning point towards everyday memory research was demanded by changes in society such as the introduction of technologies and demographic changes. Ulrich Neisser (1976) argued that traditional laboratory-based memory research had little relevance to the demands and functions of memory in everyday life and highlighted the importance of ecological validity of memory research. Today, many researchers investigate memory in everyday life including autobiographical memory, prospective memory, eyewitness memory, emotional memory, and so forth. Others focus on applied problems such as curing memory disorders, developing techniques for improving memory, and designing more effective teaching methods.

The third major development in memory research is the use of increasingly diverse methodologies and collaborations across multiple fields. In recent years we have witnessed the proliferation of new neuroscience methods that have made it possible to investigate brain events such as changes in blood flow that co-occur with mental events. Similarly, the recent exponential increases in affordability as well as the raw computing power of modern computers allowed researchers to develop new complex models of human memory cognition and to test these models with ease. This history demonstrates that memory research has benefited tremendously from the availability of new methods, cross-fertilization of ideas and collaborations across multiple research fields. This trend is reflected in the birth of Cognitive Science as a new field and in the introduction of many new scientific journals devoted to research inspired by ideas and methods from multiple fields.

One reason why traditional memory research has been so influenced by other sciences is that the traditional research had exhausted, in some sense, the limits of purely cognitive methods and run up against a brick wall. The new methods developed in adjacent fields sparked new research aims. The researchers adopted neuroimaging techniques, computer-simulation methods, and so on. Others espoused ideas from related social sciences including social constructionism and evolution theory. Thus, modern memory research has been making progress by adopting methods and ideas from related fields.

Memory research in the 21st century

What will become of the three characteristics describing the first 100 years of memory research in the 21st century? I believe that they will grow more dominant. Cognitive approaches will continue to dominate memory research. Everyday memory research and research focused on solving everyday problems will increase in importance. Advances in related fields will continue to influence memory research.

The characteristics outlined above are related to the continuum between principle-seeking research and problem-solving research. Whereas the former research focus is largely academic, the latter research focus is mostly pragmatic. At one end of the continuum, principle-seeking research seeks to describe memory phenomena and to develop theories, models and laws of memory. At the other end of the continuum, the problem-solving research aims to solve problems arising in the real world. Even though these two research orientations often appear dichotomous on the surface, they are part of the same continuum as most researchers are motivated by both foci at least to some degree.

The first characteristic, the cognitive approach, encourages principle-seeking research. The second characteristic, the focus on everyday memory and real-life applications, facilitates finding solutions to real-life problems. The third characteristic, the use of diverse methods and collaboration with related scientific fields, helps to advance both of these research aims; principle-seeking as well as problem-solving research.

The continuum between principle-seeking and problem-solving research is orthogonal to the continuum between the laboratory and everyday research. Both principle-seeking and problem-solving research can be conducted in laboratories as well as in real-life settings. However, the distinction between principle-seeking and problem-solving research is becoming more important because it highlights researchers' motivation and research goals.

The urgency to focus on problem-solving research is increasing and will continue to increase in the 21st century. The first few years have already presented us with many new problems, problems that seem to be getting more serious and more complicated. Accordingly, there will be greater pressures to focus more resources on solving these everyday problems. However, many researchers will continue to be driven by intellectual curiosity towards the discovery of the principles underlying human behaviour. Our hope is that these two approaches to research will interact in harmony, that principle-seeking research will enlighten pathways towards solving everyday problems and that the everyday problems will provide motives for the principle-solving research.

References

Baddeley, A. D., & Hitch, G. (1974). Working memory. In G. A. Bower (Ed.), *Recent advances in learning and motivation* (Vol. 8). New York: Academic Press.

Bartlett, F. C. (1932). *Remembering: A study in experimental and social psychology.* Cambridge, UK: Cambridge University Press.

Broadbent, D. E. (1958). *Perception and communication.* Oxford, UK: Pergamon.

Collins, A. M., & Quillian, M. R. (1969). Retrieval time from semantic memory. *Journal of Verbal Learning and Verbal Behavior, 8,* 240–247.

Ebbinghaus, H. (1885). *Uber das Gedachtnis.* Leipzig, Germany: Duncker and Humblot.

Neisser, U. (1976). *Cognition and reality.* San Francisco, CA: Freedman.

Schacter, D. L., & Graf, P. (1986). Effects of elaborative processing on implicit and explicit memory for new associations. *Journal of Experimental Psychology: Learning, Memory, & Cognition, 12,* 432–444.

Part I

Self, society, and culture

Lars-Göran Nilsson and Nobuo Ohta

Important memory research is presently being carried out in many laboratories all over the world. Most of this research is directed to the understanding of the structure and function of different forms of memory. This is not an undertaking for cognitive psychologists alone. Scientists from other disciplines are deeply involved as well. Experts on brain imaging techniques and genetics often collaborate with cognitive psychologists in trying to understand memory of the individual at a basic neurobiological level.

Acknowledging the importance of this neuroscientific approach to memory, the present book will point out some other directions that are also of importance for understanding memory, but often neglected in cognitive neuroscience of memory. These other directions often include factors that are much broader than those dealt with in cognitive neuroscience. In one way or another they are related to the society we live in and the general culture that the society is embedded in. At present, such factors are ignored in the neuroscientific approach to memory. Only the future will tell whether any joint enterprise will be possible in the study of such a multifacorial component of the human mind as memory.

The purpose of this book is to bring forward other factors influencing memory, emphasizing factors in society that influence memory. In the first chapter of this first section of the book, Wang and Conway describe the role of self in episodic remembering. As the authors show, including self as a concept in memory theory leads naturally to the insight that society and culture come to play important roles in understanding memory. This domain of episodic remembering goes under the general umbrella term of autobiographical memory. Conway and his colleagues have made important contributions to the understanding of memory by emphasizing the concept of self in autobiographical memory. Self-consciousness has long been conceived of as one unique feature of episodic memory. The notion of self is a way to conceptualize this feature of episodic memory. According to Wang and Conway the self is shaped by society and it is the self that encodes and constructs memories. Autobiographical memory grounds the self in remembered reality. Memory is viewed as the database of the self. Along with others, Wang and Conway conceive of the self as developed, expressed, and reconstructed through narrative creations of the past with temporal and causal dimensions.

A key notion in the chapter by Wang and Conway is that the present forms the basis for remembering the past. Memories of past events are often changed to fit the present and this is a process conceived of as being guided by the self. Wang and Conway illustrate the model proposed with data about childhood amnesia, the reminiscence bump and attachment. Wang and Conway part company with mainstream cognitive neuroscience on explanations in memory research when stating that the impact of the self on personal remembering does not occur in the mind or in the brain but in the context of socio-cultural participation. During such participation individuals actively construct their life stories guided by their culture's presuppositions and perspectives about the self. Wang and Conway review some interesting differences in both self and memory on the basis of cultural differences and propose that early social-linguistic environments are an important source from which children learn to construct life stories in culturally canonical forms. Cultural goals of the family and the society form the beliefs about the purpose of personal remembering. Wang and Conway conclude that the cultural similarities and differences they describe in accessibility, content, and lifespan distribution of autobiographical memory rule out any simple explanation in terms of self, and instead suggest a complex relation between the nature of the self, memory, and culture.

In the same way as Wang and Conway, Joslyn and Schooler argue that the present forms the basis for remembering the past. They suggest a model for memory of previously unremembered life events like abuse. The phenomenon of all of a sudden being able to remember a sexual abuse that occurred a long time ago has been a hot topic in theory and practice for quite some time, and it still is. How can it be possible not to remember such an event for many years and then at a given moment manage to do so? In Freudian terms, some have argued that these memories were repressed in the meantime, in order for the abused person to be able to cope with the fact that the shocking event has occurred. With the help of psychotherapists of various kinds, the abused person has then been able to unlock the repression.

Joslyn and Schooler use a conceptual framework from memory research to explain how it is possible to remember a previously unremembered abusive event. Their key approaches for this are shifts of perspective and a reinterpretation of what a sexual abuse is. They argue that changing the perspective on what to categorize as a sexual abuse can enhance memory by bringing forward additional details. Joslyn and Schooler review two questionnaire studies showing that a large majority of respondents who had reported unwanted sexual experiences as children excluded themselves from belonging to the category of people who had been sexually abused. Despite the fact that they regarded an abstract description of an event as sexual abuse, they did not consider the same event as sexual abuse when personally experienced. Joslyn and Schooler also suggest that poorly categorized events may be recalled less often simply because they are less well connected to autobiographical memory as a whole and hence are accessible by fewer retrieval paths, which is pretty much in line with the thesis put forward by Wang and Conway in their chapter. On the basis of case-study data, Joslyn and Schooler also point out an important methodological issue in questionnaire data that should be seriously considered, namely that the order in which questions are asked can meaningfully impact the responses that individuals provide. Joslyn and Schooler argue that memory for sexual abuse falls into a special category of memory because memories of such social interactions undergo changes in interpretation throughout life more than memory of other social interactions and events. This may certainly be so, but the model proposed by Joslyn and Schooler may provide a good framework for understanding any kind of memory that is now highly salient but was previously forgotten.

Memory is no longer conceived of as a storehouse in which one can search for the event to be remembered and then simply read out from this event if it is found there. Rather, memory is reconstructive and the rememberer's beliefs, desires and interpretations play a major role in this reconstruction. The chapters by Wang and Conway, and Joslyn and Schooler provide strong evidence for this. Lindsay and Read approach the reconstructive notion in their chapter in that they claim that many memory theorists still overestimate the completeness of autobiographical memory and underestimate human susceptibility to reconstructive errors regarding long-past autobiographical events. By this they mean that the episodic information has not disappeared from the brain, the information is still available, but because effective cues are lacking these reconstructive errors occur. The methods used for studying memories of long-past events are based on people's diaries, childhood memories questionnaires, adults' memories of high school, and childhood photographs and false memories and the interview has been the method used to collect data from these sources. Lindsay and Read review the advantages and disadvantages of these methods in a clear way. The overall finding of studies on memory for long-past events, using these methods, is that autobiographical memory is incomplete and easily susceptible to suggestion. One limitation of diary and questionnaire methods is that it is difficult to know whether a certain memory reported actually occurred, but it is interesting to note that participants in these studies frequently report that they had completely forgotten a certain event although this event should, it seems, have affected their lives considerably. These findings have various implications worth noting. For one thing, despite the fact that most people seem to believe that they know their past, at least the most important things in that past, these results show that autobiographical memory is rather incomplete. Another aspect that these data implicate at a more societal level, Lindsay and Read argue, is that it is extremely unwise to assume that an incomplete memory of childhood is indicative of abuse.

The final chapter in this first section of the book by Pezdek is about memory for the traumatic events occurring in New York on 11 September

2001. Pezdek assessed memory for September 11 seven weeks after the event in five samples that varied in their involvement in the event. There were: (1) college students from Manhattan in New York; (2) college students from California; (3) college students from Hawaii; (4) flight attendants from United and American Airlines; and (5) fire fighters from California. Pezdek reports several interesting findings from the study. Perhaps the most interesting of them all is that episodic memory of the events occurring was most accurate in the most involved New York sample whereas autobiographical memory was least accurately reported in this sample. Pezdek interprets these data as showing that the emotional response to the experience was more likely to be attached to the external event than to participants' autobiographical experience of the event. Thus, the external event was more likely to be narratively rehearsed and subsequently more accurately recalled, especially by participants more directly involved. Pezdek's overall conclusion is that it is the synergy of arousal and rehearsal that affects memory for traumatic events.

A common theme in the four chapters of this first section of the book is of course the interest in the specific features of autobiographical memory. However, the four chapters also seem to converge on the notion that memory of the past is based on how the individual conceives of the present, and that this conceptualization of the present is built up in a narrative way throughout life – perhaps in much the same way that a society or a culture is built up by oral or written narrative in that society (Rubin, 1995). Although articles on autobiographical memory often describe dramatic events like sexual abuse and terrorist attacks, the self for most people is built up of rather mundane happenings in the family in conversations at the dinner table, reflections before going to sleep, positive, negative, or mostly neutral events at work. But it is these kinds of moments that make up a life, just like the steady attempts to go on in a society that make up a culture.

Reference

Rubin, D. C. (1995). *Memory in oral traditions*. New York: Oxford University Press.

1 Autobiographical memory, self, and culture

Qi Wang and Martin A. Conway

In this chapter we outline some of our recent work on autobiographical memory in different cultures. The striking similarities and differences that we and others have observed reflect the way in which the focus of the self is shaped by society and, subsequently, how the self encodes and constructs memories in culturally canonical fashions. Our perspective derives from our view of autobiographical memory in which memory is regarded as the database of the self.

Autobiographical memory grounds the self in remembered reality, it constrains what the self can be and in turn is itself constrained by what we call the *working self*, which modulates access to memories. Of especial importance in this model is the notion of motivation or goals, which are viewed as a central component of the working self. It is the highly active complex hierarchy of working self goals that profoundly influences memory accessibility and content and it is this model that we briefly outline first (full accounts can be found in Conway & Pleydell-Pearce, 2000; Conway & Holmes, 2003; or Conway, in press). We then discuss the manifestation of the working self during remembering as exemplified in the phenomena of childhood amnesia, reminiscence bump, and attachment. Then we turn to cross-cultural data to demonstrate how motivation and goals of the working self are rooted in a culture's belief systems, which prioritize some self goals over others. This, in turn, determines which memories and which aspects of the memories are most likely to be accessible and enduring.

Self-memory system model of autobiographical remembering

According to this view long-term memory contains autobiographical memory knowledge structures that are conceptual or semantic in nature. Autobiographical knowledge can be used to access episodic memories. Episodic memories represent sensory-perceptual and conceptual-affective summaries of recent processing derived from short time slices of experience (Conway, 2001, in press). It is proposed that episodic memories are formed when the active goal structure is deactivated or dysfacilitated and another goal structure becomes active, e.g., switching from writing to making a cup of tea.

Thus, dozens, perhaps even hundreds, of episodic memories are formed each day. However, episodic memories do not endure unless they become linked to other representations in long-term memory, especially autobiographical memory knowledge structures, e.g., writing a chapter for the Tsukuba book. And even then only highly goal-relevant memories will become very integrated and endure for long retention intervals. This then is the knowledge base of the self and when autobiographical knowledge becomes associated with episodic memories during memory construction then a specific autobiographical memory is formed.

A memory, then, is a stable but transitory pattern of activation over knowledge structures and episodic memories in long-term memory. This pattern of activation is generated by cues that map on to the content of knowledge structures and episodic memories and which then activate those to which they most closely correspond. For example, returning to this sentence after a tea-break brings to mind memories of thoughts from ten minutes ago. More generally the chapter is a potent cue to the conference in Japan and leads to the recall of specific episodes from that meeting. Day dreaming about pleasant memories of visiting Tsukuba will not, however, facilitate production of this chapter. The working self then refocuses attention on the writing by raising the activation levels of the appropriate goals so that writing is prioritized over day dreaming. In general the working self modulates remembering and mostly acts to inhibit because of the attentional cost of memories entering consciousness. The working self also acts to prioritize access to goal-relevant autobiographical knowledge and it does this by elaborating the cues that are used in intentional acts of remembering to access knowledge. The autobiographical knowledge base and the working self constitute, then, what we have called the *self-memory system* (SMS). In the sections that follow we consider how the SMS, and particularly the goals of the working self, can influence memory accessibility and can in turn be influenced by culture that shapes self-focus and in so doing shapes the goals of the self.

The self and the remembering of the self

Autobiographical memory and self exhibit a dynamic, reciprocal relation. Indeed, as James Mill (1829/2001) pointed out, "The phenomenon of Self and that of Memory are merely two sides of the same fact." On the one side, autobiographical memory plays a central role in constituting one's sense of self. Instead of defining the self as mental (the soul) or physical (the body) substance, many contemporary theorists conceive of the self as developed, expressed, and reconstructed through narrative creations of the past with temporal and causal dimensions (Bruner, 1990; Conway, 1990; McAdams, 1988; Ochs & Capps, 1996; Singer & Salovey, 1993). Autobiographical memory thus provides the substance to the self-construction and serves to facilitate the maintenance of a dynamic self-concept. Loss of memory, which occurs in such situations as memory repression or brain injury, destroys one's personality and deprives life of meaning (Crites, 1986).

On the other hand, the self directs the ways in which autobiographical memories are encoded, represented, organized, and retrieved. Although past events cannot be changed, one often alters memories of those events so as to connect them to the present, the process of which is largely guided by one's current self-concept or working self goals (Conway & Pleydell-Pearce, 2000; Greenwald, 1980; Ross & Wilson, 2000). Indeed, when autobiographical recollections are consistent with one's present sense of self, they are remembered with high confidence and, often, great accuracy (Barclay, 1996). And the recall of inconsistent information tends to appear in distortion and with changes in perspective so that the memory can be fitted into the current working self (Libby & Eibach, 2002; Story, 1998). In addition, events with great self-relevance are generally better remembered (more detailed, more vivid, more persistent, and more readily accessible) than events that are of little or no personal importance (Rogers, Kuiper, & Kirker, 1977; Singer & Salovey, 1993; Thompson, Skowronski, Larsen, & Betz, 1996). Thus, auto-biographical memory and the self are inextricably connected, often in such a way that "the self who constructs the past is changed by the outcome of its own construction" (Bruner & Feldman, 1996, p. 292).

We here focus on the impact of the self on various aspects of remembering processes. Researchers have conducted studies to empirically document the mnemonic effects of the self. Three topics are of particular importance in generating theoretical debates and research findings: childhood amnesia; reminiscence bump; and attachment. We discuss these topics in turn.

Childhood amnesia

Freud (1905/1949) observed among his patients a common inability to access autobiographical events from the earliest years of life, a phenomenon he referred to as *infantile amnesia*. Empirical studies have confirmed the wide existence of this phenomenon, showing that most adults are not able to recall events occurring before age 2 or 3, forget at an accelerated rate experiences that happened before age 5, and yet remember events from age 5 onward with sharply increasing accessibility and elaboration (for reviews, see Pillemer & White, 1989; and Rubin, 2000). Researchers have proposed that the emergence of autobiographical memory is associated with a host of neurological, cognitive, linguistic, and social mechanisms (Conway & Pleydell-Pearce, 2000; Fivush, 1994; Howe & Courage, 1997; Nelson, 1996; Pillemer, 1998; Reese, 2002; Wang, 2003; Wang, Leichtman, & White, 1998).

One important cognitive mechanism proposed by researchers is the development of self-concept, which is thought to be a critical precursor to the offset of childhood amnesia. According to Howe and Courage (1993, 1997), the onset of a cognitive self at about 18 to 24 months, as indicated by mirror self-recognition, provides "a knowledge structure whose features serve to organize memories of experiences that happened to 'me' " (Howe & Courage, 1997, p. 499). The cognitive self is conceived of as a rudimentary form of the conceptual self or self-concept (Neisser, 1988) that continues to evolve with age and experiences. Other researchers (e.g., Foulkes, 1999; Povinelli, 1995; Welch-Ross, 2000) argue that the onset of autobiographical memory requires a more sophisticated self-conceptual system that emerges at about 3½ to 4 years, the same age period from which adults, on average, recall their earliest childhood memories (Pillemer & White, 1989). In spite of the disagreement over the nature and timing of the self required, there is a consensus among the theories that a functional self-system is a prerequisite to the emergence of autobiographical memory. It makes possible the organization of autobiographical information in a structured fashion, thus facilitating the retention of the information in long-term memory.

Evidence for the self-concept account is mixed, however. Reese and colleagues conducted a longitudinal study to empirically test Howe and Courage's (1993, 1997) proposal of the determining role of the cognitive self in the acquisition of autobiographical memory. It was found that individual differences in self-recognition skill at 19 months predicted the abilities of 2½-year-olds to independently report autobiographical events and to share memories with others (Harley & Reese, 1999). However, findings from a follow-up study (Reese, 2002) indicated that this effect was in fact moderated by other factors such as maternal reminiscing style and children's initial language skill. Reese suggests that self-recognition may be only an indirect contributor to later verbal memory of children. Studies by Welch-Ross (2000) on the other hand have yielded preliminary findings showing that the development of an organized self-concept in the preschool years facilitates children's recall of past events. Moreover, from 4 or 5 years of age, children begin to ask such questions as, "What kind of person am I?" when others around start asking them the same questions. Such personal and social processes of forging the basic underpinnings of a sense of identity may further facilitate the development of the autobiographical memory system (Fitzgerald, 1996).

From the present perspective a development of the self system that is of critical importance is that which occurs in the goal structure of the working self. It seems reasonable to assume that at birth the goal structure will be in some relatively unelaborated form and largely dominated by limbic-system drives related to survival, i.e., appetitive, attachment, etc. If we assume that the ability to form episodic memories – summary sensory-perceptual representations of short time-slices of goal-related activities (see Conway, 2001) – is present at least from birth (Conway, in press), then these will be represented in terms of the goals from which they arose. As the self-system develops survival goals become embedded in a more complex and elaborate hierarchy of goals in which goal–sub-goal structures modulate the attainment of limbic goals. The Conway and Pleydell-Pearce (2000) model proposed that memories are encoded and retrieved through the goal structure of the working self and one implication of this, together with the above reasoning (Conway, in press), is that childhood amnesia may arise, at least in part, because of incompatibilities between infant and child/adult goal hierarchies. The idea being that the episodic memories of the infant and very young child are represented in terms of unmodulated survival goals. These are goals that the older child and adult cannot directly access because during the course of development they become embedded in a much more elaborate working self goal hierarchy in which they are not directly accessible. Episodic memories encoded in terms of survival goals cannot then themselves be accessed, perhaps because effective goal-related cues cannot be generated, and hence childhood amnesia results.

The reminiscence bump

The reminiscence bump was first observed by Franklin and Holding (1977; see too Fitzgerald & Lawrence, 1984) and in a meta-analysis further explored and originally named by Rubin and colleagues (Rubin, Wetzler, & Nebes, 1986). The reminiscence bump has been frequently observed since then under a very wide range of procedures, to such an extent that Rubin concluded that it was one of the most reliable phenomena in cognitive psychology (Conway & Rubin, 1993). The reminiscence bump occurs when individuals (aged about 35 years and older) recall specific memories or other types of autobiographical knowledge from across their lifespan, in either free or cued recall. Memories are plotted in terms of age at encoding of the remembered experiences and the resulting lifespan retrieval curve typically takes a form similar to that shown in Figure 1.1 (Rubin, Wetzler, & Nebes, 1986; Rubin, Rahhal, & Poon, 1998). As can be seen in Figure 1.1 the lifespan retrieval curve consists of three components: the period of childhood amnesia (from birth to approximately 5 years of age); the period of the reminiscence bump (from 10 to 30

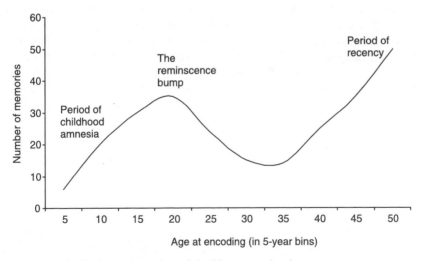

Figure 1.1 Idealized representation of the lifespan retrieval curve.

years); and the period of recency (from the present declining back to the period of the reminiscence bump).

From the present perspective the reminiscence bump is of most interest because it relates to a period when a stable self system finally forms as the individual passes from adolescence into adulthood (cf. Erikson 1950/1963). One theoretical account of the bump is that memories are more accessible from this period because they remain intricately linked to the (final) formation of a stable self and so come to mind first when autobiographical knowledge is sampled across the lifespan by older adults (Conway & Pleydell-Pearce, 2000; Holmes & Conway, 1999; see Rubin et al., 1998, for a review of other theoretical perspectives on the bump). Indeed, Conway and Holmes (2003) found that in older adults there may be several "bumps" across the lifespan each consisting of raised accessibility to memories of events in which major experiences relating to the existential problems of that period of life had occurred, e.g., from the period of middle-age older adults recalled more events to do with generativity-stagnation than with other psychosocial themes (see Erikson, 1950/1963). Thus, there appeared to be a powerful connection between the goals of the self and the accessibility of memories over the lifespan.

Attachment

According to Bowlby (1973), infants form internal working models about themselves and their caregivers through dyadic interactions early in life. They then use these models to organize information related to their emotional bonds with significant others and to form expectations and predictions of others' behaviour and affect. In a relationship of secure attachment where the caregiver responds to the infant in a sensitive, responsive, and consistent manner, the internal working model tends to be coherently organized and highly predictable. In contrast, unfavourable interaction patterns in an insecure relationship may render the young child vulnerable to the development of multiple internal working models of the attachment figure and the self. These simultaneously existing but incompatible working models may impede the insecurely attached individual's ability to perceive and remember personal experiences. Main (1991) found that, compared to children with insecure attachment styles, secure 10-year-olds were better able to access personal life events and recalled more and earlier memories. In addition, secure adults also seemed to have easier access to childhood memories than insecure adults in the Adult Attachment Interview.

In a recent study we investigated the relation between attachment style and recollection of early childhood events (Conway, Wang, & Hou, unpublished raw data). The sample consisted of 349 college students from the USA (all Caucasian), England, Russia, and China. Participants were asked to recall within a 5-minute period as many childhood memories as they could about events occurring before age 5. They then rated each of their memories on several dimensions and filled out a self-assessment attachment questionnaire (Hazan & Shaver, 1987), where they read three attachment descriptions (dismissing, secure, preoccupied) and chose the one that best described themselves. There was no significant culture or gender difference in attachment styles. However, further one-way ANOVAs examining each of the memory measures as a function of attachment style revealed intriguing findings. As expected, participants with secure attachments (M = 10.13, SD = 5.06) provided a greater number of childhood memories than did those with dismissing (M = 8.36, SD = 4.85) or preoccupied (M = 8.67, SD = 4.96) attachments. In addition, securely attached participants rated their memories as more vivid, more positive, and more being remembered on their own than did those who were preoccupied. These findings provided further evidence of a relation between aspects of the early self system and memory accessibility in later life.

Self and memory in the context of culture

The impact of the self on personal remembering does not just occur in the mind or in the brain. Instead, it takes place in the context of social-cultural participation during which individuals actively experience and construct their life stories guided by their culture's presuppositions and perspectives about selfhood (Bruner, 1990, 2002; Wang, 2001a; Wang & Brockmeier, 2000). The prevailing views of the self in each society may shape the ways in which the self manifests in the process of remembering (Mullen, 1994; Wang, 2001a; Wang et al., 1998). The societal emphasis on individuality and personal sufficiency in many Western cultures, particularly in the USA, promotes the development and expression of an autonomous sense of self. Individuals are encouraged to attend to their private beliefs, attributes, and personality traits in order to maintain their independence from other people, social groups, or interpersonal contexts. In contrast, the great emphasis on group solidarity and interpersonal connectedness in many East-Asian cultures facilitates the development of a relational sense of self. Individuals are expected to be attuned to significant social roles, duties, and responsibilities that constitute the critical features of one's self (Geertz, 1973; Kagitcibasi, 1996; Markus & Kitayama, 1991). Importantly, these differences in cultural self-construct should be viewed as only a matter of degree such that the self in any given society is bound to comprise both autonomy and relatedness, with the relative salience and prominence of each component differing markedly across cultures (e.g., Barth, 1997; Harter, 1998; Spiro, 1993; Wang & Li, 2003).

As an overarching mental schema, the cultural self-construct seems to have profound effects on "the ways in which knowledge about self and other is processed, organized, and retrieved from memory" (Markus & Kitayama, 1991, p. 232). It shapes individuals' anticipations, perceptions, interpretations, emotions, and motivations during an ongoing event and subsequent remembering and/or recounting of the event. Consequently, it affects both the accessibility and the content of autobiographical memories across cultures.

Memory accessibility

An autonomous self that focuses on the individual as a centrally important agent authoring life experiences may exert a powerful facilitating effect on the development of an organized, durable memory system. Specifically, the emphasis on individuality will not only enact in the larger social sphere but also be present in interactions with infants and children, which may drive the early emergence of an articulated, autonomous self: one that is structured and verbal and serves to organize experiences that happened to "me". In contrast, a self-construct focusing on community rather than agency may de-emphasize individuality and promote cultural practices of social integration and dependence. Under such influences the development of an autonomous and structured self-system (which would include autobiographical memory, see Conway & Pleydell-Pearce, 2000) would not be prioritized and this might lead to a longer period of childhood amnesia.

The nature of the self, its focus (agentic versus communal), and concomitant development may then influence individuals' ability to retrieve their earliest childhood memories typically accessible in a culture (see Wang, 2003, for a review). Indeed, research has already established that when asked to recall their earliest childhood memory, Asians, including native Koreans and Chinese and overseas Asians, report events dating from more than 6 months later than do Europeans and European Americans, who remember earliest events occurring, on average, at age 3½ (MacDonald, Uesiliana, & Hayne, 2000; Mullen, 1994; Wang, 2001a). To determine whether cultural self-construct has a more widespread influence on a range of earliest memories, rather than just on the first memory, we recently conducted a study using an exhaustive-search method. Participants recalled as many childhood memories (of events occurring below the age of 5 years, including their earliest memory) as they could in a 5-minute period (Wang, Conway, & Hou, 2004). This method allowed us to examine the earliest age of recall (thus replicating previous cross-cultural studies) and assess adults' ability to access memories from the period of infantile amnesia more generally. Three hundred and two college students participated, 101 from the USA (all Caucasian, 76 females, 25 males), 104 from England (87 females, 17 males), and 97 from China (47 females, 50 males). We chose to focus on the three culture groups because they differ in the degree to which they value individuality and an autonomous self. American culture puts a prime value on personal autonomy and self-sufficiency, qualities that are also emphasized but less strongly so in English culture and the least in Chinese culture, which promotes interdependence and a relational self (Hofstede, 1980; Hsu, 1970).

The resulting retrieval curve is shown in Figure 1.2 for each culture. All culture groups showed the phenomenon of childhood amnesia. That is, they all retrieved very little memory information from the first 2 to 3 years of life, and all showed increasing ability to recall events occurring in the later part of the 5-year period. However, US participants recalled the greatest

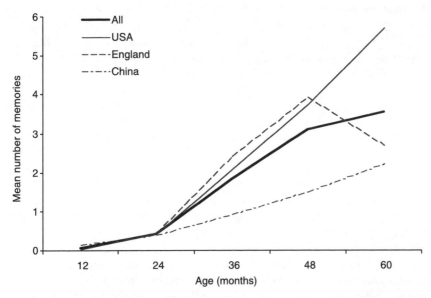

Figure 1.2 Memory retrieval curves as a function of culture and age of the memory.

number of childhood memories (M = 12.24, SD = 5.47) and showed the greatest age-linked increase in memory accessibility, followed by British participants (M = 9.83, SD = 4.45), and then Chinese (M = 5.68, SD = 1.68). In addition, consistent with previous findings (MacDonald et al., 2000; Mullen, 1994; Wang, 2001a), Chinese participants' earliest childhood memories (M = 37.60, SD = 12.01) were approximately 6 months later than their Western counterparts who, in turn, did not differ (USA M = 32.37, SD = 9.32; England M = 31.00, SD = 7.34). Thus, childhood amnesia differs in the degree of severity across cultures, with Chinese showing the strongest effect and Caucasian-Americans the weakest and the English group falling in-between.

Thus, an autonomous self-construct may prioritize the early formation of a unique, detailed and articulate personal history, resulting in earlier first memories and more childhood memories generally. It seems that the powerful emphasis on individuality in Western cultures, particularly in the USA, has positive consequences on the retention of childhood autobiographical memories. These early memories may be functionally important for the individuals in reaffirming the self as a unique, autonomous entity (Mullen, 1994; Pillemer, 1998; Wang, 2001a). Moreover, the autonomous self-focus that will endure over the lifespan as favoured by the pertinent cultural context will be represented by goals of the working self, e.g., goals of mastery, independence, and adventure, and so provided a structure that can be used to access earliest memories.

In a related study (Conway, Wang, Hanyu, & Haque, 2005), we tested the phenomenon of reminiscence bump in five different culture groups: Japan (19 females, 14 males), Bangladesh (15 females, 25 males), England (11 females, 17 males), China (32 females, 22 males), and the USA (44 females, 10 males, all Caucasians). All participants were in the age range of 38 to 60 years, mean age was 52 years. They were asked to fill out a questionnaire in which they free recalled, described, and dated twenty specific autobiographical memories from any period of their lives. When memories were plotted in terms of age-at-encoding, highly similar lifespan memory retrieval curves were observed: the periods of childhood amnesia and the reminiscence bump were the same across cultures (Figure 1.3). However, consistent with the findings we described earlier, the US sample recalled a greater number of childhood memories than any other group. They also recalled reliably fewer memories from the period of the reminiscence bump. This bias towards the retrieval of childhood autobiographical memories at the expense of recall of memories from adolescence and early adulthood suggests potentially important differences in the development of the relation between memory and self in North American culture compared with other cultures. In particular it suggests a preoccupation with individuality from the earliest age, a preoccupation that must feature in interaction between the infant and its caregivers.

Memory content

As cognitive theories suggest (Conway & Pleydell-Pearce, 2000; Markus, 1977; Neisser, 1994; Thompson et al., 1996), the way in which the self is structured – e.g., which aspects of self-related information are active, well-elaborated, salient and accessible – influences how autobiographical memory

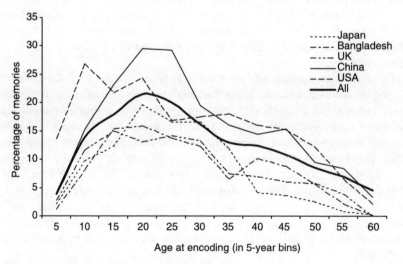

Figure 1.3 Lifespan retrieval curves from five countries.

is represented, evaluated, and reconstructed over time. Individuals with a salient autonomous self-focus may be particularly sensitive and responsive to event information unique to the self and with the self being the leading player (e.g., "the time I was elected as the class president"). In contrast, individuals who focus on the relational aspects of the self may be more attuned to information about social interactions and collective activities (e.g., "going to church with family every Sunday"), with exclusively self-focused information being less salient to them (Wang et al., 1998).

To test this hypothesis, Wang (2001a) conducted a study in which 256 Caucasian-American and Chinese college students reported their earliest childhood memory on a memory questionnaire and provided self-descriptions on a shortened Twenty Statements Test (TST) (Kuhn & McPartland, 1954). The average age at earliest memory of Americans (41.9 months) was approximately 6 months earlier than that of Chinese (47.5 months). Americans often reported voluminous, specific, self-focused, and emotionally elaborate memories; they also placed emphasis on individual attributes in describing themselves (e.g., "I am honest, happy, intelligent"). In comparison, Chinese provided relatively brief accounts of earliest experiences centring on collective activities, general routines, and emotionally neutral events; they also included a great number of social roles and group memberships in their self-descriptions (e.g., "I am a Buddhist, a son, a student"). Across the entire sample, individuals who described themselves in more self-focused and positive terms provided more specific and self-focused memories. It appears that an autonomous self-construct is linked with the early establishment of an elaborate, specific, emotionally charged, self-focused autobiographical history, whereas a relational self-construct is linked with the later establishment of a skeletal, generic, emotionally unexpressive, relation-centred autobiographical history. Two memory examples are presented below to illustrate the cultural differences in memory content (Wang, 2001a, pp. 232–233).

American, male
It was the summer of '81. I was in the backseat of our car, and we were driving to the Hamptons for the weekend. I was sorting some baseball cards when I dropped them on the front of the car. As I reached down to get them, I knocked over a jug of iced tea all over them and the car. A Tony Gwynn card was destroyed. (Participant was 3 years 2 months old at the time of the memory.)

Chinese, male
I used to play with friends when I was little. We went to the bush to pick up wild fruits to eat. And I watched them catch birds. (Participant was 4 years 6 months old at the time of the memory.)

Thus, autobiographical memory varies in content and timing of emergence, depending on whether the culture views the self as essentially separated from or bonded to other selves. Focusing on the self as an autonomous agent increases the chances of encoding durable, consciously accessible, self-focused memories for later retrieval. Focusing on the self as part of larger groups engaged in collective activities, on the other hand, may attenuate remembering detailed, individual-centred autobiographical information. Moreover, from the present perspective memory content may be reconstructed, over time to reflect and further reinforce the dominant goals of the working self as prioritized by one's culture. These self goals, in turn, provide structures that make pertinent memory content easier to access and more enduring.

Similar cultural differences in memory content are further observed among children as young as age 3 or 4 (Han, Leichtman, & Wang, 1998; Wang & Leichtman, 2000; Wang, 2004). For example, in a recent study, Wang (2004) examined autobiographical memory and self-description in Euro-American and Chinese children in preschool through second grade ($N = 180$). During individual interviews, children were invited to play a "question-and-answer game" in which they recounted four autobiographical events, e.g., one thing they did recently that was really special and fun, and described themselves in response to open-ended questions. US children tended to provide lengthy, detailed, and emotionally elaborate memories and to focus on their own roles, preferences, and feelings in telling the story; they also frequently described themselves in terms of personal attributes, abstract dispositions, and inner traits in a positive light. Chinese children, in contrast, provided relatively skeletal accounts of past experiences centred on social interactions and daily routines; and they often described themselves in terms of social roles, context-specific characteristics, and overt behaviours in a neutral or modest tone. This pattern of cultural differences was consonant across different age groups and became more prominent among older children. It appears, then, that children's autobiographical memory and self-description show systematic differences mirroring those among adults (Wang, 2001a). They reflect divergent views of selfhood as well as contrasting emphases on autonomy versus relatedness in different cultures (Hsu, 1970; Kagitcibasi, 1996; Markus & Kitayama, 1991). The early appearance of cultural variations in the self and autobiographical memory further suggests the influence of family socialization early in life.

The social origins of culture–self effects

Early social-linguistic environments are an important source from which children learn to construct life stories in culturally canonical forms (Fivush, 1994; Nelson, 1996; Pillemer, 1998; Wang & Brockmeier, 2002). Culture, as a process of symbolic mediation (Bruner, 1990; Vygotsky, 1978), manifests itself in the actions, thoughts, emotions, beliefs, and moral values of individuals, as well as in the surrounding social institutions, including the family.

Family reminiscing activities are thus bound to reflect the values and orientations of the larger society, particularly with regard to the self as an autonomous or a relational being (see Wang & Spillane, 2003, for a review). As a result, children grow up in different narrative environments that comprise culturally prescribed role-negotiation between parents and children (e.g., hierarchical or equal), parents' implicit and explicit child-rearing goals (e.g., to emphasize autonomy or relatedness), and general cultural beliefs about the purpose of personal remembering (e.g., to facilitate independence or interdependence).

Cross-cultural studies have revealed different conversational amounts and styles of parent–child memory-sharing in European American and East Asian cultures (Mullen & Yi, 1995; Wang, 2001b; Wang, Leichtman, & Davies, 2000). For instance, Mullen and Yi (1995) conducted a one-day observation of conversational interactions between Euro-American and Korean mothers and their 3-year-old children. Mother and child each wore a vest containing a small tape-recorder during the day that recorded all naturally occurring conversations between them. American mother–child pairs engaged in conversations about past events nearly three times as often when compared with Korean mother–child pairs. In another study, Wang, Leichtman, and Davies (2000) asked Euro-American and Chinese mothers to talk with their 3-year-old children about two specific recent events in which they had both participated. Mother and child discussed the events alone in a quiet place in the home and their conversations were tape-recorded. It was found that American mothers showed a high-elaborative conversational style where they dwelled upon specific episodes, supplemented children's responses with rich and embellished information, and invited children to co-construct stories of the shared past. Chinese mothers, in contrast, showed a relatively low-elaborative conversational style in which they frequently posed and repeated factual questions, provided little embellishment or feedback to assist the child's participation, and often tried to elicit correct answers in a way that emulated a memory test.

The different self-focuses on autonomy or relationship are further reflected in the content of sharing memory narratives between Euro-American and Asian parents and their children (Miller, Fung, & Mintz, 1996; Miller, Wiley, Fung, & Liang, 1997; Mullen & Yi, 1995; Wang, 2001b; Wang et al., 2000). Memory talk between American parents and children often takes a child-centred approach, where the child remains the focal point of the conversation and the mother frequently refers to the child's interests, preferences, opinions, and personal attributes. In contrast, memory talk in Korean (Mullen & Yi, 1995) and Chinese (Miller et al., 1996, 1997; Wang, 2001b; Wang et al., 2000) families often take a mother-centred, hierarchically organized approach in which mothers set the direction of the conversation, emphasize interpersonal relations, and frequently talk about moral rules and behavioural expectations with their children.

Like their mothers, American youngsters often used an elaborative conversational style where they frequently volunteered new and descriptive information about the events under discussion, assuming an equal partnership with their mothers during the conversation. They also talked frequently about their personal preferences and judgements. In contrast, Chinese children often simply replied to their mother's inquiries, especially repeated prompts, with either short answers or no new information. They also tended to play a passive role when responding to their mothers' inquiries, and made spontaneous references to significant others and to rules and disciplines during memory sharing (Wang, 2001b; Wang et al., 2000).

Thus, parent–child reminiscing serves socialization purposes that align with the dominant cultural orientations and self views in the society. The low-elaborative, interdependently oriented conversations between East-Asian parents and children are well-suited to the goal of imparting social norms and behavioural expectations to build affiliation with significant others. The highly elaborative, independently oriented conversations between Euro-American parents and children facilitate the development of children's autonomy and autobiographical remembering. Thus the culturally valued self goals are transmitted to children through these early narrative practices and further provide children with the proper organizational framework around which to structure their personal memories. Through parents' modelling of conversational styles and ways of thinking and talking about the past, children actively construct culture-specific genres of life stories and further develop culturally desirable qualities (Wang & Spillane, 2003). The early differences in the structural organization and thematic content of parent–child reminiscing across cultures appear to have long-term consequences on autobiographical memory in older children and adults (Han et al., 1998; MacDonald et al., 2000; Mullen, 1994; Wang, 2001a; Wang & Leichtman, 2000).

Conclusion: Culture can modulate the self-memory system

In this chapter, we started from the proposal that the self and its working goals play a central role in autobiographical remembering. Then, by elaborating on the phenomena of childhood amnesia, reminiscence bump, and attachment, we showed the manifesting ways in which the self affects the retention and reconstruction of memories of personal events. The subsequent analyses based on empirical cross-cultural data further indicate the importance of "putting culture in the middle" (Cole, 1996) when considering the influence of the self on autobiographical remembering. Individuals across cultures show a similar inability to recall events from early childhood, over sample memories from their youth, and remember personal experiences differently depending on their attachment styles. However, those with a salient autonomous sense of self are better able to retrieve personal information, especially that from the distant past, and tend to remember specific details that are self-focused, emotional, and unique to the individual. Those with a salient relational sense of self, in contrast, have a more prolonged period of childhood amnesia and tend to remember events that focus on social or communal activities and significant others.

These cultural similarities and differences in the accessibility, content, and lifespan distribution of autobiographical memory rule out any simple explanation in terms of self, and instead suggest a complex relation between the nature of the self, memory, and culture. In this relation the developmental stages of the self may be universal given the similar divisions of life periods across cultures. Each life period (early childhood, adolescence, mid life, etc.) is associated with similar social demands imposed by society as well as similar levels of biological maturation (or ageing) across cultures. For instance, children in all (industrialized) societies start schooling at about 5 to 6 years of age, a societal demand corresponding with physical and intellectual maturation. Given such similarities, we see the universal existence of childhood amnesia and reminiscence bump. Cultures may differ, however, in how much they weight each life period. For example, in some cultures (USA) childhood is extremely important for an early development of individuality and an autonomous self, whereas in other cultures (China, Japan) older adulthood is perhaps more important as it represents the final establishment of a moral and social self. Personal memories from the more valued life periods are conceivably highly functional in constituting the self goals and identity features prioritized by the culture, and therefore are particularly rich and accessible. This proposition applies to the cultural differences in the accessibility of childhood memory. It also applies to the universal reminiscence bump. It seems true across cultures that young adulthood is an important period in life and memories from this period are crucial for identity-formation and development.

Patently, within each life period, memory and self interact and substantiate each other while they both incorporate the belief systems of the culture. The working self enables privileged encoding of, and access to, autobiographical knowledge relevant to the self goals prioritized by the culture. This process is further facilitated by the elaboration of cues embodied in an individual's immediate social context (e.g., parent–child interaction) and distal cultural environment (e.g., cultural conception of selfhood). Autobiographical memories, in turn, are reconstructed to confirm the motivation and goals of the working self moulded by the culture, a process that takes places when the individual is in defence of his or her independence and autonomy, in compliance with authority or social pressure, and in a myriad of daily exchanges with significant others. Thus, culture can modulate the self-memory system in ways that create both commonality and diversity in human memory and cognition.

References

Barclay, C. R. (1996). Autobiographical remembering: Narrative constraints on objectified selves. In D. C. Rubin (Ed.), *Remembering our past: Studies in autobiographical memory* (pp. 94–125). New York: Cambridge University Press.

Barth, F. (1997). How is the self conceptualized? Variations among cultures. In U. Neisser & D. A. Jopling, *The conceptual self in context* (pp. 75–91). New York: Cambridge University Press.

Bowlby, J. (1973). *Attachment and loss, Vol. 2. Separation: Anxiety and anger.* New York: Basic Books.

Bruner, J. (1990). *Acts of meaning.* Cambridge, MA: Harvard University Press.

Bruner, J. (2002). *Making stories: Law, literature, life.* New York: Farrar, Straus & Giroux.

Bruner, J., & Feldman, C. F. (1996). Group narrative as a cultural context of autobiography. In D. C. Rubin (Ed.), *Remembering our past: Studies in autobiographical memory* (pp. 291–317). New York: Cambridge University Press.

Cole, M. (1996). *Cultural psychology.* Cambridge, MA: Harvard University Press.

Conway, M. A. (1990). *Autobiographical memory: An introduction.* Philadelphia, PA: Open University Press.

Conway, M. A. (2001). Sensory perceptual episodic memory and its context: Autobiographical memory. *Phil. Trans. R. Soc. Lond.*, B 356 (1413), 1375–1384.

Conway, M. A. (in press). Memory and the self. *Journal of Memory and Language.*

Conway, M. A., & Holmes, E. A. (2003). Autobiographical memory and the working self. Buckingham, UK: Open University Press.

Conway, M. A., & Holmes, A. (2004). Psychosocial stages and the availability of autobiographical memories. *Journal of Personality, 72,* 461–480.

Conway, M. A., & Pleydell-Pearce, C. W. (2000). The construction of autobiographical memories in the self-memory system. *Psychological Review, 107*(2), 261–288.

Conway, M. A., & Rubin, D. C. (1993). The structure of autobiographical memory. In A. E. Collins, S. E. Gathercole, M. A. Conway, & P. E. M. Morris (Eds.), *Theories of memory* (pp. 103–137). Hove, UK: Lawrence Erlbaum Associates Ltd.

Conway, M. A., Wang, Q., Hanyu, K., & Haque, S. (2005). A cross-cultural investigation of autobiographical memory: On the universality and cultural variation of the "Reminiscence Bump." *Journal of Cross-Cultural Psychology, 36,* 739–749.

Crites, S. (1986). Storytime: Recollecting the past and projecting the future. In T. R. Sarbin (Ed.), *Narrative psychology: The storied nature of human conduct* (pp. 152–173). New York: Praeger Publishers.

Erikson, E. H. (1963). *Childhood and society.* New York: W.W. Norton & Company. (Originally published 1950)

Fitzgerald, J. M. (1996). Intersecting meanings of reminiscence in adult development and aging. In D. C. Rubin (Ed.), *Remembering our past: Studies in autobiographical memory* (pp. 360–383). New York: Cambridge University Press.

Fitzgerald, J. M., & Lawrence, R. (1984). Autobiographical memory across the lifespan. *Journal of Gerontology, 39,* 692–698.

Fivush, R. (1994). Constructing narrative, emotions, and self in parent–child conversations about the past. In U. Neisser & R. Fivush (Eds.), *The remembering self: Construction and accuracy in the self-narrative* (pp. 136–157). New York: Cambridge University Press.

Foulkes, D. (1999). *Children's dreaming and the development of consciousness.* Cambridge, MA: Harvard University Press.

Franklin, H. C., & Holding, D. H. (1977). Personal memories at different ages. *Quarterly Journal of Experimental Psychology, 29,* 527–532.

Freud, S. (1949). *Three essays on the theory of sexuality* (J. Strachey, Trans.). London: Imago Publishing Company Ltd. (Original work published 1905)

Geertz, C. (1973). *The interpretation of cultures.* New York: Basic Books.

Greenwald, A. G. (1980). The totalitarian ego: Fabrication and revision of personal history. *American Psychologist, 35*(7), 603–618.

Han, J. J., Leichtman, M. D., & Wang, Q. (1998). Autobiographical memory in Korean, Chinese, and American children. *Developmental Psychology, 34*(4), 701–713.

Harley, K., & Reese, E. (1999). Origins of autobiographical memory. *Developmental Psychology, 35*(5), 1338–1348.

Harter, S. (1998). The development of self-representations. In W. Damon (Series Ed.) & N. Eisenberg (Vol. Ed.), *Handbook of child psychology: Vol. 3. Social, emotional, and personality development* (5th ed., pp. 553–617). New York: Wiley.

Hazan, C., & Shaver, P. R. (1987). Romantic love conceptualized as an attachment process. *Journal of Personality and Social Psychology, 52*(3), 511–524.

Hofstede, G. (1980). *Culture's consequences: International differences in work-related values.* Beverly Hills, CA: Sage Publications.

Holmes, A., & Conway, M. A. (1999). Generation identity and the reminiscence bump: Memories for public and private events. *Journal of Adult Development, 6,* 21–34.

Howe, M. L., & Courage, M. L. (1993). On resolving the enigma of infantile amnesia. *Psychological Bulletin, 113,* 305–326.

Howe, M. L., & Courage, M. L. (1997). The emergence and early development of autobiographical memory. *Psychological Review, 104*(3), 499–523.

Hsu, F. L. K. (1970). *Americans and Chinese: Purpose and fulfillment in great civilizations.* New York: The Natural History Press.

Kagitcibasi, C. (1996). *Family and human development across cultures: A view from the other side.* Hillsdale, NJ: Lawrence Erlbaum Associates, Inc.

Kuhn, M. H., & McPartland, T. S. (1954). An empirical investigation of self-attitudes. *American Sociological Review, 19,* 68–76.

Libby, L. K., & Eibach, R. P. (2002). Looking back in time: Self-concept change affects visual perspective in autobiographical memory. *Journal of Personality and Social Psychology, 82*(2), 167–179.

MacDonald, S., Uesiliana, K., & Hayne, H. (2000). Cross-cultural and gender differences in childhood amnesia. *Memory, 8*(6), 365–376.

Main, M. (1991). Metacognitive knowledge, metacognitive monitoring, and singular (coherent) vs. multiple (incoherent) model of attachment: Findings and directions for future research. In C. M. Parkes, J. Stevenson-Hinde, & P. Marris (Eds.), *Attachment across the life cycle* (pp. 127–159). London: Tavistock/Routledge.

Markus, H. (1977). Self-schemata and processing information about the self. *Journal of Personality and Social Psychology, 35,* 63–78.

Markus, H. R., & Kitayama, S. (1991). Culture and the self: Implications for cognition, emotion, and motivation. *Psychological Review, 98*(2), 224–253.

McAdams, D. P. (1988). *Power, intimacy, and the life story: Personological inquiries into identity.* New York: Guilford Press.

Mill, J. (2001). *Analysis of the phenomena of the human mind*. Chicago, IL: The University of Chicago Press. (Original work published 1829)

Miller, P. J., Fung, H., & Mintz, J. (1996). Self-construction through narrative practices: A Chinese and American comparison of early socialization. *Ethos, 24*(2), 237–280.

Miller, P. J., Wiley, A. R., Fung, H., & Liang, C. H. (1997). Personal storytelling as a medium of socialization in Chinese and American families. *Child Development, 68*(3), 557–568.

Mullen, M. K. (1994). Earliest recollections of childhood: A demographic analysis. *Cognition, 52*(1), 55–79.

Mullen, M. K., & Yi, S. (1995). The cultural context of talk about the past: Implications for the development of autobiographical memory. *Cognitive Development, 10*, 407–419.

Neisser, U. (1988). Five kinds of self-knowledge. *Philosophical Psychology, 1*, 35–59.

Neisser, U. (1994). Self narratives: True and false. In U. Neisser & R. Fivush (Eds.), *The remembering self: Construction and accuracy in the self-narrative* (pp. 1–18). New York: Cambridge University Press.

Nelson, K. (1996). *Language in cognitive development: The emergence of the mediated mind*. New York: Cambridge University Press.

Ochs, E., & Capps, L. (1996). Narrating the self. *Annual Review of Anthropology, 25*, 19–43.

Pillemer, D. B. (1998). *Momentous events, vivid memories*. Cambridge, MA: Harvard University Press.

Pillemer, D. B., & White, S. H. (1989). Childhood events recalled by children and adults. In H. W. Reese (Ed.), *Advances in child development and behavior* (Vol. 21, pp. 297–340). New York: Academic Press.

Povinelli, D. J. (1995). The unduplicated self. In P. Rochat (Ed.), *The self in infancy: Theory and research. Advances in Psychology, 112* (pp. 161–192). Amsterdam, Netherlands: North-Holland/Elsevier Science Publishers.

Reese, E. (2002). A model of the origins of autobiographical memory. In J. Fagen & H. Hayne (Eds.), *Progress in infancy research* (Vol. 2). Mahwah, NJ: Lawrence Erlbaum Associates, Inc.

Rogers, T. B., Kuiper, N. A., & Kirker, W. S. (1977). Self-reference and the encoding of personal information. *Journal of Personality and Social Psychology, 35*(9), 677–688.

Ross, M., & Wilson, A. E. (2000). Constructing and appraising past selves. In D. L. Schacter & E. Scarry, (Eds.), *Memory, brain, and belief* (pp. 231–259). Cambridge, MA: Harvard University Press.

Rubin, D. C. (2000). The distribution of early childhood memories. *Memory, 8*(4), 265–269.

Rubin, D. C., Rahhal, T. A., & Poon, L. W. (1998). Things learned in early adulthood are remembered best. *Memory & Cognition, 26*(1), 3–19.

Rubin, D. C., Wetzler, S. E., & Nebes, R. D. (1986). Autobiographical memory across the adult lifespan. In D. C. Rubin (Ed.), *Autobiographical memory* (pp. 202–221). Cambridge: Cambridge University Press.

Singer, J. A., & Salovey, P. (1993). *The remembered self: Emotion and memory in personality*. New York: The Free Press.

Spiro, M. E. (1993). Is the Western conception of the self "peculiar" within the context of the world cultures? *Ethos, 21*(2), 107–153.

Story, A. L. (1998). Self-esteem and memory for favorable and unfavorable personality feedback. *Personality and Social Psychology Bulletin, 24*, 51–64.

Thompson, C. P., Skowronski, J. J., Larsen, S. F., & Betz, A. L. (1996). *Autobiographical memory: Remembering what and remembering when.* Mahwah, NJ: Lawrence Erlbaum Associates, Inc.

Vygotsky, L. (1978). *Mind in society.* Cambridge, MA: Harvard University Press.

Wang, Q. (2001a). Cultural effects on adults' earliest childhood recollection and self-description: Implications for the relation between memory and the self. *Journal of Personality and Social Psychology, 81*(2), 220–233.

Wang, Q. (2001b). "Did you have fun?": American and Chinese mother–child conversations about shared emotional experiences. *Cognitive Development, 16,* 693–715.

Wang, Q. (2003). Infantile amnesia reconsidered: A cross-cultural analysis. *Memory, 11*(1), 65–80.

Wang, Q. (2004). The emergence of cultural self-construct: Autobiographical memory and self-description in American and Chinese children. *Developmental Psychology, 40,* 3–15.

Wang, Q., & Brockmeier, J. (2002). Autobiographical remembering as cultural practice: Understanding the interplay between memory, self and culture. *Culture & Psychology, 8,* 45–64.

Wang, Q., Conway, M. A., & Hou, Y. (2004). Infantile amnesia: A cross-cultural investigation. *Cognitive Sciences, 1,* 123–135.

Wang, Q., & Leichtman, M. D. (2000). Same beginnings, different stories: A comparison of American and Chinese children's narratives. *Child Development, 71*(5), 1329–1346.

Wang, Q., Leichtman, M. D., & Davies, K. I. (2000). Sharing memories and telling stories: American and Chinese mothers and their 3-year-olds. *Memory, 8*(3), 159–177.

Wang, Q., Leichtman, M. D., & White, S. H. (1998). Childhood memory and self-description in young Chinese adults: The impact of growing up an only child. *Cognition, 69*(1), 73–103.

Wang, Q., & Li, J. (2003). Chinese children's self-concepts in the domains of learning and social relations. *Psychology in the Schools, 40*(1), 85–101.

Wang, Q., & Spillane, E. L. (2003). Developing autobiographical memory in the cultural contexts of parent–child reminiscing. *Advances in Psychology Research, 21,* 3–18.

Welch-Ross, M. (2000). Personalizing the temporally extended self: Evaluative self-awareness and the development of autobiographical memory. In C. Moore & K. Lemmon (Eds.), *The self in time: Developmental perspective* (pp. 97–120). Mahwah, NJ: Lawrence Erlbaum Associates, Inc.

2 Influences of the present on the past: The impact of interpretation on memory for abuse

Susan Joslyn and Jonathan W. Schooler

Although the future may be open, it is tempting to think of the past as set. However, there is a sense in which the past too is changeable. New perspectives sometimes colour or even alter our view of the past. In some cases, new perspectives offer a deeper understanding of our own past experience. For example, in reflecting on what at the time seemed like a minor spat, an estranged spouse may look back and recognize unappreciated tensions. On other occasions a fresh perspective may distort memory. From the bitter vantage of a relationship gone awry, one might come to misconstrue innocent bickerings as the reflection of dark feelings that never actually occurred. If memories for prior social interactions are indeed influenced by present understanding then they may be particularly vulnerable when our understanding of the social relationship changes over time. Memory for sexual abuse may fall into this category. The label of "sexual abuse" is somewhat fuzzy, particularly as it is applied to oneself (Joslyn, Carlin, & Loftus, 1998). One could experience an abusive event, but not categorize it as such at the time. Later, if the experience is recalled in the context of abuse, it may be remembered quite differently than if it were recalled in some other context.

In this chapter, we first review evidence that memory for experimentally controlled stimuli is coloured by changes in perspective. We then consider the potential for shifts in perspective for events in one's own life, reviewing survey studies that illustrate the manner in which people may initially avoid interpreting their own experiences as childhood sexual abuse (CSA). Next, we consider the impact that a shift in interpretation might have on memory. We review several case studies of individuals who reported recovering allegedly long-forgotten memories of sexual abuse. We consider the possible role that shifts in abuse perspective had in convincing people to think that the memories were previously forgotten, when in fact they were not. Finally, we discuss a new survey study that illustrates the potential impact that changes to an abuse perspective can have on memory for the emotional content of the event. We conclude with some speculations about the possible role that shifts in perspective may have in contributing to memory discovery experiences.

The impact of shifting perspectives on memory for the past

The events of the past are inevitably viewed through the interpretive lens of the present. Sometimes this lens offers clarification not previously available. At other times it distorts the past in order to make it more consistent with the present. Numerous laboratory studies have demonstrated that the manner in which we interpret the present colours what we recall from the past. Beginning with paired associate learning, Tulving and Thompson (1973) found that items encoded in one context (e.g., "palm tree") were difficult to recognize when tested in a different context (e.g., "palm hand").

Research on memory for previously read text passages demonstrated that shifts in perspective can have both positive and negative effects on memory. Anderson and Pitchert (1978) induced participants to recall previously unreported details by offering them a new vantage from which to consider a passage read earlier in the session. After reading about an old house from the perspective of either a potential homebuyer or a burglar, participants who were encouraged to recall it from the alternative perspective recalled more facts than those who maintained the same perspective. Although shifts in perspective can sometimes enhance memory for text, other studies have illustrated that such shifts can produce systematic distortions. For example, Snyder and Uranowitz (1978) presented participants with an extensive narrative about the life of a woman (Betty K). Later, some participants were told that Betty K was living a lesbian lifestyle whereas others were told that she was living a heterosexual lifestyle. On a subsequent recognition test, participants' memories were found to be systematically biased towards their new interpretation of Betty K, i.e., those given information about the lesbian lifestyle remembering details consistent with lesbian stereotypes and vice versa for those given heterosexual information. In a similar vein, Carli (1999) had participants read identical scenarios about a date, with the one difference being the ending. For some subjects the date ended in a rape, whereas in the other condition it ended in a marriage proposal. On a subsequent memory test, participants' recollections were biased by the perspectives highlighted by the respective endings.

Given the established effects that new perspectives can have on people's recollections of laboratory materials, it is intriguing to speculate about whether similar effects may occur when people recall their own lives. Is it the case, as suggested at the outset, that new perspectives can bias individuals' memories of their own personal lives? Although less research has investigated this question, a number of studies suggest that changing perspectives may also systematically colour how people recall their own past. For example, Levine and colleagues demonstrated in a series of studies that memory for emotions is systematically distorted to conform to present-day appraisals of the remembered event. In one study, people who became more convinced of OJ Simpson's guilt over time overestimated how angry they felt when Simpson was first acquitted. People who became more convinced of his innocence underestimated how angry they felt when they heard that he had been acquitted (Levine, Prohaska, Burgess, Rice, & Laulhere, 2001). In another study (Levine, 1997), loyal Ross Perot supporters significantly underestimated their feelings of anger and sadness reported immediately after hearing of his withdrawal from the presidential race. Those who later abandoned him significantly underestimated their feelings of hope reported when they heard that he had withdrawn.

Although the above studies are suggestive, their interpretation is somewhat complicated by the fact that they are ultimately correlational in nature. Perhaps, for example, the individuals whose support for Perot waned were actually less committed to him than those whose support was unwavering. However, more recent experimental studies have demonstrated a causal link between perspective shifts and memory for emotion. Specifically, in a study of students' memory for pre-exam anxiety, students who were informed of their mid-term exam scores underestimated pre-exam anxiety when they received a good grade and overestimated pre-exam anxiety when they received a poor grade. Importantly, this pattern was not observed among students who had *not* been informed of their score (Safer, Levin, & Drapalsky, 2002), suggesting that one's present-day view causes the emotional shift rather than vice versa.

In sum, a significant body of evidence is consistent with the claim that shifts in perspective can systematically colour individuals' initial recollections of events. New perspectives can hinder people's access to information that is inconsistent with the current context (Tulving & Thompson, 1973) and it can enhance memory for otherwise forgotten information that takes on new-found significance (Anderson & Pichert, 1978). It can systematically bias people to recall laboratory-based materials in a manner consistent with the new-found understanding (e.g., Snyder & Uranowitz, 1978), and it can even cause people to re-construe their own experiences to make them more consistent with their current appraisals (e.g., Levine, 1997). Given the potentially pronounced effect of shifts in perspective on memory, it stands to reason that domains vulnerable to changes in perspective may be especially susceptible to the associated memory effects. In the following discussion we consider the impact of shifts in perspective on an often confusing type of personal experience, sexual abuse.

The role of interpretation in characterizing memories of childhood sexual abuse

CSA might be particularly vulnerable to shifts in perspective because people are hesitant to place personal experiences in that category. In a survey study, the majority of those reporting an unwanted sexual experience failed to classify it as CSA (Joslyn, Carlin, & Loftus, 1998). Responding to an anonymous questionnaire, undergraduate psychology students answered questions about whether they had experienced, as children aged 15 years or less, seven specific sexual events (e.g., fondling, exposure to masturbation, etc.). A complete list of questions appears in Table 2.1. Those who answered "yes" to one of the seven main questions also answered a series of subquestions about their understanding of the event and about their subsequent memory for the event (see Table 2.2). In a separate question, participants were simply asked if they had ever been "sexually abused" (generic abuse question). The purpose of this question was to ascertain the individual's classification of the event. Surprisingly, most of those who experienced at least one of the seven events (76%), failed to classify themselves as abused in answer to the generic abuse question. It did not matter whether the generic abuse question was answered first or last.

Uncertain categorization of potential CSA events may be due in part to the fact that there is little consensus, even among professionals, on the definition

Table 2.1 Main questions asked including seven specifically described events questions (1–7) and the generic abuse question (8).

(1) During childhood, were you ever exposed to adults' sexual private parts in a way that made you uncomfortable?	
	Yes☐ No☐ Don't know☐
(2) During childhood, did an adult ever masturbate in front of you?	
	Yes☐ No☐ Don't know☐
(3) During childhood, did an adult ever touch your body, including your breasts or private parts, in a way that made you uncomfortable?	
	Yes☐ No☐ Don't know☐
(4) During childhood, did an adult rub their private parts against you in a way that made you uncomfortable?	
	Yes☐ No☐ Don't know☐
(5) During childhood, did an adult put their mouth on your body in a manner that made you uncomfortable?	
	Yes☐ No☐ Don't know☐
(6) During childhood, were you ever forced to touch the sexual private parts of an adult in a way that made you uncomfortable?	
	Yes☐ No☐ Don't know☐
(7) Were you forced to have intercourse with an adult against your will during childhood?	
	Yes☐ No☐ Don't know☐
(8) Were you sexually abused by an adult during childhood?	
	Yes☐ No☐ Don't know☐

Table 2.2 Subquestions asked under each specific event question on the questionnaire.

If YES

(1a) After it happened, was there ever a time lasting a
few weeks or more, during which you did not
think about it at all?

Yes☐ No☐ Don't know☐

(1b) Was there ever a period during which you would
not have remembered this event, even if you were
asked about it directly?

Yes☐ No☐ Don't know☐

(1c) Do you think of this event as sexual in nature?

Yes☐ No☐ Don't know☐

If yes, did you understand it as sexual when it
happened?

Yes☐ No☐ Don't know☐

Table 2.3 Question number 9 on the questionnaire.

In your opinion, do any of the following acts constitute sex abuse?

(1) Being exposed to someone's sexual private parts in a way that makes you
uncomfortable?

(2) Someone masturbating in front of you?

(3) Someone touching your body, including your breasts or private parts, in a way
that makes you uncomfortable?

(4) Someone rubbing their private parts against you in a way that makes you
uncomfortable?

(5) Someone putting their mouth on your body in a manner that makes you
uncomfortable?

(6) Being forced to touch the sexual private parts of another person in a way that
makes you uncomfortable?

(7) Being forced to have intercourse against your will?

---

of "childhood sexual abuse". Contentious elements in the definition of CSA
include the age range that constitutes "childhood", the amount of discrep-
ancy in age between the victim and the perpetrator, what acts are considered
"sexual", and the criteria by which the experience is described as "abusive".
Thus a personally experienced event may fit under one version of this definition but fail to be classified as CSA under another definition. To get at this
issue, respondents were also asked questions about their definition of sexual
abuse. They were asked which of the same seven events would constitute
sexual abuse in the abstract. We refer to these as definition questions. The
description of the events, shown in Table 2.3, was identical to that included in

the questions about personal experience. Of those who reported at least one event but denied being sexually abused in answer to the generic question, 90% contradicted their own definition of sexual abuse to do so. Thus, 62% of those who reported at least one event, such as being fondled, also indicated that the same event constituted sexual abuse in the abstract but failed to classify themselves as sexually abused. We will refer to such participants as "self-excluders" because they exclude themselves from the category of sexually abused people. This result suggests that people are extremely reluctant to classify personally experienced events as CSA. The reluctance is so strong that it leads them to classify identically described events differently on a one-page questionnaire, depending on whether or not they were personally experienced.

The fact that so many people's classification of personal events contradicted their own definition of sexual abuse was quite surprising and led to a follow-up study (Joslyn & Loftus, unpublished) to uncover the reasoning behind this behaviour. Using the identical paradigm, a new group of respondents was asked an open-ended question about why they failed to classify themselves as abused. Again, the majority of those (74%) reporting at least one event failed to classify themselves as abused in response to the generic abuse question. Three quarters of those offered written explanations for their decision. For about 14% the written descriptions revealed that the event might well *not* have been sexual abuse (e.g., accidental viewing of undressed family member). For another 10% the perpetrator was another child and the events were excluded for that reason. However, approximately half indicated that the event that they had experienced did not constitute sexual abuse because of some mitigating factor such as the perpetrator being drunk. An 18-year-old female wrote that the event she reported was not abuse because "The man was drunk and apologized to me when he sobered up". Several others wrote that they did not consider their experience CSA because they did not voice their objections sufficiently strongly. A 19-year-old female wrote, "I don't feel what happened was abusive because I let it happen". Another quarter simply took issue with the term "sexual abuse" and preferred to call it something else such as "harassment". Thus the majority of those who answered the question appeared to be searching for some loophole that would allow them to exclude themselves from the category of sexually abused.

This elaborate reasoning may be motivated by the fact that "sexually abused" is seen as a negative label. People's reluctance to assume what is perceived as a negative label is well documented (Knutson & Selner, 1994; Savin-Williams, 1989). This too could have an impact on autobiographical memory. There is evidence that the way in which we view ourselves, the "self-schema", influences memory (Greenwald, 1980). Information that is less consistent with the self-schema or less self-relevant is less well remembered (Markus, 1977; Mischel, Ebbesen, & Zeiss, 1976). There is support for this notion in the survey study reported above (Joslyn et al., 1998). There was an association between respondents' interpretation of the event (whether or not they saw it as sexual) and their reported memory of the event. Those who failed to classify the event as sexual reported more forgetting. Whether or not they actually remembered the event less often in the past is open to question. Evidence reviewed below suggests that people are not always accurate when reporting whether or not they remembered something in the past. This is especially true in situations involving a shift in perspective.

The role of changes of interpretation in discovered memories of abuse

Although people may succeed in avoiding viewing their experiences as sexual abuse for some time, events may occur that compel them to re-examine and reclassify their experiences. In such cases there may be memorial consequences to changing one's view of the experience to an incident of sexual abuse. People may regard the reclassified event as a newly recovered memory. This appears to be the explanation for several cases of allegedly recovered CSA memories for which Schooler and colleagues (Schooler, Bendiksen, & Ambadar, 1997; Schooler 2001) attempted to corroborate the original event. In these studies, Schooler et al. reported two cases in which individuals' perspectives on their abuse experiences appeared to have changed significantly, potentially altering both their construal of the experience and perhaps their characterizations of their forgetting. In one case, WB, a 40-year-old female, described a memory discovery experience wherein she recalled being raped while hitchhiking as a teenager. Although her former husband indicated that she had mentioned this experience several times prior to this discovery experience (including the day that it happened, and subsequently over the years in a matter of fact non-emotional manner), at the time of the discovery experience she experienced a sense of emotional shock reporting "complete chaos in my emotions" and sense of being overwhelmed, "I was overwhelmed, rather than surprised, surprised is too neutral a feeling for what I felt." She also reported a seemingly new awareness of the meaning of the experience. In a letter written several days after her discovery she wrote that her initial thoughts after recalling this experience were "My God . . . I had been raped! . . . That's a crime! I was 16, just a kid! I couldn't defend myself." This characterization conflicted with the manner in which she recalled herself originally construing the event as a teenager. Originally she considered this event a sexual experience gone awry: "I made such a mess out of it by resisting what I thought was supposed to be a sexual experience." Indeed, although WB reported that she believed she had forgotten the experience, she also speculated that this might have occurred because she downplayed its significance noting, "In a way, I have managed to repress the meaning of what happened all of these years. I have pushed it away, minimized it . . . It wasn't a real rape." Notably, her discovery of a new understanding of the experience may have been confused with her discovery of the memory itself, leading her to believe that she had entirely forgotten the experience when in fact she was found to have repeatedly talked about it. This suggests that memory for remembering an event encoded under one classification may be difficult with the cues available after a shift in classification has taken place.

A similar role of reinterpretation in discovered memories was implicated in the case of TW, who like WB, had a memory-discovery experience for abuse that she had previously repeatedly mentioned to her husband. TW's memory discovery occurred in the context of considering seeing a lecture on sexual abuse. Reflecting on the topic, she suddenly recalled having been fondled by a family friend when she was nine. At the time of the memory discovery she similarly recalled a sense of shock and an onrush of emotion: "When I first remembered it I was surprised. Completely taken back by it. Then I . . . I don't even remember speaking . . . I was completely out of it." However, like WB, TW's husband reported that she had mentioned (with flat affect) the experience several times during the period that TW believed she had forgotten it. Indeed TW was startled to learn that she had talked about this experience with her husband noting that when she found out she had told him of this experience she "Felt like falling over. Absolutely shocked and floored that it happened. And I still am . . . I can't remember telling him, I can't think of anything about the memory before [the recovery], and it's very disturbing, actually."

As in the case of WB, TW recalled her initial interpretation of the experience as being different to the characterization of abuse at which she ultimately arrived. Initially she recalled the experience as a socially awkward moment for which she was responsible. As TW put it, "I mean it sounds very silly actually to me. Because I remember this guy was making some kind of disgusted sound . . . then he pushed me away. And my immediate interpretation was that I had done something wrong, and that I was somehow at fault." In short, both TW and WB presented cases in which a significant change in interpretation of the experience was associated both with increased appraisal of the severity of the experience, and a sense that the memory had previously been forgotten, even though evidence indicated that they talked about it repeatedly.

A number of recent empirical studies also support the notion that memory for prior episodes of remembering, like memory in general, can be quite fallible (Joslyn et al., 2001). Studies have shown that that people sometimes forget recalling a childhood event that was brought to mind only minutes earlier (Parks, 1999). Memory for remembering may also be subject to reconstruction. People's memory for memory judgements are influenced by recent retrieval attempts (Belli, Winkielman, Read, Schwarz, & Lynn, 1998) the type of memory test (Padilla-Walker & Poole, 2002) and the similarity of cues between encoding and test (Arnold & Lindsay, 2002).

This body of evidence supports the notion that if an autobiographical event is remembered under one categorization at an earlier time, it may be very difficult to recall *remembering* it later, after a shift in categorization.

Because recalling an awkward physical encounter may be quite different from remembering being sexually abused, it seems plausible that a shift in interpretation could lead to the impression that the event was previous forgotten, when in fact it was consistently available. In short, changes in the interpretation of an abuse experience could influence both one's recollections of the abuse itself (perhaps imbuing it with greater emotional intensity than was originally present) as well as one's metamemory understanding (perhaps confusing the new understanding of the experience with the discovery of a previously hidden memory).

The impact of interpretation on memory for abuse: A recent study

In the final study we will discuss, Joslyn and Schooler (2005) explored the impact of a shift in interpretation of an autobiographical event on memory for the emotional content of that event. We were interested in the self-exclusion phenomenon associated with CSA described above (Joslyn et al., 1998), i.e., many people who report an unwanted sexual abuse experience that fits their own definition of sexual abuse, fail to classify themselves as having been sexually abused. We wondered what would happen if we brought the definition of sexual abuse to the fore. Would respondents be less likely to exclude themselves from the abused category? If so, what impact would that have on their memory for the event?

We asked the same main questions about experience of specific unwanted sexual events as were asked in Joslyn et al. (1997).[1] Under each main question we asked a series of subquestions. Here, we focus on the questions asking how upset respondents were when the event occurred and how upset they were in the present as they thought back on it.[2] In addition, we asked participants a separate generic abuse question, "Were you ever sexually abused?". Finally, we asked whether the same seven specific events were considered sexual abuse in the abstract; the definition questions. Crucially, we varied the position of the definition questions. In the control condition, all of the definition questions were presented at the end of the questionnaire as they had been in Joslyn et al. (1998). In the experimental condition, however, we presented each definition question just prior to the corresponding question that asked about personal experience of that event (definition-salient).

We hypothesized that respondents would be less likely to exclude themselves from the category of "sexually abused" if the abstract definition question was asked first, emphasizing the fact that the event they experienced fell into their own general definition of sexual abuse. In other words we thought

---

1 Although we amended them to include the phrase "by an adult, someone 18 years old or older".
2 We also asked how recently the respondent had thought about the event, and whether it was ever completely forgotten.

that increasing the salience of the definition would compel some respondents to reclassify personal experiences as CSA, i.e., to become non-excluders. As a result we expected to see fewer self-excluders in the definition-salient condition. We also expected to see a difference in the remembered emotion that accompanied that event.

We replicated the basic findings of Joslyn et al. (1998). Of the 705 respondents, 92 (13%) said "yes" to at least one of the events. Again, the majority of those who experienced an unwanted sexual event refused to call themselves sexually abused (58%) when answering the generic question. The vast majority of those (80%) did so despite the fact that they indicated that the same event constituted abuse in the abstract. For example, they reported being fondled, they considered fondling to be CSA but said that they were not sexually abused. The distribution of all four responses (abused, self-excluders, don't knows, and those who did not regard the personally experienced event as abuse when described in the abstract) appears in Figure 2.1.

Placing the definition question first seems to have had an impact on self-exclusion. As seen in Figure 2.2, self-excluders were the majority of respondents in the control condition of the questionnaire. The pattern was reversed in the definition-salient condition. There were fewer self-excluders than others.[3] This suggests that, as predicted, answering the definition question prior to the personal experience question prevented some individuals from excluding themselves for the CSA category. Nonetheless a surprising number held on to their misclassification despite being forced to answer the two questions side by side.

We hypothesized that the ensuing shift in classification would influence reported feelings about the event as well. We expected participants in the definition-salient condition to report being more upset about the event because they would be less likely to exclude themselves from the CSA category. This

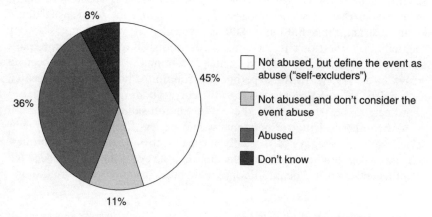

Figure 2.1 Distribution of respondents who said "yes" to at least one event.

3   This pattern was marginally significant in a one-tailed Chi-square analysis ($p =. 07$).

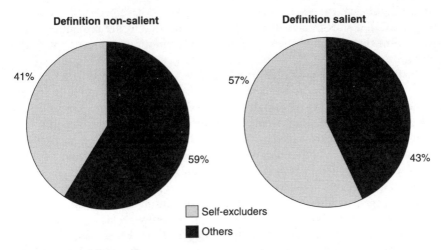

Figure 2.2 Definition salience.

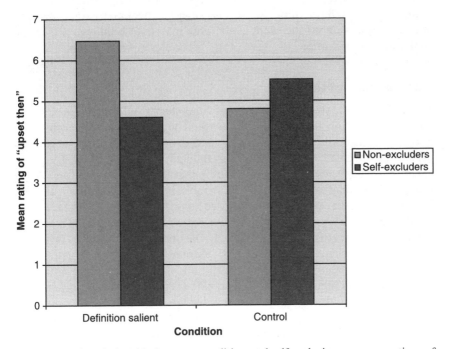

Figure 2.3 The relationship between condition and self-exclusion on mean ratings of participants' recalled upsetness at the time of the abuse.

hypothesis was supported. Note in Figure 2.3 that non-excluders reported having been more upset in the definition-salient condition than did self-excluders. In the control condition the pattern was reversed. Self-excluders were slightly more upset than were non-excluders. This suggests that many of those in the definition-salient condition who would have been self-excluders, experienced a shift in classification of the event due to the proximity of the definition that coloured their memory for the emotions associated with the event.

In the final study presented here, there was a smaller proportion of self-excluders in the definition-salient condition (albeit only marginally significant) suggesting an experimentally induced shift in respondents' classification of personally experienced events. This implies that some participants who would otherwise have failed to do so, reclassified autobiographical events as sexual abuse. When consciously thinking about the definition of CSA they were compelled to regard some personally experienced events as sexual abuse. They became non-excluders. Moreover, reclassification appears to have coloured their memory of the event. In the definition-salient condition, non-excluders, presumably including those who recently reclassified the event, reported having been more upset about it at the time. There were no systematic differences between conditions in terms of the type or number of events reported. Consequently, the difference in reported distress was very likely due to the salience of the definition itself. This suggests that participants' memory of how they felt about the event at the time may have been changed in the course of reclassification.

Summary and conclusions

To summarize, the studies reviewed here suggest that shifts in perspective can impact memory in several different ways. They can enhance memory by bringing forth additional details, they can distort memory to conform to present perspectives and they can even influence metamemory judgements. Personal events, such a CSA, which are particularly vulnerable to shifts in interpretation may be particularly vulnerable in terms of memory as well. Whether a personal experience is regarded as CSA may impact the accessibility of that memory, as well as whether one remembers remembering it and the emotional content that one remembers. In the questionnaire studies reviewed, young adult participants appeared to be extremely reluctant to regard themselves as having been sexually abused. In both studies, a large percentage of respondents who reported unwanted sexual experiences as children were self-excluders. Although self-excluders regarded an abstract description of the event as sexual abuse, their pattern of responses indicated that they did not consider the same event, when personally experienced, to be CSA. Moreover, respondents' understanding of the unwanted sexual event impacted their reported memory. Poorly categorized events may be recalled less often simply because they are less well connected to autobiographical memory as a whole and hence are accessible by fewer retrieval paths. Events that are likely to be inadequately categorized are events that are poorly understood or events for which the proper category is regarded as negative.

The case-study evidence reviewed suggests that a shift in categorization also impacts metamemory. Events, which are originally poorly categorized, may eventually be categorized as CSA. This in turn gives the impression of previous forgetting. The evidence reviewed here suggests that although the events were remembered under some other categorization, they were difficult to recall when they were later considered CSA. In addition, we presented new evidence that suggests that a shift in classification affects one's memory for the emotions that accompanied that event. The same events when interpreted as CSA appear to be remembered as being more upsetting. These results imply that simply changing the order in which the questions were asked influenced both participants' tendency to describe themselves as victims of abuse, as well as their memory for how upset they were at the time. This raises important methodological issues about the use of questionnaire data for assessing such experiences, reinforcing the well-established fact (Schwarz, 1999) that the order in which questions are asked can meaningfully impact the responses that individuals provide. For memory researchers it means that the manner in which one probes memory determines, to a certain degree, what one finds out.

In closing we note that although this chapter has primarily focused on the impact of categorization of autobiographical events on the recollection of childhood sexual abuse, it seems likely that similar factors influence various other kinds of autobiographical events for which interpretations can change. Understanding how fluctuations in the interpretations of experiences influence recollections may be an important new avenue for exploring the dynamic quality of memory. Shifts in interpretation may also provide one approach to understanding why people report that seemingly highly salient experiences were previously forgotten.

References

Anderson, R. C., & Pichert, J. W. (1978). Recall of previously unrecallable information following a shift in perspective. *Journal of Verbal Learning and Verbal Behavior*, *17*, 1–12.

Arnold, M. M., & Lindsay, D. S. (2002). Remembering remembering. *Journal of Experimental Psychology: Learning, Memory, and Cognition*, *28*, 521–529.

Belli, R. F., Winkielman, P., Read, J. D., Schwarz, N., & Lynn, S. J. (1998). Recalling more childhood events leads to judgments of poorer memory: Implications for the recovered/false memory debate. *Psychonomic Bulletin and Review*, *5*(2), 318–323.

Carli, L. L. (1999). Cognitive reconstruction, hindsight, and reactions to victims and perpetrators. *Personality and Social Psychology Bulletin*, *25*(8), 966–979.

Greenwald, A. G. (1980). The totalitarian ego: Fabrication and revision of personal history. *American Psychologist*, *35*, 603–618.

Joslyn, S. L., Carlin, L., & Loftus, E. F. (1998). Remembering and forgetting childhood sexual abuse. *Memory*, *5*, 701–724.

Joslyn, S. L., Loftus, E. F., McNoughton, A. & Powers, J. (2001). Memory for Memory. *Memory & Cognition*, *29*, 789–797.

Joslyn, S. L., & Schooler, J. W. (2005). *If it was abuse it must have been upsetting: The salience of abuse definitions and recollections of childhood sexual contact.* Unpublished manuscript, University of Washington.

Knutson, J. F., & Selner, M. B. (1994). Punitive childhood experiences reported by young adults over a 10-year period. *Child Abuse and Neglect, 18*(2), 155–166.

Levine, L. J. (1997). Reconstructing memory for emotion. Journal of Experimental Psychology: *General, 126*(2), 165–177.

Levine, L. J., Prohaska, V., Burgess, S. L., Rice, J. A., & Laulhere, T. M. (2001). Remembering past emotions: The role of current appraisals. *Cognition and Emotion, 15*(4), 393–417.

Markus, H. (1977). Self-schemas and processing information about the self. *Journal of Personality and Social Psychology, 35*, 63–78.

Mischel, W., Ebbesen, B., & Zeiss, A. M. (1976). Determinants of selective memory about the self. *Journal of Consulting and Clinical Psychology, 44*(1), 92–103.

Padilla-Walker, L. M., & Poole, D. A. (2002). Memory for previous recall: A comparison of free and cued recall. [References]. *Applied Cognitive Psychology, 16*, 515–524.

Parks, T. E. (1999). On one aspect of the evidence for recovered memories. *American Journal of Psychology, 112*, 365–370.

Safer, M. A., Levine, L. J., & Drapalski, A. L. (2002). Distortion in memory for emotions: The contributions of personality and post-event knowledge. [References]. *Personality & Social Psychology Bulletin, 28*, 1495–1507.

Savin-Williams, R. C. (1989). Gay and lesbian adolescents. *Marriage & Family Review, 14*(3–4), 197–216.

Schwarz, N. (1999). Self-reports of behaviors and opinions: Cognitive and communicative processes. In N. Schwarz & D. C. Park (Eds.), *Cognition, aging, and self-reports* (pp. 17–43). Hove, UK: Psychology Press.

Snyder, M., & Uranowitz, S. W. (1978). Reconstructing the past: Some cognitive consequences of person perception. *Journal of Personality and Social Psychology, 36*(9), 941–950.

Schooler, J. W. (2001). Discovering memories in the light of meta-awareness. *The Journal of Aggression, Maltreatment and Trauma, 4*, 105–136.

Schooler, J. W., Ambadar, Z., & Bendiksen, M. A. (1997). A cognitive corroborative case study approach for investigating discovered memories of sexual abuse. In J. D. Read & D. S. Lindsay (Eds.) *Recollections of trauma: Scientific research and clinical practices* (pp. 379–388). New York: Plenum.

Schooler, J. W., Bendiksen, M., & Ambadar, Z. (1997). Taking the middle line: Can we accommodate both fabricated and recovered memories of sexual abuse? In M. Conway (Ed.), *False and recovered memories* (pp. 251–292). Oxford, UK: Oxford University Press.

Tulving, E., & Thomson, D. (1973). Encoding specificity and retrieval processes in episodic memory. *Psychological Review, 80*, 352–373.

3 Adults' memories of long-past events

D. Stephen Lindsay and J. Don Read

What do you know of your own past? We suspect that most persons asked this question would reply, "Why, everything!" Perhaps after a pause the person would go on to say, "Well, everything *important*, at least!" Our knowledge of our own personal past seems to roll like a carpet, stretching continuously behind us from the present beneath our feet into the distance of childhood and on toward the vanishing point of infantile amnesia. People know that they quickly forget many of the minutiae of daily life (e.g., what shoes did you wear to work last Wednesday?), and most people occasionally discover that their recollections of a past event differ from those of others who also experienced that event. But people nonetheless seem to have an intuitive sense that their autobiographical memories are *in all important respects* complete and accurate. Indeed, people who report very poor memory for substantial periods of their personal pasts may be diagnosed as suffering mental illness (C. A. Ross, 1989) or brain damage (Kopelman, 1997).

Related to this intuitive sense that autobiographical memory is essentially complete and accurate is the naive assumption that memories are somewhat like videotapes, with each experience stored on its own cassette and housed in a vast autobiographical library. From this perspective, although it is sometimes difficult to locate a tape, and details may become blurred with the passage of time, the stored essence of each experience is in principle available for playback. (For a discussion of metaphors of memory, see Roediger, 1980.)

During the last quarter of a century many memory researchers have published findings and arguments that challenge this naive view of autobiographical memory as a storehouse, and of autobiographical remembering as playback (e.g., Schacter, 1999). It is now well established that memory is not a simple storehouse of unitized records of past experience, and that remembering is not merely a matter of locating and playing back such records. Researchers have shown that recollections (including autobiographical reminiscences) are influenced by the rememberers' beliefs and desires (e.g., Conway & Pleydell-Pearce, 2000; Jacoby, Kelley, & Dywan, 1989; Johnson, Hashtroudi, & Lindsay, 1993; M. Ross, 1989; Whittlesea, 2003).

Despite this emphasis on the reconstructive nature of memory, we believe that many memory theorists still overestimate the completeness of autobiographical memory and underestimate human susceptibility to reconstructive memory errors regarding long-past autobiographical events. In this chapter we describe some of the findings that have led us to suspect that most people have forgotten (in the sense of not being able volitionally to recall, given verbal cues) much of their own personal histories.[1] Some of the work we summarize also explores the relationship between memory phenomenology for long-past events and the emotion associated with those events. We also consider the implications of autobiographical forgetting for susceptibility to suggestive influences that can lead people to experience pseudomemories (i.e., illusions of remembering an event that did not really occur in the person's past).

Diary studies

In the late 1990s, we conducted two studies (with Jonathan Schooler and Ira Hyman) of memory for long-past events recorded in personal diaries. Participants in these studies were recruited via newspaper advertisements seeking individuals who had kept a personal diary years in the past. In an initial screening interview, we identified a target year for each individual, selecting the oldest year unless participants indicated that they had reviewed entries from that year, in which case we selected the oldest non-reviewed year.

In the first of these diary studies, the participants were 19 residents of Bangor, Wales, who ranged in age from 27 to 77 years ($M = 50$ years). The target year of the diary ranged from 7 to 60 years previous to the date when the study was conducted ($M = 28$ years). The second diary study involved 17 participants from Victoria, British Columbia, Canada, ranging in age from 24 to 58 years ($M = 44$ years), with target diaries ranging from 8 to 39 years old ($M = 19$ years). In each study, all but two participants were women.

In both studies, participants were asked to read eight entries from the target year of their diary (beginning with the first large entry in the year, then casually flipping forward a month or two to another large entry). For each entry, they were asked to complete a questionnaire that asked about three sorts of subjective experiences that might or might not arise when reading the entry: "Ordinary-memory experiences", in which reading the entry reminds the person of an event that they feel they have always known about and remembered (although they might not have thought of it in years); "No-memory experiences", in which there is a surprising failure to recognize a seemingly memorable event described in the diary; and "Recovered-memory

---

1   We do not assume that episodic memory information disappears from the brain (i.e., becomes non-available). It is possible, given sufficiently distinctive cues, to recover memories of long-forgotten events that had initially been encoded in ways that support long-term retention. Thus our claim is that individuals do not have access to effective cues for memories of vast portions of their past experiences.

experiences", in which there is a surprising feeling of recovering long-forgotten memories. Here we will summarize responses regarding the latter two sorts of memory experiences (recovered-memory and no-memory experiences).

Recovered-memory experiences

In each study, 16 participants (84% and 94% in Studies 1 and 2, respectively) reported one or more recovered-memory experiences (RMEs), with means of 2.5 (Study 1) and 3.2 (Study 2) of the eight diary entries being described by participants as giving rise to an RME. Many of these appeared to us to be events that it would not be particularly surprising to have forgotten about and then remembered when reading the diary (e.g., "Traveling to Berlin and meeting my uncle for the first time"; "At night off X Islands, sides of ship lit up brightly as ship moved through water, caused by phosphorous plankton in the sea"; "Xmas – first one in New York: Had totally forgotten that all the kids were there"; "A colleague who I had forgotten about").[2] Some of the reported RMEs, however, were more dramatic. One respondent, for example, reported that she had long forgotten a serious romantic relationship that she recalled when re-reading her diary:

> Jeff gave me a spray of cream rosebuds to wear. We were very emotional as we danced the last waltz. I knew I had to make a choice – Jeff or a career – and I was only 17 years old. I chose a career . . . I had put Jeff out of my mind.

Two participants reported recovering memories about their parents being injured in car crashes. Two others described RMEs involving family fights ("My oldest brother lost his temper with his wife . . . Threw his dinner at the wall" and "A fight between my sister and stepfather that involved verbal and physical abuse . . . I started picturing the event in my mind only after reading the entry several times . . . I called my sister and she didn't remember it at all"). Another participant wrote about being surprised to recover memories of holding very strong anti-abortion views to which she no longer subscribed (and had forgotten she had ever held until she re-read the diary entry). The relatively "dramatic" recovered memories cited here tended to be emotionally negative (perhaps in part because strong negative emotion contributes to their drama), but overall the self-reported RMEs ranged fairly evenly from negative to neutral to positive.

The diary study findings regarding RMEs converge with results reported by Read (1997), who asked 413 Canadian adults, "Have you ever recalled an experience or series of related experiences that you had 'forgotten' about for

---

2 Surface details of participants' reports were altered to protect their anonymity.

some extended period of time?" More than half (60.3%) indicated that they had experienced such memory-recovery experiences. A substantial minority of these reports concerned traumatic events such as sexual abuse (7.3%) or other trauma (20.6%), but most involved more mundane or positive events. Interestingly, some respondents in Read's study indicated that they had forgotten and then recovered memories of long-term, oft-repeated experiences. Here again, in some cases these RMEs for repeated events involved traumatic experiences such as sexual abuse but in others they did not (e.g., one respondent reported having forgotten for years, and then recovering memories of, taking piano lessons for several years as a child).

It is probably not unusual for individuals to recover memories of long-forgotten experiences when they encounter appropriate cues. Of course, it is one thing to recover memories of piano lessons, and quite another to recover memories of being sexually molested by a parent. In the former case, the individual might think, "That's funny, I'd completely forgotten about those lessons", whereas in the latter the person's beliefs about fundamental parts of his or her personal history would be shattered. Despite this dramatic difference in the implications and emotional impact of RMEs of positive or neutral events versus RMEs of traumatic events, we suspect that the basic mechanisms underlying the memory recovery phenomenon itself is essentially the same (excepting cases in which RME reports emerge through a prolonged and suggestive effort to recover memories, which we believe can give rise to false memories).

No-memory experiences

Typically, before a person can experience an RME he or she must first have forgotten a memorable autobiographical event.[3] As mentioned at the outset of this chapter, intuition suggests that people rarely forget the important, dramatic, consequential events of their lives. It is in regard to this issue that the diary-study results strike us as particularly interesting. Across the two studies, 29 of the 36 participants (80%) reported one or more "no-memory experiences" (i.e., self-reported a surprising lack of memories for a seemingly memorable event), with a mean of 2.4 of the eight diary entries being said to give rise to such reports. Here are some examples:

---

3 Schooler and co-workers (Schooler, 2001; Schooler, Ambadar, & Bendiksen, 1997) reported two case studies of women who had full-blown RMEs of childhood sexual abuse but who had told confidants about the abuse during the period of supposed amnesia; they had forgotten that they had previously remembered the abuse. For laboratory analogues of this phenomenon (which Schooler termed the "forgot it all along" effect), see Arnold and Lindsay (2002, 2005); Joslyn, Loftus, McNoughton, and Powers (2001); and Padilla-Walker and Poole (2002).

"Teaching my sister to ride a bike."

"The people and everything I did this day doesn't mean anything to me."

"It says 'Mike likes me', but I wonder who on earth Mike was."

"It was my 17th birthday ... The mother of my dead girlfriend phoned me. It was an emotional time for me and I can't believe I can't remember it."

"I mention studying painting and singing at the boarding school I'm attending for 12th grade, yet this surprises me because I have no memory of it."

"Have recorded that I heard my dad threaten to hit my mother."

"I made efforts to be 'Fred's' dance partner. I had a crush on him and chased after him. But now I have no idea who this guy is, much less did I have a crush on him."

"I had totally forgotten some of the things that went on at my sister's wedding ... I wrote that I cried when a song was played at the dance, than walked off to a nearby field and cried."

"I was 14 when I wrote these entries ... I was a monarchist. I'm not now, and it's embarrassing. I thought I never was."

"I can't believe I suffered from and apparently was treated for depression – at that age! If I had been asked whether I have ever been depressed, I would have said NO."

Here again, although some of the no-memory reports involved negative events, others involved positive or neutral events. Also, although the examples given above are at least somewhat dramatic and surprising (i.e., one might be surprised that a person who experienced the event would not remember it), other events for which participants claimed a "surprising" lack of memories do not seem to us to warrant such surprise. In any case, the point for current purposes is that participants frequently reported that they were surprised by their lack of memories of events described in their own diaries.

After completing the questionnaires for the eight diary events, participants were invited to make general comments about the experience of re-reading their old diary entries. Many participants did volunteer such comments, and most of them shared a common theme. That theme is readily apparent in the following examples (each of which comes from a different participant):

"I was surprised at not remembering some of the entries ... Reading something that you have done and now do not remember is quite unnerving."

"Found it odd, the things I had totally forgotten."

"I was surprised at how many experiences I had no recollection of at all."

"I was actually surprised, and a little concerned, about my lack of ability to recall events and, more importantly, people."

"I was amazed by the number of people mentioned who I cannot remember now . . . I thought I had a good memory – I've changed my mind."

"I could have been reading someone else's diary."

"I feel as if I'm reading something that someone else wrote."

As these examples illustrate, many of the participants spontaneously expressed surprise (and, in some cases, dismay) at how many of the events described in their diary seemed utterly unfamiliar, as though they had happened to someone else. Similarly, Loftus, Garry, and Feldman (1994) cited evidence that people sometimes appear to have forgotten dramatic adulthood events, such as serious motor vehicle accidents, hospitalizations, and crime victimizations. The implication, of course, is that you too have likely forgotten substantial portions of your own personal history, including events that you would be surprised to learn ever happened to you.

The findings of these diary studies are related to fascinating research by Winkielman, Schwarz, and coauthors (Belli, Winkielman, Read, Schwarz, & Lynn, 1998; Winkielman & Schwarz, 2001; Winkielman, Schwarz, & Belli, 1998; see also Merckelbach, Wiers, Horselenberg, & Wessel, 2001). Their core finding is that asking young adults to recall more than just a few childhood memories leads participants to downgrade their estimates of the completeness and accessibility of their memories for childhood. That finding suggests that people typically assume it will be easy for them to recall multiple childhood experiences. Likewise, the diary study results demonstrate that people are surprised at the number and kinds of events described in their own diaries that they fail even to recognize as familiar.

Other memory researchers have reported a variety of different sorts of diary studies of autobiographical knowledge. For example, several researchers have kept structured records of events in their own lives and then tested their ability to remember those events (e.g., Conway, Collins, Gathercole, & Anderson, 1996; Linton, 1982; Wagenaar, 1986). Others have asked undergraduate participants to complete daily records of life events for periods of weeks or months and then tested them on those records (e.g., Bower, 1981; Rubin, 1982; Thompson, Skowronski, Larsen, & Betz, 1996; Thomson, 1930). Our procedure, in which participants are ordinary people who, for reasons of their own, had kept diaries in the distant past, is similar to the method used by Burt (1992; Burt, Kemp, & Conway, 2001) (see also Smith, 1952). The method is weak in terms of control, but it could potentially be improved in this regard. For example, we had little control over which entries subjects read, but Burt obtained subjects' diaries before they re-read them and selected the events on which participants were tested (although, given our evidence that participants are likely to have forgotten much of what is in the diaries, it is not clear that subjects can give informed consent for researchers to read their diaries). In any case, the paucity of control is offset by the advantages of testing memory for spontaneously recorded real-life experiences with very long delays (up to 58 years in our studies) and of being relatively easy to conduct.

Childhood memories questionnaire studies

Lindsay, Wade, Hunter, and Read (2004) reported questionnaire studies in which adult respondents were asked about a number (28 to 32, depending on the study) of events that they might or might not have experienced during childhood. In Study 1 ($N = 96$) and in a replication of Study 1 with another 92 participants (not reported in detail in our article), respondents were undergraduates at a university in the midwestern USA, whereas Study 2 ($N = 93$) tested a community sample of residents of Victoria, British Columbia, Canada, who ranged in age from 21 to 93 years. The questionnaire asked about childhood events ranging in base rate from events that most respondents would have experienced during childhood (such as playing in a sand box) to events that relatively few would likely have experienced (such as having surgery), and in emotional quality from events that most people would view as negative (such as being bitten by a dog) to events that most would view as positive (such as playing with finger paints). For each event listed on the questionnaire, participants were asked to indicate whether they had experienced that event during childhood and, if so, if they remembered the experience (that is, recollected details of it) or merely knew it had happened. Respondents also rated the emotion of each event (on a 5-point scale, from very negative to very positive).

False memories

The reconstructive nature of autobiographical remembering may be revealed by asking people to remember plausible events that they have never experienced. One event on the questionnaire was selected because few if any of the respondents would have experienced that event, "As a young child, did you ever see a cigarette ad on TV?" Because US and Canadian television stopped advertising cigarettes in 1971, few if any of our respondents 27 years of age or younger would have seen such advertisements. Nonetheless, more than half of the respondents who were born after TV in Canada and the USA stopped airing such ads indicated that they had seen such ads during childhood. It is possible that some respondents had seen cigarette ads on television during childhood trips to other countries, but this was almost certainly the exception rather than the rule. Not only did many participants indicate they had seen such ads during childhood, but approximately a third of the respondents also claimed that they had memories of seeing those ads. In Study 2, which included a wide age range, respondents born after cigarette ads were banned from TV were just as likely as older respondents to claim to have seen and to remember seeing such ads.

Why did respondents so often falsely claim to have seen cigarette ads on

TV, and to remembering seeing those ads? We speculate that having seen other sorts of television ads, print ads for cigarettes in magazines and on billboards, and movies and TV shows in which characters are shown smoking cigarettes lays fertile ground for the creation of false memories of having seen cigarette ads on TV. Asked if they had seen cigarette ads on television during childhood, these prior experiences would be a source of thoughts and images coming to mind that respondents might misattribute to memories of TV ads.

Positivity bias in reports of experience

Most of the events listed on the questionnaires were of events that respondents might well have experienced during childhood. One measure of interest was whether or not participants said they had experienced particular events. Responses of "No, I never experienced that event during childhood" seemed suspiciously high for some events. For example, more than a third of respondents indicated that they had never "peed their pants in public" during childhood, but it seems likely that most children experience such accidents early in toilet training (including after the age of two or three years – that is, beyond the offset of infantile amnesia). As per the results of the diary studies described above, it is tempting to speculate that some responses of "No, never experienced" reflected forgetting of events that actually had been experienced.

We also examined the relationship between respondents' reports as to whether or not they had experienced particular events and their ratings of the emotional quality of those events. Respondents rated each event on a 5-point scale ranging from "very negative" to "very positive". Ratings were to indicate emotion during the experience itself; for reportedly non-experienced events ratings were to indicate the emotion the respondent believed s/he would have had if the event had been experienced. Previous explorations of such relationships have been difficult to interpret because of potential confounding differences between events rated as negative vs. neutral vs. positive. For example, it could be that the negative events tested in a particular study were rarer, or occurred earlier in childhood, or were in some other way less memorable than the positive events. To reduce these interpretive problems, we analysed our data with random-effects regression models (deLeeuw & Kreft, 1986). These statistical analyses treated event (e.g., "ride a pony or horse") as a fixed within-subjects effect, and assessed event-varying predictors (such as reportedly experienced vs. non-experienced or remembered vs. non-remembered) as random within-subject effects. This enabled us to evaluate the relationship between the event-varying predictors (in this case, rated emotion) and the dependent variables of interest (in this case, whether the event was or was not reportedly experienced during childhood) while controlling for overall mean event effects (i.e., potentially confounding characteristics of particular events). Thus we could be confident that a statistically reliable relationship between rated emotion and memory reports could not be an artifact of confounding differences between inherently negative versus inherently positive events, because the random-effect regression model statistically controlled for event.

A random-effects regression analysis revealed that there was a substantial relationship between whether or not participants reported that they had experienced an event and their rating of the emotion of that event. Reportedly experienced events tended to be rated as positive, whereas reportedly non-experienced events tended to be rated as negative. This finding is consistent with prior evidence of a "positivity" bias in autobiographical recall (e.g., Bahrick, 1998; Rubin & Berntsen, 2003; Thomson, 1930; Walker, Skowronski, & Thompson, 2003). Importantly, our analyses statistically controlled for event, so this relationship cannot be an artifact of confounding differences between commonly experienced versus rarely experienced events.

Why were reportedly experienced events rated as more positive than non-experienced events? One possible explanation has to do with the fact that some of the events asked about on our questionnaires were things that our respondents chose to do or not to do when they were children (e.g., playing with finger paints, riding a pony or horse). Presumably, people would more often choose to do something if they liked it, and would choose not to do things they didn't like, which would lead to more positive ratings for experienced than non-experienced events. This cannot be the sole explanation for the effect, however, because the tendency to rate reportedly experienced events as more positive than reportedly non-experienced events was also observed for events that people do not choose to do but that simply happen to them. For example, for each of the following events people who reported that they had experienced the event gave more positive (or less negative) emotion ratings for that event than did people who reported they had not experienced it: had your tonsils removed; got checked for head lice; became lost alone and scared; laughed when drinking so that the drink came out your nose; broke a bone.

It could be that people have a bias to assume that childhood events are less positive than they really are; hence, they give non-experienced events less positive ratings than experienced events. It could also be that people tend to remember past experiences as being more positive than they really were (retrospective Pollyannaism). Along the lines of that idea, Walker et al. (2003) argued that the positivity bias in autobiographical remembering is partly due to a tendency for the intensity of remembered affect to fade with time more quickly for negative than positive events. Regardless of whether the effect reflected a tendency to underestimate the positivity of non-experienced events or to exaggerate the positivity of experienced events (or both), it would lead people to tend to view the events they believe they had experienced during childhood as more positive than the events they believe they never experienced.

It's likely that multiple mechanisms contribute to the tendency for people to rate events they think they experienced as children more positively than events they think they did not experience. It would be interesting to conduct follow-up research to see if this bias is related to individual differences on various personality measures (e.g., are depressed people less likely to rate reportedly experienced events more positively than reportedly non-experienced events?) (cf. Christensen, Wood, & Barrett, 2003).

Emotion and memory phenomenology

Inspired by work by Tulving (1985) and Gardiner and co-authors (e.g., Gardiner & Java, 1991), many memory theorists have become interested in the subjective phenomenology of recognition memory. In particular, researchers have distinguished between recognition that is accompanied by a subjective feeling of recollecting specific details of a prior encounter with a recognized item ("Remembering") versus recognition that is not accompanied by such episodic recollections ("Knowing"). Most research in this area has examined recognition memory for words or pictures. For example, subjects might study a list of words and later be shown test words one at a time and asked to indicate, for each word, whether they recognized it from the study list and, if so, whether they recollected encountering that word on the study list (e.g., could remember something about what they perceived, thought, or felt when the word was presented) or merely have a feeling of knowing that the word was on the study list.

A central aim of our questionnaire studies was to examine the phenomenology of memories of childhood experiences (cf. Byrne, Hyman, & Scott, 2001; Bruce, Dolan, & Phillips-Grant, 2000; D'Argembeau, Comblain, & Van der Linden, 2003; Hyman, Gilstrap, Decker, & Wilkinson, 1998; Read & Lindsay, 2000; Rubin, Schrauf, & Greenberg, 2003). Respondents often reported that they had experienced an event during childhood but had no recollections of the experience itself (i.e., that they merely "knew" they had experienced the event). That finding is not surprising for some of the events asked about on the questionnaire. For example, respondents often indicated that they had their fingernails cut by their parents but that they had no recollections of experiencing this event. This is unsurprising because respondents could reasonably infer that their parents had probably cut their fingernails for them during early childhood. Similarly, Chambliss (1996) found that only 12% of a sample of 340 college students reported that they could recall sitting on a parent's lap when they were under 5 years of age; doubtless virtually all knew that they had done so on innumerable occasions, but few reported specific recollections of even a single such occasion.

Reports of knowing without remembering are more interesting in other cases. For example, across studies 147 of the 281 respondents indicated that they had been bitten by a dog during childhood, 22 of whom (15%) indicated that they had no memories of the incident. Being bitten by a dog during childhood is not culturally normative in the USA and Canada, so (unlike the fingernail-cutting event) respondents probably did not simply infer that they must have experienced that event. Being bitten by a dog is also likely to be a unique event, as well as a quite salient and emotional experience (arguably even a traumatic one). In some cases, an adult might know that she or he experienced a particular dramatic event because of having heard parents or other family members talk about that event. It is also possible, however, that a feeling of knowing that one has experienced a particular event without remembering that experience could arise more spontaneously; that is, such a feeling of knowing might not be based on second-hand knowledge but rather on the same sorts of memory influences that give rise to a feeling of knowing in list-learning experiments (for theoretical accounts of the remember/know distinction, see, e.g., Bodner & Lindsay, 2003; Donaldson, MacKenzie, & Underhill, 1996; Gardiner, Ramponi, & Richardson-Klavehn, 2002).

It is especially interesting that, among reportedly experienced events, those rated as emotional were more often recollected (as opposed to merely "known") than those rated as neutral. This result converges with Hyman et al.'s (1998) finding that when participants were asked to generate one remembered childhood event and one known childhood event the former was rated as more emotional. It is also consistent with laboratory research indicating that emotional materials are better remembered than neutral ones (e.g., Bower, 1992; Reisberg & Heuer, 1995). Our finding is novel, however, in that the effect was reliable even when statistically controlling for event (and, in Study 2, also when statistically controlling for reported age of oldest occurrence and reported number of times experienced).

Perhaps the most exciting of the findings in our questionnaire studies is that reportedly experienced events rated as positive were more often said to be remembered (as opposed to merely known) than those rated as negative. This relationship was not merely an artifact of confounding differences between inherently negative versus positive events on our questionnaires, because this pattern was observed even when event and reported age of oldest occurrence and reported number of times experienced were statistically controlled. This finding might reflect enhanced recollection of positive events (e.g., due to greater rehearsal of such events) and/or impaired recollection of negative events (e.g., due to poorer encoding of negative events or the operation of an inhibitory "repression" mechanism such as avoidance of relevant cues [Anderson, 2003; Basden, Basden, & Morales, 2003; Sahakyan & Kelley, 2002]). Via either or both of these sorts of mechanisms, our results join other evidence of positivity bias in echoing an old popular song, "It's the good times we will remember". Events viewed as negative were less often said to have been experienced and, among reportedly experienced events, less often said to be remembered.

Adults' memories of high school

One limitation of the questionnaire studies described above (and of many prior studies of very long-term autobiographical memory) is that we have no way of knowing whether a respondent had or had not experienced a particular event in childhood. Even in the diary studies, we cannot know for sure that events described in a participant's diary had actually occurred as recorded. As a means of addressing this issue, we conducted a study testing adults' memories for events that had happened during their senior year of high school (for other studies of memory for school, see, e.g., Bahrick, Bahrick, & Wittlinger, 1974; Walls, Sperling, & Weber, 2001). We recruited individuals who had graduated from a particular high school in Victoria, British Columbia, Canada, and used that high school's archival materials (e.g., old school newspapers, the class year book, the programme for the commencement ceremony) to construct customized memory tests for each participant's year of graduation.

Our 42 participants had all graduated from the same high school 10 to 38 years before participating in the study. These people were probably not a representative sample of high-school graduates. For one thing, the high school from which they graduated is a relatively old and prestigious school in a relatively affluent neighbourhood. For another, we recruited participants with newspaper ads soliciting graduates of this high school, and those who responded to the ad and went to the trouble of completing the study (which involved two in-person interviews with an intervening homework exercise) were probably unusually enthusiastic alumni.

Despite these likely subject-selection factors, which may have yielded a sample of individuals with particularly good memory for their high-school years, the most striking aspect of our results is how poorly participants did on most of the tests of memory for specific senior-year events. For example, participants were asked about specific events recorded in the school newspaper, yearbook, or other archival material, with questions such as, "What musical play was put on in your senior year?" and, "For which sport did the school team win a provincial trophy in your senior year?" Only about a quarter to a third of these questions were answered correctly. We also asked various questions about respondents' graduation (commencement) ceremony. Accuracy was perfect on a question about the location of the ceremony (the school's gymnasium), but only 11% of participants correctly remembered the time of day at which the ceremony was held, and only 53% remembered the name of their class valedictorian. We also showed participants four photos from their high-school yearbook mixed with three photos from another school's year book from approximately the same year; participants indicated no familiarity for nearly half (46%) of the photos from their yearbook. In general, participants performed well on questions for which the correct answer conformed closely to a "script" of what a Canadian would expect to have happened, but performed poorly on other questions.

Each participant was tested twice, with a delay of one to a few weeks between the two interviews. On average, performance improved between the first and second sessions. For example, during the first interview only 36% of participants correctly remembered the name of a piece of music played during their commencement ceremony, but by the second interview 64% did so. Although performance improved across interviews for some questions, the opposite occurred for other questions: For example, 75% of participants correctly reported the date of the graduation ceremony in Session 1, but only 36% did so in Session 2.

Individual participants were surprisingly inconsistent in their responses. For example, it was not unusual for a subject to report in the first session that he or she had belonged to a particular high-school club (e.g., the chess club), but not to report having been in the club during the second session (or vice versa). Similarly, participants demonstrated both losses and gains (in about equal proportions) in their responses to specific-event questions. That is, quite often a question that was not answered or was answered incorrectly in Session 1 was answered correctly in Session 2, and approximately as often a question that was answered correctly in Session 1 was answered incorrectly (or not at all) in Session 2.

During both interview sessions, participants were asked to spend 10 minutes recalling names of classmates, teachers, and other school-related individuals, with the aim of recalling as many names as they could. There was tremendous variability across participants in the number of names recalled, and we will not discuss those findings here, but will instead highlight an interesting effect of the name-recall task on participants' ratings of their memories. Participants were asked to estimate the percentage of people they had known in high school whose names they could remember if they spent time working at doing so. In both the first and second interviews, half of the participants were asked to make this estimation before working on the name-recall task, whereas others were asked this question only after they had worked on the name-recall task. Two interesting effects emerged. In the first interview, participants who made the estimate before working on the name-recall task predicted that they would be able to remember 50% of the names, whereas those who made the estimate after working on the name-recall task for 10 minutes estimated that they would be able to remember only 33%. In the second session, predicted percentage recallable declined for both groups (to 36% among those who gave the estimate before repeating the name-recall task, and to 26% among those who repeated the name-recall task before giving the estimate). Like the diary studies described above (and the work by Winkielman and co-authors cited earlier), these findings suggest that people expect their autobiographical memories to be more complete than they are.

Childhood photographs and false memories

The controversy regarding reported recovered memories of childhood sexual abuse (e.g., Porter, Campbell, Birt, & Woodworth, 2003; Read & Lindsay, 1997) motivated several memory researchers to conduct studies designed to test the hypothesis that suggestive influences can lead adults to report illusory memories of non-experienced childhood events. Prior research had demonstrated that suggestive influences can lead substantial percentages of subjects to report false memories of peripheral details in pallid laboratory events (such as a slide show, as in the classic studies by Loftus, Miller, & Burns, 1978), but this new research aimed to test the generalizability of those effects to false memories of autobiographical events comparable in some (albeit not all) respects to instances of childhood sexual abuse. Of course, researchers are bound by ethical principles that prohibit suggestions regarding childhood sexual abuse, so such studies used less traumatic events such as being lost in a shopping mall, spilling punch at a wedding reception, or breaking a window. It is possible that laboratory procedures that lead to false memories of such events would not produce false memories of incestuous abuse (see Pezdek, 2001), but given such effects the onus is on those who wish to argue against generalization.[4]

The dominant method in such studies was first introduced by Loftus (e.g., Loftus & Pickrell, 1995) and subsequently used with various modifications by researchers such as Ira Hyman (e.g., Hyman, Husband, & Billings, 1995) and Steve Porter (e.g., Porter, Yuille, & Lehman, 1999). Participants are led to believe that their parents or a sibling reported the childhood events that participants are asked to remember. Participants listen to a brief narrative description of each event, and then work at remembering more about it (typically over two or three sessions). Most of the events that participants are asked about really were reported by a parent or sibling informant, but the critical event is one that the informant reported the participant had *not* experienced. Across eight studies using this sort of procedure published in refereed journals, 116 of 374 participants (31%) were judged to have partial or complete false memories of the suggested event.

Wade, Garry, Read, and Lindsay (2002) used a novel procedure to foment false memories. Rather than reading narrative descriptions of actual and false childhood events, participants in this study were shown photographs of actual childhood events (obtained from a sibling or other relative) and

---

4   As noted in Lindsay and Briere (1997), two aspects of generalizability should be differentiated. One has to do with whether or not qualitatively different mechanisms underlie memories (and false memories) of traumatic versus mundane events, such that variables that affect trauma memories might not affect (or have qualitatively different effects on) mundane memories. The other aspect of generalizability has to do with whether or not memory for traumatic versus mundane events is affected to the same degree by particular variables. It is clear that the absolute size of effects differs for memories of salient experiences versus trivial events. For example, a single passing suggestion is sufficient to lead a large proportion of people falsely to report remembering a trivial detail in a slide show, but much stronger suggestive influences are typically required to produce pseudomemories of dramatic life events. Likewise, we suspect that stronger suggestive influences are required to produce a given prevalence of false memories of childhood sexual abuse than of, say, a childhood prank. Nonetheless, we believe the same basic mechanisms can give rise to false memories of a wide range of kinds of pseudoevents.

a doctored photograph of an event that (according to the informant) the participant had not experienced during childhood (namely, taking a ride in a hot air balloon). The false photographs were produced by using a computer program to insert a digitized image from an actual childhood photo of the participant and a family member into a stock photo of a hot air balloon. In two in-person interviews and an intervening telephone interview, participants attempted to remember the events depicted in the photographs. Of the 20 participants, 10 (50%) reported memories of the balloon-ride event by the end of the second in-person interview.

The 50% false-memory rate in the Wade et al. (2002) study is unusually high. The false-photograph procedure thus provides a useful method for producing false-memory reports for research purposes. The real-world implications of the findings are somewhat limited, however, because people rarely encounter doctored photographs of themselves doing things that they have not really done. (If people did encounter doctored photos of themselves frequently, the effect of such photographs on false memories would likely be somewhat attenuated because people would be less inclined to assume that photographs never lie.)

Although people rarely encounter doctored photographs depicting themselves in childhood psedo-events, they do sometimes look at family photo albums containing pictures of themselves during childhood. Some popular self-help books and some professional publications in the trauma-memory-oriented literature (e.g., Weiser, 1990) have recommended that people who do not remember childhood sexual abuse but suffer any of a wide variety of symptoms should work at recovering potentially repressed memories of such abuse, and one recommended technique for doing so is to review family photograph albums. In surveys of qualified therapists, Poole, Lindsay, Memon, and Bull (1995) found that 38% of respondents reported the use of family photo albums as a way of helping clients remember childhood sexual abuse. The idea is that such photographs provide rich cues that may trigger memories of long-forgotten abuse.

Childhood photographs probably are powerful cues for childhood memories. Although we have been unable to find any published experiments specifically testing the power of childhood photographs versus narratives as autobiographical memory cues, we know that recognition memory for naturalistic photographs tends to be extremely good, and it is reasonable to assume on theoretical grounds that photographs are peculiarly potent recall cues because of their high degree of distinctiveness. Unfortunately, from the perspective of the source-monitoring framework (e.g., Johnson, Hashtroudi, & Lindsay, 1993; cf. Jacoby, Kelley, & Dywan, 1989), it is also likely that childhood photographs, combined with suggestions to the effect that a person has a non-remembered history of incestuous abuse, could contribute to the formation of false memories (see Schacter, Koutstaal, Gross, Johnson, & Angell, 1997). Images derived from a photograph and from essentially veridical recollections cued by the photograph could combine with products of imagination driven by suggestions to produce vivid and perceptually detailed illusory memories.

Lindsay, Hagen, Read, Wade, and Garry (2004) tested the hypothesis that the effect of misleading suggestions regarding a childhood pseudo-event can be increased by exposure to a true photograph depicting the subject in a situation loosely related to the suggested pseduo-event. The parents of 46 university undergraduates provided us with brief descriptions of school-related events experienced by their children in grades 5 or 6 and in grades 3 or 4, along with the child's class photograph for each of the two corresponding years and for grade 1 or 2. Parents also confirmed that, to the best of their knowledge, their child had not experienced our target false event. Each participant was individually interviewed twice in person, with an intervening telephone interview. In the first interview participants were asked to remember the grade 5 or 6 event, followed by the grade 3 or 4 event, followed by the grade 1 or 2 event. The last of these (the false narrative) suggested that the participant and a classmate had put "Slime" (a gooey toy substance) into the teacher's desk while the teacher was out of the room. The follow-up telephone and final interviews focused on the target event. By random selection, half of the participants were shown the corresponding class photo when asked to recall each event. The procedure for the two conditions was otherwise identical.

Some previous studies in this area have differentiated between "partial" and "complete" false memories. The criteria to define these categories (and the exact labels used to refer to them) have varied across studies. In our study, judges blind to condition rated typed transcripts of participants' spoken interview responses and judged whether the participant: (a) believed that s/he remembered the suggested event ("memories"); (b) accepted that the event happened and reported images relevant to the suggested event but did not seem to believe that s/he remembered it; or (c) reported neither memories nor images of the suggested event. Here we focus exclusively on reports classified as memories of the suggested event.

Consistent with prior research, at the end of the final interview 27% of the participants in the no-photos condition were classified as reporting memories of the suggested pseudo-event.[5] As in the prior studies, those false-memory reports presumably arose from the suggestive influence of the narrative describing the pseudo-event, in a context in which participants believed their parents had supplied the narrative as a true story of something that had happened to them, and in which the experimenter encouraged them to work at remembering that event. Our main interest was in whether or not adding the class photograph to those suggestive influences would increase the percentage of participants who reported memories of the

---

5 Our criteria for "false memories" were comparable to what some other researchers have termed "complete" or "clear" false memories.

pseudo-event. Indeed it did. At the end of the final interview 65% of those shown the class photo were classified as reporting memories of putting Slime in their teacher's desk (the highest rate of apparent false memories yet reported in the literature).

It is worth emphasizing that the class photographs in this study did not depict the pseudo-event. Indeed, the photographs rarely if ever depicted the classroom or the teacher's desk, let alone the Slime prank itself. The photographs did, however, depict the participant and his or her classmates (one of whom was allegedly the participant's collaborator in the Slime prank) as well as the teacher. We speculate that these elements of the photographic image encouraged and supported subjects' imaginations of what the Slime prank would have been like, thereby enabling many of them to imagine the event with a degree of perceptual vividness more characteristic of memories than of fantasies. Of course, there are important differences between false memories of a harmless school prank and false memories of incestuous abuse. Nonetheless, an individual who has been led to believe she or he has a non-remembered history of incestuous abuse, and who reviews family photographs looking for cues to such memories, may be influenced to fabricate vivid images of events that are not depicted in the photographs themselves but that involve people and contextual details (e.g., articles of clothing, furniture, etc.) represented in the photographs.

The incompleteness of autobiographical memory and susceptibility to suggestion

The incompleteness of normal autobiographical memory (dramatically evidenced in the diary studies described earlier) likely heightens susceptibility to suggestive influences regarding childhood pseudo-events. For one thing, studies have shown that, all else being equal, suggestions are more likely to lead to false reports if they concern poorly remembered than well remembered materials (e.g., Heath & Erickson, 1998). Thus the fact that much of childhood is poorly remembered likely makes it easier to foster the development of false memories of childhood than adulthood pseudo-events.

The evidence reviewed in this chapter also suggests that it is normal for people to forget many of their childhood experiences, but people seem to assume that their autobiographical memories are largely complete. Consequently, individuals who are encouraged to try to remember childhood events are likely to be surprised by how little they remember. Moreover, trauma-memory-oriented therapists and self-help books sometimes claim that incomplete memory of childhood is indicative of abuse, and clients or readers who accept that claim may interpret the paucity of their memories of childhood as evidence that they must indeed have been abused. Consistent with that possibility, Winkielman and Schwarz (2001) reported a very clever study in which participants were led to believe that poor memory of childhood either (a) indicates a normal, happy childhood (things flowed along smoothly so there's not much to remember) or (b) indicates a troubled child-hood (bad things happened so memories were repressed). Participants were subsequently asked to report on either a small or a relatively large number of memories of childhood experiences. Later, all participants completed a questionnaire that included ratings of the happiness of their childhoods. The key finding was that participants rated their childhoods as less happy if they had been both (a) led to believe that poor memory for childhood is indicative of a troubled childhood and (b) asked to remember a relatively large number of childhood events.

Conclusion

People seem to assume that they remember all of the "memorable" (that is, important, dramatic, and significant) events of their lives. Yet our findings (and especially the results of the diary studies) indicate that people quite often forget seemingly memorable autobiographical events. It may be that a systematic bias leads people to have inaccurate intuitions about the likelihood of forgetting dramatic childhood experiences. Adults can recollect all of the important, dramatic, consequential childhood experiences that they can recollect, and they rarely encounter evidence of the important, dramatic, consequential childhood experiences that they have forgotten. If you don't know that you experienced a particular event, how would you know that you have forgotten it?

References

Anderson, M. C. (2003). Rethinking interference theory: Executive control and the mechanisms of forgetting. *Journal of Memory and Language, 49*, 415–445.

Arnold, M. M., & Lindsay, D. S. (2002). Remembering remembering. *Journal of Experimental Psychology: Learning, Memory, & Cognition, 28*, 521–529.

Arnold, M. M., & Lindsay, D. S. (2005). Remembrance of remembrance past. *Memory, 13*, 533–549.

Bahrick, H. P. (1998). Loss and distortion of autobiographical memory content. In C. P. Thompson & D. J. Herrmann (Eds.), *Autobiographical memory: Theoretical and applied perspectives* (pp. 69–78). Mahwah, NJ: Lawrence Erlbaum Associates, Inc.

Bahrick, H. P., Bahrick, P. O., & Wittlinger, R. P. (1974). Long-term memory: Those unforgettable high-school days. *Psychology Today, 8*, 50–56.

Basden, B. H., Basden, D. R., & Morales, E. (2003). The role of retrieval practice in directed forgetting. *Journal of Experimental Psychology: Learning, Memory, & Cognition, 29*, 389–397.

Belli, R. F., Winkielman, P., Read, J. D., Schwarz, N., & Lynn, S. J. (1998). Recalling more childhood events leads to judgments of poorer memory: Implications for the recovered/false memory debate. *Psychonomic Bulletin and Review, 5*, 318–323.

Bodner, G. E., & Lindsay, D. S. (2003). Remembering and knowing in context. *Journal of Memory and Language, 48*, 563–580.

Bower, G. H. (1981). Mood and memory. *American Psychologist, 36*, 129–148.

Bower, G. H. (1992). How might emotions affect learning? In S. A. Christianson (Ed.), *The handbook of emotion and memory: Research and theory* (pp. 3–31). Hillsdale, NJ: Lawrence Erlbaum Associates, Inc.

Bruce, D., Dolan, A., & Phillips-Grant, K. (2000). On the transition from childhood amnesia to the recall of personal memories. *Psychological Science, 11*, 360–364.

Burt, C. D. B. (1992). Reconstruction of the duration of autobiographical events. *Memory & Cognition, 20*, 124–132.

Burt, C. D. B., Kemp, S., & Conway, M. (2001). What happens if you retest autobiographical memory 10 years on? *Memory & Cognition, 29*, 127–136.

Byrne, C. A., Hyman, I. E., Jr., & Scott, K. L. (2001). Comparisons of memories for traumatic events and other experiences. *Applied Cognitive Psychology, 15*, S119–S133.

Chambliss, C. (1996). Less is sometimes more in therapy: Avoiding the false memory syndrome. *ERIC Research Report* (http://www.eric.ed.gov/ERICwebPortal/Home.-portal?_nfpb=true&_pageLabel=Home_page).

Christensen, T. C., Wood, J. V., & Barrett, L. F. (2003). Remembering everyday experience through the prism of self-esteem. *Personality & Social Psychology Bulletin, 29*, 51–62.

Conway, M. A., Collins, A. F., Gathercole, S. E., & Anderson, S. J. (1996). Recollections of true and false autobiographical memories. *Journal of Experimental Psychology: General, 125*, 69–95.

Conway, M. A., & Pleydell-Pearce, C. W. (2000). The construction of autobiographical memories in the self-memory system. *Psychological Review, 107*, 261–288.

D'Argembeau, A., Comblain, C., & Van der Linden, M. (2003). Phenomenal characteristics of autobiographical memories for positive, negative, and neutral events. *Applied Cognitive Psychology, 17*, 281–294.

deLeeuw, J., & Kreft, I. (1986). Random coefficient models for multilevel analysis. *Journal of Educational Statistics, 11*, 57–85.

Donaldson, W., MacKenzie, T. M., & Underhill, C. F. (1996). A comparison of recollective memory and source monitoring. *Psychonomic Bulletin & Review, 3*, 486–490.

Gardiner, J. M., & Java, R. I. (1991). Forgetting in recognition memory with and without recollective experience. *Memory and Cognition, 19*, 617–623.

Gardiner, J. M., Ramponi, C., & Richardson-Klavehn, A. (2002). Recognition memory and decision processes: A meta-analysis of remember, know, and guess responses. *Memory, 10*, 83–98.

Heath, W. P., & Erickson, J. R. (1998). Memory for central and peripheral actions and props after varied post-event presentation. *Legal and Criminological Psychology, 3*, 321–346.

Hyman, I. E., Jr., & Billings, F. J. (1998). Individual differences and the creation of false childhood memories. *Memory, 6*, 1–20.

Hyman, I. E., Jr., Gilstrap, L. L., Decker, K., & Wilkinson, C. (1998). Manipulating remember and know judgements of autobiographical memories: An investigation of false memory creation. *Applied Cognitive Psychology, 12*, 371–386.

Hyman, I. E., Jr., Husband, T. H., & Billings, F. J. (1995). False memories of childhood experiences. *Applied Cognitive Psychology, 9*, 181–197.

Jacoby, L. L., Kelley, C. M., & Dywan, J. (1989). Memory attributions. In H. L.

Roediger, III & F. I. M. Craik (Eds.), *Varieties of memory and consciousness: Essays in honour of Endel Tulving* (pp. 391–422). Hillsdale, NJ: Lawrence Erlbaum Associates, Inc.

Johnson, M. K., Hashtroudi, S., & Lindsay, D. S. (1993). Source monitoring. *Psychological Bulletin, 114*, 3–28.

Joslyn, S., Loftus, E. F., McNoughton, A., & Powers, J. (2001). Memory for memory. *Memory & Cognition, 29*, 789–797.

Kopelman, M. D. (1997). Anomalies of autobiographical memory: Retrograde amnesia, confabulation, delusional memory, psychogenic amnesia, and false memories. In J. D. Read & D. S. Lindsay (Eds.), *Recollections of trauma: Scientific evidence and clinical practice. NATO ASI series: Series A: Life sciences* (Vol. 291, pp. 273–303). New York: Plenum Press.

Lindsay, D. S., & Briere, J. (1997). The controversy regarding recovered memories of childhood sexual abuse: Pitfalls, bridges, and future directions. *Journal of Interpersonal Violence, 12*, 631–647.

Lindsay, D. S., Hagen, L., Read, J. D., Wade, K. A., & Garry, M. (2004). True photographs and false memories. *Psychological Science, 15*, 149–154.

Lindsay, D. S., Wade, K. A., Hunter, M. A., & Read, J. D. (2004). Adults' memories of childhood: Affect, knowing, and remembering. *Memory, 12*, 27–43.

Linton, M. (1982). Transformations of memory in everyday life. In U. Neisser (Ed.), *Memory observed: Remembering in natural contexts* (pp. 77–91). San Francisco: WH Freeman & Co.

Loftus, E. F., Garry, M., & Feldman, J. (1994). Forgetting sexual trauma: What does it mean when 38% forget? *Journal of Consulting and Clinical Psychology, 62*, 1177–1181.

Loftus, E. F., Miller, D. G., & Burns, H. J. (1978). Semantic integration of verbal information into a visual memory. *Journal of Experimental Psychology: Human Learning and Memory, 4*, 19–31.

Loftus, E. F., & Pickrell, J. E. (1995). The formation of false memories. *Psychiatric Annals, 25*, 720–725.

Merckelbach, H., Wiers, R., Horselenberg, R., & Wessel, I. (2001). Effects of retrieving childhood events on metamemory judgments depend on the questions you ask. *British Journal of Clinical Psychology, 40*, 215–220.

Padilla-Walker, L. M., & Poole, D. A. (2002). Memory for previous recall: A comparison of free and cued recall. *Applied Cognitive Psychology, 16*, 515–524.

Pezdek, K. (2001). A cognitive analysis of the role of suggestibility in explaining memories for abuse. *Journal of Aggression, Maltreatment and Trauma, 4*, 73–85.

Poole, D. A., Lindsay, D. S., Memon, A., & Bull, R. (1995). Psychotherapy and the recovery of memories of childhood sexual abuse: US and British practitioners' opinions, practices, and experiences. *Journal of Consulting and Clinical Psychology, 63*, 426–437.

Porter, S., Campbell, M. A., Birt, A. R., & Woodworth, M. T. (2003). "He said, she said": A psychological perspective on historical memory evidence in the courtroom. *Canadian Psychology, 44*, 190–206.

Porter, S., Yuille, J. C., & Lehman, D. R. (1999). The nature of real, implanted, and fabricated memories for emotional childhood events: Implications for the recovered memory debate. *Law and Human Behavior, 23*, 517–537.

Read, J. D. (1997). Memory issues in the diagnosis of unreported trauma. In J. D.

Read & D. S. Lindsay (Eds.), *Recollections of trauma: Scientific evidence and clinical practice. NATO ASI series: Series A: Life sciences* (Vol. 291, pp. 79–108). New York: Plenum Press.

Read, J. D., & Lindsay, D. S. (Eds.). (1997). Recollections of trauma: Scientific evidence and clinical practice. *NATO ASI series: Series A: Life sciences* (Vol. 291, pp. 273–303). New York: Plenum Press.

Read, J. D., & Lindsay, D. S. (2000). "Amnesia" for summer camps and high school graduation: Memory work increases reports of prior periods of remembering less. *Journal of Traumatic Stress, 13*, 129–147.

Reisberg, D., & Heuer, F. (1995). Emotion's multiple effects on memory. In J. L. W. McGaugh & M. Norman (Eds.), *Brain and memory: Modulation and mediation of neuroplasticity.* (pp. 84–92). Oxford: Oxford University Press.

Roediger, H. L. (1980). Memory metaphors in cognitive psychology. *Memory and Cognition, 8*, 231–246.

Ross, C. A. (1989). *Multiple personality disorder: Diagnosis, clinical features, and treatment.* New York: Wiley.

Ross, M. (1989). Relation of implicit theories to the construction of personal histories. *Psychological Review, 96*, 341–357.

Rubin, D. C. (1982). On the retention function for autobiographical memory. *Journal of Verbal Learning and Verbal Behavior, 21*, 21–38.

Rubin, D. C., & Berntsen, D. (2003). Life scripts help to maintain autobiographical memories of highly positive, but not highly negative, events. *Memory and Cognition, 31*, 1–14.

Rubin, D. C., Schrauf, R. W., & Greenberg, D. L. (2003). Belief and recollection of autobiographical memories. *Memory and Cognition, 31*, 887–901.

Sahakyan, L., & Kelley, C. M. (2002). A contextual change account of the directed forgetting effect. *Journal of Experimental Psychology: Learning, Memory, & Cognition, 28*, 1064–1072.

Schacter, D. L. (1999). The seven sins of memory: Insights from psychology and cognitive neuroscience. *American Psychologist, 54*, 182–203.

Schacter, D. L., Koutstaal, W., Gross, M. S., Johnson, M. K., & Angell, K. E. (1997). False recollection induced by photographs: A comparison of older and younger adults. *Psychology and Aging, 12*, 203–215.

Schooler, J. W. (2001). Discovering memories of abuse in the light of meta-awareness. *Journal of Aggression, Maltreatment and Trauma, 4*, 105–136.

Schooler, J. W., Ambadar, Z., & Bendiksen, M. (1997). A cognitive corroborative case study approach for investigating discovered memories of sexual abuse. In J. D. Read & D. S. Lindsay (Eds.), *Recollections of trauma: Scientific evidence and clinical practice. NATO ASI series: Series A: Life sciences* (Vol. 291, pp. 379–387). New York: Plenum Press.

Smith, M. E. (1952). Childhood memories compared with those of adult life. *Journal of Genetic Psychology, 80*, 151–182.

Thompson, C. P., Skowronski, J. J., Larsen, S. F., & Betz, A. (1996). *Autobiographical memory: Remembering what and remembering when.* Hillsdale, NJ: Lawrence Erlbaum Associates, Inc.

Thomson, R. H. (1930). An experimental study of memory as influenced by feeling tone. *Journal of Experimental Psychology, 13*, 462–467.

Tulving, E. (1985). Memory and consciousness. *Canadian Psychology, 26*, 1–12.

Wade, K. A., Garry, M., Read, J. D., & Lindsay, D. S. (2002). A picture is worth a thousand lies: Using false photographs to create false childhood memories. *Psychonomic Bulletin and Review, 9,* 597–603.

Wagenaar, W. A. (1986). My memory: A study of autobiographical memory over six years. *Cognitive Psychology, 18,* 225–252.

Walker, W. R., Skowronski, J. J., & Thompson, C. P. (2003). Life is pleasant – and memory helps to keep it that way! *Review of General Psychology, 7,* 203–210.

Walls, R. T., Sperling, R. A., & Weber, K. D. (2001). Autobiographical memory of school. *Journal of Educational Research, 95,* 116–127.

Weiser, J. (1990). "More than meets the eye": Using ordinary snapshots as tools for therapy. In T. Laidlaw, C. Malmo, & Associates (Eds.), *Healing voices: Feminist approaches to therapy with women* (pp. 83–117). San Francisco, CA: Jossey-Bass.

Whittlesea, B. W. A. (2003). On the construction of behavior and subjective experience: The production and evaluation of performance. In J. S. M. Bowers & J. Chad (Eds.), *Rethinking implicit memory* (pp. 239–260). Oxford: Oxford University Press.

Winkielman, P., & Schwarz, N. (2001). How pleasant was your childhood? Beliefs about memory shape inferences from experienced difficulty of recall. *Psychological Science, 121,* 176–179.

Winkielman, P., Schwarz, N., & Belli, R. F. (1998). The role of ease of retrieval and attribution in memory judgments: Judging your memory as worse despite recalling more events. *Psychological Science, 9,* 124–126.

4 Memory for the events of September 11, 2001

Kathy Pezdek

On the morning of September 11, 2001, a series of events transpired that changed the world. As first one passenger airliner, and then another, and then a third crashed into significant landmarks of US prosperity and security, it became clear that the United States was the victim of the most deadly terrorist attack ever to have occurred. Further, the fact that this level of destruction could occur so easily and so successfully made it clear that life as we know it in a free democratic country was forever changed. The implications of the terrorist bombing on September 11 were vast, they were unparalleled and they were immediate.

In the aftermath of September 11, like most Americans, I was coping with my own depression over the loss of human life and the loss of my general sense of security and well being as a US citizen. Even when I was not reading about the attacks or talking about the attacks, I was – day and night – experiencing intrusive thoughts about these events. Although I was not watching the television coverage of the events in the days after September 11 – I found it too overwhelming – most people in my world were glued to the television during this period, literally obsessed with what was occurring. In light of this devotion of our consciousness to the events of September 11 and our reactions to these, one might imagine that these events would provide the "flashbulb memories" that cognitive psychologists have been hunting for since Brown and Kulik (1977) first introduced the concept 25 years ago. The events of September 11 provided an opportunity for testing the accuracy and the persistence of memory for a salient life event that simultaneously shocked a wide cross-section of the US population. Counterintuitively, however, based on what I knew about memory, my prediction was that although most Americans would never forget the horrific events of September 11, few would remember the events as clearly as they probably thought they would.

Seven weeks after September 11, I had five samples of people complete a questionnaire on (a) memory for the events of September 11 and (b) their autobiographical memory for September 11. These five samples were: (1) 275 college students from Manhattan, New York; (2) 167 college students from California; (3) 127 college students from Hawaii; (4) 53 United and

American Airlines flight attendants and pilots; and (5) 68 fire fighters from California. This chapter focuses on the first wave of this longitudinal study. These results primarily involve comparisons among the three college samples who, because of differences in time zones, first heard of the terrorists' attack at different time intervals after the first World Trade Center tower had been struck.

The North Tower of the World Trade Center was struck by a 767 passenger airliner at 8:45 Eastern Standard Time (EST). The South Tower of the World Trade Center was struck 18 minutes later by a second 767. At 9:50 the South Tower began to collapse. At 10:28 the North Tower began to collapse. The entire event transpired over an hour and 48 minutes. In the midst of this, in Washington, DC, a third passenger airliner crashed into the Pentagon at 9:41, and at 10:06, in Shanksville, Pennsylvania, a fourth passenger airliner crashed to the ground.

People in New York City experienced the events in real time, and they experienced the events as a disjointed sequence of terrifying and incomprehensible incidents. It took some time for them to realize that the events of September 11 constituted a coordinated terrorists' attack. People in California and Hawaii, on the other hand, were more likely to have first learned of the events of September 11 after they had transpired, and consequently these people were more likely to have heard of the events in a coherent narrative describing a coordinated terrorists' attack. It was predicted that people would remember the events quite differently as a function of how the events were perceived. Comparisons across time zones avail a test of this prediction.

Episodic memory for a traumatic event

The primary motivation for this study was to assess the accuracy of episodic memory for a traumatic event. It is important for each of us to believe that our memory for past events is reasonably accurate. In some very central way, our sense of self relies on our memory for our past experiences. To the extent that these episodic memories are inaccurate, our sense of self is a distortion of reality. Our every day interactions with people also rely on shared beliefs about past experiences. These transactions usually go smoothly because our episodic memories for past experiences are usually "accurate enough". However, there are some conditions under which episodic memories are predictably less reliable.

The literature on eyewitness memory is replete with research supporting the role of specific factors affecting the accuracy of eyewitness memory. (See Cutler & Penrod, 1995, for a review of this research.) Also, dating back to the early research by Bartlett (1932), cognitive psychologists have known that story recall is a highly constructive process. People do not simply copy in memory stories or events that they experience in the world. People, for example, use schemas to comprehend events and consequently remember along with the event experienced, the embellishments and inferences that they derived from the schema. Although this constructive characteristic of memory aids in our comprehension, it is often the basis for memory flaws and distortions including suggestive influences (Holtz & Pezdek, 1992) and confabulations (Mazzoni, Loftus, Seitz, & Lynn, 1999).

What about memory for traumatic and highly emotional events? Are these memories subjected to the same type of distortions that everyday memories suffer from? The early research on "flashbulb memories" suggested that highly emotional events "leave a *scar* upon the cerebral tissues" (James, 1890/ 1950, p. 670). Brown and Kulik (1977) discussed their data on memory for the assassination of President Kennedy by postulating that "all ongoing brain patterns are subject to the order, 'Now print!' " (p. 96). Although a debate has ensued for the past two decades regarding whether it is necessary to postulate a special memory mechanism to explain the processing of traumatic events (McCloskey, Wible, & Cohen, 1988; Nadel & Jacobs, 1998; Neisser, 1982), in fact, many characteristics of memory for non-traumatic events apply to memory for traumatic events as well (Pezdek & Taylor, 2002).

Specific aims

At the most global level, this study on memory for the events of September 11 assesses the accuracy of episodic memory for a traumatic event. More specifically, this study was designed to examine whether episodic memory for a traumatic event is constructive in nature and whether the errors in episodic memory for a traumatic event follow predictable patterns. The results of this study will also allow a comparison of the accuracy of memory for the external events of September 11 (i.e., event memory) with memory for the personal circumstances in which one first learned of the events (i.e., autobiographical memory). Although Brown and Kulik (1977) first attributed the term "flashbulb memory" to the latter of these two types of memory, the concept is frequently assumed to characterize event memory as well. This is one of the few studies that separately examines event memories and autobiographical memories that were derived from the same event.

This study is also unique in that the events of September 11 were experienced to be more traumatic with more significant and widespread consequences, than were perhaps any other events that have been the focus of previous research on this topic, including memory for the 1986 explosion of the space shuttle *Challenger* (Neisser & Harsch, 1992), memory for the 1989 Loma Prieta earthquake (Neisser, Winograd, Bergman, Schreiber, Palmer, & Weldon, 1996), and even memory for the 1963 assassination of President Kennedy (Brown & Kulik, 1977). Because the "arousal hypothesis" is often proposed to explain why experiencing an event directly is more memorable than just hearing about it (Christianson, 1992; Gold, 1992), it is important to examine memory for events that were highly arousing and truly traumatic.

Methodology

The three principal samples were undergraduate college students at: (1) Baruch College at City University of New York in lower Manhattan (n = 275); (2) Pomona College in Claremont, California (n = 167); and (3) the University of Hawaii, Manoa and Hilo (n = 127). Questionnaires were completed by the college students in the seventh week after September 11. This was the earliest date possible given the time required to obtain an expedited IRB approval from each of the four participating universities. Faculty members or graduate students at each site recruited volunteers to complete the questionnaire from Introductory Psychology courses. Questionnaires were completed on site and were collected immediately.

The percentage of females (M = 62%) exceeded the percentage of males (M = 38%) at each site. The three groups were ethnically diverse. The dominant ethnic groups in New York were Caucasian (35%) and Asian (34%). The dominant ethnic group in California was Caucasian (73%). In Hawaii, the dominant ethnic group was Asian (52%), and 26% of this sample was Caucasian. As can be seen on the last page of the questionnaire in the appendix, the mean age of the three college samples was quite similar (NY: 18.91 years; CA: 19.15 years; HI: 20.78 years).

In addition to the three college samples, two other groups of participants were included. These were 53 pilots and flight attendants from United and American Airlines (the airliners that crashed were United and American Airlines flights) and 68 Californian fire fighters (the New York fire fighters were national heroes on September 11). Participants in these two groups were recruited by coworkers who were acquaintances of the author. Participants volunteered to complete the questionnaire at work and return it to their coworker. These were samples of convenience that in many ways were not comparable to the college samples, however, they were included because of the relevance of the events of September 11 to them. As can be seen on the last page of the questionnaire in the appendix, the pilots and flight attendants (M age = 42.02 years) and the fire fighters (M age = 39.37) were older than the college students, and they completed the questionnaires after a shorter time delay following September 11 (between five and six weeks following September 11 as compared to seven weeks for the college students). Nonetheless, these data are included because they provide interesting points of comparison with the college samples, and because they increase the generalizability of the findings.

A copy of the questionnaire is included as an appendix with the mean response per group indicated for each question. The significance level indicated for each item in the appendix is for statistical comparisons made across all five groups. The multiple components of question 1 probed *autobiographical memory* for the events of September 11. In addition to prompting open ended free recall, this question prompted for information regarding location, activity, informant, time, and others present – the five attributes focused on in previous research on flashbulb memory (cf. Neisser & Harsch, 1992). The remaining questions probed *event memory* for September 11. Accuracy and confidence for the event memory questions were obtained.

Results

The three college samples were selected because they spanned different time zones, and consequently were predicted to have heard of the attacks at different time intervals after the first World Trade Center tower had been struck. In fact, this was true. As can be seen in the responses to question 1 in the appendix, the mean time that the participants first heard of the terrorists' attack after the first World Trade Center tower had been struck was 0.99 hour in New York, 2.50 hours in California, and 4.10 hours in Hawaii. The difference among these three groups was highly significant, $F(2, 520) = 253.85$, $p < .001$. Correspondingly, as predicted, in response to question 3, "When you *first heard* of the attack on New York, did you know that it was a terrorists' attack?", 55% of the Californian sample and 59% of the Hawaiian sample responded affirmatively compared to only 39% of the New York sample, $X^2 (2, N = 569) = 19.43$, $p < .01$.

We also know that the participants in the New York sample were highly involved in the incident; they were on average 27 blocks from the World Trade Center when they learned of the terrorists' attack. Further, 12% of the New York sample were within 10 blocks, and 40% were within 20 blocks of the World Trade Center. In response to question 12, 28% of the New Yorkers had friends or family members in the World Trade Center or on one of the four hijacked airplanes, compared to only 9% of the Californians and 4% of the Hawaiians. In addition, in response to question 11, "Please circle the number indicating how you felt when you first realized that this was a terrorist attack on New York", (range = 1–7), the New Yorkers rated this event as more distressing ($M = 5.49$, $SD = 1.46$) than the Californians ($M = 4.96$, $SD = 1.49$) or the Hawaiians ($M = 5.17$, $SD = 1.41$). The difference among these three groups was significant, $F(2, 564) = 7.12$, $p < .001$.

Interestingly, the flight attendants and pilots reported high levels of distress (question 11) that were comparable to those of the New Yorkers ($M = 5.70$, $SD = 1.31$), and 25% of them had a friend or family member in the World Trade Center or on one of the hijacked airplanes (question 12). Further, for the flight attendants and pilots who knew someone involved in the event, 21% of these acquaintances did not survive, compared to 9% of the New York sample.

Event memory

The results are reported separately for event memory and autobiographical memory. Regarding how participants first heard about the terrorists' attack, as indicated at the bottom of Table 4.2, whereas the large majority of the college students first heard the news from some form of media (i.e., television, radio, online news, etc.), the large majority of the fire fighters and the flight attendants and pilots first heard the news from an individual (either live or by telephone). Regardless of how they first heard of the terrorists' attack, throughout the day on September 11 the primary source of information regarding the events was television. Although there were significant differences in the amount of television watched across the five samples, the mean number of hours watched (question 14) was 6.00 ($SD = 3.81$). In the week following September 11, the mean number of hours that people in the five groups reported that they watched television coverage of the events of September 11 (question 15) was 19.55 hours ($SD = 19.63$), to be compared with a mean of 6.85 hours ($SD = 9.84$) that people reported that they read about the events of September 11 in print and electronic news sources (question 16). For each of these three questions, the two most involved groups, the New Yorkers and the flight attendants and pilots, reported the highest levels of watching television and reading about these events. In light of this excessive exposure to information it would be predicted that memory for the details of the events of September 11 would be quite good.

Regarding event memory, one of the most interesting questions in the questionnaire was question 4, "On September 11, did you see the videotape on television of the first plane striking the first tower?" In fact, the video recording of the first plane striking the first tower was not available on September 11 and was not broadcast until the next day. Thus, responses to this question assess the extent to which memory is a constructive process. That is, the first plane flying into the first tower was the first event in the sequence of terrorists' events that occurred, and most participants did see the televised segment of this event. Therefore, in reconstructing their memory they retained memory for the televised segment presenting this event as having occurred first, that is, on September 11.

Across the five samples, the majority of the respondents (overall $M = 73\%$) incorrectly reported "yes" that on September 11 they did see the videotape on television of the first plane striking the first tower, and this pattern was evident in each of the five samples. This finding is made even more compelling by the fact that across all five samples, the mean confidence rating was significantly higher (indicating more confidence in their response) for people who incorrectly reported "yes" to question 4 (overall $M = 6.56$, $SD = 1.13$) than to those who correctly reported "no" to question 4 (overall $M = 5.59$, $SD = 1.77$), $t(664) = 8.38$, $p < .001$. Question 4 was the only question for which the correlation between accuracy and confidence was significant and negative, $r = -.31$, ($N = 666$), $p < .001$. Even among the New York participants, the majority (76%) incorrectly responded "yes" to question 4, and those who incorrectly responded "yes" were significantly more confident ($M = 6.59$) than those who correctly responded "no" ($M = 5.48$), $t(267) = 5.82$, $p < .001$. It is also interesting to note that the correlation between accuracy on this question and the amount of television watched on September 11 (question 14) was not significant, $r = -.02$, ($N = 627$). The effect is thus not simply a consequence of the amount of media exposure to the event. Together these findings support the constructive nature of memory, even memory for a salient traumatic event to which people had excessive amounts of exposure.

The responses to question 5, "Was the Pentagon struck before the first tower collapsed?" also support the constructive nature of memory for the events of September 11. Across the five samples, only 62% of the participants responded correctly "yes" and the pattern of responding did not differ significantly across groups, X^2 (4) = 5.76, $p > .05$. The first tower was struck at 8:45 and it began to collapse at 10:28. The Pentagon was struck at 9:41. One explanation for the low accuracy rate on this question (given that the chance accuracy rate was 50%) is that the participants experienced the attack on New York first and more intensely than they experienced the attack on the Pentagon. Consequently, the events in New York were clustered in memory and reconstructed as having occurred prior to the attack on the Pentagon. This interpretation is supported by the finding that accuracy on this question was significantly negatively correlated with the mean time that the participants first heard of the terrorists' attack after the first World Trade Center tower had been struck (question 1), $r = -.14$, ($N = 616$), $p < .001$. Thus, participants who first heard of the events later, were less likely to correctly sequence the events in memory.

Responses to question 7, "How much time passed between when the first tower was struck and when it collapsed?" indicate memory for the duration of the complete event in New York. The correct answer to this question was 1 hour and 48 minutes (or 108 minutes). The mean response across the five groups was 61.86 minutes ($SD = 81.16$), substantially less than the correct response, and the responses did not differ significantly across the five samples, $F(4, 599) = 0.05$. It is interesting to note that by seven weeks after September 11, for participants in all five samples, already memory for the events had been temporally compressed. This pattern was consistent across the five samples despite significant differences in (a) the degree of media exposure regarding the events (questions 14 and 15), (b) self-reports of the level of distress experienced (question 11), and (c) the mean time that the participants first heard of the terrorists' attack after the first tower was struck (question 1). Perhaps this result occurred because so few participants actually experienced the event – from the first airliner crashing into the North Tower to the collapse of this tower – in real time. The temporal compression might thus reflect that the resulting memory preserved the event as it was perceived (primarily on television) rather than as it occurred.

In terms of temporal memory for the more specific details of the events of September 11, response accuracy did significantly differ across the five samples. The mean response to question 8, "How much time passed between when the first tower was struck and when the second tower was struck?" was 23.25 minutes (SD = 21.65), slightly more than the correct response of 18 minutes. As can be seen in the appendix, responses differed significantly across the five samples, $F(4, 623) = 4.26$, $p < .01$, with the Californian and Hawaiian samples being least accurate, exaggerating the duration. Responses to question 9, "How much time passed between when the first tower was struck and when the second tower collapsed?" followed the same pattern.

The responses to questions 6 and 10 probe memory for specific details of the events of September 11. In response to question 6, "The point of impact, where the first plane hit the North Tower, was between what floors?" there was a significant difference in accuracy across the five samples, $F(4, 512) = 14.42$, $p < .001$, with the Californian and Hawaiian samples being the least accurate. In response to question 10, "The New York Stock Exchange was closed for how many business days following September 11?" there was also a significant difference in accuracy across the five samples, $F(4, 633) = 6.35$, $p < .001$. However, for question 10, although again the Hawaiian sample was the least accurate, exaggerating the number of days from the correct response of 3 to an average of 5.15, the Californian sample was most accurate ($M = 3.69$ days). Responses to this question most likely reflect the familiarity of each sample with the functioning of the stock market.

Autobiographical memory

Autobiographical memory was assessed from the responses to the first question in the questionnaire. In coding these data, we followed the procedure of Neisser and Harsch (1992) to obtain *Weighted Attribute Scores* (WAS). The five most salient attributes of autobiographical memory typically include *location*, *informant*, *activity*, *day and time*, and *others present*. For each participant, each of the five attributes was coded 0, 1, or 2 to reflect how much detail was included in the response regarding that attribute. A score of 0 reflected that no information or incorrect information was provided; a score of 2 reflected that accurate detailed information was provided. The author and one graduate student together read and coded the responses of all participants. Any differences in ratings were reconciled by discussion. *Location*, *informant* and *activity* were considered major attributes. *Day and time* and *others present* were considered minor attributes. The WAS is the sum of the scores on the three major attributes, plus a bonus point if the subject scored 3 or more (of 4 possible) on the minor attributes. The WAS thus ranged from 0 to 7.

Mean WAS and mean scores on each of the five attributes of autobiographical memory are presented for each of the five groups in Table 4.1. Although the WAS were generally very high (overall mean = 6.63) analyses revealed significant differences both among the three college samples, $F(2, 568) = 38.79$, $p < .001$, and among all five samples, $F(4, 689) = 22.14$, $p < .001$. The autobiographical memory data present a pattern of results that is quite different from that reported with the event memory data. As can be seen in Table 4.1, the WAS were lowest for the New York sample. This finding was consistent for each of the five attributes that composed the WAS. The finding that autobiographical memory was lower for the New York participants than for

Table 4.1 Mean weighted attribute scores (range = 0–7) and mean scores (range = 0–2) for each of the five attributes of autobiographical memory for each of the five groups

Attribute	NY	CA	HI	Air	Fire
Location	1.88	1.99	1.98	2.00	1.95
Informant	1.65	1.89	1.95	1.94	1.85
Activity	1.93	1.99	1.99	1.96	1.99
Time	1.81	1.82	1.83	1.85	1.71
Others present	1.87	1.97	1.97	1.98	1.87
WAS	6.37	6.83	6.87	6.83	6.63

participants in the other samples is inconsistent with the results reported by Neisser et al. (1996) that level of involvement was associated with better memory for participants' personal experience upon hearing of the Loma Prieta earthquake.

To assess whether autobiographical memory was significantly related to the degree of self-reported arousal, the correlation was computed between the WAS and degree of distress indicated in responses to question 11. Computed across all participants, this correlation was not significant, $r = .04$, ($N = 686$), nor was the correlation significant within any of the five samples except for the fire fighters, $r = .27$, ($N = 66$), $p < .05$. Although this result may be an artifact of ceiling effects with both measures, a consistent relationship between arousal and memory was also reported by Neisser et al. (1996).

In addition to the WAS, responses to the autobiographical memory questions were also coded from 0 (no information provided) to 2 (specific information provided) for (a) memory of the first thing said to you, (b) memory of the first thing that you said, (c) degree of emotional reaction noted, (d) degree of disbelief noted (i.e., "I couldn't believe it had happened"; "I thought I was watching a movie"), and (e) the extent to which the respondent indicated that they went about their regularly scheduled day after hearing of the terrorists' attacks. The mean rating per group, with the significance level for each indicated, are reported in Table 4.2. One way Analyses of Variance (ANOVA) across all five groups revealed significant differences among groups on each item. More specifically, the New York participants, along with the fire fighters, were less likely to remember the specific thing first said to them and the specific thing they first said upon hearing of the terrorists' attack. Also, the New York sample, along with the flight attendants and pilots, was more likely to express disbelief, more likely to express an emotional reaction and less likely to have gone about their regularly scheduled day after hearing of the terrorists' attacks than were the other three groups.

Discussion

This research extends the findings of other studies of memory for traumatic events and specifically compares event memory and autobiographical mem-

Table 4.2. Mean rating for qualities indicated in autobiographical memory responses (range = 0–2) and percentages indicated regarding source of first information for each of the five groups

	NY	CA	HI	Air	Fire	
First thing said to you	1.67	1.9	1.8	1.87	1.68	$F(4, 689) = 6.62, p < .001$
First thing you said	1.8	1.95	1.87	1.96	1.76	$F(4, 89) = 3.93, p < .01$
Disbelief expressed?	0.39	0.22	0.42	0.51	0.26	$F(4,689) = 34.52, p < .001$
Emotion expressed?	0.59	0.36	0.46	0.75	0.24	$F(4, 689) = 6.32, p < .001$
Go about your day?	1.44	0.84	0.72	1.32	0.87	$F(4, 689) = 29.20, p < .001$
First heard from media	82%	87%	72%	34%	29%	
First heard from a person	18%	13%	28%	66%	71%	$X^2 (4) = 132, p < .001$

ory for an event that was experienced to be more traumatic, with more significant and widespread consequences, than was perhaps any other event that has been the focus of previous research on this topic. The most interesting finding in this study is the result that whereas event memory was most accurate in the sample most directly affected and the most distressed by the events of September 11, autobiographical memory was least accurately reported in this sample. This finding is a novel one because this is one of the few studies that has separately examined event memory and autobiographical memory for the same event. The discussion will focus first on an explanation for this finding and second on patterns of errors that occurred in event memory.

The effect of arousal on event memory and autobiographical memory

The landmark studies of "flashbulb memory" include memory for the 1986 explosion of the space shuttle *Challenger* (Neisser & Harsch, 1992), memory for the 1989 Loma Prieta earthquake (Neisser et al., 1996), and memory for the 1963 assassination of President Kennedy (Brown & Kulik, 1977). From these studies it has been concluded that "personal involvement . . . led to greatly improved recall" (Neisser et al., 1996, p. 337). That is, that people more aroused by a traumatic event will remember their experience of the event better than will people less aroused by the event. The results of the present study suggest that this conclusion is too simple.

I propose that in these studies, as well as in the present study, the traumatic event and people's experience of it were perceived and processed separately, resulting in separate memories. Accordingly, the emotions produced by the events could be attached to either the external event or to one's personal experience of the event, whichever is more vivid. As a consequence, it is the more vivid and emotionally arousing aspect of the experience – either event memory or autobiographical memory – that will receive more narrative rehearsal and be more accurately retained. In this way, it is the synergy of arousal and rehearsal that affects memory.

In the present study, 73% of the participants first heard of the terrorists' attack from the media, primarily from television, and on September 11, the participants watched an average of six hours of television coverage of the attacks. Even in New York, although many of the participants experienced the events directly, they too watched a tremendous amount of television on September 11 – an average of more than seven hours. The televised images of the airliner crashing into the World Trade Center and the subsequent collapse of two of the tallest buildings in the world in one of the most densely populated areas of the world were vivid and horrifying. By comparison, participants' personal experience upon hearing of the terrorists' attack was relatively minor.

It is thus proposed that the emotional response to the experience was more likely to be attached to the external event than to an individual's personal experience, and the external event was more likely to be narratively rehearsed and subsequently more accurately recalled, especially by participants in the more involved samples. According to this interpretation of the results, participants in the college sample reporting the highest levels of distress, specifically those in New York, were more likely to narratively rehearse the events of September 11 and the focus of their narration was more likely to be the external event itself rather than their experience upon hearing of the event. This would explain why event memory was most accurate (as reflected in the responses to questions 6, 8, 9, and 10) and autobiographical memory was least accurate (as reflected in the results reported in Tables 4.1 and 4.2) in the New York sample.

What type of narrative rehearsal occurred for the events of September 11? A remarkable observation was the finding that the large majority of the participants sought out social contact upon first hearing of the terrorists' attack, and the social contact extended well beyond the individuals in their immediate environment. Students in New York phoned friends and relatives for updates on what had transpired and to see if they were all right. The fact that the cell phone service in New York was disrupted by the collapse of the World Trade Center was reported to be extremely upsetting to most New Yorkers. Students in California and Hawaii were on the phone, primarily with their parents, as if needing to be reassured that some aspect of life was unchanged. The process of talking about the terrorists' attack seemed to serve to make the events more comprehensible by providing a coherent narrative. It was this narrative rehearsal that shaped their memory for the events.

Keep in mind that in the present study, the terrorists' attack on September 11 was experienced to be highly distressing to participants (mean response to question 11 was 5.21, SD = 1.51, on a 7-point scale). In addition, autobiographical memory was recalled with a high level of detail (mean WAS, range = 0–7, was 6.63, SD = .66) and except for·the suggestibility questions, event memory was quite accurate as well. By comparison, the mean emotion-ality rating by the Californian participants in the Neisser et al. (1996) study of memory for the Loma Prieta earthquake was around 4, the middle of a 7-point scale, and the WAS reported by Neisser and Harsch (1992) in the study of memory for the *Challenger* disaster was about 3 (range = 0–7). The terrorists' attack on September 11 was, in fact, more distressing than were the events focused on in other studies of "flashbulb memory". Nonetheless, even in the New York sample in the present study, autobiographical memory and event memory were quite accurately retained. However, errors in event memory did occur, and they followed a predictable pattern.

Patterns of errors in event memory

This study afforded the opportunity to see if memory for a salient traumatic event is subjected to the same type of distortions that everyday memories suffer from. In a recent review of the literature, Pezdek and Taylor (2002) reported that many characteristics of memory for non-traumatic events apply to memory for traumatic events as well. Specifically, I wanted to see if con-structive features of memory were observable in memories for the events of September 11. Two questions were included to address this issue, question 4, "On September 11, did you see the videotape on television of the first plane striking the first tower?" and question 5, "Was the Pentagon struck before the first tower collapsed?" Regarding question 4, 72% of the participants incor-rectly reported "yes" that on September 11 they did see the videotape on television of the first plane striking the first tower. Even more compelling is the finding that across all five samples, the mean confidence rating was sig-nificantly higher for people who incorrectly reported "yes" to question 4 than to those who correctly reported "no".

Regarding question 5, 38% of the participants incorrectly reported "yes" that the Pentagon was struck before the first tower collapsed. One explan-ation for the low accuracy rate on this question is that the participants experi-enced the attack on New York first and more intensely than they experienced the attack on the Pentagon. Consequently, the events in New York were clustered in memory and reconstructed as having occurred prior to the attack on the Pentagon. Together, these findings suggest that memory for at least some aspects of the events of September 11 were constructed rather than being retained as they had in fact occurred.

Memory for the temporal duration of the events of September 11 also suggests that memory is a constructive process and events are not retained in memory as they in fact occur. Relevant are responses to question 7, "How much time passed between when the first tower was struck and when it col-lapsed?" The terrorists' attack began with the first airliner striking the North Tower of the World Trade Center and ended when this tower collapsed. Thus, answers to this question reflect the duration of the entire incident in the participants' memory. The correct answer to this question was 108 minutes.

The mean response across the five groups was about 62 minutes, substantially less than the correct response, and responses did not differ across groups. Although several researchers have reported that witnesses' estimates of the duration of a stressful event tend to be exaggerated (Buckhout, 1974; Loftus, Schooler, Boone, & Kline, 1987), the current finding of compressed memory for the events of September 11 does not necessarily contradict these results. In the previous research, the events focused on were experienced in real time, and it was the duration of these events that was temporally expanded. In contrast, few participants actually experienced the events of September 11 in real time. The temporal compression might thus reflect that the resulting memory preserved the events as they were perceived (primarily on television) rather than as they occurred.

These findings are likely to generalize to eyewitness memory. If the emotions produced by a stressful and traumatic event are attached to the witness's autobiographical experience, then memory for this aspect of event is more likely to be rehearsed and consequently will be well retained in memory. On the other hand, if the emotions produced by an event are attached to the witness's experience of the event itself, then details of the event itself are more likely to be rehearsed and consequently will be well retained. Future research is necessary to understand the conditions under which the emotions produced by an event become attached to memory for the event itself or the autobiographical memory. The next wave of this study will address changes in event memory and autobiographical memory over time to assess whether the patterns of results reported here are also apparent in participants' memories one year after September 11, 2001.

Acknowledgements

Several people made it possible to conduct this study in a timely manner, and I am grateful to each of them for their generosity. I am indebted to Melanie Rogers at Baruch College at City University of New York, Joie Acosta at the University of Hawaii, Manoa and Mark Runco at the University of Hawaii, Hilo, for their assistance in collecting data at their institutions. I also appreciate Robbin Hutchison's willingness to distribute questionnaires to the flight attendants and pilots. Finally, I thank Aris Karagiorgakis and Anne Schimmelbusch for their help with data coding and analysis, and Dani Hodge for suggesting question 4.

References

Bartlett, F. C. (1932). *Remembering: A study of experimental and social psychology.* New York & Cambridge: Cambridge University Press.

Brown, R., & Kulik, J. (1977). Flashbulb memories. *Cognition, 5,* 73–99.

Buckhout, R. (1974). Eyewitness testimony. *Scientific American, 231,* 23–31.

Christianson, S.-A. (Ed.). (1992). *Handbook of emotion and memory: Research and theory.* Hillsdale, NJ: Lawrence Erlbaum Associates, Inc.

Cutler, B. L., & Penrod, S. D. (1995). *Mistaken identification: The eyewitness, psychology, and the law.* New York & Cambridge: Cambridge University Press.

Gold, P. E. (1992). A proposed neurobiological basis for regulating memory storage for significant events. In E. Winograd & U. Neisser (Eds.), *Affect and accuracy in recall* (pp. 141–161). New York: Cambridge University Press.

Holtz, V. F., & Pezdek, K. (1992). Scripts for typical crimes and their effects on memory for eyewitness testimony. *Applied Cognitive Psychology, 6,* 573–587.

James, W. (1950). *Principles of psychology.* New York: Dover. (Original work published in 1890)

Loftus, E. F., Schooler, J. W., Boone, S. M., & Kline, D. (1987). Time went by so slowly: Overestimation of event duration by males and females. *Applied Cognitive Psychology, 1,* 3–13.

Mazzoni, G. A. L., Loftus, E. F., Seitz, A., & Lynn, S. J. (1999). Changing beliefs and memories through dream interpretation. *Applied Cognitive Psychology, 13,* 125–44.

McCloskey, M., Wible, C. G., & Cohen, N. J. (1988). Is there a special flashbulb memory mechanism? *Journal of Experimental Psychology: General, 117,* 171–181.

Nadel, L., & Jacobs, W. J. (1998). Traumatic memory is special. *Current Directions in Psychological Science, 7,* 154–157.

Neisser, U. (1982). Snapshots or benchmarks? In U. Neisser (Ed.), *Memory observed: Remembering in natural contexts.* New York: Freeman.

Neisser, U., & Harsch, N. (1992). Phantom flashbulbs: False recollections of hearing the news about *Challenger.* In E. Winograd & U. Neisser (Eds.), *Affect and accuracy in recall* (pp. 9–31). New York & Cambridge: Cambridge University Press.

Neisser, U., Winograd, E., Bergman, E. T., Schreiber, C. A., Palmer, S. E., & Weldon, M. S. (1996). Remembering the earthquake: Direct experience vs. hearing the news. *Memory, 4,* 337–357.

Pezdek, K., & Taylor, J. (2002). Memory for traumatic events. In M. L. Eisen, G. S. Goodman, & J. A. Quas (Eds.), *Memory and suggestibility in the forensic interview.* Mahwah, NJ: Lawrence Erlbaum Associates, Inc.

APPENDIX

Questionnaire with mean response per group indicated along with the results of the corresponding significance test conducted across the five groups

---

**Questionnaire Regarding Your Memory for
The Terrorists' Attack on New York, September 11, 2001**

*Thank you for participating in this study. Please answer the following questions from memory without consulting print material or anyone else.
Your responses will remain confidential.*

1. Please describe what you remember about where you were and what you were doing at the time that you *first heard* of the attack on New York.

Day and time:

**Mean ' hours after first impact @ 8:45 EST:
NY: 0.99   CA: 2.50   HI: 4.10   Air: 1.17   Fire: 1.05
Sig: $F(4, 621) = 152.38, p < .001$**

Where you were:

What were you doing:

Who told you (If TV/radio, what program/newscaster; if person, who?)

Specify as precisely as you remember, what was the first thing *said to you* regarding the attack:

Specify as precisely as you remember, what was the first thing that *you said* upon hearing of the attack:

Specify who else was present when you first heard of the attack:

> Please describe in as much detail as possible, everything you remember about where you were and what you were doing when you *first heard of the attack on New York and in the hour or so thereafter*. (Please continue on to back of page.)

2. When you *first viewed* the television reports of the attack on New York, what had already occurred at the World Trade Center? (Check all that apply.)

a. The first tower (North Tower) had been struck _____
b. The second tower (South Tower) had been struck _____
c. The first tower had collapsed _____
d. The second tower had collapsed _____
e. You did not view this incident on television on September 11 _____

3. When you *first heard* of the attack on New York, did you know that it was a terrorists' attack? Yes ____ No ____
    Indicate your confidence in this response: 1   2   3   4   5   6   7
                                              (uncertain)   (absolutely certain)

Responded "yes":
   NY: 39%   CA: 55%   HI: 59%   Air: 32%   Fire: 29%
   Sig: $X^2(4) = 31.90, p < .001$
Confidence ratings:
   NY: 5.63   CA: 5.58   HI: 5.88   Air: 6.52   Fire: 5.82
   Sig: $F(4, 668) = 4.5, p < .001$

4. On September 11, did you see the videotape on television of the first plane striking the first tower?   Yes   ____No ____   ____
    Indicate your confidence in this response: 1   2   3   4   5   6   7
                                              (uncertain)   (absolutely certain)

Responded incorrectly *"Yes"*:
   NY: 76%   CA: 61%   HI: 84%   Air: 62%   Fire: 73%
   Sig: $X^2(4) = 23.88, p < .001$

5. Was the Pentagon struck before the first tower collapsed?   ____Yes   ____No   ____
    Indicate your confidence in this response: 1   2   3   4   5   6   7
                                              (uncertain)   (absolutely certain)

Responded correctly, "Yes":
   NY: 62%   CA: 62%   HI: 56%   Air: 68%   Fire: 73%
   Sig: $X^2(4) = 5.76, p > .05$

Confidence ratings:
   NY: 4.40   CA: 3.76   HI: 4.08   Air: 4.90   Fire: 5.25
   Sig: $F(4, 657) = 9.25, p < 0.001$

6. The point of impact, where the first plane hit the North Tower, was between what floors? _____
    Indicate your confidence in this response: 1   2   3   4   5   6   7
    (uncertain)   (absolutely certain)

Response (correct: ~90th):
   NY: 88.89   CA: 71.72   HI: 78.03   Air: 86.20   Fire: 83.67
   Sig: $F(4, 512) = 14.42, p < .001$

Confidence ratings:
   NY: 3.68   CA: 2.78   HI: 2.74   Air: 3.66   Fire: 4.21
   Sig: $F(4, 509) = 11.72, p < .001$

7. How much time passed between when the first tower was struck and when it collapsed? _____
    Indicate your confidence in this response: 1   2   3   4   5   6   7
    (uncertain)   (absolutely certain)

Response (correct: 108 min):
   NY: 62.21   CA: 61.51   HI: 63.33   Air: 62.56   Fire: 57.21
   Sig: $F(4, 599) = .05, p > .05$

Confidence ratings:
   NY: 3.97   CA: 3.07   HI: 3.00   Air: 4.23   Fire: 4.30
   Sig: $F(4, 590) = 16.94, p < .001$

8. How much time passed between when the first tower was struck and when the second tower was struck? _____
    Indicate your confidence in this response: 1   2   3   4   5   6   7
    (uncertain)   (absolutely certain)

Response (correct: 18 min):
   NY: 20.61   CA: 26.56   HI: 28.29   Air: 17.93   Fire: 21.94
   Sig: $F(4, 623) = 4.26, p < .01$

Confidence ratings:
   NY: 4.65   CA: 3.48   HI: 3.46   Air: 4.76   Fire: 4.55
   Sig: $F(4, 614) = 19.56, p < .001$

9. How much time passed between when the first tower was struck and when the second tower collapsed? _____
    Indicate your confidence in this response: 1   2   3   4   5   6   7
    (uncertain)   (absolutely certain)

Response (correct: 65 min):
   NY: 76.61   CA:107.46   HI: 87.03   Air: 70.65   Fire: 56.76
   Sig: $F(4, 559) = 3.50, p < .01$

Confidence ratings:
   NY: 3.75   CA: 2.65   HI: 2.76   Air: 3.89   Fire: 4.10
   Sig: $F(4, 548) = 18.48, p < .001$

10. The New York Stock Exchange was closed for how many business days following September 11? _____
    Indicate your confidence in this response: 1   2   3   4   5   6   7
    (uncertain)   (absolutely certain)

Response (correct: 3 days)
   NY: 4.26   CA: 3.69   HI: 5.15   Air: 3.70   Fire: 4.16
   Sig: $F(4, 633) = 6.35, p < .001$

Confidence Ratings:
   NY: 4.67   CA: 3.36   HI: 3.40   Air: 5.20   Fire: 4.86
   Sig: $F(4, 620) = 27.55, p < .001$

11. Please circle the number indicating how you felt when you first realized that this was a terrorist attack on New York:

   1   2   3   4   5   6   7
   (very calm)   (as distressed as I have ever felt)

Mean response:
   NY: 5.49   CA: 4.96   HI: 5.17   Air: 5.70   Fire: 4.35
   Sig: $F(4, 681) = 10.80, p < .001$

12. On September 11, 2001, did you have any friends or family members in the World Trade Center or on any of the four airplanes that were hijacked?
   Yes _____No _____

Responded "yes":
   NY: 28%   CA: 9%   HI: 4%   Air: 25%   Fire: 2%
   If yes, did they survive?   Yes _____   No _____

Responded "no":
   NY: 9%   CA: 4%   HI: 2%   Air: 21%   Fire: 0%

13. On September 11, 2001, did you have any friends or family members in New York City?
   Yes _____   No _____

Responded "yes":
NY: 99%   CA: 72%   HI: 44%   Air: 55%   Fire: 22%
Sig: $X^2(4) = 234.58, p < .001$

14. On the day of September 11, estimate how many hours you watched the television coverage of the attack on New York.

Mean response:
   NY: 7.31   CA: 3.89   HI: 5.46   Air: 8.00   Fire: 6.11
   Sig: $F(4, 622) = 27.27, p < .001$

15. In the week following September 11, how extensively did you watch *television* coverage of the attack on New York?
   For about _____ days, I watched about _____ hours of television per day.

Response in total hours:
   NY: 26.59   CA: 8.17   HI: 17.14   Air: 29.23   Fire: 17.07
   Sig: $F(4, 663) = 30.96, p < .001$

16. In the week following September 11, how extensively did you *read about* the attack on New York in print and electronic news sources?
   For about _____ days, I spent about _____ hours per day.

Response in total hours:
   NY: 7.67   CA: 6.70   HI: 5.35   Air: 8.82   Fire: 5.12
   Sig: $F(4, 664) = 2.22, p > .05$

17.   Check which *one* of the following applied to you on September 11, 2001

____You were a college student on the East Coast.
What college? ____   What year in college? ____
If you were in NY City when the World Trade Center was struck, how many blocks were you from the World Trade Center? ____
____ You were a college student in California.
What college? ____   What year in college? ____
____ You were a college student in Hawaii.
What college? ____   What year in college? ____

18.   Gender: _____

19.   Ethnicity: _____

20.   What is your primary language? _____

21.   What country were you born in? _____

22.   If you were not born in the US, how long have you lived in the US? _____

23.   Your age (in years) on September 11, 2001 _____

Mean age:
   NY: 18.91   CA: 19.15   HI: 20.78   Air: 42.02   Fire: 39.37
   Sig: $F(4, 666) = 387.99, p < .001$

24.   Today's date _____

Mean days after 9/11:
   NY: 49.98   CA: 50.86   HI: 50.07   Air: 35.80   Fire: 40.48
   Sig: $F(4, 660) = 154.66, p < .001$

Part II

Learning in social settings

Lars-Göran Nilsson and Nobuo Ohta

Hermann Ebbinghaus is generally regarded as the father of the scientific study of memory. And indeed, as pointed out by Ohta in the indroductory chapter of this book, Ebbinghaus was the first person to do regular experiments on memory; he was the first to report the results from his experiments in graphs and tables and the first to draw conclusions about memory on the basis of these results and he communicated these results and interpretations about memory to others in scientific publications.

However, as memory research has developed, one can hardly say that Ebbinghaus was the father of what is now the mainstream investigation of memory, but rather the father of what has developed as the application of scientific studies of memory. This section of the book describes some aspects of how the basic principles gained in laboratory settings can be applied to learning and memory in more social settings.

The claim that Ebbinghaus rather was the father of applied research on memory might need a few words of comment. Danzinger (2001) recently described the core features of a debate between Wilhelm Wundt and Ebbinghaus that is not generally known among memory researchers of today. Wundt and Ebbinghaus distinguished between something that they called "memory proper" (*das eigentliche Gedächtnis*) and memory as it was conceived of and used by people outside the laboratory, in the real world. They both believed that the former was available for scientific investigation, whereas the latter was not. However, Wundt and Ebbinghaus had different opinions about what was memory proper. According to Wundt, memory proper involved the renewal of conscious contents, in particular self-consciousness, which comes close to what later has been called episodic memory. At the time, Wundt and others did not manage to find the means to explore this renewal of the conscious content and, as we all know, it took almost a century before methods were available to study such memories. Ebbinghaus had a different idea about how to set about examining memory proper. He felt that conscious contents should be avoided in order to make the scientific task manageable. This could be accomplished, he postulated, by studying retention, which, he argued, was another aspect of memory proper that did not involve self-consciousness.

As is known to all by now, Ebbinghaus used nonsense syllables as the to-be-remembered materials and the purpose of this was to avoid the influence of self-consciousness. The basic reason that Ebbinghaus was so eager to start studies on learning and memory by doing this detour around self-consciousness was that he wanted to establish methods for measuring the learning capacity of school children. Thus, the aim was to find a method that could be used in a practical setting and the means for this was an objective experimental technique that provided a measurement, but had little to do with memory, at least it had little to do with memory as we conceive of it today.

Ebbinghaus' efforts to develop methods to assess retention can hardly be said to be in a social setting as the rubric of this section of the book is. The chapter by Albert, Hockemeyer and Mori is certainly describing a social setting of the modern world, namely memory and e-learning. The authors point out that much memory research has been conducted that can be applied to this domain of investigation. However, they say, this previous research misses one important aspect of understanding e-learning in a more basic manner, namely that the concept of knowledge is not included as a core concept in the development of models for e-learning. The aim of all teaching, including e-learning, is of course, as they argue, to create knowledge and competence. Thus, the application of the psychology of memory to teaching and education must be accompanied by the application of the psychology of knowledge. The authors present very specific aims for applying psychology to e-learning more than has been done previously. The authors present the Knowledge Space Theory not only to be used for e-learning issues, but also, they claim, for use in improving basic and applied memory research.

The second chapter in this section by R. A. Bjork and E. L. Bjork presents an interesting theory about how to optimize treatment and training. On the basis of various basic-research findings, the authors have observed that the regular way of measuring performance during treatment and training may not be optimal for carryover effects to real-world environments. Bjork and Bjork argue that introducing certain difficulties, slowing the progress of therapy and training, may enhance long-term retention and transfer of desired changes or knowledge. The framework proposed, called the New Theory of Disuse, suggests how treatment and training should be structured to produce long-term effects and transfer.

The third chapter of this section on learning in social settings by E. L. Bjork, R. A. Bjork and MacLeod deals with intended and unintended forgetting. The essence of the chapter is that forgetting is a necessary and critical component of an efficient and adaptive memory system. The authors make the distinction between intentional or directed forgetting and retrieval-induced forgetting and make the claim that these two forms of forgetting play an important role in the everyday functioning of memory. They provide a series of illustrative examples of each type of forgetting showing the validity of their thesis. However, they also point out that the forgetting in order to avoid competition from competing memories is accompanied by some costs.

The obvious cost is that forgetting of a certain event, directed or retrieval induced, will hinder recall of this event if retrieval is wanted on a later occasion. More strikingly, a cost with respect to retrieval-induced forgetting is that the individual may unintentionally be led to accept misleading information as correct, as for example in witness situations, or to maintain certain beliefs he or she would prefer not to maintain.

The last chapter of this section, by Itsukushima, Hanyu, Okabe, Naka, Itoh, and Hara, reviews the literature on eyewitness testimony and uses the data from one empirical study to illustrate the role of conformity on memory accuracy. The method used was similarity rating of faces after manipulation of conformity by means of a confederate of the experimenter who was asked to give their responses before each other participant in the experiment. The authors claim that no such studies have been conducted previously in a similar setting. The results showed that similarity ratings on face recognition conformed to impacts given by the confederate, that the influence-of-conformity effects remain for at least one week and that the degree of conformity reflects the intensity of the impact given by the confederate. The authors conclude that, for example in an eyewitness-testimony situation, the performance of the eyewitness does not just depend on his or her individual memory, but also on the influence of society, in this case simulated by the testimony given by the confederate.

Reference

Danzinger, K. (2001). Sealing off the discipline: Wilhelm Wundt and the psychology of memory. In C. D. Green, M. Shore, & T. Teo (Eds.), *The transformation of psychology* (pp. 45–62). Washington, DC: American Psychological Association.

5 Memory, knowledge, and e-learning

Dietrich Albert, Cord Hockemeyer,
and Toshiaki Mori

Introduction

The aims of this chapter are to stimulate ecologically valid research in the psychology of memory and of knowledge, as well as stimulating the future development of e-learning. Hermann Ebbinghaus, the founder of modern memory psychology, called attention to the application of his results to educational practice; especially his results concerning distributed practice and retention. An early textbook about memory psychology written by Offner (1913) *Das Gedächtnis (Memory)*, also focused on the pedagogical applications of the scientific results. Nevertheless, more than 100 years later, Ebbinghaus' and his successors' results on massed and distributed practice have still not been applied in schools. This is more or less the general picture of applied memory psychology in education — even after Neisser (1978) called it "scandalous" and demanded more ecological memory research.

More recently, Harry P. Bahrick (2000) pointed out the following reasons for this ignorance. Traditional memory research had little impact on education, since it was focused on the short-term retention of episodic content, a domain that has little relevance to the concerns of educators. Furthermore, educators have emphasized the immediate achievements of students, paying little attention to the effects of their instruction on long-term retention of content.

Bjork (1994) pointed out that making training too quick and easy has the additional disadvantage of giving trainees an unrealistically inflated metacognitive self-assessment of knowledge and of the likelihood of long-term retention of knowledge and skills. Overestimations of competence can have disastrous consequences in particular work environments, for example air traffic control, police or military operations, or nuclear power plants.

Christina and Bjork (1991, p. 47) concluded that, "the effectiveness of a training program should be measured not by the speed of acquisition of a task during training or by the level of performance reached at the end of training, but rather by a learner's performance in the post-training tasks and real-world settings that are the target of training".

The results of Bahrick and others can be applied to long-term predictions of retention, to maintaining knowledge and – if necessary – to refreshing knowledge at a later date, thereby obtaining permanent storage of the memory contents. As this example already demonstrates, not only the models of memory but also the empirical results themselves can be used to substantially improve e-learning systems.

We would like to add the following comment. In the past the influence of psychology on practical teaching processes was indirect and complicated. Influencing both teacher training and teachers' behaviour in the classroom involves many stages. Even ecologically valid memory research probably could not have been successfully transformed into the educational practice of classroom teaching. However, by developing e-learning systems, memory psychologists can influence learning and teaching more directly by improving the teaching systems. It may be much easier to shape the "behaviour" of the e-learning systems than that of the teachers.

Indeed, there exist at least three successful examples. More than 30 years ago, the multi-talented Richard Atkinson and Patrick Suppes co-founded a very successful company (Computer Curriculum Corporation; now integrated into Pearson Education Technologies) for computer-based learning and teaching. John R. Anderson's ACT model has successfully been applied to e-learning applications. Recently, Jean-Claude Falmagne and his group created the fully automated, interactive, adaptive, and integrated math-tutor ALEKS (Assessment and Learning in Knowledge Spaces) — available only on the Internet – and founded the ALEKS Corporation.

Furthermore, if ecologically valid memory research is used to improve e-learning systems, these systems can then be used to improve the results of ecologically valid memory research. E-learning systems may be used as a kind of worldwide learning- and memory-research laboratory.

The aim of teaching is, of course, to create knowledge and competence. Thus, in addition to the psychology of memory, teaching must also be based on the psychology of knowledge (see, e.g., Albert, 1994; Albert & Lukas, 1999). As a result, the psychology of memory may profit methodologically from the psychology of knowledge.

Thus, three subdisciplines have to be combined, namely the psychology of memory, the psychology of knowledge, and the psychology of e-learning. On Monday 4 March 2002, at 23:00 CET, with "offensive content reduction", the search engine FAST SEARCH found 7,975,787 pages for "memory", 14,512,585 pages for "knowledge", and 620,650 pages for "e-learning OR eLearning" on the Internet. For "memory AND knowledge AND (e-learning OR eLearning)" 4,136 entries were found. Even if we take into account that all these terms are also used in technological research and development, it does not seem to be necessary to search any other data bases, e.g., for psychological literature, to demonstrate how huge each of the three subdisciplines are. Thus, we have to focus in this chapter on the intersections of memory, knowledge, and e-learning.

Former and recent contributions of psychology to e-learning

Technicians' e-learning definition

Current definition or aims of e-learning by technicians are: having access to electronically based learning resources anywhere, at anytime, for anyone.

Nowadays the most advanced technology for e-learning is the World Wide Web, WWW, Web, or Internet. Thus our aim is Web-based or Internet-based e-learning, directed by psychology and psychologists.

A psychological structure for e-learning systems

Depending on the point of view taken (e.g., computer and network technology, artificial intelligence, service, educational, or psychological), an e-learning system consists of a special set of components (see, e.g., Albert & Mori, 2001). In psychology, usually four components of a computer-based learning and teaching system are included:

Knowledge base

The *knowledge base* contains the structured expert knowledge about the knowledge domain.

Student model

The *student model* represents the hypothetical knowledge state and other attributes of the student. It may capture, e.g., the student's knowledge, misconceptions and general skills. It is the basis for individualized pedagogical intervention. It has to be adapted to the learning process.

Teaching model

The *teaching model* calculates the pedagogical interventions after taking into account the knowledge base and the student model.

Interactive human computer interfaces

The *interactive human computer interfaces* are needed to present information to the student and receive information from the student.

Cognitive psychology contributes to the development of e-learning systems by improving these four components by the application of its theoretical and empirical results.

Former and recent contributions

Programmed learning

The use of the computer for teaching aims based on psychological findings started with *programmed learning*, which is based on Skinnerian principles of operant conditioning. The basic idea was to break the information into small simple pieces presented to the student sequentially with immediate feedback ("reinforcement") given after each learning step – depending on the student's answer. Thus, programmed learning is addressed to the systems teaching model. It is the first of the psychological models realizing the principles of adaptive, personalized testing and teaching. However, programmed teaching machines were limited in their ability to adapt to individual differences among students and to provide a stimulating, responsive environment for students. Programmed learning was popular in the 1960s but in the end was not successful. The main reason for this was theoretical in character. In traditional operant conditioning, contingencies between already available and easily accessible behaviour and the contingent behavioural outcomes have to be learned. In classroom learning, for instance, new and difficult cognitive contents and operations have to be both acquired and applied. However, some aspects of programmed learning are still used nowadays in computer-based training of the drill type.

Mathematical models of rote learning

Mathematical models of rote learning assume that the learning process is described either by incremental growth or by stepwise transitions between learning states. The knowledge domain and the students are represented by individualized parameters for learning-task difficulties and learning ability. The models were developed in the 1950s and 1960s based on Estes' Stimulus Sampling Theory or Bush and Mosteller's Linear Operator approach. "Computer Assisted/Aided Instruction" (CAI) applications starting with language acquisition were initiated by Atkinson and Suppes. The latter, especially, is one of the pioneers and leading figures in educational computer applications on the basis of psychology. He is still active in this field, e.g., by contributing to Stanford University's e-learning program for gifted youth.

Cognitive modelling

The *cognitive modelling* approach aims to simulate the cognitive processes of humans by the use of computers, e.g., the cognitive processes involved in storing information, solving problems, metacognitions, detecting inconsistencies, etc. By means of Intelligent Tutorial Systems (ITS) or Intelligent Computer Aided Instruction (ICAI) these models have been used as the student model component in e-learning systems with a strong impact on the teaching model component of the system. Since the 1980s, learning to program a computer language, to solve complex physical problems and so on have been modelled. Among others, the working groups around John R. Anderson, Hans Spada, and Karl F. Wender should be mentioned. Until recently, several of these approaches have been more or less of academic value only, and while interesting results have been reached, many of them still remain theoretical and difficult to apply in the real world of broader field applications. However, in 1998 the Pittsburgh Advanced Cognitive Tutoring (PACT) Center together with the company Carnegie Learning was founded by the group around John R. Anderson. Their algebra tutor and other courses, originally developed at Carnegie Mellon University, based on Anderson's ACT-theory, have been very successfully applied in the field.

Knowledge space theory

Knowledge space theory (KST) is a mathematical psychological framework (based on order and lattice theory) for representing knowledge structures. The theory uses dependencies between problems and other learning objects in a knowledge domain in order to structure the assessment process and the teaching process for adaptive, personalized teaching – like a private teacher. KST was founded by Doignon and Falmagne in 1985 and has been enormously extended and applied to knowledge assessment and Web-based teaching since that time (see, e.g., Albert & Lukas, 1999; Doignon & Falmagne, 1999). Key concepts of KST are surmise or prerequisite relationships between test items or learning objects, knowledge states and the knowledge space, and learning paths. E-learning applications based on KST are the systems ALEKS, and RATH, which is a prototype. Some basic concepts of KST will be introduced in more detail below.

Current aims of applying psychology to e-learning

Psychology should have a strong impact on e-learning systems (see Albert, Hockemeyer, & Wesiak, 2002), as has been demonstrated by, e.g., Clark and Mayer (2002). Here we would like to focus on only a few aspects.

Psychological expertise in methodology

Psychologists' expertise in computer- and Internet-based presentation, assessment, data collection and experimentation will improve e-learning systems and their usability. The most advanced technology in e-learning is the Internet. Also from a psychological point of view Internet-based e-learning systems are preferable. Why is cognitive psychology a strong partner in developing Internet-based e-learning systems? The main methodological reasons are:

- Applying empirical findings to structuring content, creating student models and teaching models.
- Theory-based models of learning, reasoning, problem solving, knowledge retrieval, remembering and retention, which have been proven to be empirically valid.
- Test theories for assessment and diagnosis of performances, knowledge, and acquisition processes.
- Methodology for creating and presenting learning objects.
- Clearly defined learning objects and strict control of learning objects.
- Clearly defined and specified (classes of) actions of the teaching system.
- Methodology for recording the students' data, their traces of learning behaviour.
- Methodology for collecting, analysing and interpreting behavioural data, which are not only answers to multiple-choice questionnaires or solutions of problems, but also latencies, eye-tracking data, movements, e.g., of the computer mouse, video recordings, as well as psycho-physiological data.
- Expertise in computer-based and Web-based experimental methodology for assessing and shaping behaviour and the processes and structures behind the behaviour – no other discipline offers this.
- World-wide collection of data and information for testing the psychological and educational models or theories of teaching and improving or refining the e-learning systems.

Individualisation and adaptivity

The aim is to make the Internet-based systems behave like a private teacher. A private teacher has only one student at a time and can adapt his/her teaching behaviour to the individual student, to the student's learning state, his/her abilities, needs and so on, using his/her knowledge about this student. However, a private teacher is also using his/her knowledge about the theories, results, methods, procedures and techniques of learning and cognitive science, including the psychology of memory, cognition, and knowledge.

Already in the 1960s Patrick Suppes focused on "using computers to individualize instruction". By far the most important topic in current e-learning research and development (R&D) is adaptivity. Adaptive hypermedia systems bridge the gap between technology-driven tutoring systems – the risks: mental overload, demotivation – and student-driven learning environments – the risk: being lost in the hyperspace. We distinguish between the directions and objectives of adaptivity, the objects of adaptivity, and the level of individualization of adaptivity (Albert & Mori, 2001; Riley et al., 2001, Section 2.3).

Directions and objectives of adaptivity

Directions and objectives are the adaptivity to the requirements of different learning cultures, the adaptivity to the teacher's/student's aims and goals, the adaptivity to the student's properties, e.g., his or her (pre-)knowledge, preferences in Human Computer Interaction (HCI), communication style and needs, cognitive and learning style, and cultural background.

Learning itself is an adaptive process; the e-learning system has to support this process by being adaptive itself. Supporting the student by an adaptive e-learning system means: (a) the intended individual learning process has to be optimized according to specified criteria; (b) "learning to learn", i.e., control processes and metacognitive processes may also be a learning aim; and (c) other learning processes and demands on the student have to be minimized to overcome limited cognitive processing capacity and time constraints.

Objects of adaptivity

The question of what is adapting in an e-learning system has a strong relationship with the objectives of adaptation. Certainly, from a psychological point of view the four components of the e-learning system: knowledge base; student model; teaching model; and the interactive human computer interface, have to be made adaptive by the documents' contents, their kind of presentation, the documents' granularity, courses' contents and structure, navigation by dynamically generated learning paths, and navigation support methods.

Level of individualization of adaptivity

The level of individualization of adaptivity may differ depending on the learning culture, the status of technology and the status of research. In some cultures a large amount of standardization is required. Group level adaptivity is common for subgroups or minorities in a culture, e.g., for people with special needs. Individual level is usually the aim in Western cultures with the model of private teaching following.

However, in many cases the actual status of research allows only group level adaptivity, e.g., based on an empirical effect that has been found valid for a special group of persons.

Some of these objectives of adaptivity have already been realized in existing e-learning systems. We will introduce two of them, which are based on KST.

E-learning and knowledge space theory

KST was originally developed for the efficient, adaptive assessment of knowledge (Doignon & Falmagne, 1985). Meanwhile, however, the focus of applying KST has moved to e-learning. We will first introduce some basic concepts of KST and afterwards look at some e-learning systems based on it.

Basic concepts in knowledge space theory

Within the scope of this chapter only some basics of KST are presented. Here we want to mention that the theory is not merely a psychometric model but that it is linked to cognitive psychology, including memory psychology. For a more detailed and more technical description, the reader is referred to Doignon and Falmagne (1999) and Albert and Lukas (1999); a comprehensive list of literature can be found at http://css.uni-graz.at/staff/hockemeyer/kst-bib.html.

Example problems

Without going into details, obviously a structure is inherent in the problems presented in Figure 5.1. For instance, the solution process of problem (a) is included in the solution process of problem (d). Thus, (d) is more difficult than (a), and mastering (a) is a prerequisite for mastering (d).

Prerequisite relation

For another set of problems *u*, *v*, *w*, and *x* a prerequisite relation (surmise relation) is illustrated by the graph in Figure 5.2 (a). For instance, problem *w* is more difficult than problem *x*. Problem *x* is a prerequisite for problem *w*. (From solving problem *w* solving problem *x* can be surmised.) Problems *v* and *w*, also *w* and *x* are independent.

Knowledge space

For each prerequisite relation (surmise relation), there exists exactly one knowledge space (a theorem of Birkhoff), which is the set of knowledge states, i.e., the set of expected answer patterns corresponding to the respective prerequisite relation. For the prerequisite relation exemplified in Figure 5.2 (a), the corresponding knowledge space is illustrated in Figure 5.2 (b).

(a) Differentiate	$f(x) = x^2$
(b) Integrate	$f(x) = x^3 + x$
(c) Integrate	$f(x) = \dfrac{1}{14x^3}$
(d) Differentiate	$f(x) = x^2 - 2x - 3$
(e) Differentiate	$f(x) = \dfrac{ax^3 - bx - c}{x^2}$
(f) Integrate	$f(x) = \cos.x$

Figure 5.1. Example problems for the knowledge domain "Elementary Calculus" (Lukas & Albert, 1999, p. 5).

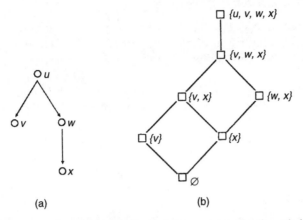

(a)   (b)

Figure 5.2. Example of a surmise relation and its corresponding knowledge space.

Doignon and Falmagne's generalization of basic knowledge space theory

Until now for each item we have taken into account only one set of prerequisite items. The illustrating graph is an AND-graph. However, in practical applications items are often solved by different kinds of prerequisite knowledge. In these cases the illustrating graph is an AND-OR-graph. A proof by Doignon and Falmagne also shows that in these cases a one-to-one correspondence exists between surmise/prerequisite structures and knowledge spaces.

Learning systems based on knowledge space theory

Adaptive learning environment based on knowledge spaces

Adaptive learning environment based on knowledge spaces (ALEKS) is based on Doignon and Falmagne's generalization of their KST. ALEKS has been developed at the University of California by a team based around J-C. Falmagne with the support of a multi-million dollar grant from the US National Science Foundation. Falmagne is also the founder and chairman of ALEKS Corporation (http://www.aleks.com).

ALEKS contains the complete K-12 mathematics contents. The structure of the objects was obtained in a two-step procedure: first, experts were queried about prerequisite relationships and, second, the preliminary structure was refined based on student data (Cosyn & Thiéry, 2000).

The system itself is not a classical e-learning system insofar as it is centred on test items. After adaptively assessing a new learner's knowledge state, appropriate new items are suggested as training items. Whenever the learner has shown a certain performance level on such a new item, it is included in their knowledge state, which also leads to a change in the set of appropriate items.

Relational adaptive tutoring hypertext

A teaching-centred system based on KST is the internet-based tutorial system relational adaptive tutoring hypertext (RATH) (Hockemeyer, Held, & Albert, 1998; http://css.uni-graz.at/rath). It is a prototype demonstrating adaptive presentation of learning objects depending on the specific (pre-) knowledge of the student. This is done through link-hiding, i.e., links to learning objects for which the student does not yet fulfil all prerequisites are hidden.

Due to its prototypical nature, RATH starts with the assumption of a complete novice. Whenever a teaching document is presented to a learner, it is preliminarily assumed that its content is acquired by that learner. However, if there are test items within the prerequisite structure, the learner has to solve them in order to get beyond that point.

Currently, RATH contains a tiny course on elementary probability theory structured through demand analysis and component-wise ordering (see below). However, system and content were developed independently, i.e., a different course can be installed into RATH at any time given an appropriate specification of the prerequisite relationships between the objects.

How to obtain knowledge spaces

In order to apply a knowledge space to adaptive assessment, to classroom teaching, or to adaptive tutoring, to develop or restructure a curriculum, and to describe learning objects by computer-readable metadata, one has first to obtain the knowledge space and, second, the knowledge space has to be investigated for its empirical validity. Here we focus on the first question, that is, on how to get the knowledge space.

There exist three traditional, straightforward methods of getting knowledge spaces: by analysing mass data from performance tests with respect to prerequisite relationships; by getting answer patterns that may correspond to knowledge states; and by asking experts about the surmise and prerequisite relationships. From these kinds of data the missing other structure, the knowledge space or the surmise/prerequisite relation, can be derived easily because of the one-to-one correspondence between the two structures.

In the following, we discuss approaches based on psychological analysis, taking into account the cognitive demands, latent, unobservable knowledge, and the cognitive processes (see Albert & Lukas, 1999).

Demand analysis and component-wise ordering

Learning objects can be described by attributes of several components. The attributes can be ordered according to difficulty (Figure 5.3, upper part) based on analysing the related cognitive demands (Albert & Held, 1994; Held, 1999). The learning objects can be located in a structure obtained by a

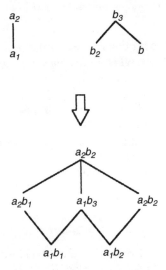

Figure 5.3. Component-wise ordering of learning objects.

Cartesian product of the components. Thus, the prerequisite relationships between the learning objects (Figure 5.3, lower part) can be obtained by component-wise ordering (dominance). This method has been applied successfully for different knowledge domains. A detailed example is shown below.

Direct skill and competence assignment

Using direct skill and competence assignment (elaborated by Doignon, 1994; Düntsch & Gediga, 1995; and Korossy, 1993, 1997) each item, problem, or learning object is mapped on to a subset of skills and competencies. The advantage of this approach is that the number of items and objects can increase without increasing the number of skills and competencies. Applications have been made, e.g., in the fields of geometry and algebra. The aim is to assess the competencies and to learn and teach competencies instead of performances.

Process analysis

Process analysis (Schrepp, 1999) uses process models of cognitive psychology, individualizes these models, e.g., by means of submodels of expert production systems, and derives the knowledge space for a set of items in the respective domain. Successful applications have been made in inductive reasoning tasks, e.g., letter series continuation.

Demands, component-wise orders, and indirect skill assignment in RATH

Demand analysis and component-wise ordering have been successfully applied for developing the RATH course based on the work by Held (1999). The methods used for the course development have been described in more detail by Albert and Hockemeyer (2002). Learning objects can be described by attributes of components. Types of learning objects are obtained by a Cartesian product. The attributes are ordered according to difficulty. The attributes' difficulty orders are obtained by the inclusion principle applied to the sets of demands assigned to the attributes. The prerequisite relationship of the learning objects are obtained by component-wise ordering (dominance).

An example problem in elementary probability theory

A typical example of a problem used in the RATH tutor is, "An urn contains three red and three blue balls. Two balls are drawn successively. Drawing is performed with replacement. The drawn balls are red. Compute the probability of this event."

Six problems of this kind, labelled *A*, *B*, *C*, . . ., *F*, have been structured. The resulting prerequisite structure and its corresponding knowledge space are shown in Figure 5.4.

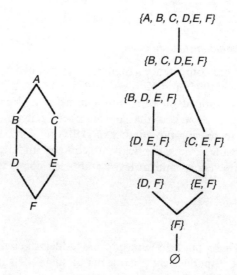

Figure 5.4. Prerequisite structure (left) and knowledge space (right) for exercises in the RATH course.

Problem components and their attributes

Three components are used to describe the problem types with two or three attributes for each component (in parentheses).

(a) Numerical ratio of differently coloured balls
   (equal to one, not equal to one)
(b) The way of drawing
   (one-off, with replacement, without replacement)
(c) Specification of the asked event
   (only equally coloured balls are drawn, exactly *m* of the drawn balls have the same colour, at least *m* of the . . .)

Attribute ordering by demand and competence assignment

Two examples for attribute sets (components) ordered by inclusion of the demand sets which are assigned to the attributes, are presented in Figure 5.5 for illustration. On the left side we obtain a linear order while on the right side we have a partial order due to the differently structured demand assignments.

Demands of the problems

The following demands have been used for assigning to the attributes.

(1) Knowledge that, in general, Laplace probabilities are computed as the ratio between the number of favourable events and the number of possible events.
(2) Ability to determine the number of possible events.
(3) Ability to determine the number of favourable events if one ball is drawn.
(4) Ability to determine a favourable event if one ball is drawn, or if the sample for which the probability has to be computed consists of equally coloured balls.
(5) Knowledge that if an outcome like "exact/at least *n* balls are of colour *x*" is asked for, all possible sequences of drawing are favourable events.
(6) Knowledge that probabilities are added for two disjoint events A and B.

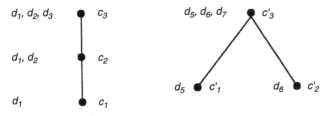

Figure 5.5. Attribute orderings based on demand analysis.

(7) Knowledge that probabilities are multiplied for two events A and B that are (stochastically) independent.

(8) Knowledge that the probability of drawing a ball of a specific colour is not equal to 0.5 if there are different numbers of balls of different colours in the urn.

(9) Knowledge that drawing without replacement reduces both the total number of balls in the urn and the number of balls that have the same colour as the drawn ball.

(10) Knowledge that drawing at least a number of certain balls includes the – not explicitly stated – results of drawing more balls of the certain kind.

Teaching units

We took the demands as teaching contents in our prototype RATH. Thus, they are the to-be-taught competencies that have to be learned to solve the problems. Each of these ten demands/competencies is represented by a teaching unit containing a teaching lesson (an instruction). Furthermore, most of these teaching units also contain some examples. These examples have the respective lesson as a prerequisite but are not prerequisites of any other learning object themselves.

RATH's learning paths

During the tutoring process, the student's knowledge state can be updated at any step corresponding to the lessons learned. At any time, the student has access to those learning objects that are the next step on some learning path from the current state to the destination or goal state (Figure 5.6).

Key concepts of RATH

Prerequisite relationships establish possible knowledge states and learning paths. Depending on the student's actual knowledge state she or he can choose from among the next steps for those learning paths for which he or she has the necessary prerequisite knowledge to understand a lesson or solve an exercise. Other lessons or exercises are hidden from the student and are not accessible. The system adapts to the student's changing knowledge. The knowledge of a student is also defined by his/her performance and his/her competencies.

RATH is an example of an adaptive system that applies results from cognitive psychology. Based on this, the question arises about how such systems might be improved by the integration of results from memory psychology.

Potential of memory research for e-learning

The human memory and memory traces are the basis and the substrate of human learning and knowledge. Certainly, the psychology of memory (see,

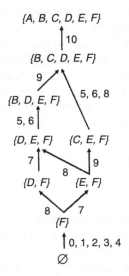

Figure 5.6. Learning paths in RATH. Letters refer to exercises, numbers refer to teaching units/demands.

e.g., Albert & Stapf, 1996; Tulving & Craik, 2000) has the potential to improve e-learning systems such as the RATH system. To make this explicit, some examples will be given.

Optimizing speed of learning and duration of retention

Guiding the student during the acquisition of new knowledge aiming not only at effective learning but also at long-term retention has been requested already by Bjork. The models and results of memory psychology referring to massed and distributed practice for learning and life-long retention are the basis of individual guidance during the acquisition process.

Optimizing by maintaining and refreshment

Weeks, months and years after new learning, introducing the individual student to activities both to maintain knowledge and to avoid forgetting prior knowledge is another aim, as mentioned already by Bahrick. The models and results in the fields of forgetting, retention and maintenance of knowledge can be the basis for the system's individual guidance.

Optimising coding and cognitive representation

The methods and results for multi-attribute coding, multiple-modality coding and deeper levels of processing are the basis for optimal coding and adequate rehearsal strategies. The different kinds of cognitive representations, e.g., pictorial or verbal, are important for cognitive functioning in learning, problem solving and creative processing. The same content can be represented mentally in different ways. Knowledge about KST is a good example, because different representations are possible: sets, graphs, vectors, matrices, formulas, orders, lattices, and logical operations are all used in representing the concepts of KST. Furthermore, the representations' interrelationships and their relations with the external learning environment have to be specified. The aim is to facilitate the generation and interpretation as well as the flexible and creative usage of the suitable representations by e-learning and e-teaching for problem solving and storage.

Optimizing mental load

Since G. E. Müller and A. Pilzecker the concept of narrow consciousness or limited working memory has been worked out in memory psychology, and many empirical results demonstrate the importance of this concept. Thus, also in applied settings, like e-learning, the model of working memories in combination with coding and rehearsal strategies may be the basis for optimizing mental load.

Optimizing the conditions for successful retrieval and usage

In order to apply KST, it is essential that all available competencies and knowledge are accessible and used. Thus retrieval problems and decision failures have to be minimized or coped with. The results on context effects, fan effect, recall latencies and so on are the basis for optimizing retrieval and use of available knowledge.

Recall and recognition

In e-learning the matter of answer-formats is of great importance because it has been shown that performance strongly depends on the answer format. Psychology of memory has elaborated different types of retrieval methods, like recall and recognition, cued recall and prompting. The retrieval methods correspond to some extent to the different answer formats and may explain performance differences. Thus, the results and models on retrieval can be used in e-learning systems in order to optimize performance measurement.

Optimizing transfer

The aim of at least higher education is to enable the student to use his or her knowledge not only for tasks used in learning and training but rather in other contexts and environments. The research on general and specific transfer as well as on context effects is the basis not only for acquiring specific competencies and for learning how to apply them, but also for transferring them.

Levels and hurdles in applying memory research

Modern memory psychology has existed for more than 100 years and a great deal of wisdom about human memory has been accumulated since Ebbinghaus, but this has not been finally integrated. The one and only theory of human memory is missing and many empirical facts have still not been integrated by any of the existing models and theories. Thus different levels of memory research have to be distinguished in application. Applications can be based on:

- Empirical effects and phenomena explained ad hoc;
- Partial models;
- Global memory models;
- Global cognition model; or
- The theory of the human mind.

Empirical effects and phenomena explained ad hoc

We may blame ourselves, however, as former memory researchers and current teachers of experimental psychology, that we are not able to overview all the empirical effects and phenomena in memory research. Experts on special fields in memory psychology may be helpful in developing e-learning systems. However, are they willing to participate not only in research but also in development – like engineers?

(1) Needed are even more standardized, and computer readable descriptions of the investigations and their results in memory research.
(2) Availability of the rough data in a computer database is necessary.
(3) An expert system is necessary for scientific handling of (1) and (2) for basic research, applied research, and applications like e-learning.
(4) Interfaces between these three components, the programs for computing or simulating memory models, and e-learning systems are required and should be developed.

Partial memory models

Partial models are good candidates for applications in specified learning situations, for instance a model for recognition (e.g., Signal Detection Theory-based or Random Walk Model-based) or for free recall (e.g., Linear Death Process Model-based or Associative Network-based) depending on the kind of knowledge retrieval. However, in applications different models usually have to be used simultaneously, both recognition and recall are often involved in the same situation, e.g., in comprehending an instruction or solving a problem. Thus, in applied settings, the question is how to combine different partial models or how to find a global model.

Global memory models

Recovering from the decline of behaviourism first partial and then global models of memory have been developed. The problem is that there are several of them, all of which are excellent candidates for applications, however with a lot of overlap, e.g., SAM, MINERVA2, TODAM, REM. Which one should be used for e-learning applications? Two aims are involved in applying the models: (1) the relationships between the models have to be analysed; and (2) it needs to specified how the memory models are to be linked to other models of cognitive functioning, e.g., for problem solving, or for reading and comprehension. Alternatively, we can take one of the global cognition models for application.

Global cognition models

With the availability of powerful computers several schools have developed global models of human cognition, e.g., the teams around John R. Anderson and Dietrich Dörner. Anderson's ACT model has already stimulated success-ful applications in e-learning. Often, however, the following problem arises in applying these approaches to cognitive modelling. One has to be a member of the respective school in order to be informed in enough detail about the functioning of the computer-based models to be able to understand and apply them.

The theory of human mind

As far as we know, a theory of the human mind that takes into account the empirical facts of cognitive psychology does not exist.

The impact of KST on memory research methodology

The impact of KST on memory research methodology will be at least two-fold, regarding folk data analysis and the validation of hypotheses and models.

Data analysis (an example)

Correlational analyses are very popular in psychology and have been performed also in memory research, e.g., recently by Kahana (2000). He recommends contingency analyses of memory performance data using Yule's Q-equation. The quasi-order used in KST allows high or low contingency – corresponding to high or low Q-values, which in KST means "equivalence" or independence. A moderate Q-value, however, can correspond to a strong dependency of the surmise or prerequisite type.

Kahana, for instance, presents a contingency table for the number of items, which are recognized and recalled by the same subjects or not (Figure 5.7).

Recognition test

		1	0
Recall test	1	9	2
	0	9	6

Figure 5.7. Contingency table for hypothetical data. 1 = correct; 0 = incorrect. Correlation: a moderate relationship with Q = 0.5 (Kahana, 2000, p. 62).

From the viewpoint of KST there exists a strong relationship between recall and recognition in this case – with only two exceptions because (1,0) = 2 instead of zero. From recalling an item, recognizing it can be surmised. Recognition and recall are in a prerequisite relationship. For (1,0) = 0, instead of two, the relationship would be perfect. This is not captured by using Q-values.

Validation of hypotheses/models

Because of the one-to-one correspondence between surmise relations and knowledge spaces, confidence table data as well as the answer pattern of the individual subjects can be used for validating hypotheses and models. Very convenient is Schrepp's (1999) method of individualizing the models. Creating a variety of submodels we expect different knowledge states for the different subjects. These can be compared with the observed answer patterns for validating the models. This procedure can also be applied to latencies. The models are explaining individual differences and they can be tested by taking individual differences into account, which is seldom done in memory research.

The impact of e-learning on memory research methodology

The impact of memory research on e-learning and that of e-learning on memory research is a reciprocal relationship. Memory research methodology can be used to prepare and improve e-learning systems, and Internet-based e-learning can be a very useful application of the results of memory research (see above). E-learning systems, on the other hand, can provide powerful research tools for applied memory research in an ecological setting using field experiments as well as prediction and control methods.

Applied field experiments

Internet experiments are already used in basic memory research (see, e.g., http://psych.hanover.edu/research/exponnet.html). From a methodological point of view, Internet experiments have a lot of disadvantages, e.g., the control of the experimental conditions is reduced, and the sample of participants is not representative of a given population.

Even by planning the experiments according to the state of the art, not all of the disadvantages can be avoided. This is the price of an ecological setting.

Thus, applied Internet experiments in the e-learning setting are meaningful for verifying the results of lab experiments in the field and as a control before applying the results of basic lab or Web experiments to the improvement of e-learning and e-teaching.

However Internet-based e-learning experiments are, in the case of applied memory research, based on carefully designed memory lab experiments. Thus, the convergence of the results of both kinds of experiments are important criteria for the successful application of basic research.

Prediction and control by application

Results from basic research may be applied directly to e-learning systems without prior applied field experimentation. The models and experimental results of basic memory research will be implemented directly in improving the e-learning environment. The convergence between the predicted and the observed behaviour or performance of the student is the criterion for successful application of basic research. In computer-based learning and teaching this method has a long tradition, see, e.g., the work of Patrick Suppes in the 1970s.

Even in the case of discrepancies between predictions and observations, the e-learning system can be improved by adjustments of the models or their parameters – and the models can be improved, too! In the case of unexplainable discrepancies, basic research will be stimulated. Memory psychology has the chance to verify its models and results in an ecological e-learning setting through field experiments and the control of predictions.

Concluding remarks

One of the traditional and most elaborated fields in cognitive psychology is the psychology of memory. The substrate of learning is memory. Thus the theories and results of memory psychology should be systematically applied to create the e-learning systems of the future.

On the other hand, besides using ecological memory research to improve them, the e-learning systems can be used to improve ecological memory research, using them as a kind of world-wide learning- and memory-research laboratory for testing and validating the models of memory in ecological settings.

The aim of teaching is to create knowledge, of course. Thus the psychology of knowledge – which is already much closer to e-learning than memory research – has to be linked with the psychology of memory to improve e-learning systems. KST provides methods for data analysis, validation of hypotheses, and models, which may improve basic and applied memory research.

Some hurdles in applying memory research results and models have to be overcome. Modern information technology has to be used for storing the descriptions of investigations and the data in computer-searchable and readable form for applications and model testing.

The relationships between the models in memory psychology have to be analysed between as well as within the partial and the global models.

We would like to conclude this chapter by the proposition that e-learning and KST offer a lot of chances and challenges for memory psychologists.

Authors Note

The work reported in this paper was contacted during the first author's stay as a visiting professor at Hiroshima University, Japan, during the academic year 2001/2002.

References

Albert, D. (Ed.). (1994). *Knowledge structures*. Berlin: Springer-Verlag.

Albert, D., & Held, T. (1994). Establishing knowledge spaces by systematical problem construction. In D. Albert (Ed.), *Knowledge structures* (pp. 78–112). New York: Springer Verlag.

Albert, D., & Hockemeyer, C. (2002). Applying demand analysis of a set of test problems for developing an adaptive course. In *Proceedings of the International Conference on Computers in Education ICCE 2002* (pp. 69–70). Los Alamitos, CA: ICCE Computer Society.

Albert, D., Hockemeyer, C., & Wesiak, G. (2002). Current trends in e-learning based on knowledge space theory and cognitive psychology. *Psychologische Beiträge, 44*, 478–494.

Albert, D., & Lukas, J. (Eds.). (1999). *Knowledge spaces: Theories, empirical research, applications*. Mahwah, NJ: Lawrence Erlbaum Associates, Inc.

Albert, D., & Mori, T. (2001). Contributions of cognitive psychology to the future of e-learning. *Bulletin of the Graduate School of Education, Hiroshima University, Part I (Learning and Curriculum Development)*, *50*, 25–34.

Albert, D., & Stapf, K.-H. (Eds.). (1996). *Gedächtnis. Enzyklopädie der Psychologie, Themenbereich C, Serie II, Band 4* [Memory. Encyclopedia of Psychology]. Göttingen: Hogrefe.

Bahrick, H. P. (2000). Long-term maintenance of knowledge. In E. Tulving & F. I. M. Craik (Eds.), *The Oxford handbook of memory* (pp. 347–362). Oxford: Oxford University Press.

Bjork, R. A. (1994). Memory and metamemory: Considerations in the training of human beings. In J. Metcalfe & A. Shimamura (Eds.), *Metacognition: Knowing about knowing* (pp. 185–206). Cambridge, MA: MIT Press.

Christina, R. W., & Bjork, R. A. (1991). Optimizing long-term retention and transfer. In D. Druckman & R. A. Bjork (Eds.), *In the mind's eye: Enhancing human performance* (pp. 23–56). Washington, DC: National Academy Press. (Also available online: http://www.nap.edu/books/0309047471/html/; access July 17, 2003)

Clark, R. C., & Mayer, R. E. (2002). *E-learning and the science of instruction: Proven guidelines for consumers and designers of multimedia learning.* San Francisco, CA: Wiley.

Cosyn, E., & Thiéry, N. (2000). A practical procedure to build a knowledge structure. *Journal of Mathematical Psychology, 44,* 383–407.

Doignon, J.-P. (1994). Knowledge spaces and skill assignments. In G. H. Fischer & D. Laming (Eds.), *Contributions to mathematical psychology, psychometrics, and methodology* (pp. 111–121). New York: Springer-Verlag.

Doignon, J.-P., & Falmagne, J.-C. (1985). Spaces for the assessment of knowledge. *International Journal of Man–Machine Studies, 23,* 175–196.

Doignon, J.-P., & Falmagne, J.-C. (1999). *Knowledge spaces.* Berlin: Springer Verlag.

Düntsch, I., & Gediga, G. (1995). Skills and knowledge structures. *British Journal of Mathematical and Statistical Psychology, 48,* 9–27.

Held, T. (1999). An integrated approach for constructing, coding, and structuring a body of word problems. In D. Albert & J. Lukas (Eds.), *Knowledge spaces: Theories, empirical research, applications* (pp. 67–102). Mahwah, NJ : Lawrence Erlbaum Associates, Inc.

Hockemeyer, C., Held, T., & Albert, D. (1998). RATH – a relational adaptive tutoring hypertext WWW-environment based on knowledge space theory. In C. Alvegård (Ed.), *CALISCE'98: Proceedings of the Fourth International Conference on Computer Aided Learning in Science and Engineering* (pp. 417–423). Göteborg, Sweden: Chalmers University of Technology.

Kahana, M. J. (2000). Contingency analysis of memory. In E. Tulving & F. I. M. Craik (Eds.), *The Oxford handbook of memory* (pp. 59–72). Oxford: Oxford University Press.

Korossy, K. (1993). *Modellierung von Wissen als Kompetenz und Performanz* [Modelling knowledge as competence and performance]. Inauguraldissertation, Fakultät für Sozial- und Verhaltenswissenschaften, Universität Heidelberg.

Korossy, K. (1997). Extending the theory of knowledge spaces: A competence–performance approach. *Zeitschrift für Psychologie, 205,* 53–82.

Lukas, J., & Albert, D. (1999). Knowledge structures: What they are and how they can be used in cognitive psychology, test theory, and the design of learning environments. In D. Albert & J. Lukas (Eds.), *Knowledge spaces: Theories, empirical research, applications* (pp. 3–12). Mahwah, NJ: Lawrence Erlbaum Associates, Inc.

Neisser, U. (1978). Memory: What are the important questions? In M. M. Grunenberg, P. E. Morris, & R. E. Sykes (Eds.), *Practical aspects of memory* (pp. 3–24). London: Academic Press.

Offner, M. (1913). *Das Gedächtnis. Die Ergebnisse der experimentellen Psychologie und ihre Anwendung in Unterricht u. Erziehung* [Memory. Results of experimental psychology and its applications in teaching and education]. Dritte, vermehrte u. teilweise umgearbeitete Aufl. Berlin: Reuther & Reichard.

Riley, K., Pavlidou, T., Wade, V., Conlan, O., Akeroyd, J., Sandford, P., Albert, D., Hockemeyer, C., Lefrere, P., Grant, J., Romano, L., Da Bormida, G., Trabucchi, R., & Cardinali, F. (2001). *EASEL D03 – Requirements specification,* version 1.2. Available online at http://css.uni-graz.at/projects/easel/D03.doc;access7nov2005.

Schrepp, M. (1999). An empirical test of a process model for letter series completion problems. In D. Albert & J. Lukas (Eds.), *Knowledge spaces: Theories, empirical research, applications* (pp. 133–154). Mahwah, NJ: Lawrence Erlbaum Associates, Inc.

Tulving, E., & Craik, F. I. M. (Eds.). (2000). *The Oxford handbook of memory.* Oxford: Oxford University Press.

6 Optimizing treatment and instruction: Implications of a new theory of disuse

Robert A. Bjork and
Elizabeth L. Bjork

With few or no exceptions, the goals of both treatment and instruction (or training) are long-term goals. In the case of instruction, we would like the conditions of instruction and practice to yield knowledge and skills that are durable and flexible – that is, knowledge and skills that are not only accessible within the instructional context, but that are also accessible in the various post-instructional real-world settings to which they are applicable. In the case of treatment, we would like therapy to be structured in a way that produces long-term changes in behaviour – that is, changes that last beyond the end of treatment and are not confined to the treatment context.

Knowledge and skills acquired during instruction, however, often prove to be neither durable nor flexible. Individuals who perform well at the end of instruction frequently perform poorly at a later time when it really matters, especially if a prolonged period of disuse of that knowledge or skill has intervened, or if the post-instructional environment differs – even super-ficially – from the instructional environment. Similarly, changes in behaviour that are evident during treatment are often short-lived after treatment, or fail to transfer to the real-world settings in which they are most needed, or both. Individuals who overcome fearful responding during treatment, or appear to make progress in overcoming some other problem, frequently suffer a return of that fear or problem as time passes after treatment (e.g., Clark, Salkovskis, Hackmann, Middleton, Anastasiades, & Gelder 1994; Craske, Brown, & Barlow, 1991; Heimberg, Salzman, Holt, & Blendell, 1993; Ost, 1996; and see Craske, 1999, and Rachman, 1989, for reviews).

Learning versus performance

Why are programmes of instruction and treatment often less than successful in achieving the long-term goals of instruction or treatment? One reason, as we and our colleagues have argued elsewhere (e.g., Bjork, 1994, 1999; Bjork & Bjork, 1992; Christina & Bjork, 1991; Jacoby, Bjork, & Kelley, 1994; Schmidt & Bjork, 1992; Simon & Bjork, 2001), is that teachers, trainers, and therapists are at risk of assuming that *performance* during instruction, train-ing, or treatment is a reliable index of *learning* – that is, that performance during instruction provides a valid basis for judging whether the relatively permanent changes that will support long-term performance have or have not taken place. In fact, such performance is often *not* a reliable index of learning.

The need to distinguish between learning and performance traces back to the heydays of learning research – the 1930s, 1940s, and 1950s – when latent-learning experiments with animals (e.g., Tolman & Honzik, 1930) and motor-learning experiments with humans (e.g., Adams & Reynolds, 1954) demonstrated that considerable learning could happen across a period when there were few or no changes in performance. More recent findings have demonstrated that the converse is true as well – that is, it is also the case that little or no learning can happen across periods when there are substantial changes in performance (for reviews, see Bjork, 1994, 1999; Christina & Bjork, 1991; Schmidt & Bjork, 1992).

Thus, a major problem confronting any designer of treatment or instruction is that performance *during* treatment or instruction does not provide a reliable index of whether the goals of treatment or instruction have been achieved. Conditions of treatment or instruction that enhance performance, or accelerate the rate of desirable changes in behaviour, can fail to support long-term retention and transfer. Conversely, conditions that introduce difficulties for students, trainees, or patients – slowing their apparent rate of progress – may prove optimal, as measured by the long-term consequences of instruction or treatment.

Our goal in the present chapter is to examine the optimization problem from the standpoint of a theoretical framework we have come to call a "new theory of disuse" (Bjork & Bjork, 1992). The theory distinguishes between *storage strength*, a measure of learning, and *retrieval strength*, a measure of current ease of access – a distinction that is consistent with the time-honoured distinction between *learning* and *performance*. From the standpoint of the theory, programmes of treatment and instruction are frequently far from optimal for two reasons: (1) retrieval strength is confused with learning; and (2) manipulations that – according to the theory – optimize the gain of retrieval strength are *not* those that will optimize the gain of storage strength that is necessary to support long-term retention and transfer, or in the case of treatment, to maintain the newly learned desired behaviour and to prevent the return of the old, undesirable behaviour. In the present chapter, we focus on implications of the theory for optimizing treatment, especially of fears and phobias; for a discussion of the implications of the theory for the optimization of instruction and training, see Bjork (1999).

Before moving on to the assumptions of the new theory of disuse in greater detail, we need to characterize treatment, and the problem of changing behaviours, as a learning problem. In the following characterization we lean heavily on the work of Mark Bouton and his collaborators (e. g., Bouton, 1994, 2000; Bouton & Swartzentruber 1991), who have provided an insightful analysis of clinical treatment – and the maintenance or lapse of behavioural changes – from a learning-theory perspective. We also lean heavily on the work of Michelle Craske and her collaborators (Lang & Craske, 2000; Lang, Craske, & Bjork, 1999; Mystkowski, Craske, & Echiverri, 2002; Rodriguez, Craske, Mineka, & Hladek, 1999; Rowe & Craske, 1998a, 1998b; Tsao & Craske, 2001), who have provided innovative and systematic research on the exposure treatment of fears and phobias from a therapy-as-learning perspective.

Behavioural change as new learning

At the risk of oversimplification, the challenge confronting a therapist – from a learning-theory perspective – is to structure the conditions of treatment so as to enable a patient to replace earlier-learned non-adaptive behaviours with newly-learned more-adaptive behaviours. Someone suffering a debilitating fear of spiders, heights, or public speaking, for example, has learned – prior to entering treatment and perhaps over a long period of time – a pattern of emotional and behavioural responding to certain situational cues that inter-feres with and constrains his or her daily life. The problem for the therapist (and the patient) is to replace that pattern of responding with a more adap-tive pattern of responding. From a learning-theory standpoint, the problem is one of *counterconditioning*.

Evidence abounds, however, from both human and animal research, that new learning does not replace or overwrite old learning. Extinction or coun-terconditioning procedures that might seem to have eliminated a particular response to a particular stimulus configuration, or replaced that response with another response, do not actually replace the original stimulus–response association. By some measures, in fact, such procedures leave the original stimulus–response association at full strength (see, e.g., Rescorla, 1993, 1996, 2001). Some of the types of evidence from the animal-learning literature for that assertion (as summarized by Bouton, 1994) are *renewal, reinstatement*, and *spontaneous recovery*, phenomena that we describe in the next section.

Recovery effects in extinction and counterconditioning

Renewal The phenomenon of *renewal* refers to the recovery of the original stimulus–response association when an animal is brought back to the original conditioning context after undergoing extinction in a different context. Bouton (1993), for example, has shown that when conditioning (e.g., tone–footshock) occurs in one context (say, A) and then extinction (e.g., tone presentation alone) occurs in another context (say, B), presentation of the tone alone back in context A will result in a full recovery of the original conditioned fear response to it. Furthermore, renewal can also occur when the tone is presented alone in a third context (say, C); that is, a context in which neither the original conditioning nor the extinction took place. In contrast, however, extinction performance seems to depend on testing in the context in which extinction occurred. In other words, whereas the original conditioned fear response generalizes to new contexts, the learned extinction response does not (e.g., Bouton & Bolles, 1979; Bouton & Brooks, 1993).

Reinstatement   The phenomenon of *reinstatement* refers to the reappearance or reinstatement of an extinguished stimulus–response association following presentation alone of the original unconditioned stimulus (e.g., Rescorla & Heth, 1975). If, for example, following the extinction of a conditioned fear response to a tone, the unconditioned stimulus of footshock is presented by itself, the fear response will return when the tone is presented again in that same context (e.g., Bouton, 1984; Bouton & King, 1983). As interpreted by Bouton and colleagues, the presentation of the unconditioned stimulus alone creates an association between it and the contextual cues present at the time. Those contextual cues then give rise to the expectation of the unconditioned stimulus, resulting in a return of the extinguished response when the tone alone is presented.

Spontaneous recovery   The phenomenon of *spontaneous recovery* refers to the return of a previously extinguished response to a conditioned stimulus with the passage of time since extinction. If, as suggested by Bouton (2000) and, previously, by Estes (1955), the passage of time is assumed to allow a new contextual background to emerge, then spontaneous recovery can be thought of as a renewal effect that occurs when the previously extinguished stimulus is encountered in a new temporal context.

Of considerable relevance for treatment, all three of these recovery effects have also been shown to occur after counter-conditioning. Peck and Bouton (1990), for example, have demonstrated a dramatic renewal effect when tone–shock pairings (or tone–shock conditioning) occur in context A, then tone–food pairings (or tone–food conditioning) occur in context B, and then the tone is presented back in context A. Even when fear responding to the tone has completely disappeared and been replaced by food responding by the end of the second conditioning phase, when back in context A, fear responding returns in response to the tone. (It should be noted that this effect does not depend on the tone–shock pairings occurring first; that is, renewal of the first learned response also occurs when tone–food pairings are followed by tone–shock pairings.)

Additionally, Brooks, Hale, Nelson and Bouton (1995) have shown that reinstatement occurs following a few presentations of shock alone after the originally learned fear responding to tone–shock pairings has been replaced by food responding to tone–food pairings. As with extinction, however, the shock-alone presentations have to be presented in the testing context, causing the expectancy of shock in that context and, thus, a return of the fear response to the tone. And, finally, spontaneous recovery of the first conditioned response has also been shown to occur simply with the passage of time. If tone–shock conditioning is followed by tone–food counterconditioning, for example, the behaviour that is most likely to occur in response to the tone sounded alone depends on when the tone is subsequently presented. After a short delay, such as one day, the behaviour that dominates tends to be the recently learned (food-appropriate) behaviour, whereas after a long delay, such as a month, the first-learned (shock-appropriate) behaviour becomes dominant (Bouton & Peck, 1992).

Thus, to the extent that behavioural changes acquired during the treatment of fears and phobias constitute learning new responses to the same cues with which undesirable responses are associated, such as a debilitating fearful response to spiders, then someone undergoing treatment is vulnerable to all of the recovery effects described above – that is, renewal, reinstatement, and spontaneous recovery. The fact that the old fearful responding is not replaced or overwritten by the new non-fearful responding means that both associations remain in memory and compete for retrieval – with, unfortunately, the odds often stacked in favour of fearful responding, given the dynamics of renewal, reinstatement, and recovery and the longer period over which the fearful responding was acquired.

In the next sections, we turn to a description of the new theory of disuse, a framework that we have proposed to explain several distinctive qualities of human memory, which is also quite compatible with the just described perspective of new learning in conditioning and counterconditioning terms, advanced by Bouton and his colleagues (e.g., Bouton, 1994, 2000; Bouton & Swartzentruber, 1991). We first describe the new theory of disuse and its assumptions. We then indicate how these assumptions are compatible with the characterization of treatment and the problem of changing behaviours as a problem of new learning and how its assumptions can thus point the way to improved conditions of treatment; that is, conditions that can enhance its long-term effectiveness. We then describe studies involving exposure therapy that were designed to test some implications of the new theory of disuse respecting how treatment conditions should be structured to enhance the effectiveness of therapy.

COMPETITIVE DYNAMICS IN LEARNING AND MEMORY: A NEW THEORY OF DISUSE

The new theory of disuse (Bjork & Bjork, 1992) was formulated to provide an account of certain fundamental phenomena that characterize human learning and memory. The assumptions of the theory were influenced heavily by certain "important peculiarities" of human memory. Among these peculiarities are the following: (1) a remarkable capacity for storing information coupled with a highly fallible retrieval process; (2) what can be accessed from memory at any one time is heavily dependent on the current environmental, interpersonal, emotional, and body-state cues; (3) the act of retrieving information from memory is a dynamic process that alters the subsequent state of the system; and (4) access to competing memory representations regresses over time – that is, with the passage of time and accompanying intervening events, memory representations learned earlier become more accessible and competing memory representations learned more recently become less accessible (for a discussion of such regression effects, see Bjork, 2001).

Such important peculiarities are both important and strange because they describe characteristics of human memory that differ markedly from the characteristics of man-made memory devices, such as a videotape recorder or the memory in a computer. In that sense, they provide a kind of guide to the functional architecture of human learning and memory and, especially, how that architecture differs from the architecture that characterizes man-made recording devices of various kinds.

The new theory of disuse versus Thorndike's (1914) "law of disuse"

A kind of conceptual starting point for the new theory of disuse derives from a real-world observation – namely, that no matter how well learned items are at some point in time they eventually become non-recallable given a long enough period of disuse. Thus, a home phone number, or street address, or friend's name, which may have been effortlessly recallable at one point in time, will nonetheless become non-recallable given a long enough period of disuse. As measured by other indices, however, such as recognition and, especially, relearning, it is possible to demonstrate that such information still resides in your memory and at essentially full strength. That is, what is lost to us with disuse is not the memories per se, but access to those memories.

In Thorndike's (1914) original "law of disuse," disuse was assumed to lead to decay of the actual memory representations. In the *new* theory of disuse, memory representations, once encoded in long-term memory, are assumed to remain in memory, but – without intermittent access to those representations – they eventually become non-retrievable.

In short, the momentary ease of access to a memory representation, which may be a product of recency or prevailing contextual and other cues, needs to be distinguished from the more permanent/learned representation of that information in memory. In the new theory of disuse, this distinction is captured by assuming that items in memory are represented by two types of strengths: (1) *retrieval strength*, which refers to momentary ease of access; and (2) *storage strength*, which refers to how "entrenched" or interassociated a given item is with other items in memory – that is, how well learned that item is.

Such a distinction is not new. In fact, learning theorists dating back to the heydays of learning theories in the 1930s, 1940s, and 1950s, all found it necessary to make such a distinction in order to account for a variety of phenomena, all of which pointed to the necessity to distinguish between *performance* and *learning*. Hull (1943), for example, distinguished between "momentary reaction potential" and "habit strength", and Estes (1955) distinguished between "response strength" and "habit strength". What is new are the assumptions of the new theory of disuse as to how retrieval strength and storage strength interact and change as a function of study and retrieval events.

Assumptions of the new theory of disuse

The following assumptions attempt to capture the dynamic interplay between the storage and retrieval strengths of a memory representation.

Assumption 1 An item or representation in memory is indexed by two strengths: (1) *storage strength*, which represents how well learned, or inter-associated, that representation is with other representations in memory; and (2) *retrieval strength*, which reflects how accessible, primed, or activated, that representation is with respect to the cue or cues guiding retrieval. The probability that an item can be recalled is completely determined by its retrieval strength (and on the retrieval strength of other items associated with the same cue as described in Assumption 3, below) and is independent of its storage strength.

That is, storage strength is a latent variable that has no direct effect on performance. Items with high storage strength can have low retrieval strength (e.g., a phone number you previously had for 5 years but not for the last 20 years), and items with low storage strength can have high retrieval strength (e.g., your hotel room number on the third day of your stay at a resort hotel on a summer vacation).

Assumption 2 The storage strength of an item is assumed to grow as a pure accumulation process in response to opportunities to study or recall that item; that is, it is assumed that storage strength, once accumulated, is never lost. Consequently, there is essentially no limit on the amount of information that can be stored in long-term memory; that is, on the sum of storage strengths across items. Storage strength for a given item, however, is assumed to grow in a negatively accelerated fashion; that is, the increment in its storage strength owing to a study or test event is a decreasing function of its current storage strength. Furthermore, increments in storage strength are also assumed to be a decreasing function of an item's current retrieval strength; that is, high retrieval strength is assumed to retard the accumulation of additional storage strength. Or, stated differently, the more accessible or activated an item's representation in memory is at the time of a study or test event, the less its storage strength can be increased as a result of those events.

Assumption 3 Whereas storage capacity is assumed to be unlimited, retrieval capacity is not; that is, there is a limit on the total number of items that are retrievable at any one point in time in response to a retrieval cue or configuration of cues. Two limits on retrieval capacity are assumed. First, because retrieval strength – in contrast to storage strength – is lost as a function of subsequent study and test events on other items, there is an overall limit on retrieval strength. At some point, a kind of dynamic equilibrium is reached where any gain in retrieval strength for items being studied or tested is offset by a corresponding loss in retrieval strength summed across other items in memory. Second, owing to the cue-dependent nature of retrieval assumed in the model, for a given item to be recalled in response to a given cue, (a) its representation must be discriminated from other representations in memory associated to that same cue, and (b) it must be reconstructed or integrated from its representation. Discriminating a given item is assumed to be a function of its retrieval strength relative to the strength of other items in the cued set. Reconstructing the item for output is assumed to be a straightforward function of its absolute retrieval strength.

Together, these two limits on retrieval strength imply that as items are added to memory, or as the relative strengths of certain items are increased, other items become less recallable.

Assumption 4　　Both the act of retrieving an item from memory and the act of studying that item result in increments to its retrieval strength and storage strength, but retrieval is the more potent event. That is, the act of successfully retrieving an item results in larger increments to its storage and retrieval strengths than does the act of studying it again. In either case, however, increments in an item's retrieval strength are assumed to be a decreasing function of its current retrieval strength and an increasing function of its current storage strength. Consequently, the benefits of a successful retrieval, in terms of its influence on that item's subsequent retrievability, are larger the more difficult or involved the act of retrieval (low retrieval strength) and the better registered the item is in memory (high storage strength).

Assumption 5　　Decrements in an item's retrieval strength, owing to the learning or retrieval of other items, are assumed to be greater the higher the item's current retrieval strength and the lower the item's current storage strength. Importantly, then, storage strength acts to enhance the gain and to retard the loss of retrieval strength.

On the basis of the foregoing assumptions, it follows that increasing the retrieval strengths of certain items through study or test events makes other items less retrievable. Furthermore, according to the theory, this competition for retrieval strength takes place at the level of retrieval cues, which are assumed to consist of current environmental, interpersonal, emotional, and body-state stimuli, real or imagined, that have been associated with a given item in the past.

Of particular relevance to issues of treatment, then, the theory states that when a cue is reinstated, either physically or imaginally, competition for retrieval among the representations in memory associated with that cue (or context) takes place, and whether a given memory representation is retrieved (or is the representation that determines the behavioural response produced in response to that cue) depends, not only on the absolute strength of its association to that cue, but also on the strengths of the associations of other memory representations to that cue. That is, in the presence of a given cue or context, whether a given memory representation will determine the behavioural response that occurs, depends on its relative as well as absolute retrieval strength with respect to those cues or context.

Also of particular relevance to issues of treatment and therapy is the theory's assumption that storage strength, once accumulated, is never lost. Thus, the retrieval strength of a given response can be decreased and eventually lost with disuse, but the learned representation of a response and its association to relevant cues remains in memory.

In general, as we have argued elsewhere (Bjork, 1989; Bjork & Bjork, 1988; Bjork & Bjork, 1992), the fact that retrieval strength, but not storage strength, is lost plays an adaptive role in the everyday use of our memories. Because old, out of date, information becomes non-retrievable, owing to the learning and use of new information, it does not interfere in the recall of the new information. The old information, however, remains in memory, meaning that it remains familiar and identifiable when it reoccurs, and – should circumstances change making the old information relevant again – it can be relearned rapidly, becoming readily accessible again, with significant savings compared to its original learning. In the case of therapy, however, the goal is to replace an old way of responding with a new way of responding. From that standpoint, it is a major problem that old associations and ways of responding remain in memory and are susceptible to relearning and recovery.

THE NEW THEORY OF DISUSE AS A GUIDE TO OPTIMIZING TREATMENT

With respect to the interplay of new associations and competing old associations, one broad implication of the new theory of disuse is that treatment conditions should be structured to optimize the storage strength of new, non-fearful, responding, rather than the retrieval strength of such responding. This implication is especially important because a therapist can easily be fooled by the current retrieval strength of non-fearful responding. That is, to the degree that those responsible for treatment interpret current performance – retrieval strength – as learning, they can not only be fooled as to the success of treatment, they can also be influenced to structure the conditions of treatment in far from optimal ways, as we describe below.

Spacing of practice, retention intervals, and their interaction

The effects of spacing or distributed practice on learning are complex. The ideal spacing interval (i.e., the temporal spacing of practice, learning episodes, study attempts, or training trials) has been shown (e.g., Glenberg & Lehmann, 1980) to be a function of the length of the final retention interval – that is, of the interval between the last presentation of the to-be-learned material and the testing of it and, thus, the interval over which it must be maintained. More specifically, when the retention interval is short, closely spaced study or learning episodes (i.e., *massed* practice, such as cramming all night before a morning exam) tend to produce somewhat better test performance than do study or learning episodes that are spaced further apart (i.e., *distributed* practice). When, however, the retention interval is long, distributed practice produces significantly better retention – often performance that is more than twice as good as that produced by massed practice. This latter effect – that distributed or spaced practice enhances long-term retention and performance, often referred to as the *spacing effect* – is one of the more robust and general findings in learning research. It holds for multiple time scales, types of to-be-learned material, and types of learners (see, e.g., Baddeley & Longman, 1978; Bahrick, Bahrick, Bahrick, & Bahrick, 1993; Lee & Genovese, 1988; for reviews see Dempster, 1996; Glenberg, 1992).

To the degree that the effects of treatment trials are subject to the same interaction of spacing interval and retention interval, which seems a safe assumption given the generality of such effects, therapists are clearly at risk of choosing massed practice over spaced practice. That is, if current performance is assumed to reflect treatment success, then the schedule of trials that will appear optimal is massing of practice, because it will result in more rapid apparent progress.

The new theory of disuse provides a quite natural account of the observed interaction of spacing interval and retention interval. According to the theory, the advantage of massed practice at short retention intervals arises because massed study episodes lead to a more rapid growth in retrieval strength than do spaced study episodes, owing to the greater loss of retrieval strength between successive spaced trials, versus between successive massed trials. When retention is tested at a short interval, retrieval strength – which determines momentary performance – will be higher in the case of massed than distributed practice. On the other hand, distributed practice produces greater increases in storage strength than does massed practice because, as outlined in Assumption 2, above, increments in storage strength are a negatively accelerated function of current retrieval strength. With distributed practice, there is more forgetting or loss of retrieval strength between the repeated study or learning episodes, which creates better conditions for new learning – that is, greater increments in storage strength. In turn, the greater accumulation of storage strength with distributed practice slows the loss of retrieval strength with disuse (i.e., across the retention interval), resulting in better performance after a delay, such as a delay from the end of treatment to a real-world context in which non-fearful responding is desired.

It is important to emphasize that a therapist is not the only one susceptible to being fooled by retrieval strength. Patients, too, can interpret rapid progress as success and be unaware that a rapid reduction in fearful responding during treatment, or rapid progress in, say, a behavioural approach test in the case of spider phobia, does not ensure success at a delay and outside of the treatment context. In fact, according to the new theory of disuse, rapid progress may constitute a kind of warning sign – that retrieval strength is being accumulated at the expense of storage strength.

In the context of instruction, Bjork (1994) has referred to conditions such as spaced practice as *desirable difficulties*. Other such difficulties include interleaving, rather than blocking, practice on separate tasks; varying, rather than keeping constant, the conditions of practice; reducing, rather than increasing feedback to the learner; and using tests, rather than study trials, as learning events. They are all "difficulties" because they introduce challenges for the learner and typically slow the apparent rate of acquisition. They are "desirable" because they then, typically, enhance long-term retention and transfer.

Retrieval as a learning event

When treatment sessions are spaced, retrievals of new non-fearful responses in the next training session will be more difficult, owing to the decrease in retrieval strength between sessions, but such retrievals – provided they are successful – will (owing to Assumption 4 above) be powerful learning events, far more powerful than when the act of retrieving is easy. That is, when retrieval strength is high (as it would be in massed practice) versus when low (as it would be in spaced practice), the act of retrieval is easier, but also less effective from the standpoint of increments in storage strength.

It is important to emphasize, however, that for a retrieval attempt to lead to a large gain in storage strength it not only needs to be difficult, but also successful. The challenge, therefore, is to structure the timing of sessions such that there is a drop off in the retrieval strength of the non-fearful behaviour between sessions, but not so great a drop off that the retrieval attempt in the next session is not successful. If retrieval of the non-fearful response is not successful, and, if instead, the old fearful response is retrieved, then the beginning of a relapse may be set in motion. Such an outcome is likely because, while the retrieval strength of the old fear response will be lowered owing to the intervening treatment sessions, its storage strength will remain high, built up by years of the patient responding fearfully to the fear-evoking stimulus on a variety of occasions and in a variety of contexts. Thus, a single retrieval of it could return its retrieval strength to its nearly full pretreatment level; thus, beginning a relapse to the old way of responding.

A potentially promising way to optimize the scheduling of treatment sessions across an intervention is to use what has come to be called *expanding retrieval practice* (Landauer & Bjork, 1978). In this method of scheduling practice, the first retrieval attempt is scheduled shortly after the first study or learning episode, the next retrieval attempt is scheduled after a slightly longer retention interval, the third after a still longer interval, and so forth. Ideally, each retrieval attempt should occur at the point when retrieval would be maximally difficult, but still possible, given the present level of retrieval strength. Each successive retrieval attempt would then act as a potent learning event, producing increases to storage strength as well as retrieval strength and, thereby, enabling the next retrieval attempt to be successful at a still longer interval.

Expanding retrieval practice has been shown to have an advantage compared to both massed and evenly spaced retrieval practice for the learning of verbal material as well as motor skills (for reviews see Bjork, 1988; Cull, Shaughnessy, & Zechmeister, 1996; Schmidt & Bjork, 1992) and for patients with memory disorders (Schacter, Rich, & Stampp, 1985). Again, however, in the context of fear-reduction therapy, it would be of critical importance to manage the spacing of training sessions such that the likelihood of successfully retrieving the new non-fearful behavioural response is kept high, while the likelihood of retrieving the old fearful behaviour response is kept low to avoid its being accidentally evoked in the training context.

Variation as a desirable difficulty

Introducing variation into the learning of a new task has been demonstrated to benefit both the long-term retention of the learning and its generalizability (e.g., Shea & Morgan, 1979; Simon & Bjork, 2001; Smith, Glenberg, & Bjork, 1978; Smith & Rothkopf, 1984; for a discussion of such findings, see Schmidt & Bjork, 1992). These benefits of variation are thought to occur for a number of reasons. First, in terms of the new theory of disuse, retrieval is made more difficult via the variation because the cues available from the just prior learning episode will be at least somewhat changed from those of the current learning episode, thus producing greater increments to storage strength as well as retrieval strength (for reasons why conditions that create forgetting can also enable learning, see Bjork, 1999; Cuddy & Jacoby, 1982; Estes, 1955; Jacoby, 1978). Second, each time the new learning occurs in a slightly different context, it becomes associated with different retrieval cues and, thus, it becomes retrievable in response to a greater variety of cues and contexts, improving the generalizability of the newly learned response or task. Third, variation in the task or tasks to be learned is assumed to force the learner to engage in certain types of higher-order learning in order to overcome the interference among the tasks – for example, to discover similarities and differences among the tasks to be learned, or to develop a common strategy that enables performance of the basic task despite variations in it (e.g., Battig, 1972).

In the case of fear-reduction therapy, variation in the task to be learned (i.e., responding in a non-fearful manner to the previous fear-evoking stimulus) could be accomplished by varying the nature of the feared stimulus (say, exposing the learner to different types of spiders or snakes) or by varying the treatment context (say, having the learner encounter the spider or snake in different physical or environmental settings and when experiencing different types of internal states). Introducing these types of variation into the treatment tasks or learning episodes should result in the build up of both the storage and retrieval strength of the new non-fearful response to a variety of cues, both external and internal, and thus increase the likelihood that there will be at least some retrieval cues for the new learning present in situations likely to be encountered by the learner after treatment. The practice of having the learner retrieve the non-fearful behaviour when in different internal states would have the benefit of building up the retrieval strength of the new behaviour to such cues – such as elevated heart rate or increased respiration. Thus, such internal states can become retrieval cues for the new non-fearful behavioural response, not just the old fearful behavioural response.

Overlearning and repeated learning

As we have previously pointed out (Bjork & Bjork, 1992), a long-established result in the study of learning is that additional trials given after an animal or human participant has achieved perfect performance (overlearning), or additional relearning sessions to bring performance back to the original criterion level (repeated learning) both serve to slow the rate of subsequent forgetting (e.g., Ebbinghaus, 1885/1964; Krueger, 1929). In the new theory of disuse, the assumed distinction between storage and retrieval strengths readily accounts for these two effects. Performance is a function of momentary retrieval strength, and performance cannot go beyond 100% correct. Storage strength, however, can continue to accumulate in response to overlearning or repeated learning, and increased storage strength acts to slow the loss of retrieval strength, which would be revealed in the observed slower rate of forgetting following overlearning or repeated learning.

In the context of fear-reduction therapy, overlearning results would imply that continuing fear-reducing sessions beyond the point where the patient or learner reports little or no fear in the presence of the previously fear-evoking stimulus might have the benefit of slowing the forgetting of the newly learned behaviour once treatment is stopped. Furthermore, repeated learning or refresher treatments could be used to help return the retrieval strength of the new non-fearful response to the level it had attained at the end of treatment. Additionally, because the retrieval strength of the new behaviour would typically be lower at the time of relearning than it was at the end of treatment, these relearning trials would be highly beneficial as far as increasing the storage strength of the new behaviour, not just its retrieval strength. It would be critical, however, as was discussed with respect to devising an optimal spacing interval for treatment sessions across the original period of intervention, to administer any relearning trials for the new non-fearful response before its retrieval strength has been so diminished with disuse as to make it non-retrievable.

When thinking about how to optimally structure the spacing of relearning trials in the context of fear reduction, some work by Bjork and Fritz (1994) in the context of the new theory of disuse – suggesting that massing trials in a relearning treatment phase might be as effective as distributing them – seems of great relevance. Working with a quantitative version of the theory, Bjork and Fritz showed that the theory predicted that massed relearning not only produced more rapid reacquisition during training than does spaced relearning, but also that this advantage was maintained over a much longer retention interval than is the case for initial learning.

This prediction, though initially very surprising, is quite understandable. Because storage strength, once accumulated, is assumed to be permanent, the storage strength that results from original learning carries over to relearning. The disadvantage that massed practice would typically have during training – a limited accumulation of storage strength – is, therefore, mitigated. As pointed out by Lang, Craske, and Bjork (1999), this prediction of the new theory of disuse has both positive and negative clinical implications. On the one hand, it suggests that providing a client or patient with a single massed relearning treatment session could be just as effective as several, spaced relearning treatment sessions. On the other hand, however, it implies that a single massed fear-inducing episode in which the old fearful response is evoked could not only restore fearful responding to its pretreatment retrieval strength, but also increase its storage strength, undoing many of the gains made during treatment. But again, as retrieval strength decreases over time with disuse, well-timed relearning treatment trials could be the best way both to maintain the retrieval strength of the newly learned non-fearful behaviour and to prevent an inadvertent relapse to the old fearful behaviour.

In the next section, we describe and discuss examples of exposure-therapy experiments carried out by Craske and her collaborators, experiments that were designed to test a broad implication of the new theory of disuse – namely, that treatment conditions should be structured to optimize the storage strength, not simply the retrieval strength, of non-fearful responding.

OPTIMIZING STORAGE STRENGTH IN THE TREATMENT OF FEARS

Applying the new theory of disuse to exposure-based treatment of fears, the new to-be-learned or to-be-remembered information is a new association between a previous fear-evoking stimulus (e.g., a snake or spider, a closed space, public speaking, etc.) and a new non-fearful response. Because storage strength is not lost, however, the newly acquired association or memory representation does not replace the old fearful association or memory representation; rather, both representations will be stored in memory and compete for retrieval. In a post-treatment encounter with the previously feared stimulus, the representation that will determine how the patient responds – with fearful or non-fearful feelings and behaviour – will depend on the relative retrieval strengths of the two associations to the available retrieval cues. Thus, a goal of treatment is not only to associate a new non-fearful response to the previously feared stimulus, but also to increase its retrievability; that is, the likelihood that it will be the response retrieved rather than the old fearful response. In the studies described next, Craske and collaborators examined different procedures – suggested by the new theory of disuse – in an attempt to maximize both the storage and the retrieval strength of new, non-fearful, associations.

Exposure therapy and the effects of spacing

According to the new theory of disuse, massing exposure trials during treatment should result in a more rapid reduction in the retrieval strength of old, fearful, responses and a rapid build up of retrieval strength for new, non-fearful, responses, but a limited build up of the storage strength of the non-fearful responses. Distributed spacing of exposure trials, on the other hand, in particular the use of an expanding schedule of retrieval practice, should lead to a greater increase in the storage strength of the new, non-fearful, response and, thus also, to its slower loss of retrieval strength following the end of treatment. In other words, whereas massed exposure trials may produce faster apparent learning of the new non-fearful response than do spaced exposure trials, the potential for return of fear to occur (that is, the reinstatement of the old fearful way of responding) should be greater in the former than in the latter case. Additionally, because the spacing of exposure trials (or retrieval opportunities) allows for a greater change in temporal context cues across exposure trials, the new non-fearful response should build up retrieval strength to more different types of cues across the duration of the intervention when exposure trials are spaced versus massed, leading to a greater generalizability of the newly learned response when acquired under distributed versus massed conditions. To assess the validity of these predictions, Rowe and Craske (1998a) compared the relative benefits of a massed versus an expanding-spaced exposure schedule for treating fear of spiders.

In their study, participants reporting a fear of spiders were randomly assigned to receive massed exposure trials or expanding-spaced exposure trials, and the two groups were compared on a number of measures on three different occasions: pre-training, post-training, and at a one-month follow-up. Participants in the massed-exposure condition received four exposure trials that were conducted consecutively on the same day as the pre-and post-assessments. Participants in the expanding-exposure condition received exposure trials on four different occasions that were spaced in a 1–2–4–8 pattern; that is, with the time between successive exposure trials expanding from only one day, to two days, to four days, and then eight days.

The assessment measures included several behavioural assessment tests (BATs), such as patients being required to approach the glass cage containing the training (or control) spider (a tarantula with an abdomen of approximately 7.5 cm [3 inches] in length), and touching the tarantula with either a pencil or a Q-Tip. In addition, heart rate was recorded and several self-report measures, designed to reveal the strength of certain fear-related feelings, such as the participant's maximum level of anxiety during the task, perceived degree of danger during the task, and perceived chances of being bitten, were collected. In the post-training and follow-up assessments, participants were exposed to the original control spider to assess fear reduction. Additionally, to assess generalization effects, participants were also exposed to a novel spider that differed in size, colour, hairiness, and speed of movement to the control spider.

Consistent with the predictions of the new theory of disuse, although both groups exhibited fear reduction or habituation across exposure trials, participants in the expanding-exposure condition exhibited less habituation than did the participants in the massed-exposure condition. Across trials, all measures of fear revealed a linear decline for the massed-exposure group; whereas the same means revealed a more erratic course of fear reduction or habituation for the expanding-exposure group, consistent with the assumption that spaced exposure trials would increase the difficulty of retrieval of the non-fearful response and, thus, slow down the course of habituation. Indeed, the heart rate of the expanding-exposure participants continued to increase across exposure trials, consistent with the notion that retrieval of the non-fearful response is more difficult given an expanding, versus a massed, schedule of exposure trials. Additionally, on the immediate post-training assessment tests with the control spider, the expanding-exposure participants responded more poorly in terms of maximum reported fear, danger ratings, and heart rate compared to the massed-exposure participants.

Thus, as in many previous studies demonstrating more rapid improvement in performance with massed practice versus spaced practice during instruction or training, it appeared that a massed scheduling of exposure trials was superior to a spaced scheduling of exposure trials for the reduction of fear. But Rowe and Craske's inclusion of a generalization test at the immediate post-treatment assessment revealed this apparent superiority of massed exposure trials to be misleading. Consistent with the new theory of disuse, when exposed to the novel spider, massed-exposure participants evidenced significant return of fear both on the post-assessment BAT and in terms of their self-reported maximum fear and danger ratings. In contrast, the expanding-exposure participants did not show increases in these measures.

Finally, of critical importance is the question of how participants in the two groups performed at the one-month follow-up assessment. In terms of the new theory of disuse, it should be the case that participants in the expanding-exposure condition – despite having shown less habituation during treatment and poorer performance on the immediate post-treatment assessment with the control spider than did the massed-exposure participants – should nonetheless show superior maintenance of fear reduction. As reported by Rowe and Craske (1998a), this prediction was "strikingly demonstrated" in the self-reported measures of maximum fear, which showed a significant increase for the massed-exposure participants and a significant decrease for the expanded-exposure participants. Thus, although showing significantly better habituation across exposure trials as well as better performance on the immediate post-treatment assessment with the control spider, only the massed-exposure participants demonstrated a return of fear at the follow-up assessment. Furthermore, as they had done on the immediate post-treatment assessment, the massed-exposure participants also showed return of fear to the novel spider at the one-month follow-up assessment, whereas the expanding-exposure participants did not.

In summary, the pattern of results obtained by Rowe and Craske (1998a) strongly indicate that the structuring of exposure trials to maximize the growth of storage strength as opposed to the growth of retrieval strength, as is assumed to occur in spaced versus massed practice in the new theory of disuse, is one way to increase the long-term effectiveness of fear-reduction therapy – specifically, a decrease in the return of fear following treatment. It must be pointed out, however, that a study by Lang and Craske (2000) comparing massed-exposure training to expanded-exposure training in the treatment of fear of heights did not find a difference in return of fear between the two groups. Participants in this study, however, received nearly four hours of direct exposure and neither group showed a detectable return of fear between the end of treatment assessment and the one-month follow-up assessment. Possibly, with a longer delay, enhanced long-term retention of the non-fearful response for the expanded-exposure training would have emerged. In a similar study by Tsao and Craske (2001), which examined the effects of different spacing manipulations (massed, uniform, and expanding) on the reduction of fear of public speaking, participants in the massed-spacing condition showed the greatest return of fear at the one-month follow-up – in fact, their fear ratings at this time did not differ from their pre-treatment levels – whereas participants in both of the spaced conditions showed an impressive lack of return of fear at the one-month follow-up.

Based on these promising results, and as has been argued by Lang, Craske, and Bjork (1999), additional research in this area is clearly needed, both to extend it to clinically fearful populations and to determine the optimal spacing and follow-up intervals for the prevention of return of fear. According to the new theory of disuse, the optimal intervals would be those that allow some forgetting or decrease in the retrieval strength of the new non-fearful behaviour to occur between successive exposure trials, in order to make the retrieval of the newly learned response increasingly difficult (thus producing a larger increment to its storage strength), but not so difficult that successful retrieval during the next exposure trial is rendered impossible.

Exposure therapy and the effects of variation

As previously discussed, Bouton and colleagues (e.g., Bouton & Peck, 1992; Peck & Bouton, 1990; Brooks et al., 1995) have demonstrated that the recovery phenomena of renewal, reinstatement, and spontaneous recovery all occur following counterconditioning as well as extinction. Of particular relevance for fear therapy, Peck and Bouton (1990) have demonstrated renewal when tone–shock conditioning occurs first in context A, then tone–food conditioning in context B, and then the tone is encountered again back in the original context A. In other words, even though a new non-fearful response has been learned to the tone stimulus, when back in the context of the original learning of the fearful response to the tone, the fearful behaviour returns.

In addition, as demonstrated by Bouton and Swartzentruber (1991), even when placed in a new context C – that is, not the context of original learning – renewal of the old fearful response often occurs. Taken together these results suggest, as Bouton and colleagues have emphasized (e.g., Bouton & Nelson, 1994, 1998), that first learning generalizes, but second learning does not. That is, second learning appears to remain contextualized and highly dependent on the context in which it was acquired. In discussing these results with respect to the problem of relapse in behaviour therapy, Bouton and colleagues (Bouton, 1994, 2000; Bouton & Swartzentrauber, 1991) have argued that it is important to think of how to make the new learning generalize beyond the immediate context or the context present in therapy and, when so doing, to think of the context more broadly; that is, as including any background event or any changes in the features of the stimulus. An immediate implication of such an argument is that, during exposure therapy, contextual variation across exposure trials in either the background or the features of the stimulus should help to reduce return of fear.

In terms of the new theory of disuse, contextual variation during training would decrease the potential for return of fear in at least two ways. First, because retrieval is assumed to be cue dependent, increasing the storage and retrieval strength of the desired response to many retrieval cues will make it more likely to be the response retrieved in a future context. Second, contextual variation across exposure trials will make retrievals of the new response more difficult, thus adding to its storage strength and reducing its loss of retrieval strength across a retention interval or period of disuse. In short, according to the theory, retrieval strength of non-fearful responding should grow more rapidly without contextual variation, but long-term retention and generalizability of the to-be-remembered response should be greater with contextual variation.

To test these predictions, Rowe and Craske (1998b) compared the relative benefits of exposing participants to a constant stimulus versus multiple versions of a stimulus in the treatment of fear of spiders. As in the Rowe and Craske (1998a) study, participants reporting a fear of spiders were randomly assigned to receive either a constant-exposure treatment or a varied-exposure treatment, and the two groups were compared on a number of measures on three different occasions: pre-training, post-training, and at a three-week follow-up. Also, as before, the assessment measures included several behavioural assessment tests (BATs), heart rate, and several self-report measures designed to gauge the participant's level of anxiety.

A total of seven different tarantulas were used that varied in a number of ways, including shape, colour, hairiness, speed of movement and size. For each participant, one spider – referred to as the control spider – was presented at the pre-training, post-training, and follow-up assessments. Additionally, for each participant, a novel spider was presented at the post-training assessment, and a different novel spider at the follow-up assessment. During exposure trials, the varied-exposure participants were exposed to a different tarantula on each of four exposure trials; whereas, constant-exposure participants were exposed to only the control spider across their four exposure trials. Thus, including the spiders used for assessment (one control, and two novel), participants in the varied-exposure condition were exposed to a total of seven different spiders; whereas, participants in the constant-exposure condition were exposed to only three spiders. The seven tarantulas used were counterbalanced across the two exposure conditions so that each spider was represented an equal number of times in each of the seven possible presentations to ensure that no observed effects could be due to the particular characteristics of a given spider.

The study took place over two sessions: The first session, which included a pre-training assessment, four exposure trials, and two post-training assessment trials, lasted approximately two hours; and, the second, which occurred approximately three weeks after the first session, included two follow-up assessment trials and lasted for about half an hour.

Although not for all measures, the constant-exposure group, in general, exhibited significantly more habituation or fear reduction across the exposure trials and less reported anxiety during the immediate post-training assessment than did the varied-exposure group. With delay, however, the constant-exposure group showed a clear return of fear to the control spider, whereas the varied-exposure group did not. In terms of the new theory of disuse, the increase in retrieval difficulty, introduced by the changes in context (i.e., the characteristics of the spider) from one exposure trial to the next slowed down the reduction of fear in the varied-exposure participants during training. In the long-term, however, this increased retrieval difficulty across exposure trials, resulted in the accumulation of greater storage strength and thus a slower loss of retrieval strength across the retention interval, allowing the varied-exposure participants to retrieve the new non-fearful response when faced with the control spider after three weeks, whereas the constant-exposure participants could not.

At the three-week follow-up, however, both groups were found to exhibit return of fear when presented with the novel spider. Although disappointing, this result is consistent with the assumptions of both the new theory of disuse and the arguments of Bouton and colleagues as to the power of the context (or retrieval cues) to determine which of two competing memory representations will lead to observed behaviour. In the case of the new theory of disuse, the contextual cues present after three weeks and in the presence of a new spider are more likely to be ones for which the old fearful response has both greater storage strength and retrieval strength, built up across many years and in a variety of contexts, and thus is the response more likely to win in the competition for retrieval in the face of those cues. According to Bouton (1994), the return of fear to the new spider would be considered an example of renewal following counterconditioning.

As was the case with the earlier discussed study of Rowe and Craske (1998a), the present study also demonstrates the risk to both therapists and clients of being misled by performance during and immediately following training, which can often be a poor index of whether the type of learning that is the goal of training has actually occurred. On the basis of performance both during training and on the immediate post-training assessment task with the control spider, the constant-exposure procedure appeared to be the superior way of conducting fear-reduction therapy. Without the additional generalization test given immediately after training, or the delayed assessment with the control spider, the inadequacy of the constant-exposure procedure to that of the varied-exposure procedure would not have been revealed. Thus, the pattern of results observed by Rowe and Craske (1998a, 1998b) – like many others in the verbal-learning and motor-skills literature – emphasizes the need for both transfer tests and delayed retention tests to properly evaluate the efficacy of training procedures, as has been advocated by Schmidt and Bjork (1992). Additionally, they also demonstrate the risk of relying on the meta-cognitions of the learner or trainee to gauge the efficacy of the training procedure (see, Simon & Bjork, 2001, for a similar result with a motor-skills learning task). And, finally, they again underscore the risk to the therapist of being misled by the apparent ease of new learning or habituation during treatment into preferring what is actually a poorer method of treatment over a better method of treatment.

As with the optimal spacing of exposure trials within the period of treatment, how to vary context in order to minimize the return of fear following treatment needs additional research. One other study by Lang and Craske (1998), in which individuals who were afraid of heights were either exposed to varied stimuli and contexts (multiple heights in different locations) or to a single stimulus and context (one high location), has also shown that the varied exposure treatment leads to better performance or less return of fear at a one-month delay. Thus, contextual variation in exposure treatment seems a promising direction to take, but, as with the spacing of exposure trials, many questions remain to be investigated, such as how much variation is optimal and whether certain types of variation – such as varying the type of task versus only the features of the stimulus – might be more potent than others. And, finally, a promising line of research might be how best to combine these two manipulations – that is, the spacing of exposure trials and the variation of context across exposure trials. Perhaps there are combinations of these two manipulations that would have not just an additive effect on the learning of the new non-fearful response, but a superadditive or synergistic one, greatly enhancing the long-term effectiveness of such a treatment procedure.

CONCLUDING COMMENTS

We set out in this chapter to extend a theoretical framework, our new theory of disuse, which we developed in the context of research on verbal learning and skill acquisition, to the broad problem of changing behaviours, and, more specifically, to the treatment of fears and phobias. In drawing on, and trying to account for, the animal-learning research of Mark Bouton and his collaborators, and the exposure-therapy research of Michelle Craske and her colleagues, we are struck by the potential for cross-fertilization between research domains that, typically, have little to do with each other. We are struck as well, by the central role of memory – in learning, in treatment, and, as the title of this book states, in society. Finally, however promising the new theory of disuse may prove to be as a guide to optimizing treatment, one thing is clear: Research and theory are far better guides than are intuition and "common sense", both of which can lead us to choose poorer conditions of instruction over better conditions of instruction, and less-effective treatment over more-effective treatment.

References

Adams, J. A., & Reynolds, B. (1954). Effect of shift in distribution of practice conditions following interpolated rest. *Journal of Experimental Psychology, 47,* 32–36.

Baddeley, A. D., & Longman, D. J. A. (1978). The influence of length and frequency of training session on the rate of learning to type. *Ergonomics, 21,* 627–635.

Bahrick, H. P., Bahrick, L. E., Bahrick, A. S., & Bahrick, P. E. (1993). Maintenance of foreign language vocabulary and the spacing effect. *Psychological Science, 4,* 316–321.

Battig, W. F. (1972). Intratask interference as a source of facilitation in transfer and retention. In R. F. Thompson & J. F. Voss (Eds.), *Topics in learning and performance* (pp. 131–159). New York: Academic Press.

Benjamin, A. S., Bjork, R. A., & Schwartz, B. L. (1998). The mismeasure of memory: When retrieval fluency is misleading as a metamnemonic index. *Journal of Experimental Psychology: General, 127,* 55–68.

Bjork, E. L., & Bjork, R. A. (1988). On the adaptive aspects of retrieval failure in autobiographical memory. In M. M. Gruneberg, P. E. Morris, & R. N. Sykes (Eds.), *Practical aspects of memory II*. Chichester, UK: Wiley.

Bjork, R. A. (1988). Retrieval practice and the maintenance of knowledge. In M. M. Gruneberg, P. E. Morris, & R. N. Sykes (Eds.), *Practical aspects of memory II* (pp. 396–401). Chichester, UK: Wiley.

Bjork, R. A. (1989). Retrieval inhibition as an adaptive mechanism in human memory. In H. L. Roediger & F. I. M. Craik (Eds.), *Varieties of memory and consciousness: Essays in honor of Endel Tulving* (pp. 309–330). Hillsdale, NJ: Lawrence Erlbaum Associates, Inc.

Bjork, R. A. (1994). Memory and metamemory considerations in the training of human beings. In J. Metcalfe & A. Shimamura (Eds.), *Metacognition: Knowing about knowing* (pp. 185–205). Cambridge, MA: MIT Press.

Bjork, R. A. (1999). Assessing our own competence: Heuristics and illusions. In D. Gopher & A. Koriat (Eds.), *Attention and peformance XVII. Cognitive regulation of performance: Interaction of theory and application* (pp. 435–459). Cambridge, MA: MIT Press.

Bjork, R. A. (2001). Recency and recovery in human memory. In H. L. Roediger, J. S. Nairne, I. Neath, & A. M. Surprenant (Eds.), *The nature of remembering: Essays in honor of Robert G. Crowder* (pp. 211–232). Washington, DC: American Psychological Association Press.

Bjork, R. A., & Bjork, E. L. (1992). A new theory of disuse and an old theory of stimulus fluctuation. In A. Healy, S. Kosslyn, & R. Shiffrin (Eds.), *From learning processes to cognitive processes: Essays in honor of William K. Estes* (Vol. 2, pp. 35–67). Hillsdale, NJ: Lawrence Erlbaum Associates, Inc.

Bjork, R. A., & Fritz, C. O. (1994, August). Reinforcing and competitive dynamics in the maintenance of knowledge. In H. Bahrick (Chair), *The maintenance of knowledge*. Symposium, Practical Aspects of Memory Conference, College Park, Maryland.

Bouton, M. E. (1984). Differential control by context in the inflation and reinstatement paradigms. *Journal of Experimental Psychology: Animal Behavior Processes, 10*, 56–74.

Bouton, M. E. (1993). Context, time, and memory retrieval in the interference paradigms of Pavlovian learning. *Psychological Bulletin, 114*, 80–99.

Bouton, M. E. (1994). Context, ambiguity, and classical conditioning. *Current Directions in Psychological Science, 3*, 49–53.

Bouton, M. E. (2000). A learning theory perspective on lapse, relapse, and the maintenance of behavior change. *Health Psychology, 19*, 57–63.

Bouton, M. E., & Bolles, R. C. (1979). Contextual control of the extinction of conditioned fear. *Learning and Motivation, 10*, 445–466.

Bouton, M. E., & Brooks, D. C. (1993). Time and context effects on performance in a Pavlovian discrimination reversal. *Journal of Experimental Psychology: Animal Behavior Processes, 19*, 165–179.

Bouton, M. E., & King, D. A. (1983). Contextual control of the extinction of conditioned fear: Tests for the associative value of the context. *Journal of Experimental Psychology: Animal Behavior Processes, 9*, 248–265.

Bouton, M. E., & Nelson, J. B. (1994). Context-specificity of target versus feature inhibition in a feature-negative discrimination. *Journal of Experimental Psychology: Animal Behavior Processes, 20*, 51–65.

Bouton, M. E., & Nelson, J. B. (1998). The role of context in classical conditioning: Some implications for cognitive behavior therapy. In W. O'Donohue (Ed.), *Learning and behavior therapy* (pp. 59–84). Needham Heights, MA: Allyn & Bacon.

Bouton, M. E., & Peck, C. A. (1992). Spontaneous recovery in cross-motivational transfer (counterconditioning). *Animal Learning and Behavior, 20,* 313–321.

Bouton, M. E., & Swartzentruber, D. (1991). Sources of relapse after extinction in Pavlovian and instrumental learning. *Clinical Psychology Review, 11,* 123–140.

Brooks, D. C., Hale, B., Nelson, J. B., & Bouton, M. E. (1995). Reinstatement after counterconditioning. *Animal Learning and Behavior, 23,* 383–390.

Brown, T. A., & Barlow, D. H. (1995). Long-term outcome in cognitive-behavioral treatment of panic disorder: Clinical predictors and alternative strategies for assessment. *Journal of Consulting and Clinical Psychology, 63,* 754–765.

Christina, R. W., & Bjork, R. A. (1991). Optimizing long-term retention and transfer. In D. Druckman & R. A. Bjork (Eds.), *In the mind's eye: Enhancing human performance* (pp. 23–56). Washington, DC: National Academy Press.

Clark, D. M., Salkovskis, P. M., Hackmann, A., Middleton, H., Anastasiades, P., & Gelder, M. (1994). A comparison of cognitive therapy, applied relaxation and imipramine in the treatment of panic disorder. *British Journal of Psychiatry, 164,* 759–769.

Craske, M. G. (1999). *Anxiety disorders: Psychological approaches in theory and treatment.* Denver, CO: Westview Press/Basic Books.

Craske, M. G., Brown, T. A., & Barlow, D. H. (1991). Behavioral treatment of panic disorder: A two-year follow-up, *Behavior Therapy, 22,* 289–304.

Cuddy, L. J., & Jacoby, L. L. (1982). When forgetting helps memory: Analysis of repetition effects. *Journal of Verbal Learning and Verbal Behavior, 21,* 451–467.

Cull, W. L., Shaughnessy, J. J., & Zechmeister, E. B. (1996). Expanding our understanding of the expanding pattern of retrieval mnemonic: Toward confidence in applicability. *Journal of Experimental Psychology: Applied, 2,* 365–378.

Dempster, F. N. (1996). Distributing and managing the conditions of encoding and practice. In E. C. Carterette & M. P. Friedman (Series Eds.) and E. L. Bjork & R. A. Bjork (Vol. Eds.), *Handbook of perception and cognition: Vol. 10. Memory* (2nd ed., pp. 317–344). New York: Academic Press.

Ebbinghaus, H. (1964). *Memory: A contribution to experimental psychology* (H. A. Ruger & C. E. Bussenius, Trans.). New York: Dover. (Original work published 1885)

Estes, W. K. (1955). Statistical theory of spontaneous recovery and regression. *Psychological Review, 62,* 145–154.

Glenberg, A. M. (1992). Distributed practice effects. In L. R. Squire (Ed.), *Encyclopedia of learning and memory* (pp. 138–142). New York: Macmillan.

Glenberg, A. M., & Lehmann, T. S. (1980). Spacing repetitions over 1 week. *Memory & Cognition, 8,* 528–538.

Heimberg, R. G., Salzman, D. G., Holt, C. S., & Blendell, K. A. (1993). Cognitive-behavioral group treatment for social phobia: Effectiveness at five-year follow-up. *Cognitive Therapy and Research, 17,* 325–339.

Hull, C. L. (1943). *The principles of behavior.* New York: Appleton-Century-Crofts.

Jacoby, L. L. (1978). On interpreting the effects of repetition: Solving a problem versus remembering a solution. *Journal of Verbal Learning and Verbal Behavior, 17,* 649–667.

Jacoby, L. L., Bjork, R. A., & Kelley, C. M. (1994). Illusions of comprehension and competence. In D. Druckman & R. A. Bjork (Eds.), *Learning, remembering, believing: Enhancing human performance* (pp. 57–80). Washington, DC: National Academy Press.

Krueger, W. C. F. (1929). The effects of overleaning on retention. *Journal of Experimental Psychology, 12,* 71–78.

Landauer, T. K., & Bjork, R. A. (1978). Optimal rehearsal patterns and name learning. In M. M. Gruneberg, P. E. Morris, & R. N. Sykes (Eds.), *Practical aspects of memory* (pp. 625–632). London: Academic Press.

Lang, A. J., & Craske, M. G. (1998, July). *Long-term benefit of maximizing memory for exposure-based treatment of fear.* Paper presented at the World Congress of Cognitive and Behavioral Therapies, Acapulco, Mexico.

Lang, A. J., & Craske, M. G. (2000). Manipulations of exposure based therapy to reduce return of fear: A replication. *Behaviour Research and Therapy, 38,* 1–12.

Lang, A. J., Craske, M. G., & Bjork, R. A. (1999). Implications of a new theory of disuse for the treatment of emotional disorders. *Clinical Psychology: Science and Practice, 6,* 80–94.

Lee, T. D., & Genovese, E. D. (1988). Distribution of practice in motor skill acquisition: Learning and performance effects reconsidered. *Research Quarterly for Exercise and Sport, 59,* 277–287.

Mystkowski, J., Craske, M. G., & Echiverri, E. (2002). Treatment context and return of fear in spider phobia. *Behavior Therapy, 33,* 399–416.

Ost, L-G. (1996). Long-term effects of behavior therapy for specific phobia. In M. R. Mavissakalian & R. F. Prien (Eds.), *Long-term treatment of anxiety disorders* (pp. 121–170). Washington, DC: American Psychiatric Press.

Peck, C. A., & Bouton, M. E. (1990). Context and performance in aversive-to-appetitive and appetitive-to-aversive transfer. *Learning and Motivation, 21,* 1–31.

Rachman, S. (1989). The return of fear: Review and prospect. *Clinical Psychology Review, 9,* 147–168.

Rescorla, R. A. (1993). Preservation of response-outcome associations through extinction. *Animal Learning and Behavior, 21,* 238–245.

Rescorla, R. A. (1996). Preservation of Pavlovian associations through extinction. *Quarterly Journal of Experimental Psychology: Comparative and Physiological Psychology, 49(B),* 245–258.

Rescorla, R. A. (2001). Experimental extinction: In R. R. Mowrer & S. Klein (Eds.), *Handbook of contemporary learning theories* (pp. 119–154). Hillsdale, NJ: Lawrence Erlbaum Associates, Inc.

Rescorla, R. A., & Heth, C. D. (1975). Reinstatement of fear to an extinguished conditioned stimulus. *Journal of Experimental Psychology: Animal Behavior Processes, 1,* 88–96.

Rodriguez, B. I., Craske, M. G., Mineka, S., & Hladek, D. (1999). Context-specificity of relapse: Effects of therapist and environmental context on return of fear. *Behaviour Research and Therapy, 37,* 845–862.

Rowe, M. K., & Craske, M. G. (1998a). Effects of an expanding-spaced vs. massed exposure schedule on fear reduction and return of fear. *Behaviour Research and Therapy, 36,* 701–717.

Rowe, M. K., & Craske, M. G. (1998b). Effects of varied-stimulus exposure training on fear reduction and return of fear. *Behaviour Research and Therapy, 36,* 719–734.

Schacter, D. L., Rich, S. A., & Stampp, M. S. (1985). Remediation of memory disorders: Experimental evaluation of the spaced-retrieval technique. *Journal of Clinical and Experimental Neuropsychology, 7,* 79–96.

Schmidt, R. A., & Bjork, R. A. (1992). New conceptualizations of practice: Common principles in three paradigms suggest new concepts for training. *Psychological Science, 3*, 207–217.

Shea, J. B., & Morgan, R. L. (1979). Contextual interference effects on the acquisition, retention, and transfer of a motor skill. *Journal of Experimental Psychology: Human Learning and Memory, 5*, 179–187.

Simon, D., & Bjork, R. A. (2001). Metacognition in motor learning. *Journal of Experimental Psychology: Learning, Memory, and Cognition, 27*, 907–912.

Smith, S. M., Glenberg, A. M., & Bjork, R. A. (1978). Environmental context and human memory. *Memory & Cognition, 6*, 342–353.

Smith, S. M., & Rothkopf, E. Z. (1984). Contextual enrichment and distribution of practice in the classroom. *Cognition and Instruction, 1*, 341–358.

Thorndike, E. L. (1914). *The psychology of learning*. New York: Teachers College.

Tolman, E. C., & Honzik, C. H. (1930). Introduction and removal of reward and maze performance of rats. *University of California Publications in Psychology, 4*, 257–275.

Tsao, J. C. I., & Craske, M. G. (2001). Timing of treatment and return of fear: Effects of massed, uniform and expanding spaced exposure schedules. *Behavior Therapy, 31*, 479–497.

7 Types and consequences of forgetting: Intended and unintended

Elizabeth L. Bjork, Robert A. Bjork, and Malcolm D. MacLeod

For most of us, remembering is good; forgetting is bad – something we wish to avoid. For most of us, in fact, "forgetting things" is the biggest complaint we have about our memories. Contrary to such intuitions, however, forgetting is a necessary and critical aspect of an efficient and adaptive memory system and, often, exactly what we must do to keep our memories functioning optimally. When previously stored information becomes out of date or no longer functional, we need some way to set aside, suppress, or forget that old information. Additionally, when we search our memories for some desired piece of information, such as the name of a former colleague or the source of an article that we have recently read, we need to inhibit or "forget" closely related, but incorrect, pieces of information that compete for retrieval with the target of our search. As we and others have previously argued (e.g., R. A. Bjork, 1989; E. L. Bjork & Bjork, 1996; E. L. Bjork, Bjork, & Anderson, 1998; Macrae & MacLeod, 1999), without such active forgetting mechanisms, we would soon become incapable of retrieving the information we need now, owing to interference from all the related information we have learned in the past.

In some cases, the types of forgetting that serve our goals and needs seem intentional, or at least not unintentional, as when we deliberately try to update our memories by forgetting or replacing an old phone number or an old password with a new one, or when we try to avoid retrieving uncomfortable or painful past events in our lives as a way of reducing their potentially aversive influences on our present lives. Such goal-directed forgetting may occur in response to explicit or implicit cues to forget, initiated either by ourselves or others, in both real-world and laboratory situations. And, contrary to what our intuitions about our memories might suggest – that even should we wish to forget certain previously stored information in response to an explicit cue, we would not be able to do so – extensive research using a procedure known as the intentional- or directed-forgetting paradigm (e.g., R. A. Bjork, 1972, 1989) shows that individuals can, in fact, forget previously stored information when instructed to do so.

In other types of forgetting important for the efficient functioning of our memories, however, the forgetting is unintended, may not be consistent with our long-term goals, and is instigated by cues of a more subtle and implicit nature. In the process of updating our memories so as to remember, for example, where we parked our car this morning, rather than yesterday morning, we typically do not give ourselves an explicit cue to forget the previous parking spot; rather, the cue to forget is implicit, and the forgetting or suppression of the old parking spot most likely occurs as a consequence of our noting and retrieving to ourselves the current parking spot. Analogously, in laboratory research on this type of forgetting using the retrieval-practice procedure of Anderson, Bjork, and Bjork (1994), the instruction to forget is not explicit, as it is in the intentional- or directed-forgetting paradigm; rather, it arises as an implicit and subtle component of the procedure itself. As participants practice retrieving some of the items associated with a particular cue during a retrieval-practice phase, there is an implicit instruction to forget, inhibit, or suppress the other items that were associated with that same cue during a preceding study phase and are now competing with the desired target of retrieval. In selecting for the desired target and against these competitors, the latter become suppressed or forgotten. Although such retrieval-induced forgetting serves the immediate goal of the participant – successful retrieval of the desired target during the retrieval-practice phase – it is difficult to conceive of such forgetting as being consciously intentional, nor does it serve the participant's long-term goal, which is to remember as many of the cue–target pairs presented during the original study episode as possible.

Whether occurring intentionally or unintentionally, however, or in response to an explicit or implicit cue, we believe that these types of forgetting are critical to the efficient functioning of human memory and are driven by a common underlying inhibitory process or mechanism, which we and others have called retrieval inhibition (e.g., R. A. Bjork, 1989; E. L. Bjork, Bjork, & Anderson, 1998; Geiselman, Bjork, & Fishman, 1983; Macrae & MacLeod, 1999; Roediger, 1974), and by which we mean the loss of retrieval access to information that nonetheless remains available in memory. That is, although our retrieval access to such inhibited information has become impaired or diminished, the inhibited or suppressed information still remains stored and available in memory, as can be demonstrated by other measures, such as recognition tests.

In the remainder of this chapter, we first briefly describe the principal paradigms used to study intentional forgetting, the basic characteristics of such forgetting, and the role of retrieval inhibition in its production. We then discuss more fully the type of forgetting that is our primary focus – retrieval-induced forgetting – including a description of the retrieval-practice paradigm recently developed to study it, the basic characteristics of such forgetting that implicate the role of inhibition or suppression in its produc-tion, and certain recently discovered extensions and boundary conditions of retrieval-induced forgetting. Finally, we explore several areas in which retrieval-induced forgetting may have unintended, but nonetheless profound, consequences in our lives: reliability of witness memory, stereotyping and other forms of impression formation, and – possibly – repression.

Intentional forgetting: Basic paradigms, results, and the role of retrieval inhibition

In perhaps the most typical instantiation of the paradigm used to study intentional forgetting, following the presentation of a list of words (List 1) that is to be learned for a later memory test, some participants are then directed "to forget" that list, which they are told was presented just for practice or by mistake, and are then presented with the "real" or the "correct" list to learn (List 2). In contrast, a different group of participants are presented with List 1, told to keep remembering it, and are then presented with List 2 to learn as well. In another variation of this paradigm, the instruction "to forget" does not come as a surprise; rather, all participants are informed at the beginning of the study that half way through each list of words presented, a cue either to forget or to remember the preceding words (i.e., List 1) will occur. Then, immediately following this mid-list cue, the remaining words, which are always to be remembered, are presented (i.e., List 2). Occasionally, a control condition is also employed in which the pre-cue or List-1 words are replaced by non-verbal materials to be processed in some way, and then the List-2 words are presented for study.

Across many studies employing such directed-forgetting procedures, a basic pattern of results has emerged that can be summarized in terms of three robust findings. First, List-2 words are significantly better recalled when participants are instructed to forget the preceding List-1 words than when they are told to keep remembering them; and, second, if a control condition was employed, List-2 words are frequently remembered just as well when participants were instructed to forget the List-1 words as when no words were presented at all in List 1. Third, if participants are unexpectedly asked to recall words that they were instructed to forget, their ability to do so is significantly impaired compared to their ability to recall words that they were instructed to remember. On the basis of the first two findings, it appears that directing people to forget previously studied material significantly reduces, and can even eliminate, the proactive interference of the to-be-forgotten material on subsequent learning. Based on the third finding, directing people to forget previously studied material appears to impede their later conscious access to that material or to the original learning episode that is the target of the forget instruction. (For a review of the studies from which this basic pattern of intentional-forgetting results has been extrapolated, see R. A. Bjork, 1972, 1989; Johnson, 1994; and C. M, MacLeod, 1998.)

As previously indicated, we believe that the most compelling explanation for this pattern of directed-forgetting results is in terms of retrieval inhibition. Namely, when individuals are instructed to forget previously studied information and then given new information to learn in its place, a process is initiated that inhibits subsequent retrieval access to the to-be-forgotten information or the learning episode that was the object of the instruction to forget. Moreover, because the to-be-forgotten information is not retrievable, it does not interfere with the recall of the current to-be-remembered information; thus, the decrease or elimination of proactive interference owing to the to-be-forgotten information as well as its significantly diminished recall relative to that for comparable to-be-remembered information.

Furthermore, although one's retrieval access to previously studied information becomes inhibited as a consequence of being instructed to forget it, the strength in memory of such information appears to be left unaffected, as indicated by the following three findings. First, recognition memory for the to-be-forgotten information is unimpaired as compared to that for comparable to-be-remembered information (e.g., Block, 1971; Elmes, Adams, & Roediger, 1970; Geiselman et al., 1983). Second, in a relearning paradigm, to-be-forgotten items can be learned as readily as to-be-remembered items (e.g., Reed, 1970; Geiselman & Bagheri, 1985). Third, under certain conditions, the proactive interference owing to the forgotten list can be reinstated at full strength, such as when some to-be-forgotten items are encountered as foils on a recognition test for to-be-remembered items (E. L. Bjork, Bjork, & Glenberg, 1973; E. L. Bjork & Bjork, 1996). Finally, observations based on indirect measures of retention provide evidence for continuing indirect or implicit influences of information that has been intentionally forgotten, even when retrieval access to such information remains inhibited (e.g., Basden, Basden, & Gargano, 1993; E. L. Bjork, Bjork, & Kilpatrick, 1990; E. L. Bjork & Bjork, 1996). Indeed, under certain circumstances, the indirect influences of previously studied information appear to be larger when that information has been intentionally forgotten versus intentionally remembered (E. L. Bjork & Bjork, 2003; E. L. Bjork, R. A. Bjork, Stallings, & Kimball, 1996).

Thus, in terms of the present analysis, it seems reasonable to think of the type of forgetting observed in response to an instruction to forget – whether implicit or explicit and whether administered by ourselves in everyday life or by an experimenter in the laboratory – to have two intended consequences of a positive nature, and one unintended consequence that, under certain circumstances at least, could be negative. First, because the process so initiated inhibits the subsequent retrieval of the information that is the target of the forget instruction, such information does not interfere with our learning and recall of the new information that is to replace it, thereby allowing for efficient memory updating and ease of access to the new information. Second, because the representation of the intentionally forgotten information in our memories appears to remain intact and at essentially full strength, as indicated by other measures such as recognition and priming, should our circumstances change and we need to regain access to such information, we can become fluent in its use again more quickly than were we to have to learn it anew from scratch. On perhaps the negative side, however, because such intentionally forgotten information, although still inhibited, can continue to

influence our behaviour in indirect ways, there can be unintended consequences or influences of such forgetting about which we are unaware and
thus cannot consciously correct for or mitigate.

Retrieval-induced forgetting: Basic paradigms, results, and the role of retrieval inhibition

Although a considerable body of results – obtained over many years of
research employing a variety of paradigms – supports the notion that the act
of retrieving some information impairs one's ability to retrieve other related
information, we focus in the present chapter on the type of forgetting that has
come to be called retrieval-induced forgetting as demonstrated in the
retrieval-practice procedure recently developed by Anderson et al. (1994).

The standard version of this procedure employs four distinct phases: a
study phase, a directed retrieval-practice phase, a distractor phase, and a final
test phase. In the study phase, participants are presented with a list of
category-exemplar pairs to learn (e.g., *Fruit Orange; Weapon Rifle*) – typically, six such pairs from each of eight categories, presented individually and in
a mixed order. Next, participants practice retrieving half of the exemplars
from half of the studied categories (e.g., *Fruit*), and none of the exemplars
from the remaining categories (e.g., *Weapon*). This retrieval practice is directed in that a category name together with a letter stem (e.g., *Fruit Or ____*)
is presented with participants instructed to retrieve the previously studied
exemplar that fits the combined category-stem cue. Also, to increase the
effectiveness of this retrieval practice, each practiced pair is typically given
three such tests separated by expanding intervals filled with the retrieval practice of other pairs (Landaur & Bjork, 1978). Then, following the distractor
phase, originally lasting 20 minutes, the final and unexpected recall test
is administered by presenting each category cue (e.g., *Fruit, Weapon*) and
asking participants to recall all the members of that category that they can
remember from any part of the experiment.

On this final test, the recall of three types of items – defined by the preceding study and retrieval-practice phases – is of interest: (1) practiced exemplars
from practiced categories (e.g., *Orange*; called Rp+ items); (2) unpracticed
items from practiced categories (e.g., *Banana*, called Rp– items); and (3)
unpracticed items from unpracticed categories, (e.g., *Rifle*; called Nrp or
baseline items). In studies using this procedure, performance on the final test
typically reveals the following pattern: whereas, the final recall of items that
received retrieval practice, the Rp+ items, is significantly facilitated relative to
recall of the baseline Nrp items, the final recall of the unpracticed items from
the practiced categories, the Rp– items, is significantly impaired relative to
this same baseline. It is also important to note that when final-test performance
is assessed using a cued-recall procedure in which recall of non-practiced Rp–
items is required before recall of Rp+ items within a category – thus controlling for output interference or the possibility that the observed impaired

recall of Rp– items is entirely due to the earlier recall of the stronger Rp+ items during the final test – this pattern of results is still observed (e.g., Anderson et al., 1994, Experiment 2). Additionally, post-hoc analyses of free-recall performance (e.g., Macrae & MacLeod, 1999) have also precluded output interference as a significant factor in the production of the impaired recall of Rp– items.

This pattern of results, which has been replicated across a number of studies using both verbal materials such as those described above (Anderson et al., 1994; Anderson & Spellman, 1995) and visuospatial materials (Ciranni & Shimamura, 1999) is consistent with the notion that the act of retrieving some items impairs the retrieval of related items. Because the resultant impairment appears to be initiated during the retrieval-practice phase and can last at least 20 minutes, this pattern has come to be called retrieval-induced forgetting. Furthermore, as previously argued (Anderson et al., 1994; E. L. Bjork et al., 1998; Macae & MacLeod, 1999), we believe that inhibitory processes are responsible for the impaired recall of the unpracticed, related items. More specifically, our conception of the mechanism producing such inhibition is as follows: During the retrieval practice of *Orange* to the cue Fruit, other exemplars, such as *Banana*, are also activated, creating competition and interference. To retrieve the desired target, *Orange*, in the presence of this competition, *Banana* must be selected against or inhibited, with the resultant suppression of *Banana* leading to its impaired recall on the final test.

It needs to be pointed out, however, that – although our interpretation of these basic retrieval-induced forgetting results is in terms of inhibition or suppression – other explanations not involving the assumption of inhibition, such as blocking (e.g., Blaxton & Neely, 1983; Roediger, 1974; Roediger & Neely, 1982; Rundus, 1973) or response competition owing to the strengthening of the practiced exemplars (e.g., McGeoch, 1942; Mensink & Raajimakers, 1988; Raajimakers & Shiffrin, 1981) are also consistent with this basic pattern. We believe, however, that additional studies designed to test among these proposed explanations favour an account in terms of inhibition. In these studies, the research strategy has been to construct a situation in which unpracticed exemplars would not be expected to compete – and thus would not need to be selected against or inhibited – during the retrieval practice of their related category-exemplar pairs. Then, having created such a situation, to see whether the later recall of such unpracticed exemplars is nonetheless impaired, which would be consistent with blocking, response-competition, or strength-dependent explanations, or whether their later recall is not impaired, which would be consistent with the suppression explanation.

To illustrate, in one such study employing this strategy, Anderson et al. (1994) manipulated the taxonomic strength of practiced and unpracticed exemplars, with the assumption that taxonomically strong, unpracticed exemplars would compete during retrieval practice of other category-exemplar pairs and, thus, have to be suppressed; whereas, taxonomically weak, unpracticed exemplars would be less likely to compete during retrieval practice of other category-exemplar pairs and, thus, escape being suppressed. In contrast, most non-inhibitory based explanations would have to predict that the later recall of either type of unpracticed exemplar would be impaired owing to the strengthening of the related practiced pairs. The pattern of results obtained supported the inhibitory-based explanation. Recall of unpracticed taxonomically strong exemplars (i.e., the ones that should compete and thus need to be suppressed during retrieval practice for related exemplars) was impaired on the final test, whether their related practiced exemplars were taxonomically strong (e.g., *Orange*) or taxonomically weak (e.g., *Papaya*); whereas, recall of unpracticed taxonomically weak exemplars (i.e., the ones that should not compete and thus escape being suppressed during retrieval practice for related exemplars) was not impaired, whether their related practiced exemplars were taxonomically strong or weak. Furthermore, this pattern was obtained in the presence of large facilitative (or strengthening) effects of retrieval practice for both strong and weak exemplars.

Additionally, in a study manipulating the type of retrieval practice (Anderson, Bjork, & Bjork, 2000), results consistent with the inhibition explanation of retrieval-induced forgetting were likewise obtained. In this study, participants engaged in one of two types of retrieval-practice conditions: (1) competitive, which followed the same procedures of Anderson et al. (1994); and (2) non-competitive, in which, rather than recalling an exemplar in response to a category label and a two-letter stem (e.g., *Fruit Or* ___), participants were given the exemplar along with a two-letter stem for the category (e.g., *Fr* ___ *Orange*) and asked to recall the category label. Thus, in both conditions, participants practiced retrieving the same category-exemplar associations for the same number of times and, in both conditions, it was expected that those associations would be strengthened. Similar to the preceding study, however, it was assumed that only in the competitive condition would attempts to retrieve the target exemplar, *Orange*, invoke competition from other strong exemplars, such as *Banana*, which would then need to be suppressed. In contrast, in the non-competitive condition, no such competition among exemplars should arise and, thus, there should be no consequent suppression of the unpracticed exemplars, such as *Banana*. As expected, both types of practice resulted in significant strengthening of the practiced category-exemplar pairs; that is, recall of *Orange*, for example, was facilitated on the later recall test by both the *Fruit Or* ___ or *Fr* ___ *Orange* types of practice. Critically, however, recall of the unpracticed exemplars, such as *Banana*, was only impaired in the competitive condition, lending strong support to the assumption that inhibitory processes – invoked to resolve interference from competitors during attempts to recall a target item – underlie retrieval-induced forgetting.

Finally, perhaps the strongest support for an explanation of retrieval-induced forgetting in terms of inhibitory mechanisms comes from the research of Anderson and Spellman (1995) who reasoned that if competing responses were suppressed in the attempt to retrieve the designated target during retrieval practice, then those inhibited items should be more difficult to retrieve, not only from the studied retrieval cue, but from any cue used to test them. Consistent with this assumption, Anderson and Spellman found that when participants practiced retrieving some exemplars of a category (e.g., *Red Blood*), their delayed recall of other unpracticed exemplars of that category was impaired, whether those exemplars were tested with the same cue used for practice (e.g., *Red*) or a different cue not used during practice (e.g., *Food*). The critical aspect of this finding in support of an inhibitory explanation is that the ability of participants to recall such items in response to the unpracticed category cue was impaired even though that cue was unrelated to the item strengthened during retrieval practice. In this situation, then, the unpracticed cue provides a measure of the accessibility of these related, unpracticed items that is independent of associative interference from the practiced targets. As argued by Anderson and Spellman, such cue-independent impairment provides strong support for the assumption of inhibitory processes acting during retrieval to suppress competing responses in order to focus retrieval search on the desired target.

Extensions of retrieval-induced forgetting

As previously indicated, we believe retrieval-induced forgetting to be prevalent in our everyday lives, playing a critical role in our frequent need to update our memories and to resolve interference during retrieval. Our making such a claim, however, immediately raises the issue of the generality of the phenomenon of retrieval-induced forgetting and whether this type of forgetting does, in fact, extend beyond the rather constrained learning and retrieval-practice procedures represented in the standard Anderson et al. (1994) paradigm. Several relevant questions thus come to mind. For example, would such forgetting occur when we are encoding information of a more personal or social relevance to us than the learning of category-exemplar pairs, and would it occur when we are not specifically encoding or processing such information with the conscious intention of learning it for a later memory test? Conversely, would it occur if, during retrieval practice for *some* of the items, it were fully understood that there would be a later recall test for *all* of the items. In the typical instantiation of the Anderson et al. retrieval-practice paradigm, the final recall test comes as a surprise, leaving open the question of whether inhibition of unpracticed competitors would occur were participants to know in advance that a later recall test for all of the originally studied category-exemplar pairs would be given. And, lastly, would retrieval-induced forgetting occur with less retrieval practice than typically provided? If the inhibitory processes assumed to underlie retrieval-induced forgetting play the important role in memory updating and the resolution of competition in everyday memory retrieval that we are suggesting, then it seems unreasonable that such extensive retrieval practice would be a necessary condition for their elicitation.

These questions concerning the generality of retrieval-induced forgetting and the variety of conditions under which it occurs were recently raised and addressed by Macrae and MacLeod (1999) in a series of three studies. To address the first question, they presented participants with the social-cognition task of impression formation. Specifically, participants were asked to form impressions about two individuals, named *John* and *Bill*, on the basis of traits (e.g., *trustful, cheerful*), which were presented in a similar manner to that used to present the category-exemplar pairs in a typical Anderson et al. (1994) paradigm. Participants first looked through a stack of randomly ordered cards on each of which one name (i.e., *John* or *Bill*) was printed together with one of 10 traits that had been randomly paired with that name. Next, participants were presented with cue cards that probed their memory for half of the traits paired with one of the individuals, say *John*, making those traits the Rp+ items, while the remaining traits for *John* thus become Rp– items, and the traits for the other individual, *Bill*, become Nrp items. To illustrate, in this case, such a cue card would contain the name *John* along with a two-letter stem for a trait (e.g., *John tr____* as a probe for retrieving *trustful*), with each such card presented on three occasions. Then, after a distractor phase, a surprise test was given in which participants were asked to recall all the traits they could remember that had described *John* and *Bill*, respectively. As in the intentional-learning situation of the Anderson et al. paradigm, the typical pattern of retrieval-induced forgetting was observed. Specifically, recall of the Rp+ traits was significantly facilitated compared to the Nrp or baseline traits, whereas recall of the Rp– traits was significantly impaired compared to that for the Nrp traits, demonstrating the occurrence of retrieval-induced forgetting in the context of the social-information processing task of impression formation and, furthermore, its generalization to a situation in which the original encoding of information did not take place in the context of an intentional leaning set.

To address the second question – whether retrieval-induced forgetting would emerge when participants knew in advance that a final recall test would be given and are thus motivated to retain all of the originally studied information – Macrae and MacLeod (1999) attempted to create a type of situation with which students are often faced: namely, needing to prepare for an examination that will cover all of the assigned material, but with only enough time to practice retrieving some of that material before the exam. To set up such a situation, participants were instructed that they would be presented with information (to learn about two tropical islands (*Tok* and *Bilu*) in preparation for a later geography exam, and they were then given 10 facts to learn about each island (e.g., *The official language in Tok is French*). Next, participants engaged in a retrieval-practice phase in which they were presented with cue cards probing their memory for half the facts associated with one of the islands, say *Bilu*, with each card containing the name of the island and a hint about the fact to be recalled (e.g., for the fact, *"Bilu's only major export is copper"*, participants were cued with the hint, *"Bilu's only major export is c ____"*) and with each such card presented on three occasions. Then, after a distractor task, participants were given a simulated final exam in which they were asked to recall as much as they could about both of the tropical islands. As in their previous study using names and traits, the pattern of retrieval-induced forgetting was observed: participants recalled significantly more practiced facts (Rp+ items) about an island than unpracticed facts about the different island (Nrp baseline items); whereas, compared to the same baseline, they recalled significantly fewer of the unpracticed facts about the practiced island (the Rp– items). These results thus extended the occurrence of retrieval-induced forgetting to situations in which participants, before the study phase, have foreknowledge of a final test and, thus, should be highly motivated not to forget any of the originally studied information.

Lastly, to address the question of the amount of retrieval practice required to produce retrieval-induced forgetting, Macrae and MacLeod (1999) varied the number of retrieval-practice trials given to different groups of participants in the context of the previously described impression-formation task. Specifically, the Rp+ items were presented for practice on one, three, or six occasions, with the duration of each practice trial timed in a manner to equate the duration of the total retrieval-practice phase for each group. The question of primary interest, of course, was how many practices would be necessary to elicit retrieval-induced forgetting. Consistent with the notion that such forgetting plays a critical role in the regulation of everyday memory, impaired retrieval of Rp– items compared to Nrp items was obtained in all three retrieval-practice conditions, establishing that a single retrieval practice of the Rp+ items can be sufficient to produce retrieval-induced forgetting for the related, non-practiced items.

Taken together, then, the results from these three studies lend compelling support to the contention that retrieval-induced forgetting is an adaptive and pervasive mechanism of memory, playing a critical role in the type of memory updating and the resolution of interference in retrieval that occurs in everyday life. On the other hand, retrieval-induced forgetting is not all pervasive. For example, as we have already seen in the studies manipulating the taxonomic strength of category-exemplar pairs (Anderson et al., 1994) and the nature of retrieval practice (Anderson et al., 2000), there are circumstances under which successful retrieval of desired targets occurs without producing impaired retrieval of associated material in memory. Moreover, as discussed in the next section, recent research from a number of investigators has revealed additional moderating factors or boundary conditions on the occurrence of retrieval-induced forgetting.

Boundary conditions on retrieval-induced forgetting

In research by Anderson and McCulloch (1999), retrieval-induced forgetting has been shown to be significantly reduced, and even eliminated, when participants are instructed to interrelate or integrate the different exemplars within a given category during the initial study phase. Although how integration acts to limit the occurrence of retrieval-induced forgetting is not yet fully understood, the results obtained by these investigators across a series of experiments point to diminished suppression and mediated retrieval as the two most likely explanations. The notion of diminished suppression as an explanatory factor builds upon the finding from numerous studies on fact retrieval that integration reduces retrieval competition (e.g., Moeser, 1979a, 1979b; E. E. Smith, Adams, & Schorr, 1978). If, similarly, linking items associated to the same cue via integration reduces retrieval competition among them, then there should be little need to suppress non-target items during retrieval practice of target items. The notion of mediated retrieval as an explanatory factor stems from studies conducted during the classical interference era of verbal learning demonstrating that participants could use connections established between competing associates as indirect retrieval routes, thereby evading both proactive and retroactive interference (for reviews, see Anderson & Neely, 1996; Postman, 1971). As applied to the phenomenon of retrieval-induced forgetting, the notion would be that links established between exemplars of the same category during study could then, during the final recall test, be used as indirect retrieval routes to recover suppressed non-target items. Suppose, for example, that an *Orange–Banana* link had been established via integration during study. Now, even if *Banana* is suppressed during the retrieval practice of *Orange* to the cue *Fruit*, such practice should also have enhanced the accessibility of the *Orange–Banana* link, allowing *Banana* to be retrieved via this link even if still suppressed.

In the first case, integration could be thought of as insulating non-target items from the suppression that produces retrieval-induced forgetting; in the latter case, integration could be thought of as offsetting or masking the suppression that normally produces retrieval-induced forgetting. Indeed, as Anderson and McCulloch (1999) conclude, the benefits of integration in reducing retrieval-induced forgetting most likely arise from a combination of reduced suppression and mediated retrieval. Importantly, as also argued by Anderson and McCulloch, these limiting factors on the occurrence of retrieval-induced forgetting may demonstrate the means by which the complex knowledge structures of experts are spared such forgetting, even though experts may repeatedly engage in the access of some, but not all, of the knowledge accumulated within their domains of expertise.

In addition to integration apparently protecting material from retrieval-induced forgetting, research by R. E. Smith and Hunt (2000) has demonstrated that distinctive encoding of information also seems to increase its resistance to such inhibition. To illustrate, when Smith and Hunt instructed participants, during the initial study, to think about how each member of a category differed from all the other members of the category, subsequent retrieval practice given to a subset of the category members did not result in retrieval-induced forgetting of the remaining category members. (In contrast, it should be pointed out that when participants are instructed to encode, during initial study, similarities among items that are to become the competitors of the practiced targets, the retrieval inhibition suffered by such items can be significantly increased. For an in-depth discussion and theoretical explanation of how similarity relationships between practiced targets and competitors and among competitors themselves can lead to both increases and decreases in retrieval inhibition or suppression, see Anderson, Green, & McCulloch, 2000.)

The potential power of both distinctive encoding and integration to render information resistant to retrieval inhibition is illustrated in an interesting study by Macrae and Roseveare (2002). Using a variation of the standard retrieval-induced forgetting procedure, different participants were asked to learn a list of gifts by imagining them to have been purchased by (a) themselves, (b) their best friend, or (c) an unspecified other, with the expectation that participants receiving the first instruction would be led to engage in more self-relevant processing of the to-be-learned information than would the participants receiving the other two types of instruction. The intent of this manipulation was thus to test whether information encoded in terms of the self – presumed to constitute a highly complex knowledge structure (e.g., Kihlstrom & Cantor, 1984; Klein & Kihlstrom, 1986) – would spontaneously result in its being both more highly integrated and more distinctively processed, thus potentially protecting it from retrieval inhibition. As expected, whereas participants in the "best friend" and "other" instruction groups showed significant retrieval-induced forgetting on the final recall test, participants in the "self" instruction group did not.

As a check on this interpretation, Macrae and Roseveare (2002) also had participants, following the retrieval practice and final recall phases, rate the extent to which they had engaged in thoughts about potential recipients for the gifts, with the notion that such ratings would serve as a measure of the degree to which spontaneous distinctive processing in terms of the self had taken place during original study. These ratings confirmed that participants in the "self" condition had indeed engaged in more self-relevant and distinctive encoding of the gifts than had the other two groups of participants. Thus, it seems possible that the same distinctive (Smith & Hunt, 2000) and integrative (Anderson & McCulloch, 1999) encoding processes that have been shown to eliminate retrieval-induced forgetting in the laboratory may be spontaneously evoked whenever we engage in self-relevant processing of information, thereby setting another boundary condition on the occurrence of retrieval inhibition as produced via retrieval practice (see, M. D. MacLeod, Bjork, & Bjork, 2003, for a discussion of this possibility with respect to emotive material).

Finally and critically, it needs to be noted that there are temporal boundaries on the duration of retrieval inhibition as well. That is, the retrieval-induced forgetting of competing material in memory is temporary, resulting from decreases in its retrieval access, rather than its erasure or elimination from memory. (Or, as expressed in R. A. Bjork & Bjork's, 1992, new theory of disuse, resulting from decreases to its retrieval strength, not to its storage strength.) As we have also argued elsewhere (e.g., R. A. Bjork, 1989, E. L. Bjork et al., 1998; M. D. MacLeod et al., 2003; M. D. MacLeod & Macrae, 2001), this temporary nature of retrieval inhibition is adaptive. While in force, the inhibition serves to aid recall of desired information by suppressing interference from competing information. Should such inhibited information be needed in the future, however, it can become recallable again once its inhibition has been released or dissipated. Furthermore, as reasoned by M. D. MacLeod and Macrae (2001), if retrieval inhibition is to serve an adaptive memorial function, it must be transient in nature, owing to the constantly changing nature of our goal states, and, indeed, they have demonstrated that retrieval inhibition is no longer present following a 24-hour delay. If, however, a 24-hour delay is inserted between initial study and retrieval practice (rather than between retrieval practice and final recall), retrieval inhibition still occurs. Taken together, these two results demonstrate an interesting feature of retrieval inhibition – although transient in nature, it can be evoked for older memories, as well as newly established ones. It thus seems possible that selective retrieval practice over longer periods of time could well result in more permanent inhibition of competitive memories. (For further discussions of the potential relevance of repeated retrieval practice for such issues as the maintenance of one's self-image, the construction of auto-biographical memories, and the suppression of unpleasant and/or traumatic memories, see E. L. Bjork et al., 1998, and M. D. MacLeod et al., 2003.)

Unintended consequences of retrieval-induced forgetting

As we have noted, an important aspect of the inhibition that we believe to underlie the phenomenon of retrieval-induced forgetting is that it occurs automatically or without our conscious attention. As we retrieve or remember some information, other related information is inhibited, with the inhibition occurring rather like a by-product. Hence, as we have previously suggested, there can be unintended consequences of such forgetting. For example, while the retrieval inhibition of competitors produced in the retrieval-practice phase of the Anderson et al. (1994) paradigm serves the immediate goal of successfully retrieving the desired target of the retrieval practice cue, it does not serve the longer-term goal of performing well on the final recall test for all the studied pairs. Moreover, as so aptly demonstrated in the study by Macrae and MacLeod (1999) in which participants learned geography facts for a later examination, this negative consequence of retrieval-induced forgetting occurs even when participants know in advance that a final test for all the information studied will be given. Although motivated to remember all the originally studied facts in order to perform well on the expected final test, the retrieval practice given to a subset of the facts about a particular island nonetheless diminished the participants' ability to recall the remaining, unpracticed facts about that island. Worse yet, their recall for such unpracticed items was impaired relative to that of control participants who did not engage in any practice for any of the facts about either island. In the remainder of this section, several such unintended consequences of the phenomenon of retrieval-induced forgetting are discussed, some of them clearly negative, but others of perhaps a more positive nature.

Witness memory   One of the more interesting areas in which the potential negative consequences of intentional-forgetting have been investigated is that of witness memory. In the first study to look at the possible relevance of retrieval-induced forgetting effects on eyewitness testimony, Shaw, Bjork, and Handal (1995) explored potential unintended consequences of the repeated questioning of witnesses on their long-term ability to recall details about the observed event. Although it had been realized for some time that repeated post-event interrogations of witnesses could alter their memories for the information that was the target of such questioning (e.g., Wells, 1993), Shaw et al. wondered – given the retrieval-induced forgetting observed by Anderson et al. (1994) – if such post-event interrogations might also have an impact upon the ability of witnesses to recall information that was *not* the object of such interrogations.

To explore this possibility, these investigators adapted the typical retrieval-practice procedure to make it suitable for an investigation of eyewitness memory. Participants were told to imagine that they had attended a party in a fellow student's apartment and, when leaving, noticed that their wallet was missing from their jacket pocket. They were then shown a series of 21 slides depicting objects in the bedroom where their jacket had been during the party, being told to pay close attention to the contents of the slides so that they would later be able to assist the police in an investigation of the theft. Within the slides presented were an assortment of objects that could typically be found in a student's bedroom, such as a desk, a computer, a telephone, and various personal items. Additionally, two categories of target items – college sweatshirts and college schoolbooks, with eight exemplars of each – were also contained within the slide sequence. After viewing the slides, participants were exposed to an "interrogation" phase in which they were given retrieval practice on half of the items in one of the two categories (e.g., four sweatshirts). To optimize the effects of this practice as is presumably achieved in the expanding retrieval procedure of Landauer and Bjork (1978), their interrogation phase included three retrieval-practice sessions that were (a) separated by increasingly longer intervals filled with distractor tasks and (b) designed to demand progressively more difficult retrievals. Thus, in the first interrogation phase, participants were presented with fairly simple true–false questions about the four target items, asked from the standpoint of the owner of the apartment, *Janet*, and suggesting the correct response (e.g., "I think my friend Julia wore her Harvard sweatshirt. Was there a Harvard sweatshirt on my desk?"). In the second interrogation phase, participants were presented with more difficult cued-recall questions about the same target items asked from the perspective of a police officer who had arrived on the scene (e.g., "Was there a grey sweatshirt on Janet's desk? If so, what was the name of the university on that sweatshirt?"). In the third and final interrogation phase, the participants were presented with the most difficult cued-recall questions about the same items asked from the perspective of a detective investigating the case (e.g., "Were there any sweatshirts on the desk? What was written on those sweatshirts?"). Following this last interrogation phase and a distractor interval, participants engaged in a final "testimony phase", consisting of a category-cued-recall test in which they were asked to recall as many items in each of the two categories, sweatshirts and schoolbooks, as they could remember. Additionally, Shaw et al. included a group of participants who received no interrogation or retrieval practice. Instead, after viewing the slides, these no-interrogation control participants only engaged in distractor tasks until being given the same final recall test as the interrogated participants.

On the final recall test, the practiced or Rp+ items (e.g., the four sweatshirts that were the targets of the interrogation questions in the present example) were recalled at a significantly higher rate than were the Nrp items (e.g., the schoolbooks in the present example), whereas the Rp– items (e.g., the other four sweatshirts in the present example) were recalled at a significantly lower rate than were the Nrp items. Furthermore, because of the inclusion of a no-interrogation control condition, recall of the Rp+, Rp– and Nrp items by the interrogated participants could also be compared to the mean recall of participants who had not engaged in any retrieval practice for any of the items. Compared to the mean recall of this control group, the interrogated participants' recall of Rp+ items was significantly better, their recall of Rp– items was significantly worse, whereas their recall of Nrp items did not differ, indicating that Nrp items do not suffer from the retrieval practice given to a subset of items in another category. Prior to the inclusion of this no-interrogation condition by Shaw et al., it had not been clear whether Nrp items, although recalled significantly better than Rp– items, might not also suffer some ill effects from the retrieval practice given to items in the other categories. In a more recent study of retrieval-induced forgetting effects in an eyewitness context, M. D. MacLeod (2002) also obtained this same pattern of results. Thus, it seems clear that unpracticed items of unpracticed categories escape the potential negative consequences of the retrieval practice given to items belonging to different categories. Additionally and importantly, the results from these two studies demonstrate that retrieval-induced forgetting (i.e., the significant impairment in recall of Rp– items relative to Nrp items) cannot be attributable to any increase in Nrp recall in the retrieval practice condition.

The results of the Shaw et al. (1995) and M. D. MacLeod (2002) studies have both encouraging and problematical implications for the legal profession. On the one hand, they provide evidence that even minimal interrogation can have a substantial positive impact on the witness's later ability to recall the items that were the targets of that interrogation. On the other hand, they provide evidence that the repeated retrieval of certain details during interrogation might lead to the witness having impaired recall for other details; in particular, details that were not asked about but that happen to bear a category similarity to those items that were the subject of the interrogation. Moreover, the witness's ability to recall such unpracticed details can be significantly impaired compared to that of witnesses who were never interrogated at all. Although, as Shaw et al. cautioned, care should be taken in drawing inferences from these results to the interrogations occurring in actual eyewitness settings, there is no compelling reason to believe that such real-world interrogations would produce a different pattern of results. Indeed, as these investigators argued, the potential consequences – both positive and negative – resulting from the repeated questioning of witnesses in real-life cases could well be greater than those that can be produced in the laboratory.

Although the unintended forgetting by witnesses of unpracticed details as a consequence of the repeated questioning for other details would certainly be a negative consequence of retrieval inhibition, at least the errors so produced would be ones of omission. A potentially more problematical consequence of retrieval inhibition may be that it plays a role in the production of the so-called misinformation effect originally observed by E. F. Loftus and colleagues (e.g., Loftus, 1979; Loftus, Miller, & Burns, 1978; Loftus & Loftus, 1980), which refers to the introduction of errors into the reports of witnesses as a consequence of being presented with misleading information during post-event questioning. The possibility that retrieval-induced forgetting might play such a role was recently explored in research by Saunders and MacLeod (2002), whose reasoning was as follows. In the typical misinformation paradigm, participants are asked questions about, or are given a type of retrieval practice for, a subset of the items or details that they presumably encoded about a previously witnessed event. Consequently, on the basis of the earlier discussed results of Shaw et al. (1995) plus those of MacLeod and Macrae (2001) indicating that retrieval-induced forgetting can be produced by a minimal amount of retrieval practice, such questioning could result in the inhibition of related, but unpracticed, details about the same event. If post-event misinformation about such inhibited details was then introduced, the only information accessible to conscious retrieval or inspection during a later recall attempt would be that misleading post-event material, resulting in the production of misinformation effects.

To test this possible explanation of misinformation effects, Saunders and MacLeod employed an adaptation of the Anderson et al. (1994) retrieval practice procedure similar to that used by Shaw et al. (1995), but with two additional phases necessary for the introduction of misleading post-event information and the assessment of the misinformation effect. Rather than viewing slides, participants were given two narratives to read about two separate burglaries, one concerning a theft at the Joneses' house, in which 10 items were stolen (e.g., a mobile phone, a Game Boy, a wristwatch) and the other about a theft in the Smiths' house, in which 10 different items were stolen (e.g., a video recorder, rollerblades, a necklace). Following the reading of these narratives, half of the participants were assigned to a retrieval-practice condition in which they were presented with questions about half the items stolen from one of the houses (e.g., the Smiths' house), but were asked no questions about items stolen from the other house, thereby creating Rp+, Rp–, and Nrp items. Similar to the Shaw et al. study, three distinct questions were asked about each of the five practiced items in separate questioning sessions, with the questions increasing in difficulty across the three sessions, and successive sessions separated by distractor tasks. Then, after another distractor task, participants were asked to recall all the items that they could remember about both thefts as a manipulation check to ensure that retrieval-induced forgetting had actually occurred. Following this recall test and another distractor task, participants were asked 12 additional questions about the two burglaries, one of which contained misinformation about one of the stolen items presented in the original narrative (e.g., *necklace* was replaced by *earrings*) and this critical question was directed at either an Rp+, an Rp–, or an Nrp item. Then, following another distractor task, all participants engaged in a final test consisting of multiple-choice questions about the stolen items, with each question presenting three alternatives: the correct item and two new incorrect ones. One of these questions concerned the stolen item about which misleading information had been presented, and for this critical question, the three alternatives were: the original item, the erroneous misinformation, and one new incorrect item. How participants responded to this question was used to determine the occurrence, or lack thereof, of a misinformation effect.

As in the Shaw et al. (1995) study, the other half of the participants did not receive retrieval practice about any of the stolen items, engaging, instead, in retrieval practice for the names of capital cities. They did, however, engage in all other phases of the study, including the misinformation phase and the final multiple-choice test, permitting their performance to serve as an important baseline for the presence of misinformation effects in the absence of related retrieval practice.

Having first determined that retrieval-induced forgetting was produced by the first questioning phase, Saunders and MacLeod (2002) then assessed the consequences of introducing misleading post-event information about items that had been inhibited (i.e., the Rp– items) versus items that had not been inhibited (i.e., Rp+ items, or Nrp items, or control-condition items). If correct in their hypothesis that retrieval-induced forgetting leads to misinformation effects, such effects should only occur, or at least occur to a greater degree, when the misleading information was presented about inhibited (or Rp–) items versus the other types of non-inhibited items, and, indeed, this pattern of results was exactly what they observed. Significantly more misinformation was reported when such misleading information had been presented about Rp– items compared to all other types of items. Specifically, the likelihood of reporting misinformation was .60 for participants given misinformation about an Rp– item versus .16, .20, and .24 for participants given misleading information about Rp+, Nrp, or control items, respectively.

These results thus provide compelling support for the suggestion of Saunders and MacLeod (2002) that retrieval-induced forgetting could play a critical role in the production of misinformation effects. When participants were asked about or given retrieval practice on a subset of details about a crime event (e.g., some of the items stolen in one of the burglaries), other items known about that event suffered inhibition. Participants then given misinformation about those inhibited items were significantly more likely to report that misleading information, rather than the correct information, on the subsequent multiple-choice test than were participants given misleading information about non-inhibited items. In addition to predicting the pattern of results obtained by Saunders and MacLeod, a retrieval-induced forgetting or inhibitory-based account of misinformation effects would also seem to have certain advantages over other explanations that have been advanced in the literature, such as destructive updating (e.g., Loftus, 1979), retrieval competition (e.g., Bekerian & Bowers, 1983), and source monitoring (e.g., Lindsay & Johnson, 1989a). For example, an inhibitory account is not dependent on the misleading information being introduced subsequent to the encoding of the original material (Lindsay & Johnson, 1989b), and it is compatible with the observation that participants in misinformation studies respond as quickly and as confidently to false memories as they do to genuine ones (Loftus, Donders, Hoffman, & Schooler, 1989).

Stereotyping Most individuals can be thought about in two ways: as a member of some social group, and thus considered to possess some of the attributes typically thought of as characterizing members of that group (i.e., stereotypic attributes), and as an individual, and thus considered to possess attributes that one would not expect to be typical of that group (i.e., counter-stereotypic or individuating attributes). Previously, we have suggested that retrieval-induced forgetting may be an important adaptive mechanism through which we can forget or inhibit memories whose influence on our behaviour we may want to avoid, such as traumatic or disturbing memories or our stereotypic beliefs about others (E. L. Bjork et al., 1998; Macrae & MacLeod, 1999). On the negative side, however, retrieval-induced forgetting may contribute to the well-documented resistance of stereotypes to modification or change (e.g., Hamilton & Sherman, 1994; Johnston & Macrae, 1994) even in the face of disconfirming evidence (Bodenhausen & Macrae, 1998). If, when we think about members of another group, it is the stereotypic information that more readily comes to mind, then with each such retrieval, the counterstereotopic information will be inhibited, making the stereotype more and more accessible and perpetuating its ability to influence our thinking about such group members. Similarly, retrieval-induced forgetting may be the mechanism by which we maintain other types of pre-existing beliefs despite evidence to the contrary, even beliefs about ourselves.

In recent research, Dunn and Spellman (2003) have investigated some of these possibilities by investigating whether retrieval-induced forgetting could produce stereotype inhibition. For example, in one condition of one of their studies, participants learned about two women, *June* and *Cheryl*, who were presented via the use of pictures as an Asian-American woman and a White mother, respectively, and participants studied six traits associated with each individual, three of which were related to the stereotype about each woman's group (Asian-American traits for June and "mom" traits for Cheryl) and three of which were unrelated to their respective stereotypes. After studying all six traits for each woman, participants were divided into two groups: one given retrieval practice on only the stereotype traits and one given retrieval practice on only the individuating traits. All participants then engaged in a distractor phase, followed by a final test phase in which they were asked to recall all the traits originally studied with each woman. Given these two groups, Dunn and Spellman could ask whether strengthening stereotype traits through retrieval practice would impair access to individuating traits and, conversely, whether strengthening individuating traits would impair access to stereotypic traits. What they found was that retrieval practice on either type of trait produced inhibition or forgetting of the other type of trait.

Perhaps, then, retrieval-induced forgetting provides a more promising way to reduce the influence of stereotypes than seems to be the case for more intentional efforts to do so (e.g., Macrae, Bodenhausen, Milne, & Ford, 1997; Wyer, Sherman, & Stroessner, 2000). In the research by Macrae et al., for example, stereotype-congruent memories were found to be particularly difficult to inhibit intentionally and not to show typical directed-forgetting effects when participants were instructed to forget such information. In contrast, in the Dunn and Spellman study, stereotypic traits were inhibited as an unintended consequence of the retrieval practice given to the individuating traits. On the other hand, as pointed out by Dunn and Spellman, their results do not paint an entirely rosy picture. Although the degree of retrieval-induced forgetting obtained in their study was not significantly moderated by the type of traits given retrieval practice, there was a slight trend suggesting that retrieving stereotype traits inhibited individuating traits more than vice versa. Furthermore, a regression analysis showed that the stronger the participant's belief in the relevant stereotype, the less the stereotype traits were inhibited by practice of the individuating traits. As suggested by Dunn and Spellman, one possible explanation for this relationship could be that stereotype traits comprise a more highly integrated set for strong believers, and, thus, may be able to escape the effects of inhibition via mediated retrieval. That is, being strongly linked together, if one trait manages to be retrieved, it can provide a retrieval path to the others (see the earlier discussion of Anderson & McCulloch, 1999).

Additionally, as the results of M. D. MacLeod and Macrae (2001) have shown, retrieval-induced forgetting may be fairly transient, lasting for at least 20 minutes but perhaps no longer than 24 hours. Typically, given our constantly changing needs and goals, the temporary nature of such forgetting is advantageous. The information we inhibit today may be exactly what we need tomorrow, next week, or next year. With respect to some stereotypes, however, a more permanent state of inhibition may be desirable. But to keep such information in a more or less permanent state of inhibition may well require recurring practice of the counterstereotypic or individuating traits.

The role played by retrieval-induced forgetting *vis-à-vis* stereotypes is thus complex. If we mainly practice retrieving stereotypic congruent information, our stereotypes will be strengthened while our access to counterstereotypic or individuating information will become more and more inhibited – clearly, an unintended negative consequence of retrieval-induced forgetting. On the other hand, if we consciously practice retrieving the individuating information, we will automatically inhibit the stereotypic information, making it less and less likely to come to mind – clearly, an unintended positive consequence of retrieval-induced forgetting.

Suppression of negative memories   Another area in which the unintended consequences of retrieval-induced forgetting could potentially serve a positive function is in the suppression of various types of unpleasant or negative memories, thereby enabling us to avoid the potentially disabling emotions that would be aroused by the continuous presence in consciousness of such memories. For example, as we have previously suggested (E. L. Bjork et al., 1998; Macrae & MacLeod, 1999), in many abusive situations, it seems reasonable to assume that the victim of the abuse would hold both positive and negative memories about the perpetrator of the abuse. It also seems reasonable to assume that, in most such situations, there would be reasons for the victim of abuse to want to retrieve only the positive memories associated with the perpetrator, rather than dwelling on the negative ones. If so, then when thinking about the perpetrator, the victim would engage in retrieval practice for the positive memories. Thus, those memories – like the practiced exemplars of the Anderson et al. (1994) paradigm – would become more and more likely to be retrieved in the future, while the negative memories – being selected against and thus inhibited again and again – would become less and less accessible to retrieval. And, as long as the practice of the positive continued, access to the negative would remain inhibited.

Although more research is necessary to demonstrate such a consequence for retrieval-induced forgetting, some initial results point in that direction. We have found, for example, that having participants practice neutral traits associated with fictional individuals seems to be making their valenced traits (either positive or negative) less accessible for retrieval, and, furthermore, that the traits that are otherwise most recallable are the most susceptible to such effects (Storm, E. L. Bjork, & R. A. Bjork, 2005). Although few of us may have been actual victims of serious abuse, essentially all of us must interact with others whom we consider to have both positive and negative character-istics, or with whom we have had both positive and negative interactions. Thus, being able to remember or emphasize such people's positive attributes while forgetting or making their negative attributes less salient in our memor-ies, can help us to maintain positive relationships with such people – who can be our co-workers, our supervisors, members of our family, or even our spouses – that is, people with whom we want or need to maintain functional and positive relationships. Storm et al.'s results suggest that these types of unintended, but nonetheless positive, consequences of retrieval-induced forgetting could well serve as an adaptive mechanism to smooth our interactions with people with whom we must interact on a range of levels and in a variety of contexts.

CONCLUDING COMMENTS

We began this chapter with the assertion that forgetting, contrary to our intuitions, is a necessary and critical component of an efficient and adaptive memory system. More specifically, we have focused on two types of forgetting – intentional (or "directed") forgetting and retrieval-induced forgetting – each of which, in our view, plays an important role in the everyday functioning of our memories. It is important to emphasize, however, that the benefits of each type of forgetting, with respect to keeping our memories current and avoiding competition from competing memories, are accompanied by some potential costs. Each type of forgetting also has a dark side, so to speak – beyond simply making information unavailable that we might then later, for whatever reason, want to recall. In the case of intentional forgetting, our opinions and beliefs may continue to be influenced by intentionally forgotten information in ways about which we are unaware and thus cannot mitigate. In the case of retrieval-induced forgetting, for example, we may unintentionally be led to acccpt misleading information as correct or to maintain certain stereotypical beliefs that we would prefer not to maintain. Forgetting, in short, refines and updates our memories, but not without certain costs.

References

Anderson, M. C., Bjork, R. A., & Bjork, E. L. (1994). Remembering can cause forget-ting: Retrieval dynamics in long-term memory. *Journal of Experimental Psychology: Learning, Memory, and Cognition, 20*, 1063–1087.

Anderson, M. C., Bjork, E. L., & Bjork, R. A. (2000). Retrieval-induced forgetting: Evidence for a recall-specific mechanism. *Psychonomic Bulletin & Review, 7,* 522–530.

Anderson, M. C., Green, C., & McCulloch, K. C. (2000). Similarity and inhibition in long-term memory: Evidence for a two-factor theory. *Journal of Experimental Psychology: Learning, Memory, and Cognition, 26,* 1141–1159.

Anderson, M. C., & McCulloch, K. C. (1999). Integration as a general boundary condition on retrieval-induced forgetting. *Journal of Experimental Psychology: Learning, Memory, and Cognition, 25,* 608–629.

Anderson, M. C., & Neely, J. H. (1996). Interference and inhibition in memory retrieval. In E. L. Bjork & R. A. Bjork (Eds), *Handbook of perception and cognition: Vol. 10. Memory* (pp. 237–313). San Diego: Academic Press.

Anderson, M. C., & Spellman, B. A. (1995). On the status of inhibitory mechanisms in cognition: Memory retrieval as a model case. *Psychological Review, 102,* 68–100.

Basden, B. H., Basden, D. R., & Gargano, G. J. (1993). Directed forgetting in implicit and explicit memory tests: A comparison of methods. *Journal of Experimental Psychology: Learning, Memory, and Cognition, 19,* 603–616.

Bekerian, D. A., & Bowers, J. M. (1983). Eyewitness testimony: Were we misled? *Journal of Experimental Psychology: Learning, Memory, and Cognition, 9,* 139–145.

Bjork, E. L., & Bjork, R. A. (1996). Continuing influences of to-be-forgotten information. *Consciousness and Cognition, 5,* 176–196.

Bjork, E. L., & Bjork, R. A. (2003). Intentional forgetting can increase, not decrease, residual influences of to-be-forgotten information. *Journal of Experimental Psychology: Learning, Memory, and Cognition, 29,* 524–531.

Bjork, E. L., Bjork, R. A., & Anderson, M. C. (1998). Varieties of goal-directed forgetting. In J. M. Golding & C. N. MacLeod (Eds.), *Intentional forgetting* (pp. 103–137). Mahwah, NJ: Lawrence Erlbaum Associates, Inc.

Bjork, E. L., Bjork, R. A., & Glenberg, A. M. (1973, November). *The reinstatement of proactive interference owing to to-be-forgotten items.* Paper presented at the meeting of the Psychonomic Society, St Louis, MO.

Bjork, E. L., Bjork, R. A., & Kilpatrick, H. A. (1990, November). *Direct and indirect measures of inhibition in directed forgetting.* Paper presented at the meeting of the Psychonomic Society, New Orleans, LA.

Bjork, E. L., Bjork, R. A., Stallings, L., & Kimball, D. R. (1996, November). *Enhanced false fame owing to instructions to forget.* Paper presented at the meeting of the Psychonomic Society, Chicago, IL.

Bjork, R. A. (1972). Theoretical implications of directed forgetting. In A. W. Melton & E. Martin (Eds.), *Coding processes in human memory.* Washington, DC: Winston & Sons.

Bjork, R. A. (1989). Retrieval inhibition as an adaptive mechanism in human memory. In H. L. Roediger, III, & F. M. Craik (Eds.), *Varieties of memory and consciousness: Essays in honor of Endel Tulving* (pp. 309–330). Hillsdale, NJ: Lawrence Erlbaum Associates, Inc.

Bjork, R. A., & Bjork, E. L. (1992). A new theory of disuse and an old theory of stimulus fluctuation. In A. Healy, S. Kosslyn, & R. Shiffrin (Eds.), *From learning processes to cognitive processes: Essays in honor of William K. Estes* (Vol. 2, pp. 35–67). Hillsdale, NJ: Lawrence Erlbaum Associates, Inc.

Blaxton T. A., & Neely, J. H. (1983). Inhibition from semantically related primes: Evidence of a category-specific inhibition. *Memory & Cognition, 11,* 500–510.

Block, R. A. (1971). Effects of instructions to forget in short-term memory. *Journal of Experimental Psychology*, 89, 1–9.

Bodenhausen, G. V., & Macrae, C. N. (1998). Stereotype activation and inhibition. In R. S. Wyer, Jr. (Ed.), *Sterotype activation and inhibition. Advances in social cognition* (Vol. 11, pp. 1–52). Mahwah, NJ: Lawrence Erlbaum Associates, Inc.

Ciranni, M. A., & Shimamura, A. P. (1999). Retrieval-induced forgetting in episodic memory. *Journal of Experimental Psychology: Learning, Memory, and Cognition*, 25, 1403–1414.

Dunn, E. W., & Spellman, B. A. (2003). Forgetting by remembering: Stereotype inhibition through rehearsal of alternative aspects of identity. *Journal of Experimental Social Psychology*, 39, 420–433.

Elmes, D. G., Adams, C., & Roediger, H. L. (1970). Cued forgetting in short-term memory: Response selection. *Journal of Experimental Psychology*, 86, 103–107.

Geiselman, R. E., & Bagheri, B. (1985). Repetition effects in directed forgetting: Evidence for retrieval inhibition. *Memory & Cognition*, 13, 51–62.

Geiselman, R. E., Bjork, R. A., & Fishman, D. (1983). Disrupted retrieval in directed forgetting: A link with posthypnotic amnesia. *Journal of Experimental Psychology: General*, 112, 58–72.

Hamilton, D. L., & Sherman, J. W. (1994). Stereotypes. In R. S. Wyer, Jr., & T. K. Srull (Eds.), *Handbook of social cognition: Vol. 2: Applications* (pp. 1–68). Hillsdale, NJ: Lawrence Erlbaum Associates, Inc.

Johnson, H. (1994). Processes of successful intentional forgetting. *Psychological Bulletin*, 116, 274–292.

Johnston, L. C., & Macrae, C. N. (1994). Changing social stereotypes: The case of the information seeker. *European Journal of Social Psychology*, 24, 581–592.

Kihlstrom, J. F., & Cantor, N. (1984). Mental representations of the self. In L. Berkowitz (Ed.), *Advances in experimental social psychology* (Vol. 17, pp. 1–47). New York: Academic Press.

Klein, S. B., & Kihlstrom, J. F. (1986). Elaboration, organization, and the self-reference effect in memory. *Journal of Experimental Psychology: General*, 115, 26–38.

Landaur, T. K., & Bjork, R. A. (1978). Optimal rehearsal patterns and name learning. In M. M. Gruenberg, P. E. Morris, & R. N. Sykes (Eds.), *Practical aspects of memory* (pp. 625–632). London: Academic Press.

Lindsay, D. A., & Johnson, M. (1989a) The eyewitness suggestibility effect and memory for source. *Memory & Cognition*, 17, 349–358.

Lindsay, D. A., & Johnson, M. (1989b) The reversed suggestibility effect. *Bulletin of the Psychonomic Society*, 27, 111–113.

Loftus, E. F. (1979). *Eyewitness testimony*. Cambridge, MA: Harvard University Press.

Loftus, E. F., Donders, K., Hoffman, H. G., & Schooler, J. W. (1989). Creating new memories that are quickly accessed and confidently held. *Memory & Cognition, 5*, 607–616.

Loftus, E. F., Miller, D. G., & Burns, H. J. (1978). Semantic integration of verbal information into a visual memory. *Journal of Experimental Psychology: Human Learning and Memory*, 4, 19–31.

Loftus, G. R., & Loftus, E. F. (1980). On the permanence of stored information in the human brain. *American Psychologist*, 35, 409–420.

MacLeod, C. M. (1998). Directed forgetting. In J. M. Golding & C. M. MacLeod

(Eds.), *Intentional forgetting: Interdisciplinary approaches* (pp.1–57). Hillsdale, NJ: Lawrence Erlbaum Associates, Inc.

MacLeod, M. D. (2002). Retrieval-induced forgetting in eyewitness memory: Forgetting as a consequence of remembering. *Applied Cognitive Psychology, 16,* 135–149.

MacLeod, M. D., Bjork, E. L., & Bjork, R. A. (2003). The role of retrieval-induced forgetting in the construction and distortion of memories. In B. Kokinov & W. Hirst (Eds.), *Constructive memory: NBU Series in cognitive science* (pp. 55–68). Sophia: New Bulgarian University.

MacLeod, M. D., & Macrae, C. N. (2001). Gone but not forgotten: The transient nature of retrieval-induced forgetting. *Psychological Science, 121,* 148–152.

Macrae, C. N., Bodenhausen, G. V., Milne, A. B., & Ford, R. L. (1997). On the regulation of recollection: The intentional forgetting of stereotypical memories. *Journal of Personality and Social Psychology, 72,* 709–719.

Macrae, C. N., & MacLeod, M. D. (1999). On recollections lost: When practice makes imperfect. *Journal of Personality & Social Psychology, 77,* 463–473.

Macrae, C. N., & Roseveare, T. A. (2002). I was always on my mind: The self and temporary forgetting. *Psychonomic Bulletin & Review, 9,* 611–614.

McGeoch, J. A. (1942). *The psychology of human memory.* New York: Longman.

Mensink, G. J. M., & Raajimakers, J. W. (1988). A model of interference and forgetting. *Psychological Review, 95,* 434–435.

Moeser, S. D. (1979a). Retrieval interference in the independent storage of related episodic traces. *Canadian Journal of Psychology, 33,* 182–192.

Moeser, S. D. (1979b). The role of experimental design in investigations of the fan effect. *Journal of Experimental Psychology: Human Learning and Memory, 5,* 125–134.

Postman, L. (1971). Transfer, interference and forgetting. In J. W. Kling & L. A. Riggs (Eds.), *Woodworth and Scholsberg's experimental psychology* (3rd ed., pp. 1019–1132). New York: Holt, Rinehart & Winston.

Raajimakers, J. G. W., & Shiffrin, R. M. (1981). Search of associative memory. *Psychological Review, 88,* 93–134.

Reed, H. (1971). Studies of the interference processes in short-term memory. *Journal of Experimental Psychology, 84,* 452–457.

Roediger, H. L., (1974). Inhibiting effects of recall. *Memory & Cognition, 2,* 261–269.

Roediger, H. L., & Neely, J. H. (1982). Retrieval blocks in episodic and semantic memory. *Canadian Journal of Psychology, 36,* 213–242.

Rundus, D. (1973). Negative effects of using list items as retrieval cues. *Journal of Verbal Learning and Verbal Behavior, 12,* 43–50.

Saunders, J., & MacLeod, M. D. (2002). New evidence on the suggestibility of memory: The role of retrieval-induced forgetting in misinformation effects. *Journal of Experimental Psychology: Applied, 8,* 127–142.

Shaw, J. S., III, Bjork, R. A., & Handal, A. (1995). Retrieval-induced forgetting in an eyewitness-memory paradigm. *Psychonomic Bulletin & Review, 2,* 249–253.

Smith, R. E., & Hunt, R. R. (2000). The influence of distinctive processing on retrieval-induced forgetting. *Memory & Cognition, 28,* 503–508.

Smith, E. E., Adams, N., & Schorr, D. (1978). Fact retrieval and the paradox of interference. *Cognitive Psychology, 10,* 438–464.

Wells, G. L. (1993). What do we know about eyewitness identification? *American Psychologist, 48,* 553–571.

Wyer, N. A., Sherman, J. W., & Stroessner, S. J. (2000). The roles of motivation and ability in controlling the consequences of stereotype suppression. *Personality & Social Psychology Bulletin, 26*, 13–25.

8   Response conformity in face recognition memory

Yukio Itsukushima, Kazunori Hanyu, Yasunari Okabe, Makiko Naka, Yuji Itoh, and Satoshi Hara

Introduction

Since the Merkmal study conducted by Ebbinghaus (1985/1964), psychologists have devoted much effort to figuring out how human memory functions. In the tradition of Ebbinghaus's approach most of the materials used were verbal, and memory psychologists have tried to uncover the laws that govern memory processes in general and the forgetting process in particular by using such verbal materials. Although Ebbinghaus's paradigm was very strong, there existed another approach that underscored social aspects of human memory. The initiator of it was Sir Frederic Bartlett who investigated how a schema is adopted and how it works when people are faced with new information (Bartlett, 1932). Furthermore, Bartlett investigated how hearsay information deforms. That is, he showed that memory was distorted or influenced not only by the factors that were found in the research where verbal materials were used but also by the factors of both the culture and the schema. Of course, Bartlett's work was not the only research in the field of memory research that showed evidence of memory distortion. For example, Carmichael, Hogan, and Walter (1932) presented subjects with somewhat ambiguous line drawings and verbal labels. Two groups of subjects were presented with line drawings coupled with different verbal labels such as "array" to one group and "eyeglass" to another. In the recall phase of the original line drawings, the two groups of subjects tended to produce figures that were more consistent with the verbal labels given.

The significance of the study by Carmichael et al. (1932) is that memory for the original line-drawings was distorted by the information conveyed by the verbal labels. Although the Carmichael et al. (1932) study was rather primitive in methodology, the verbal influence on the original pictorial memory has been extensively examined in a series of studies by Loftus and her collaborators (e.g., Loftus, Miller, & Burns, 1978). They elaborated the method to study the effect of verbal information on memory for an event. In their method called "standard test" (McCloskey & Zaragoza, 1985) subjects saw a series of slides that depicted a fairly complex event such as a car accident. After the slide presentation, they were asked to answer questions about the scene. A critical item of misinformation (information that was similar to the original but did not actually appear in the original slides) was inserted in one of the questions. After the subjects answered the questions, a recognition test was given. The subjects who received the misinformation had a higher probability of choosing the slide that was not originally shown to them than those who did not receive the misinformation. This result indicated that memory for the original events was easily replaced by post-event misinformation. This phenomenon was called the "misinformation effect" or "post-event information effect" and there are many studies that have tested this phenomenon from various aspects such as retention interval, warning, presentation order of recognition items, types of misinformation and so on (see Greene, 1992; Lindsay, 1994, for reviews).

In the study of the misinformation effect, the misinformation is usually presented in the form of a question or a text. Despite these variations in methods and materials, the misinformation had not been presented by a third person directly. In the mid-1990s a new approach was introduced where the effect of third person's (confederate's) opinion or response on the subjects' memory was studied. The effect of the third person has been recognized as important in the field of eyewitness research, especially in studies of the identification of a suspect by eyewitnesses (Kassin, Ellsworth, & Smith, 1989; Kassin, Tubb, Hosch, & Memon, 2001). Such an effect was demonstrated by many studies and supported by the meta-analytic review by Steblay (1997). Wells and Bradfield (1998) found that positive feedback given after the identification inflated subjects' confidence in the task.

The effect of a third person's opinions, perceptual judgements, attitude or behavioural changes on others' performance has long been investigated in social psychology. Such a phenomenon was classically called the conformity effect (Asch, 1951; Deutsch & Gerard, 1955). In the traditional study of the conformity effect, a perceptual judgement task was employed and the number of confederates was controlled because it was considered to be an important factor in generating the effect. In memory experiments, however, the factor of group size has not been studied much (although one exception to this is a study by Walter, Bless, Strack, Rackstraw, Wagner, & Werth, 2002) though recently there is a growing interest how social factors affect individuals' memories.

Research on the conformity effect in memory began in the mid-1990s. Schneider and Watkins (1996) presented a list to pairs of subjects who believed that they were learning the same list of words, but a part of the list was actually different. When each member of the pairs was asked to judge whether each item was "old" or "new", and respond aloud, the first participant's responses affected the responses of the second participant. Such memory conformity was observed for memory of household objects (Meade & Roediger, 2002; Roediger, Meade, & Bergman, 2001), stories (Betz, Skowronski, & Ostrom, 1996), and drawings of familiar objects (Hoffman, Granhag, Kwong See, & Loftus, 2001; Wright, Self, & Justice, 2000.) In such studies the conformity effect occurred even in situations where there was only one confederate (or one confederate was presumed in Hunter et al.'s study), which suggests that memory conformity occurs even when the group pressure is rather moderate.

Words, household objects, stories, and drawings are not irrelevant to eye-witness studies. Nevertheless, in realistic situations, faces are the most urgent and significant materials to be studied, though no studies on memory conformity for faces have been conducted. We, therefore, explored the conformity effect in memory for faces.

Method

Participants were shown a staged event at three universities during a regular lecture course. The event that they saw was when a graduate student asked them to answer a questionnaire that was developed for another study, which is not reported here. The graduate student instructed them about the question-naire for about five minutes. After a certain period (four months in Experiment 1 and one month in Experiment 2) from the event, the same participants were tested on their memory of the graduate student, the target. The individually administered face-recognition test required participants to give level-of-similarity judgements for each face presented by using 0 to 100 numerals (11 steps). Subjects were randomly assigned to one of three conditions: the high-similarity face conformed condition (HSC for short, 47 participants in Experiment 1 and 18 participants in Experiment 2); the low-similarity face conformed condition (LSC, 52 and 19 participants, respectively), and the control (C, 32 and 16, respectively).

The participants were shown slides of 24 faces one by one. Each was pre-sented for 8 seconds. Twelve young men's faces were used as stimuli, of which four were fairly similar to the target, four were moderately similar to the target, and the remaining four were not similar to the target. These similar-ities were determined beforehand by another group of participants by rating the similarity through paired comparisons, and the data obtained were ana-lysed by a multi-dimensional scaling technique. Two types of photos were used, one was a full face without emotional expression and the other was a smiling face, for each line-up member. The order of the stimulus presentation was randomized.

In the control conditions, the participants took the recognition test in a small group. In the other two experimental conditions, the participants were tested individually. The task of participants in the control condition was to rate how similar the presented faces were to the target. In the other two conditions when the participants came to the laboratory a man was waiting. He was a confederate of the experimenter but behaved naturally as if he were another participant. Before the test, an experimenter asked the confederate to say his age, which was always older than that of the participant. Then the confederate was asked to respond aloud first in the pair. Thus, participants' responses to a stimulus face always followed a confederate's response. The confederate's rating was assigned for each stimulus beforehand by the experimenters.

A week later the same participants came back to the laboratory to take the second test. The second test was a recognition test to examine whether the conformity effect had lasted for a long interval, in this case for a week.

Results

Figure 8.1a shows the result from the HSC condition, where the high-similarity faces were given higher levels of impact for conformity than were the low-similarity faces. In this figure, the horizontal axis represents the series of face stimuli, showing the level of similarity, high, medium, and low: the ■–■ line, the ▲–▲ line, and the ◆–◆ line indicate the scores reported by confederates, the mean scores rated by the participants, and the baseline obtained from the control condition, respectively. In the first few trials, the effect of conformity did not appear. In the fifth trial, the effect of conformity appeared in response to the confederate's high report of 90. The same happened in the sixth trial. In the trials 9, 11, 14, 17, 19, and 22, the participants showed prominent conformity.

Figure 8.1b shows the result from the LSC condition, where the low-similarity faces were conformed. The result slightly differed from that of HSC. That is, although the participants showed some conformity to the confederate's high-similarity ratings, the degree of conformity was not as prominent as that in HSC. Rather, participants' rating scores stayed at a high level compared to the baseline responses.

In the trials for high-similarity faces with intense impact for conformity participants' ratings seemed to fall between confederates' ratings and the baseline. This suggests that the participants' ratings could be a function of confederates' response and the baseline scores. Figure 8.2a shows the data and regression result in HCS and Figure 8.2b shows those in LSC.

When we applied a regression analysis to these data with the confederates' responses and the baseline scores being treated as independent variables and the participants' responses as an dependent variable, the regression analysis yielded the linear formula of $y = 0.785x + 4.39$ with a high squared multiple correlation coefficient ($R^2 = .86$). This function suggests that the degree of conformity increases linearly with the increment of the given amount of impact. This implies that there may be a mechanism that follows confederates' responses but mitigates the degree of the impact.

However, when a regression analysis was applied to the data of LSC, a linear function did not account for the significant degree of variance and a power function better explained the data. The given linear function was $y = 0.575x + 15.73$ with $R^2 = .47$ whereas the given power function was $y = 3.252x^{0.677}$ with $R^2 = .71$. This implies that the mechanism of conformity in the responses for low-similarity stimuli differed from that for high-similarity stimuli.

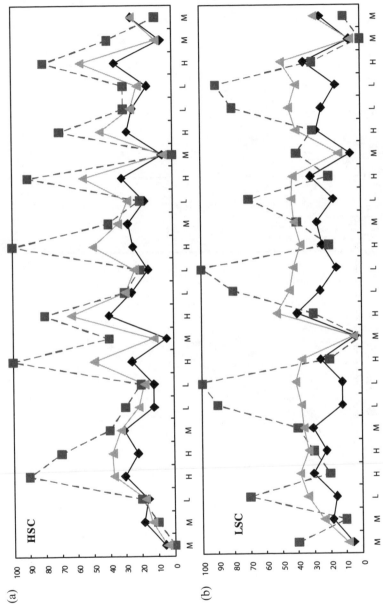

Figure 8.1 The graphs show the result of similarity ratings for HSC (a) and LSC (b). The X axis is for the series of stimulus faces where H stands for high-similarity faces, M for medium-similarity ones, and L for low-similarity ones. The Y axis is for similarity scores for each stimulus where ◆ is for the baseline score given by the control group, ■ is for the confederate's response, and ▲ is for participant's rating.

(a)

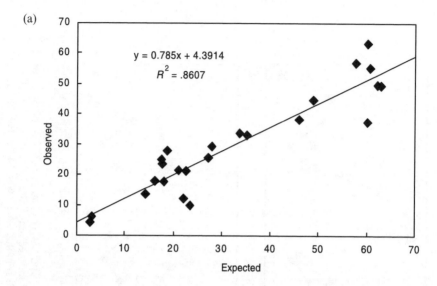

$y = 0.785x + 4.3914$

$R^2 = .8607$

(b)

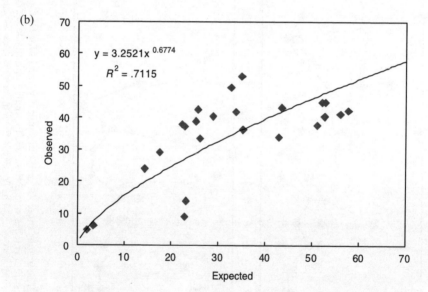

$y = 3.2521x^{0.6774}$

$R^2 = .7115$

Figure 8.2 The graphs show the results of regression analyses that fit observed scores to the average score of conformity and baseline (i.e., impact) for HSC (a) and LSC (b). The X axis is for the expected score provided by averaging the degree of conformity and the baseline score. The linear and curved linear lines in the figures show the best fitted regressed functions among the potential candidates.

There were two conformity conditions, HSC and LSC, in the similarity rating task. In this design, when the same absolute degree of impact for conformity is given in the two conditions, the relative degree of impact for conformity in LSC is greater than that in HSC. For example, when the rating 80 is given to a stimulus with 20 in similarity to the target face, the net impact for conformity is 60, 80 minus 20, whereas when the same rating is given to a stimulus with 70 in similarity, the net impact is 10. The analysis confirmed the main effect of the impact, $F(1, 97) = 4.283$, $p < .05$. More important, there was the significant interaction between the level of similarity in stimuli and the conformity conditions (HSC or LSC), which suggested that, regardless of the similarity of the stimulus face to the target face, the stimuli given larger impact made participants' responses conform more than did those given smaller impact. Figure 8.3a shows the effect of impact on HSC and LSC. The scores presented represent the difference between participants' response and the baselines provided by the controlled condition.

Another purpose of the present study was to examine whether the conformity effect remained in memory. Thus, one week later the same participants attended another rating task where the same faces (but shot from an angled direction) and nine new faces were used.

Again, we adopted similarity judgement as a dependent variable. Figure 8.3b shows the result. Our interest here was whether or not the effect that remained in the conformity task remained in the recognition task one week later, and the result shows that it significantly appeared again, $F(1, 97) = 4.57$, $p <. 05$.

We conducted a follow-up experiment because we felt the necessity of examining the validity of this amazing finding. The procedure in this Experiment 2 was the same as that in Experiment 1 except for the following points. First, compared with Experiment 1, greater ratings for conformity by a confederate were assigned to the high-similarity faces in HSC and smaller ratings were assigned to the high-similarity faces in LSC in Experiment 2. This operation was assumed to increase the contrast between the impacts of the two similarity conditions. Second, in Experiment 1 the duration between observing the target and the conformity task was 4 months whereas in Experiment 2 it was 30 days. This was to test the conformity in the shorter time interval between witnessing the target and the conformity task.

The results showed a strong conformity effect as in Experiment 1. Regression analyses were adopted and the best fit model was $y = 0.743x + 6.93$ ($R^2 = .82$) for HSC and $y = 3.19x^{0.662}$ ($R^2 = .774$) for LCS. The results showed that the response conformity for face recognition memory occurred even after the one month retention period and that the degree of conformity was expressed as linear (for HSC) and power (for LSC) functions of impacts given for stimuli. Furthermore, as impact increased the degree of expressed conformity increased. Finally, the similarity rating one week later showed the same interaction as in Experiment 1.

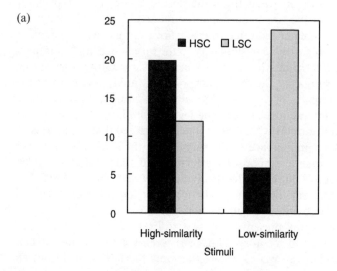

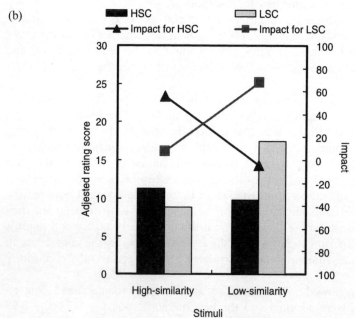

Figure 8.3 Similarity ratings at the conformity task (a) and at the recognition task (b). Bars stand for participants' adjusted response (similarity rating − baseline), with scaled by the right Y axis. Lines stand for impacts with scaled by the left Y axis.

Discussion

The results showed that similarity rating on face recognition is conformed to given impacts by another person, that the degree of conformity reflects the intensity of the impact given, that the influence of conformity remains for at least one week, and that these phenomena can occur in both 1- and 4-month retention intervals. Previous studies that reported conformity effects usually used fairly short retention intervals. For example, in Roediger et al.'s (2001) study and Hoffman et al.'s (2001) study, the retention interval was 48 hours. It is a well-known fact that a memory trace of any event gets weaker as the time passes from the experience of the original event. If the memory trace of the original event is weak, then we infer that the information from a confederate has a greater effect on that memory trace, and the subject would more easily accept the information given by the confederate. Our research results showed that this was true when a longer retention interval was adopted.

Furthermore, in our study a human face was used as the original event and the conformity effect was observed. This is the same as the results that show social influence on memory for word lists (Schneider & Watkins, 1996), stories (Betz et al., 1996), daily familiar objects (Hoffman et al., 2001; Roediger et al., 2001; Meade & Roediger, 2002), and cars (Wright et al., 2000) as described in the introduction. Our research results extend the conformity effects to the region of face recognition memory.

The uniqueness in our approach to exploring the conformity effect of human face remembering was to employ the method of similarity rating in the conformity formation and recognition phases. The employment of this method allowed us to simulate the realistic situation where law-enforcement officers asked witnesses of real crimes to identify the suspects or criminals. Even if they could not identify any person from the line-up, they were asked to show the degree of similarity of the suspect that the law enforcer indicated to the person that they had originally witnessed (see Loftus & Ketcham, 1991, Chapter 7). Our results indicated that if several witnesses see the same person in a real crime and later are asked to identify that person from a line-up where all or some of the witnesses are in a same room together and are asked to indicate the degree of similarity one by one where they can hear one another's responses, the first response may influence that of the next person, and so on.

The degree of the conformity effects in our study reflected the impact given by the confederate, and the response produced by the subjects was a linear function for the high-similarity condition and curved linear function for the low-similarity condition. These results suggest that there may exist some underlying mechanisms that produce very systematic similarity judgements. For example, participants in our studies first accepted the impact from the confederate, and then compared the impact with his/her own, then automatically calculated the output similarity. And these activities strengthen the memory trace of the similarity judgements and after a week the trace was retrieved from memory. To find out how the mechanism works under various situations, further investigations that examine the characteristics of the events that the witnesses experience, the characteristics of the confederates, the retention intervals, the degree of impacts given by the confederates, etc., are necessary.

So far, it has been proved that a kind of similarity judgement is adopted in criminal identification and that if an eyewitness gains information from a third person, it is to be expected that the testimony of the eyewitness will be strongly contaminated by the third person's direct information. Memory is composed not only within the individual but also in society. It is the nature of human memory.

Acknowledgements

We deeply appreciate Keiichiro Ichinose, a lawyer, for giving us the opportunity to start this project and Professor Sumio Hamada for his useful advice.

References

Asch, S. E. (1951). Effects of group pressure upon the modification and distortion of judgements. In H. Guetzkow (Ed.), *Group, leadership and men*. Pittsburgh, PA: Carnegie Press.

Bartlett, F. C. (1932). *Remembering: A study in experimental and social psychology*. Cambridge: Cambridge University Press.

Betz, A. L., Skowronski, J. J., & Ostrom, T. M. (1996). Shared realities: Social influence and stimulus memory. *Social Cognition, 14*, 113–140.

Carmichael, L. C., Hogan, H. P., & Walter, A. A. (1932). An experimental study of the effect of language on the reproduction of visually perceived form. *Journal of Experimental Psychology, 15*, 73–86.

Deutsch, M., & Gerard, H. B. (1955). A study of normative and informative social influence upon individual judgment. *Journal of Abnormal and Social Psychology, 51*, 629–636.

Ebbinghaus, H. (1964). *Memory: A contribution to experimental psychology* (H. A. Ruger & C. E. Buscenius, Trans.). New York: Dover. (Original work published in 1885)

Greene, R. L. (1992). *Human memory: Paradigms and paradoxes*. Hillsdale, NJ: Lawrence Erlbaum Associates, Inc.

Hoffman, H. G., Granhag, P., Kwong See, S. T., & Loftus, E. F. (2001). Social influences on reality-monitoring decisions. *Memory and Cognition, 29*, 394–404.

Kassin, S. M., Ellsworth, P. C., & Smith, V. L. (1989). The "general acceptance" of psychological research on eyewitness testimony: A survey of the experts. *American Psychologist, 44*, 1089–1098.

Kassin, S. M., Tubb, V. A., Hosch, H. M., & Memon, A. (2001). On the general acceptance of eyewitness testimony research: A new survey of the experts. *American Psychologist, 56*, 405–416.

Lindsay, D. S. (1994). Memory source monitoring and eyewitness testimony. In D. F.

Ross, J. D. Read, & M. P. Toglia (Eds.), *Adult eyewitness testimony: Current trends and developments.* New York: Cambridge University Press.

Loftus, E. F., & Ketcham, K. (1991). *Witness for the defense: The accused, the eyewitness, and the expert who puts memory on trial.* New York: St Martin's Press.

Loftus, E. F., Miller, D. G., & Burns, H. J. (1978). Semantic integration of verbal information into a visual memory. *Journal of Experimental Psychology: Human Learning and Memory, 4,* 19–31.

McCloskey, M., & Zaragoza, M. (1985). Misleading postevent information and memory for events: Arguments and evidence against memory impairment hypothesis. *Journal of Experimental Psychology: General, 114,* 381–387.

Meade, M. L., & Roediger, H. L. III, (2002). Explorations in the social contagion of memory. *Memory & Cognition, 30,* 995–1009.

Roediger, H. L., III, Meade, M. L., & Bergman, E. T. (2001). Social contagion of memory. *Psychonomic Bulletin & Review, 8,* 365–371.

Schneider, D. M., & Watkins, M. J. (1996). Response conformity in recognition testing. *Psychonomic Bulletin & Review, 3,* 481–485.

Steblay, N. M. (1997). Social influence in eyewitness recall: A meta-analytic review of lineup instruction effect. *Law and Human Behavior, 21,* 283–297.

Walter, D. B., Bless, H., Strack, F., Rackstraw, P., Wagner, D., & Werth, L. (2002). Conformity effects in memory as a function of group size: Dissenters and uncertainty. *Applied Cognitive Psychology, 16,* 793–810.

Wells, G. L., & Bradfield, A. L. (1998). "Good, you identified the suspect": Feedback to eyewitnesses distorts their reports of the witnessing experience. *Journal of Applied Psychology, 83,* 360–376.

Wright, D. B., Self, G., & Justice, C. (2000). Memory conformity: Exploring misinformation effects when presented by another person. *British Journal of Psychology, 91,* 189–202.

Part III

Memory deficits: Social costs

Lars-Göran Nilsson and Nobuo Ohta

This section of the book is about the practical consequences of various forms of memory deficits and the costs involved, both with respect to the individual and his or her family and with respect to society as a whole. The section covers a wide variety of types of memory deficits: memory deficits occurring in normal ageing and pathological changes in old age; memory deficits that are related to dyslexia; working memory problems in everyday cognition; problems in executive functions in chronic alcoholics; and Korsakoff amnesics. This section also includes one chapter on memory failures and their causes in everyday life and one chapter on the rehabilitation of memory in everyday life.

The first chapter of the section by Craik is about age-related changes in memory and to what extent these changes in normal ageing may reflect the same causes that may underlie the pathological losses seen in some dementias. Craik reviews the research literature on ageing and memory. In so doing he emphasizes certain aspects. He is arguing that in order to find effective techniques for memory rehabilitation in the elderly it is nessary to establish more precisely the nature and the location of the age-related memory loss. He also deals with some specific problems often occurring in elderly persons' memory – remembering names and remembering the future, i.e., prospective memory. Craik ends his chapter by pointing out some practical consequences of the current knowledge about how memory develops in adulthood and old age. He concludes that the dominating feature of the data reviewed is that there is a memory decline as a function of age, but that there are means by which memory can be improved in older adults. Craik identifies two useful principles of how to accomplish this. One way is to provide support for memory operations at both encoding and retrieval. Another way is to arrange the situation such that the elderly person should be able to make a successful retrieval soon after encoding as a means to improving encoding further. He also states that retrieval processes are especially costly in terms of attentional resources for older adults. Craik's final note is encouraging, namely that the memory losses in older adults can be reduced by applying the findings from experimental studies.

The second chapter by Lundberg deals with the role of working memory and reading disability. Lundberg makes several important distinctions for dealing with memory and reading, and memory and dyslexia. One is about individual memory and external storage, another is about oral and written language, still another is about speech perception and speech production. On the topic of memory and dyslexia, Lundberg concludes that developmental dyslexia is a complex biologically rooted condition resulting from impairments of phonological processes, reflecting differences in brain structures and brain functions between dyslexic and normal readers. There is also a genetic influence on the dyslexic impairment. Lundberg states that twin studies indicate a heritability of more than .50 and molecular-genetic studies suggest several significant candidate loci in the human genome. Lundberg also presents an illustrative study on the relationship between working memory and reading disability. Although he demonstrates a clear association between working memory and reading disability, he makes an observation of considerable interest in this context that he stresses, namely that the most important memory in literacy activities is related to the use of the expanding bank of information provided by media. The skill of getting access to these sources is not only a question of decoding the printed words, but the navigation in this sea of information requires complex procedural memories and advanced cognitive strategies that dyslexic individuals may not have available. Such problems have, of course, increased enormously in the explosion of information in the post-modern society.

The third chapter by Logie and Della Sala is about a workspace for memory in healthy and damaged cognition. The authors' main thesis is that a well-functioning working memory is crucial for a wide range of everyday tasks that require the retention of information on a temporary basis, together with the manipulation, transformation and reinterpretation of that information. The authors discuss some current theoretical arguments regarding working memory. They also report the results of two lines of experimental research that illustrate how the multiple-task working-memory model has been particularly useful in the study of mental imagery in healthy adults and in brain-damaged individuals, and in the study of dual-task performance impairments that arise in the early stages of Alzheimer's disease. The results presented offer insights into several important domains of cognition. In this context, the results are particularly important for some of the cognitive difficulties that brain-damaged individuals might encounter in daily life with advice for carers, and for non-invasive methods of detecting and monitoring the impact of forms of brain damage.

The chapter by Mimura examines executive functions in two different alcohol-related areas: alcoholism and alcoholic Korsakoff syndrome. The general theme in this chapter is the question of the social prognosis of amnesic patients, i.e., whether or not the patient will be able to return to society, job and normal level of functioning. Three studies are reported. In the first study, the question was whether executive functioning of alcoholics can predict further drinking behaviour or a successful return to a regular social life. The results show that executive dysfunction predicts alcohol–non-specific functioning (occupation) but not alcohol–specific-drinking outcome. In the second study, the aim was to examine whether there were any neuro-cognitive factors that determine the future social prognosis of Korsakoff amnesics. From previous research, it is not clear whether the cognitive functions of Korsakoff patients deteriorate, remain unchanged or gradually improve, although not to perfect recovery. The results show that overall social prognosis of Korsakoff patients is extremely poor as indexed by place of abode and job status. Most of the patients in the study remained institutionalized and none of the patients in the study returned to an active job. Despite these depressing results Mimura was able to determine that intelligence and attention were equivalently well preserved for both the good and the poor prognosis groups. Dense amnesia was also a common feature for both groups. The main discriminating factor between the good and poor prognosis groups was the absence of executive dysfunction. In the third study, a characteristic Korsakoff patient, who remained hospitalized for a long time, was examined. The patient depicted several pathological features of the chronic Korsakoff syndrome. It was concluded that only rehabilitation approaches for severe memory deficits may benefit such treatment-resistant patients.

In their chapter, Herrmann, Gruneberg, Fiore, Schooler and Torres describe the typical memory failures of everyday life and their causes. Frequency of memory failures was investigated as a function of whether they were retrospective or prospective. The research reported also examined how often memory failure was characterized by failing to remember (omission) or remembering incorrectly (commission). Moreover, the authors report different cause characteristics. Are there just a few causes or many causes? Are different kinds of memory failures produced by the same or different causes? Do the relative influences of causes on memory failure act directly or indirectly on memory? The results show that more failures were recalled that were prospective than retrospective and that there were more failures involving an error of omission rather than an error of commission. More memory failures in this study involved direct causes (e.g., insufficient encoding procedures, long retention intervals, misguided retrieval attempts with poor cues, doing too many things at once, being preoccupied during input or output) than indirect causes (e.g., stress, fatigue, lack of sleep). The data obtained seem to suggest that memory failures are produced by just a few rather than many causes. Being too busy or doing too many things at once was by far the most important cause of memory failure. Poor rehearsal was reported to be a cause of memory failure less often than any other cause category. The authors conclude that memory failures in everyday life can be avoided if society slows down and members of society take better care of themselves.

In the final chapter of this section and the book, Wilson discusses rehabilitation of memory in everyday life. Wilson describes in detail how the planning and implementing of a memory rehabilitation programme should be done. Many practically valuable features of such a programme are provided. Wilson then goes on to describe strategies for reducing everyday memory problems. Also this section is very rich in practical advice for people with memory problems themselves and for caregivers and other practitioners of memory rehabilitation. A final section of this valuable chapter addresses the emotional consequences of memory impairment. Anxiety, depression and social isolation are common in people with memory difficulties. According to Wilson, these states are often as handicapping as the cognitive deficits per se and should therefore be part of any memory rehabilitation programme.

This section of the book covers several areas of cognitive difficulties that are of potential importance for the individual with cognitive impairments, the families of these individuals, and for the society in which these individuals live. A potential disaster is in slow progress in society of today. When all those who were born during the 1940s reach an age when the proportion of dementia cases dramatically increases, there will be great difficulties for any society to manage the care and the financial costs of this care. About 2% of those aged 65 and older are demented. Those large numbers of people born during the 1940s are in the process of reaching this age at present. This baby boom from the 1940s will be a heavy burden on each society, but probably most societies will manage these costs. However, when the baby boomers reach the age of 80 years the proportion of dementia will be 20%, at 90 years of age and more it will be about 50%. There is still some time before societies will receive this burden, but before this happens members of the scientific community should focus on finding early signs of dementia, in order to cure, or at least postpone the development of the dementia process. Non-invasive cognitive methods will probably play an important role in such an early diagnosis of dementia. Cognitive psychologists will have the possibility, in joint efforts with cognitive neuroscientists, of making important breakthroughs that will be of great importance for the individual, the family, and society as a whole.

9 Age-related changes in human memory: Practical consequences

Fergus I. M. Craik

Some degree of memory impairment is one of the commonest complaints of older adults. After their 60th birthday, and sometimes earlier, many older people report that they experience difficulty in retrieving well-known names and occasional difficulty in finding the right word to express an idea. In addition, they report an increase in everyday forgetfulness with regard to carrying out intentions, remembering where they left a book or their spectacles, and where they met a person previously. This benign memory loss is often irritating and sometimes embarrassing (forgetting a person's name when you meet them in a social setting, for example), but it is usually remediable and rarely catastrophic. Nonetheless, it is important for memory researchers to understand the underlying causes of the condition. Two obvious reasons for such a research programme are, first, that age-related memory losses may reflect the same causes (in a milder form) that underlie the pathological losses seen in some dementias and, second, an understanding of causation is the first step in the development of methods of prevention and rehabilitation.

The experimental literature confirms that memory abilities decline with increasing age, but studies also show that the age-related decrements are differential – performance on some tasks declines greatly whereas performance on other tasks remains stable well into the 70s or 80s. One major task of the memory theorist is therefore to provide an adequate account of the factors underlying this differential pattern of loss, stability, and even gains in some situations. Reviews of these relative strengths and weaknesses are provided by Craik and Jennings (1992), Balota, Dolan, and Duchek (2000) and Zacks, Hasher, and Li (2000). Aspects of memory that hold up well with age include well-learned (and often-used) facts and knowledge, memory for cognitive and sensorimotor procedures, and "implicit memory" or priming. Primary memory for small amounts of information held briefly in mind and then given back verbatim also declines little with age, as does recognition memory for recent experiences. On the other hand, aspects that decline with age include unsupported recall of episodic events, recollection of the context in which a fact was acquired, prospective memory (remembering to carry out an intention at some future time), and working memory (the manipulation of material held in mind).

I have previously argued that this pattern of differential loss with age can be understood in terms of the types of processing necessary to carry out particular memory tasks. Some memory operations are well supported by the external environment or by well-learned schematic knowledge – procedural learning, recognition memory, and retrieval of general factual information are good examples – and performance on such tasks holds up well with age. When the appropriate encoding or retrieval operations are *not* supported by the environment, the person must "self-initiate" the required processes, and it seems that the effort to initiate, organize, and implement the processes becomes more difficult with increasing age. Figure 9.1 shows the postulated relations among environmental support, self-initiated processing, and the age-related decline in performance. The figure also shows a sample of memory retrieval tasks, ordered from tasks showing the greatest age-related loss (e.g., free recall) to tasks showing little or no loss (e.g., procedural memory tasks). Thus, the overall pattern of performance may be understood as a complex set of interactions among variables associated with individuals, tasks, and degree of environmental support. Finally, it is suggested that the age-related difficulty associated with self-initiated processing may be related to the declining efficiency with age of frontal lobe functions (Craik & Grady, 2002; Grady & Craik, 2000; West, 1996).

Locating the loss

In order to devise and develop effective techniques for memory rehabilitation in the elderly, it is necessary to establish more precisely the nature and

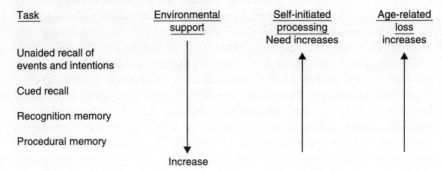

Figure 9.1 Theoretical scheme showing the relations among environmental support, self-initiated processing, and age-related decrements in memory performance.

location of the age-related memory loss. Is the major problem one of encoding, for example, or retrieval, or perhaps both encoding and retrieval? Recent evidence from neuroimaging studies of memory and ageing suggests that, in the case of episodic memory at least, encoding difficulties play a major role. These studies have shown that effective encoding operations are typically associated with activation of the left ventro-lateral prefrontal cortex, and that the level of this encoding-related activation is greatly reduced in older people (Grady et al., 1995; Grady & Craik, 2000; Kapur et al., 1994). Effective retrieval operations are associated with right prefrontal activations (Tulving, Kapur, Craik, Moscovitch, & Houle, 1994), and the level of these activations is typically less affected by ageing than are the levels of left-frontal activations.

The experimental literature on human memory contains a large number of studies showing that memory performance is enhanced by various manipulations of encoding processes. These methods of boosting encoding include presenting items as pictures as opposed to words, generating a word from its incomplete fragment as opposed to simply reading the complete word, and carrying out a simple motor command (e.g., "point to your nose", "pick up the book") as opposed to reading the command. This last method is often referred to as involving "subject-performed tasks" or SPTs; later recall of the phrases is contrasted with recall following reading the phrases without enactment ("verbal tasks" or VTs). A study by Rönnlund and his colleagues (Rönnlund, Nyberg, Bäckman, & Nilsson, 2003) compared recall levels of SPTs and VTs in groups of 100 people ranging in age from 35 to 80 years. If an encoding deficit is the major problem for older learners, it would be expected that SPTs would be differentially more helpful to older adults. However, the results (Figure 9.2) show very clearly that the advantage of SPTs over VTs is uniform across all age groups.

A similar finding was reported by Craik and Byrd (1982). In an experiment carried out by Jan Rabinowitz, groups of younger and older adults studied unrelated words and pictures of objects for a later recall test. The results (Table 9.1) show that pictures were associated with higher levels of recall than words, but that this picture superiority effect was identical (0.19) for both age groups. In this study the recall test was followed by a recognition test, and Table 9.1 also shows that the combination of picture presentation and recognition eliminated the age difference. On the assumption that a recognition test provides better retrieval support than a recall test, this result may be taken to mean that age-related memory deficits are reduced by the *combination* of favourable encoding conditions (e.g., pictures vs. words) and favourable retrieval conditions (recognition vs. recall). The same conclusion was drawn from an experiment by Naveh-Benjamin, Craik, and Ben-Shaul (2002). In their study, younger and older adults were presented with semantically related or unrelated word pairs to learn for a later cued recall test in which the first words were given and subjects attempted to recall the paired word. The retrieval test was run either under conditions in which the first letter of the

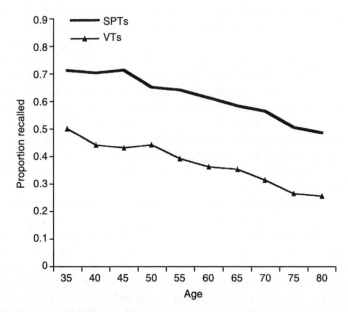

Figure 9.2 Proportions of phrases recalled by adults of different ages as a function of whether the phrases were presented as "subject-performed tasks" (SPTs) or "verbal tasks" (VTs) (Data from Rönnlund et al., 2003).

Table 9.1 Mean proportions recalled and recognized as a function of age and type of material (Craik & Byrd, 1982)

Age group	Recall		Recognition	
	Words	Pictures	Words	Pictures
Young	0.33	0.52	0.73	0.84
Old	0.17	0.36	0.63	0.83

word to be recalled was provided (Figure 9.3, right panel) or was not provided (Figure 9.3, left panel). Related pairs presumably boost encoding relative to unrelated pairs, and provision of the first letter presumably boosts retrieval. Figure 9.3 shows that the age-related deficit is again minimized by the *combination* of good encoding conditions (related pairs) and good retrieval conditions (first letter provided). Note that ceiling effects are not a factor here – maximum performance is less than 70%.

These examples of ways to reduce age-related memory impairments illustrate the general principle of environmental support (Craik, 1983, 1986) described earlier. If older adults are less able to self-initiate optimal encoding and retrieval processes, they are more reliant on aspects of the materials, tasks, and environmental contexts to perform successfully, and should benefit more than their younger counterparts when such support is provided. This

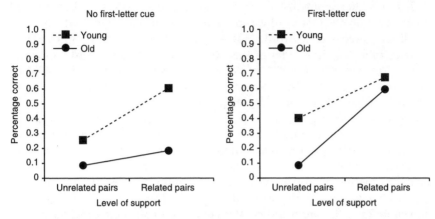

Figure 9.3 Proportions of words recalled as a function of age, relatedness, and provision of cue (Naveh-Benjamin et al., 2002).

principle is utilized by architects and engineers when designing housing, appliances, and information displays for the elderly, but could probably be drawn on to an even larger extent. Successful remembering relies partly on efficient processes of self-initiation and recollection, and partly on processes driven by the task and by the person's environmental context. As the first set of factors declines in the course of normal ageing, the second set can provide compensating support, and this fact should be borne in mind by human-factors engineers.

Successful retrieval as encoding

One problem with assessing the effectiveness of various memory encoding techniques lies in the difficulty of knowing exactly which mental operations are being performed in response to specific task demands. For example, does the advantage of SPTs over VTs reflect greater focal attention in the first case, or deeper processing, or enrichment from the motoric aspects? Without doing a concurrent neuroimaging scan we just cannot tell. This problem is reduced (but not eliminated) when successful retrieval acts as an encoding device that may boost performance in a subsequent retrieval test. Successful retrieval from secondary memory typically involves semantic processing (Morris, Bransford, & Franks, 1977), and some knowledge of the processes involved can be inferred from that observation and from the fact that retrieval *was* successful. Empirically it is the case that retrieval on a first test is effective in boosting retrieval on a subsequent test (Bjork, 1975; Götz & Jacoby, 1974).

Moshe Naveh-Benjamin and I have recently explored the effectiveness of retrieval as an encoding manipulation in older adults. The paradigm consisted of presenting a long series of moderately-related word pairs visually at a 6 s rate. Within the long list, word pairs were either *repeated* at lags of either

0, 2, 4 or 8 intervening items, or were *tested* at these same lags. In the tested condition, only the first word was presented and the participant attempted to recall its paired second word. Not all pairs were successfully retrieved of course; Table 9.2 shows that in this "online" phase, tested word pairs were successfully retrieved on 93% of occasions at lag = 0, but on only 44% of occasions at lag = 8. The online phase was followed by a final cued recall phase in which first words of all pairs (originally tested and originally repeated) were given as cues for the second word. Table 9.2 shows the values of cued recall in this final test for originally tested and originally repeated words at lags 0–8. The values shown for tested pairs are based on those items in which recall was successful in the first (online) phase. To avoid selection artifacts, specific word pairs in the tested condition were yoked across subjects with word pairs in the repeated condition. That is, the cued recall values shown in Table 9.2 are based on the same word pairs across the tested and repeated conditions.

The results show that successful retrieval is a *much* more effective method of learning than is simple repetition. There is also a positive effect of increasing lag (the "lag effect", see Murdock, 1974) and an interaction between tested/repeated and lag, in the sense that the superiority of tested over repeated is greater at longer lags. It is striking that performance in this task varies from 20% to 75% in the final recall test, despite the equivalence of materials, subjects, and the fact that all pairs were presented twice in the online phase. The clear messages for people designing learning situations for older adults are, first, repetitions should be spaced, and, second, if possible have participants *retrieve* the wanted material as part of the learning phase. One way to accomplish this would be to combine the gradually phased-in technique of errorless learning (see Wilson, Chapter 14 this volume) with retrieval viewed as an encoding device. As a final note on this topic, we have also used this technique with younger adults, and they show the same pattern of behaviour. So it is not *necessarily* the case that retrieval-as-encoding reduces the age-related difference in performance (though see Rabinowitz & Craik, 1986, where that result *was* obtained). The main point, however, is that prior retrieval functions as an excellent encoding device that can greatly improve the memory performance of older adults.

Table 9.2 Mean proportions of words recalled by older adults "online" and after repetitions that either were tested or repeated (see text for details)

	Lag			
	0	*2*	*4*	*8*
Online	.93	.41	.45	.44
Tested	.24	.64	.61	.75
Repeated	.20	.30	.22	.50

Divided attention and ageing

There are several good reasons for studying the effects of divided attention (DA) on ageing, and the effects of ageing on dual-task performance. First, older people often complain that they have difficulty "concentrating", and that irrelevant sources of information affect their ability to comprehend, to learn and to remember. It might therefore be expected that older adults should be differentially penalized by dual-task situations, and there is some evidence to this effect (Craik, 1977) although not everyone is convinced (e.g., Salthouse, 1991). Second, one theoretical approach to cognitive ageing stresses an age-related reduction in attentional resources (e.g., Craik, 1983; Craik & Byrd, 1982), so it should be possible to mimic the effects of ageing by studying young adults under dual-task conditions. That is, by diverting some processing resources to a secondary task the amount of attention available for the primary task is reduced, and under these circumstances younger adults' performance on the primary task should resemble that of older adults performing the same task under conditions of full attention. A third reason for studying division of attention is that the drop in performance on a secondary task from single task to dual-task conditions ("secondary task costs") provides an index of the attentional resources required to perform the primary task, and these costs may be different for different primary tasks and between younger and older adults. This last point will be illustrated by the results of some studies of encoding and retrieval from my laboratory.

In one set of experiments, Nicole Anderson used a visual continuous reaction-time (RT) task as the secondary task, and auditory presentation of words or word pairs as the primary memory task (Anderson, Craik, & Naveh-Benjamin, 1998). In a free recall version, lists of 15 single words were presented auditorily and subsequently retrieved by spoken recall. This memory task was carried out either under conditions of full attention at both encoding and retrieval (thus under single-task conditions) or while simultaneously performing a visual-motor four-choice RT task at *either* encoding or retrieval. The RT task was continuous in the sense that a correct response immediately brought up the next stimulus; thus the measure of RT task performance was the mean RT over the whole duration of the encoding phase (75 s) or the retrieval phase (30 s). The RT task was also performed under single-task conditions, yielding a mean RT of 414 ms for a group of young adults and a mean RT of 574 ms for the comparison group of older adults.

Performance levels in the various conditions are shown in Figure 9.4a. When the memory task was performed alone (i.e., under full attention conditions) the young adults recalled 9.8 words on average as opposed to 6.3 words recalled by the older group. When attention was divided at encoding, memory performance fell substantially, but by an equivalent amount, in the two groups. When attention was divided at retrieval, memory performance in both groups fell relative to full attention levels, but only to a slight extent. This last result replicates earlier findings (Craik, Govoni, Naveh-Benjamin, &

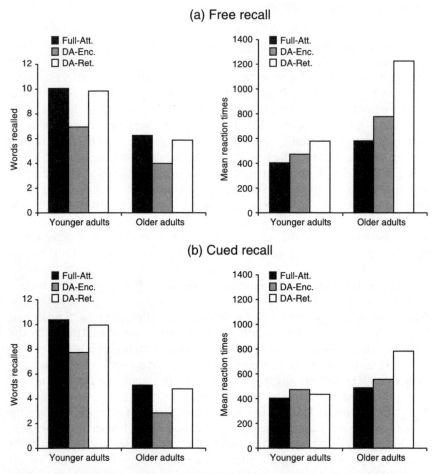

Figure 9.4 Proportions of words recalled under free recall (a) or cued recall (b) conditions as a function of attentional conditions. Right-hand graphs show
reaction times on the concurrent secondary task. (Anderson et al., 1998.)

Anderson, 1996). Thus, overall, division of attention reduced memory
performance by about the same amount in younger and older adults. The
right-hand panel of Figure 9.4a shows the mean RT scores. Now it is seen
that RT costs (the difference between full attention and divided attention
performance) are greater for the older group – substantially so in the case of
DA at retrieval. Anderson and her colleagues therefore concluded that the
attentional requirements of memory encoding and more especially retrieval
were greater in older adults. This experiment thus gave no support to the
notion that the addition of a secondary task would be more disruptive to
memory performance in an older group, but did support the position that the
efficiency of encoding and (especially) retrieval processes in the elderly may

be reduced because of the greater attentional requirements of these processes. Alternatively it might be concluded that the total supply of attentional resources is reduced in older adults, so that when they perform the memory task, performance on the concurrent RT task suffers disproportionately. A similar set of findings – equivalent losses in memory performance under DA conditions but greater secondary-task costs in a group of older adults – was reported by Nyberg, Nilsson, Olofsson, and Bäckman (1997).

Anderson also carried out a cued-recall version of the experiment. In this case, pairs of unrelated nouns were presented auditorily at encoding. At retrieval, the first words of each pair were presented auditorily as cues for the second word and participants spoke their responses. The same visual-motor RT task was used as the secondary task. Memory performance is shown in the left panel of Figure 9.4b. The results were very similar to those for free recall; that is, younger adults recalled more than older adults, the secondary task reduced performance by about the same amount for the two age groups, more so for DA at encoding than for DA at retrieval. The mean RT results (right panel of Figure 9.4b) are also similar to those for free recall, but in this case the DA costs are substantially less. The suggested explanation for this finding is that cued recall offers more environmental support to retrieval processes, and that this support is particularly beneficial to older adults.

The conclusion that encoding and retrieval processes (especially the latter) are more costly in terms of attentional resources in older compared to younger adults was borne out in a more recent study by Naveh-Benjamin, Craik, Guez, and Kreuger (2005). Word pairs were again presented auditorily to be learned during the encoding phase, and the first words of each pair were presented auditorily during the retrieval phase as cues for the corresponding second word. In this case the secondary task was a visual tracking task in which participants tracked a randomly moving dot on a computer screen by moving the computer mouse. The mouse controlled a "chaser" dot, and the participant's task was to keep the chaser as close to the randomly moving target dot as possible. The computer kept track of the distance between the chaser and the target, and how this distance changed across time. The logic here is that the chaser–target distance is a measure of attention paid to the task – if the participant is paying full attention, the distance should be small, and as attention is diverted to some other task, the chaser–target distance should increase. Participants performed this tracking task by itself (under full-attention conditions), and also performed the task while they were simultaneously encoding each word pair (6 s) or attempting to retrieve each second word (6 s). In order to measure the extra attentional *costs* of encoding and retrieval, we subtracted the average chaser–target deviations when the tracking task was performed alone from those found when the task was performed simultaneously with either encoding or retrieval. This procedure was carried out separately for each participant, and separately for each 500 ms of the memory phases.

Figure 9.5 thus shows the attentional costs of encoding and retrieval for

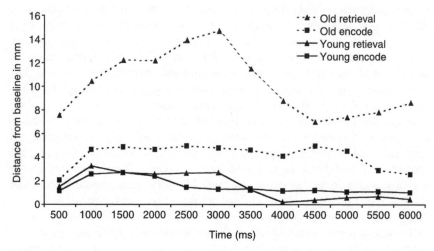

Figure 9.5 Tracking costs as a function of age and experimental condition (Naveh-Benjamin et al., 2005).

younger and older adults as a function of time within the encoding or retrieval phase. The figure shows that young adults require about the same amount of attention at encoding and retrieval, and that the attentional demands of both memory tasks are at a peak between 1 and 3 s after presentation of the word pair (encoding) or word cue (retrieval). The pattern for older subjects is very different. First, the attentional demands are much greater (that is, the deviations *from their own baseline* are larger); second, retrieval costs are substantially greater than encoding costs; and, third, deviations from baseline do not return to zero even after 6 s of memory activity. It seems, therefore, that memory retrieval requires a considerable amount of attentional resources in older people, and that they show substantial "dual-task costs" even when the memory-related costs are presumably light, at the end of each encoding or retrieval phase. That is, the simple fact of being in a dual-task situation appears to be somewhat costly, and more so for older than for younger adults. This work using a secondary tracking task thus confirms and extends the work of Anderson and colleagues (1998) using a secondary choice-RT task.

Remembering names

Perhaps the single most frequent memory complaint of older people is their experienced difficulty in remembering proper names – even names of people that they have known for many years. Clearly this is not an encoding problem, as the names were often learned decades ago, and it is not a storage problem, as the names are usually retrieved at a later time or in response to further cues and prompts. It is a problem of retrieval – of recollection. One possible reason for this age-related problem is that the retrieval of very *specific* information becomes differentially more difficult as people age. Work with depressed patients has shown this pattern – that general, gist-like information is more accessible than is specific information such as names and numbers (Williams, 1996) – so it seems possible that normal ageing and depression share some features, decreased arousal or decreased processing resources for example, that give rise to the similarity in behaviour.

In my laboratory Alan Castel has conducted a study in which he investigated the possibility that older adults have greater difficulty remembering names than remembering words that are otherwise comparable. Following an ingenious design introduced by McWeeney and colleagues (1987), Castel presented a series of photographs of people, each photograph accompanied by the person's name and occupation (both fictitious). Thus a photograph of a man might be presented along with the information that his name is Mr Johnston and that he is an engineer. Some of the names chosen were also common names of occupations, for example Baker, Fisher, Mason, Potter, and these words were used (between subjects) either as the name of the person depicted or as the description of his or her occupation. So one subject might be presented with the sentence "Mr Baker is a mason" whereas another subject was told "Mr Mason is a baker". The test consisted of showing the series of photographs, and the subject's task was to recall the name and occupation of each person. In order to disguise the fact that some names were also occupations, the list contained a number of names and occupations, that were *not* interchangeable, for example "Mr Stevens is an actor".

The results of the recall test were somewhat surprising. Both younger and older adults recalled more occupations than names (from the set of interchangeable words), and younger adults recalled more items than older adults; both of these results were expected. Surprisingly, however, the drop in recall level from occupations to names was the same for the two age groups. For the young group, occupations = 0.63, names = 0.41, a drop of 0.22, and for the older adults, occupations = 0.39 and names = 0.17, again a drop of 0.22. Thus it seems from Castel's study that whereas the recall of names is more difficult than the recall of the same words when they are presented as labels for occupations, this difference is equivalent for younger and older adults. It is difficult to reconcile this result with the common report of older people that names are particularly difficult to remember (although other studies have also failed to show an age difference in remembering names, e.g., Maylor, 1997). Perhaps there is some crucial difference between the learning and remembering of new names (as in Castel's experiment) and the recall of well-known names that the person cannot retrieve for the moment. Given the ubiquity of this reported difficulty in real life, the topic remains an interesting one to explore further.

Remembering the future

Most memory tasks involve the recollection of some event from the person's past or the retrieval of facts or ideas that have been acquired and stored at some previous time. But we also form intentions to carry out activities at some time in the future, both in the short term ("when I finish writing this section I must remember to phone my daughter") and in the long term ("my mother's birthday is in two weeks, so I should remember to buy a card some-time next week"). Such intentions are often forgotten, with consequences ranging from embarrassment (e.g., forgetting a friend's birthday) to disaster (e.g., forgetting to check crucial dials in an aircraft or in a powerplant). This type of remembering is referred to as prospective memory and it is surpris-ingly vulnerable to failure. In one study, Harris and Wilkins (1982) asked subjects to watch a movie and also carry out simple actions after various lengths of time (e.g., at intervals of 3, 9, and 3 minutes). The subjects were allowed to monitor the time by checking a clock behind them, and occasion-ally subjects would check the time, find they should respond in 20 seconds or so, yet fail to carry out the action when the 20 seconds elapsed.

With regard to age differences in such tasks, the literature reports some puzzling inconsistencies. In one early report, Moscovitch (1982) described a study in which older adults were markedly superior to young adults in remembering to phone the lab at various times over the course of several days. It seemed, however, that the superiority was largely attributable to the much greater use of cues and reminders by the older group. On the other hand, Cockburn and Smith (1991) found that older adults were poorer at spontaneously remembering to carry out future tasks in the context of com-pleting a battery of cognitive tests. Einstein and McDaniel (1990) initially reported an absence of ageing effects on a lab-based prospective memory task, but later concluded that the pattern of age-related differences depended on whether the task was time-based (e.g., carry out the action after some specified time has elapsed) or event-based (e.g., carry out the action when some event occurs). Einstein and McDaniel (1996) found age-related decre-ments in a time-based task but not in event-based tasks, which provide greater environmental support to the participant (Craik, 1983).

In my own laboratory, Peter Rendell and I explored several facets of pos-sible age differences in prospective remembering (Rendell & Craik, 2000). In previous work Rendell had found strong evidence for an age-related *superior-ity* in prospective memory using a real-life task in which participants recorded events on a time-logger at various specified times over the course of a week. Interestingly, the same subjects showed the opposite effect – that is, younger adults were superior to older adults – on two laboratory tests of prospective memory (Rendell & Thomson, 1999). We conjectured that older adults may do well on real-life tasks because their daily and weekly routines are typically more structured than are the more variable and spontaneous patterns of younger experimental participants, who are often university students. Rendell and I therefore developed a laboratory task that was intended to incorporate the salient features of real-life events, with the expectation that older adults could utilize these features to support prospective remembering.

The laboratory task was a board game called Virtual Week that required participants to make their way round a board in accordance with "shakes" of electronic dice. The board was marked out in hours of a typical waking day, from 7 a.m. to 10:30 p.m., and ten squares were marked E for event. Whenever participants landed on or passed an E square they were required to pick up an event card, which described some typical daily event such as breakfast, dinner, a phone call, visit from a friend, watching television, going to the library, and so forth. Ten prospective memory (PM) tasks were given on each of seven "virtual days". Four were the same "regular" tasks that were performed each day; they included such things as remembering to take medication connected with a particular meal. Four further tasks each day were "irregular" in the sense that they were different each day; the instructions for these tasks were given either before commencing the board circuit on that day (e.g., "When you go to the library remember to return the book about Spain") or in the course of making the board circuit (e.g., "Your friend Kate calls and asks you to call her back at 9 p.m."). Finally, two other "time-check" tasks were given on each day: subjects were asked to inform the experimenter when a stop-clock (in full view) showed 2 minutes 30 seconds, and 4 minutes 15 seconds. These time-check tasks were obviously outside the "set" of performing daily activities, and we predicted that older adults would do poorly on them although they would do well on the regular and irregular PM tasks.

Figure 9.6a shows the proportions of correct responses on the three types of PM task by each of three age groups: young adults (mean age = 21.3 yr); young-old adults (mean age = 67.8 yr); and old-old adults (mean age = 75.8 yr). Our predictions were only partially confirmed. There were age-related decrements on all three types of task, although the decrement was small for the regular tasks. Overall, though, the older adults performed less well on these laboratory tasks, in spite of our attempts to simulate real life, and so allow them to utilize their supposedly more structured daily schemas.

Out of interest, we then devised a parallel version of Virtual Week that was conducted during the course of a week of each participant's real-life activities. This version – "Actual Week" – had the same three types of PM task, and subjects recorded their responses on time-stamped portable cassette recorders. The results are shown in Figure 9.6b. The young adults are now the poorest performers, and the old-old group do as well as the young-old, except on the time-check task, on which the young-old show some superiority. The study thus replicated the results of Rendell and Thomson (1999) in the sense that younger adults do well on laboratory versions of PM tasks, but poorly on real-life versions, whereas older adults show the opposite pattern. Why should this be? We asked our subjects not to use

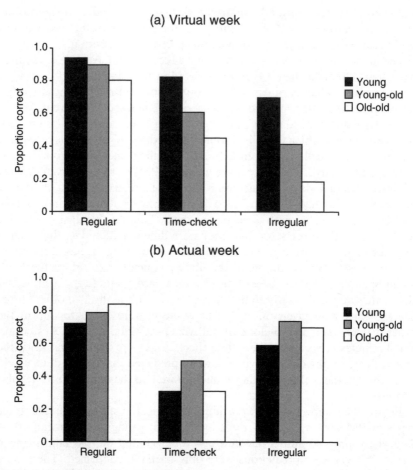

Figure 9.6 Performance on prospective memory tasks as a function of age (Rendell &
        Craik, 2000).

notes and prompts in Actual Week, and they adhered to these instructions.
It seems likely that the older groups took the tasks more seriously, however,
and that they not only rehearsed the day's instructions more times but also
thought about them in the course of the day more often than did their
younger counterparts. Perhaps younger adults are good at maintaining
intentions and carrying out the required actions over the course of a laboratory experiment when that is their primary activity, but do not do so well in
real-life settings where many other interests and priorities compete with
what is only "a psych. experiment" after all! Whatever the reasons behind
the switch in age-related patterns between laboratory and real-life versions
of PM tasks, it is heartening to see that older adults *can* perform well (even
in their mid-seventies) on PM tasks performed in their own domestic
settings.

Age and memory: Practical consequences

In this chapter I have reviewed several recent studies on memory and ageing conducted in my laboratory. In general the results bear out the generality that age-related losses are typically found, but these losses are variable depending on the specific mental operations involved. The encouraging feature of the experimental results is that memory performance in older adults *can* be improved by a variety of means. In some cases the older group improved more than the younger group, but the more important point for practical situations is that the performance levels of older adults can be increased in absolute terms. Two useful principles that emerge from the experimental work are, first, that further "support" for memory operations should be provided at both encoding and retrieval and, second, that successful retrieval acts as a very effective encoding device, especially if the initial retrieval is accomplished some time after initial encoding. Our work using secondary tasks has shown that retrieval processes are especially costly in terms of attentional resources for older adults. One practical implication of this finding is that retrieval from episodic (and probably semantic) memory should be attempted in situations where the person is able to devote full attention to the retrieval task.

The factors important for the successful recall of names and for remembering to carry out intentions require further experimental clarification. For name recall it is probably beneficial to re-establish the context in which the name was learned, but we do not know whether such reinstatement of context is differentially beneficial to older adults. In the case of prospective remembering, Einstein and McDaniel's (1996) finding of reduced age-related losses in event-based PM settings provides a useful guide. In summary, although there *are* substantial memory losses in older adults, many such losses can be reduced by applying the findings from experimental studies.

Acknowledgments

The work reported in this chapter was supported by a grant from the Natural Sciences and Engineering Research Council of Canada to the author. I am greatly indebted to my scientific collaborators whose work is described in the chapter: Nicole Anderson, Alan Castel, Moshe Naveh-Benjamin, Jan Rabinowitz, and Peter Rendell. I am also grateful for technical assistance from Sharyn Kreuger and Jennie Sawula.

References

Anderson, N. D., Craik, F. I. M., & Naveh-Benjamin, M. (1998). The attentional demands of encoding and retrieval in younger and older adults: I. Evidence from divided attention costs. *Psychology and Aging, 13*, 405–423.
Balota, D. A., Dolan, P. O., & Duchek, J. M. (2000). Memory changes in healthy

older adults. In E. Tulving & F. I. M. Craik (Eds.), *The Oxford handbook of memory* (pp. 305–409). New York: Oxford University Press.

Bjork, R. A. (1975). Retrieval as a memory modifier: An interpretation of negative recency and related phenomena. In R. L. Solso (Ed.), *Information processing and cognition* (pp. 120–142). Hillsdale, NJ: Lawrence Erlbaum Associates, Inc.

Cockburn, J., & Smith, P. T. (1991). The relative influence of intelligence and age on everyday memory. *Journal of Gerontology: Psychological Sciences, 46*, 31–36.

Craik, F. I. M. (1977). Age differences in human memory. In J. E. Birren & W. Schaie (Eds.), *Handbook of the psychology of aging* (pp. 324–420). New York: Van Nostrand Reinhold.

Craik, F. I. M. (1983). On the transfer of information from temporary to permanent memory. *Philosophical Transactions of the Royal Society of London, Series B, 302*, 341–359.

Craik, F. I. M. (1986). A functional account of age differences in memory. In F. Klix & H. Hagendorf (Eds.), *Human memory and cognitive capabilities, mechanisms and performances* (pp. 409–422). Amsterdam: North Holland.

Craik, F. I. M., & Byrd, M. (1982). Aging and cognitive deficits: The role of attentional resources. In F. I. M. Craik & S. Trehub (Eds.), *Aging and cognitive processes* (pp. 191–211). Hillsdale, NJ: Lawrence Erlbaum Associates, Inc.

Craik, F. I. M., Govoni, R., Naveh-Benjamin, M., & Anderson, N. D. (1996). The effects of divided attention on encoding and retrieval processes in human memory. *Journal of Experimental Psychology: General, 125*, 159–180.

Craik, F. I. M., & Grady, C. L. (2002). Aging, memory, and frontal lobe functioning. In D. T. Stuss & R. T. Knight (Eds.), *Principles of frontal lobe function* (pp. 528–540). New York: Oxford University Press.

Craik, F. I. M., & Jennings, J. M. (1992). Human memory. In F. I. M. Craik & T. A. Salthouse (Eds.), *The handbook of aging and cognition* (pp. 51–110). Hillsdale, NJ: Lawrence Erlbaum Associates, Inc.

Einstein, G. O., & McDaniel, M. A. (1990). Normal aging and prospective memory. *Journal of Experimental Psychology: Learning, Memory, and Cognition, 16*, 717–726.

Einstein, G. O., & McDaniel, M. A. (1996). Retrieval processes in prospective memory: Theoretical approaches and some new empirical findings. In M. Brandimonte, G. A. Einstein, & M. A. McDaniels (Eds.), *Prospective memory: Theory and applications* (pp. 115–142). Mahwah, NJ: Lawrence Erlbaum Associates, Inc.

Götz, A., & Jacoby, L. L. (1974). Encoding and retrieval processes in long-term retention. *Journal of Experimental Psychology, 102*, 291–297.

Grady, C. L., & Craik, F. I. M. (2000). Changes in memory processing with age. *Current Opinion in Neurobiology, 10*, 224–231.

Grady, C. L., McIntosh, A. R., Horwitz, B., Maisog, J., Ungerleider, L. G., Mentis, M. J., Pietrini, P., Schapiro, M. B., & Haxby, J. V. (1995). Age-related reductions in human recognition memory due to impaired encoding. *Science, 269*, 218–221.

Harris, J. E., & Wilkins, J. A. (1982). Remembering to do things: A theoretical framework and an illustrative experiment. *Human Learning, 1*, 123–136.

Kapur, S., Craik, F. I. M., Tulving, E., Wilson, A. A., Houle, S., & Brown, G. M. (1994). Neuroanatomical correlates of encoding in episodic memory: Levels of processing effect. *Proceedings of the National Academy of Sciences, USA, 91*, 2008–2011.

Maylor, E. A. (1997). Proper name retrieval in old age: Converging evidence against disproportionate impairment. *Aging, Neuropsychology, and Cognition, 4*, 211–226.

McWeeney, K. H., Young, A. W., Hay, D. C., & Ellis, A. W. (1987). Putting names to faces. *British Journal of Psychology, 78*, 143–149.

Morris, C. D., Bransford, J. D., & Franks, J. J. (1977). Levels of processing versus transfer appropriate processing. *Journal of Verbal Learning and Verbal Behavior, 16*, 519–533.

Moscovitch, M. (1982). A neuropsychological approach to memory and perception in normal and pathological aging. In F. I. M. Craik & S. Trehub (Eds.), *Advances in the study of communication and affect: Vol. 8. Aging and cognitive processes* (pp. 55–78). New York: Plenum.

Murdock, B. B., Jr. (1974). *Human memory: Theory and data.* Potomac, MD: Lawrence Erlbaum Associates, Inc.

Naveh-Benjamin, M., Craik, F. I. M., & Ben-Shaul, L. (2002). Age-related differences in cued recall: Effects of support at encoding and retrieval. *Aging, Neuropsychology, and Cognition, 9*, 276–287.

Naveh-Benjamin, M., Craik, F. I. M., Guez, J., & Kreuger, S. (2005). Divided attention in younger and older adults: Effects of strategy and relatedness on memory performance and secondary task costs. *Journal of Experimental Psychology: Learning, Memory, and Cognition, 31*, 520–537.

Nyberg, L., Nilsson, L.-G., Olofsson, U., & Bäckman, L. (1997). Effects of division of attention during encoding and retrieval on age differences in episodic memory. *Experimental Aging Research, 23*, 137–143.

Rabinowitz, J. C., & Craik, F. I. M. (1986). Prior retrieval effects in young and old adults. *Journal of Gerontology, 41*, 368–375.

Rendell, P. G., & Craik, F. I. M. (2000). Virtual Week and Actual Week: Age-related differences in prospective memory. *Applied Cognitive Psychology, 14*, S43–S62.

Rendell, P. G., & Thomson, D. A. (1999). Aging and prospective memory: Differences between naturalistic and laboratory tasks. *Journal of Gerontology: Psychological Sciences, 54B*, 256–269.

Rönnlund, M., Nyberg, L., Bäckman, L., & Nilsson, L.-G. (2003). Recall of subject-performed tasks, verbal tasks, and cognitive activities across the adult life span: Parallel age-related deficits. *Aging, Neuropsychology, and Cognition, 10*, 182–201.

Salthouse, T. A. (1991). *Theoretical perspectives on cognitive aging.* Hillsdale, NJ: Lawrence Erlbaum Associates, Inc.

Tulving, E., Kapur, S., Craik, F. I. M., Moscovitch, M., & Houle, S. (1994). Hemispheric encoding/retrieval asymmetry in episodic memory: Positron emission tomography findings. *Proceedings of the National Academy of Sciences, 91*, 2016–2020.

West, R. L. (1996). An application of prefrontal cortex function theory to cognitive aging. *Psychological Bulletin, 120*, 272–292.

Williams, J. M. G. (1996). Depression and the specificity of autobiographical memory. In D. Rubin (Ed.), *Remembering our past: Studies in autobiographical memory.* Cambridge, UK: Cambridge University Press.

Zacks, R. T., Hasher, L., & Li, K. Z. H. (2000). Human memory. In F. I. M. Craik & T. A. Salthouse (Eds.), *The handbook of aging and cognition* (2nd Ed., pp. 293–357). Mahwah, NJ: Lawrence Erlbaum Associates, Inc.

10 Working memory and reading disability

Ingvar Lundberg

A major step in the development of human culture and society has to do with the invention of a system for the external representation of the sounds of human language. As a cognitive tool the art of reading and writing has had a profound impact on society and human cognitive functioning. It can even be claimed that the evolution of mankind from "barbarism" to "civilization" was the result of literacy. Written language has obviously the character of an external memory system where its spatial lay-out and its permanence permit inspection and repeated controls of the stream of thoughts, thereby considerably reducing the working load of the human memory. As with all revolutionary inventions, however, written language has also had unintended side effects.

In Plato's dialogue *Phaedrus* (1961) Socrates tells an old myth about the Egyptian god Theuth who came to the king Thamus with his invention of writing and declared, "Here is an accomplishment, my lord the king, which will improve both the wisdom and the memory of the Egyptians. I have discovered a sure recipe for memory and wisdom." But Thamus was sceptical and answered, "Those who acquire it will cease to exercise their memory and become forgetful; they will rely on writing to bring things to their remembrance by external signs instead of on their own internal resources." And no doubt, non-literate peoples are capable of astonishing feats of memory as testified by ethnologists.

Although the art of verbatim long-term episodic memorization may have declined in literate societies, reading and writing seem to have put other demands on the memory system. Before we discuss this issue, a few comments on the characteristics of written language as a memory system will be given.

Individual memory and external storage

A distinction should be made between memory as an individual capacity and memory as part of a collective, external storage system that allows humans to accumulate experience and knowledge. Donald (1991) proposed a clarifying metaphor. You can specify what hardware and what software a given computer possesses and thereby characterize its "cognitive capacity". This is roughly the same when you characterize a human individual. The nervous system (the hardware) is studied and the cognitive skills, language and knowledge (software) are described. However, if a computer is embedded in a network of computers, the powers of the network must also be taken into account; the processor and memory are now part of a much larger computational resource. Individuals with access to written language are like computers with network capabilities. Their skills are now determined both by their network and their constitutional biological capacity. Non-literate humans are isolated from the external memory systems. "Thought moves from the relatively informal narrative ramblings of the isolated mind to the collective arena, and ideas thus accumulate over centuries until they acquire the precision of continuously refined exterior devices, of which the prime example is modern science" (Donald, 1991, p. 311). Thus external memory with its unlimited size, in the shape of texts and other cultural artifacts, is a critical feature of the modern human cognition. The cultural network of symbols, pictures and written texts, however, has not completely replaced human memory functions. Successful coding or processing of written language seems to involve new demands on working-memory functions, which will be discussed in the present paper.

Oral and written language

It does not, of course, take a scientist to point out that there is a modality difference between oral and written language. This observation may not even help much in understanding the difference in how the different forms of language are acquired. Thus, there appear to be some circumstances in which the acquisition of a visually based language is extremely rapid and easy, perhaps comparable to the acquisition of spoken language. A deaf child born into a family with deaf parents is primarily exposed to sign language, which seems to be acquired just as naturally, quickly and easily as hearing children learning the oral language (Newport & Meier, 1985).

Besides modality, written language is different from oral language in many other important respects, and some of these differences may help to account for the great difficulties that many individuals have in learning to read. I will focus on two basic dimensions, one related to the way in which words are encoded in the different media, the other related to the communicative functions.

Speech perception and speech production

In speech the phonemic segments are merged in the sound stream through complicated rules of co-articulation (Liberman, Cooper, Shankweiler, & Studdert-Kennedy, 1967). There are no separable packets of information in the acoustic stream like the sequence of separate symbols in print. There are not even discernable pauses between successive words in rapid speech. The phonemic cues are strongly affected not only by the preceding and following context, they are also altered by more global features like speech rate, stress contour, fundamental frequency, and dialectical variation (Repp & Liberman, 1984).

A given spoken utterance may be located on a continuum of articulatory precision, from extreme hypo-articulation to a very unnatural hyper-articulation. The actual location on the continuum is the result of a "tug-of-war" between two demands: on the one hand, the need to facilitate the listener's comprehension, on the other hand, the tendency to simplify articulation in order to minimize and smoothen the movements of the tongue and other parts of the articulatory apparatus. The latter reflects a general economic principle of minimizing the expenditure of physical energy in muscle activity, which also holds for all other motor systems. A dialogical situation offers conditions for rapidly reaching a point of acceptable equilibrium for the level of articulation through the listener's explicit demands for increased clarity ("What did you say?").

How is it then possible to understand spoken utterances, acoustically realized as mere hints rather than a fully articulated sequence of sounds? Apparently, we listen actively with departure from our knowledge of the language and the situational context of the speech communication. This knowledge helps us to reveal the speech signal and correctly interpret what the speaker intended to say despite ambiguous information in the acoustic event. In other words, the element of top-down processing is usually substantial in speech perception due to the reduced physical quality of the signal.

The closer the participants involved in spoken communication are, physically as well as psychologically, the stronger is the tendency to move towards the hypo-articulated region. In the following examples there are no complete correspondences for phonemes, syllables or words.

/temminsem/ for "ten minutes to seven"
/kju:/ for "thank you"

Yet, in the proper context they are completely understandable. Successful speech communication can take place with safety margins created by the listener's active perceptual strategies and the redundancy of language, which protect against disturbances and noise. The speech-perception mechanism must be able to function, even with a highly degraded stimulus.

From the speaker's point of view speech movements are designed with implicit reference to the listener's active perceptual strategy. The speaker seems to work under the assumption that the units or segments of speech need to be explicitly and physically realized only if they cannot be derived by the top-down processor of the listener. This information-governed precision of articulation is also a principle for syntactic organization implying that the working-memory load for both the speaker and the listener is minimized. In written text, however, the situation is different.

Written words

While reductions, assimilations and co-articulation are inevitable features of spoken language, printed words are fully articulated, especially in an alphabetic writing system, where the complete morpho-phonemic architecture of words is represented. Basically, of course, the hyper-articulated written representation reflects the different functions of written language. In its prototypical form, such as an expository text, the written message is essentially transmitted by linguistic means with little or no support from extra-linguistic cues. This forces an explicitness and articulated precision from syntactic structure all the way down to the word-form level. Written language is normally also intended for a larger, often unknown and variable, audience with different oral conventions (e.g., dialects).

Chafe (1985) has examined differences in structure between conversational speech and written texts. In writing, people use devices such as nominalization, subordination, and modification to pack many idea units within a single sentence. Chafe (1985) specified as many as 14 different linguistic devices that serve this function. Dependent clauses, appositives, and participial clauses are typical devices used to create a more elaborated and complex linguistic product. In written language cohesion is achieved by lexicalization, anaphoric references, and various other cohesive ties, whereas in spoken discourse cohesion is often accomplished through the situational context or through paralinguistic or prosodic cues. Deictic terms, such as "here", "he", "now", are clarified by reference to the shared situation and by pointing, nodding or other gestures. In the absence of non-verbal or paralinguistic channels, the author's attitude towards ideas must be lexicalized in writing.

All these differences between oral and written language seem to imply that the working-memory load for a reader of typical texts is higher than for a listener involved in an everyday conversation. But, somewhat paradoxically, if one and the same message is delivered, either by ear or by eye, there might be different memory demands in the other direction. In listening there are now obviously heavier demands, since it is not easy to go back to clarify what has been said. With a written text that option is easily available. The spatial lay-out of a text can be designed such that the back-tracking process is facilitated and other spatial cues are provided for guiding the comprehension process. On the other hand, more complex parsing processes are needed to compensate for the absence of prosodic cues to the sentence structure that are provided in spoken language.

To summarize the comparison between reading and listening: in processing written text a reader must integrate moment-to-moment perceptions across time, rehearse them and combine them with simultaneous access to archival information about past experience, actions and knowledge. This is what working memory involves. In oral dialogues the working-memory load is normally considerably lower than in reading, as written discourse packs linguistic information differently. The absence of prosodic information further

increases the working-memory load in reading. Even at the word level, especially in alphabetic scripts, and especially during the initial stages of reading
acquisition, the decoding process involves considerable working-memory
demands. A skilled reader processes many thousands of words each day, year
after year. No doubt, this intense and extensive activity would be expected
to have a profound impact on brain functions. And, in fact, recent studies
have shown how literate adults have brain activity patterns in response to
phonological memory tasks, which are clearly different from the patterns
of illiterate individuals from the same SES background (Castro-Caldas,
Petersson, Reis, Stone-Elander, & Ingvar, 1998). Also, dyslexic individuals
show lower activity or less integrated activity in brain areas of critical
importance for phonological processing (Paulesu, Frith, & Frackowiak, 1993;
Pugh et al., 2000).

Working memory and reading

It seems intuitively obvious that the temporary retention of information
would be important for complex cognitive activities such as mental arithmetic
or reading comprehension. As we have noted, in order to comprehend a text
one must temporarily retain representations of words, phrases, and sentences.
Text comprehension often also requires integration of information from different parts of a text. This processing demand seems to involve working
memory. Simple measures of short-term memory, such as digit span, however, do not seem to have a strong relationship to comprehension, probably
due to the fact that the digit-span task reflects a passive storage buffer not
very much involved in the processing of information. Research indicates that
poor readers do not have a general deficit in short-term memory capacity.
Their difficulties do not seem to lie in the storage of information, but
rather in the processing of that information to derive meaning from the
text. This suggests that poor comprehenders might show impaired performance on more complex memory tasks, requiring both storage and processing
functions simultaneously.

Studies of adults suggest that performance on tests of working memory is
related to reading comprehension (for a review, see Daneman & Carpenter,
1983). Skilled comprehenders are better at making inferences, monitoring
their understanding, producing and deriving the structure of stories because
they have more efficient working memory. According to Oakhill and Cain
(1998) poor comprehenders are able to build adequate representations of
parts of a text, but fail to relate and integrate these partial representations to
produce a model of the text as a whole.

Most research on working memory and reading comprehension has been
made in the context of the Baddeley and Hitch model (1974) developed more
fully by Baddeley (1986, 2000). They proposed a working-memory system that
is responsible not only for the storage of information but also for the simultaneous processing of information. As we have seen, this system, rather than

short-term memory, plays a role in complex cognition and constitutes a critical constraint in human functioning. There are three elements in this model: the visuo-spatial sketch-pad, the phonological loop and the central executive. The visuo-spatial sketchpad is not assumed to be much involved in reading comprehension and therefore will not be further discussed in this paper.

The phonological part refers to a system that includes a phonological store coupled with an articulatory loop. The phonological store maintains short-lived representations resulting from speech-based coding and appears to be particularly important in the retention of order information. The articulatory loop is required to refresh the quickly decaying representations maintained in the phonological store. The sounds of words are important, which is evident in the phonological similarity effect, first shown by Conrad (1964). Systematic errors related to phonetic similarity are made by subjects trying to memorize lists of consonants. Thus, the literal recording of sounds rather than abstract semantic categories is processed. Similar-sounding words are harder to retain than different-sounding words, regardless of their meaning. Suppression of articulation also reduces recall of auditory-verbal material indicating the role of literal phonetic information for the short-term store.

Non-phonological input, such as printed words or pictures, are transformed into phonological form by the articulatory loop to be retained in the store. The phonological storage buffer has the properties commonly attributed to short-term memory. It can hold linguistic information only briefly, perhaps just for a second or two, unless the material is maintained by continuous rehearsal. The buffer's limited capacity means that the information must be rapidly encoded in a more durable form if it is to be retained for higher-level processing.

Cabeza and Nyberg (2000) have shown that the phonological part of working memory is related to bilateral activation of frontal and parietal areas as measured by PET. Behavioural evidence suggests that the phonological store and the articulatory loop are independent processes (Longoni, Richardson, & Aiello, 1993). Neuroimaging evidence (Paulesu et al., 1993) further indicates that the phonological store is likely located in temporal/parietal areas, whereas the articulatory loop has a more frontal control. Desmond (2001) suggested that the efficiency of the articulatory loop is enhanced by the cerebellum, and the phonological store is also connected to the cerebellum via a temporal/parietal – inferior cerebellar route.

The second component of working memory, the central executive, has the task of relaying the results of the lower-level processing upwards through the system. It is assumed to be an attentional control system with limited resources for strategy selection, integration, coordination and control of information from several sources. A deficit in processing phonological information creates a bottleneck that impedes the transfer of information to the higher levels in the system. According to this processing-limitation hypothesis the poor comprehension observed among poor readers should be more pronounced in contexts that tax working memory.

One way of conceiving of reading comprehension is that it does not always proceed on line, as each new word occurs. Rather, each word is processed at a superficial level and the phonological representation is maintained until the end of a phrase or sentence or until sufficient information is obtained to come up with the correct syntactic structure and do the final wrap-up.

Sublexical processes in reading (word decoding) involve working memory because phonological information has to be retained (or even articulated, perhaps subvocally). At the same time, conceptual resources are required to amalgamate or process this information and decide which word has been encountered. So, one would expect an extra load on working memory at the initial stages of reading acquisition when word decoding is a slow and effortful process.

On developmental dyslexia

Although developmental dyslexia mostly involves reading and spelling difficulties a proper understanding of its nature requires a step beneath the manifest surface of written language problems (Lundberg, 1999). Developmental dyslexia is here viewed as a complex biologically rooted condition resulting from impairment of phonological processes, which, in turn, reflects differences in brain structures and brain functions between dyslexic and normal readers (for a review, see Grigorenko, 2001). There is also strong evidence for genetic influences on the dyslexic impairment. Twin studies indicate a heritability of more than .50 (Olson, 1999), and molecular-genetic studies suggest several significant candidate loci in the human genome (Grigorenko, 2001).

Several supplementary hypotheses concerning the phonological core deficit have been proposed, such as the magnocellular theory (Stein, Talcott, & Witton, 2001), the temporal processing deficit hypothesis (Merzenich et al., 1996) and the cerebellum hypothesis (Nicolson, Fawcett, & Dean, 2001). So far, however, the support for these supplementary hypotheses is somewhat inconsistent. No one has really challenged the phonological hypothesis, which has massive empirical support (see Hoien & Lundberg, 2000), although the issue of subgroups of developmental dyslexia is still open.

Typical indicators of the phonological impairment in dyslexia according to Hoien and Lundberg (2000) are inaccurate and slow non-word reading, difficulties in segmenting words into phonemes or manipulating these phonemes (phonemic awareness), difficulties learning new words in a foreign language, difficulties in remembering sequences of verbal material, such as letters or digits, difficulties in learning to use a secret language, such as Pig Latin, difficulties in dealing with spoonerisms (i.e., swapping the initial consonant of two words – "John Lennon" to produce "Lohn Jennon"), confusing low-frequency and phonologically complex words, and sometimes a dyslexic disposition can be expressed in indistinct articulation in speech. At the manifest reading level the difficulties are primarily seen in slow, effortful and sometimes inaccurate word decoding and lack of fluency and automaticity in reading connected text. Spelling difficulties are also typical and often persist even when the reading problems have been overcome. However, manifest problems with written language can be caused by a multitude of factors, such as caring conditions during infancy, cultural deprivation in early childhood, inadequate instructional methods, a different home language, irregular school attendance, low motivation, slow maturation, etc. The step beneath the manifest reading and writing surface offers possibilities of identifying the circumscribed cognitive-linguistic impairment underlying the literacy problems of dyslexia beyond the cultural-social factors referred to. The empirical illustration presented below is an example of the search for "fine cuts behind the hidden seams" in the syndrome of dyslexia.

An empirical illustration

A complex working-memory task is typically devised to mimic the competing cognitive demands involved in an activity such as reading. In the study to be reported in this paper the subject is orally presented with a consonant letter followed by a simple sentence verification task also orally presented ("trees can walk" yes–no). After two or more such presentations the subject is required to report the presented consonants in correct order. This is a task involving the phonological loop as well as the central executive.

This task and several other tasks were presented to adults with a proven history of reading disability and to normal readers matched on age, gender and educational level. The working-memory capacity was expected to be significantly associated with a number of phonological tasks such as spoonerism, non-word reading, and phonological distinctness of vocabulary assumed to differentiate between poor and normal readers, and whether working memory has the power to predict group membership over and above the other tasks. If working memory does not offer unique explanatory power, one may interpret this negative finding as indicating that only the phonological loop part of working memory is critical for word reading. According to Kail and Hall (2001) working memory is equal to short-term memory plus attention. If dyslexia is not an attention problem but rather a phonological problem (see also Samuelsson, Lundberg, & Herkner, 2004) one would expect a lower correlation between word decoding and working memory than between word decoding and short-term memory. A more complete study should then include simple span tests as well as more complex comprehension tasks with texts manipulated systematically to induce different working-memory loads. The study to be reported is not such a complete investigation but rather an empirical illustration of the first steps necessary to investigate the role of working memory in dyslexia.

Method

Participants

Participants were 57 students (22 males, 35 females) at adult-education centres for secondary education (high school level) in Western Sweden. Those who are enrolled in adult education centres in Sweden have not completed their secondary education above compulsory school often due to failure and are now given a second chance. About half of the students (28) attended courses especially designed for students with reading disabilities. The average age was about 30 years in both groups (a range from 21- to 45-year-olds), and the gender distribution was about the same for both groups. The recruitment of participants from adult-education centres had the advantage that the educational level, intellectual habits and professional experience in the two groups of adults were relatively similar.

Instruments

Working memory

The working-memory assessment had the format of a dual task. The participants were orally presented with a consonant letter immediately followed by two sentences. The first sentence was a statement (e.g., "Dogs sometimes bark") and the second was a question related to the statement (e.g., "Can canaries bark?"). The task was now to respond yes or no. This was followed by a new consonant and two more sentences of the same format with the verification task. After two or more sequences of this kind the final task was to report the consonants in correct order. A total of six trials was given with the following number of consonants in each trial: 2, 2, 3, 3, 4, 5. Only completely correct responses with the consonants in correct order were included in the final score. Thus, the maximum score was 19 points. The consonants and the sentences were presented by means of a tape recorder with high-quality sound. The inter-trial intervals were quite brief. By showing written tags with YES or NO the subjects indicated their sentence verification. Only very seldom were incorrect responses given.

Spoonerism – reversed

This was a completely new task designed to capture phonological skills with a limited memory load and with no production requirement. Two associated words were presented orally. However, their initial consonants were swapped (an equivalent in English could be, for example, the word pair "mystery house" which would be changed to "hystery mouse" when presented orally). The task was to choose between three alternative picture pairs and indicate which one corresponded to the non-swapped original word pair. The distractor alternatives could contain pictures of a mouse or someone in a hysterical state and thus attract subjects who were unable to do the proper phonemic analysis. A total of 35 such tasks was given. The word pairs were presented from a tape recorder at a rather high tempo. The score on the task was the total number of correctly marked picture pairs.

Phonological choice

Triplets of non-words were printed in columns in a booklet. Each non-word was pronounceable but only one corresponded to a real word when read aloud. The task was to mark in each triplet the alternative, which was a pseudo-homophone with a pronunciation equivalent to a real word. The only way to arrive at a correct decision in this task is to silently pronounce the words and find out which one matches the sound of a real word. A large number of triplets were presented in a booklet, and the task was to quickly mark as many as possible correctly within three minutes. A similar task has been used by Olson, Forsberg, Wise, and Rack (1994) and has proven to yield a valid indication of phonological ability.

Orthographic choice

The task format is similar to the format of the phonological choice task. Triplets of words are presented in columns. Only one word in a triplet is a correctly spelled word, whereas the other words are pronounceable non-words and pseudo-homophones to the target word. The task is to recognize the word with correct orthography and mark it with a pencil. This task can only be solved on the basis of orthographic knowledge, not pronunciation as in the phonological choice task. The final score was the number of correctly marked words within three minutes.

Vocabulary with phonologically confusable alternatives

A total of 24 words or brief phrases were given. Each word or phrase was accompanied by three alternative, low-frequency and phonologically complex words of which one was a true synonym to the target word. The other two alternatives were phonologically highly similar to the correct alternative. An example in English would be: memory loss: amnesty, amnesia, amenity. This task was designed to tap the distinctiveness or precision of the phonological representations.

Self-reported dyslexic problems

Each participant filled out a questionnaire including 24 items concerned with various kinds of symptoms assumed to be indicators of dyslexic problems. Each item included a statement such as, "I have difficulties remembering new words or new names", accompanied by a 4-point scale to indicate the extent to which one could agree or not with the statement. The validity of this self-report was assessed in an earlier study (Wolff & Lundberg, 2002). The correlation between a composite score of phonological skills and the score on the self-report scale amounted to .80.

Results

Table 10.1 presents a comparison between the group with reading disability and the group of normal readers on the four main variables studied.

The differences between the two groups are highly significant on all variables. The discriminative power of the self-report scale was particularly high as was shown by a logistic regression analysis, where 95% of the 57 cases were correctly classified as reading disabled or non-disabled. The phonological tests had a considerably lower discriminative power with only about 70–75% of the cases correctly classified. When self-report data were combined with the phonological measures, including working memory and orthographic choice, this set of variables could without any error classify the participants in the two groups (poor readers and normal readers).

The remarkable sensitivity of the self-report is also indicated in Figure 10.1. As can be seen, there is almost no overlap between the distributions. So, here we are rather close to a "fine cut" in the diagnosis of dyslexic problems. The validity of the self-report scale justifies the use of the scores on this scale as the dependent variable in a multiple regression analysis to examine whether the phonological tasks can provide independent contributions to the explanation of the variance in self-report scores.

Table 10.2 presents the results of a hierarchical regression analysis with the self-report scale as the dependent variable. Working memory was entered as the last step. In the earlier steps gender and age were entered first, then reversed spoonerism, phonological choice and vocabulary with phonologically confusable alternatives.

Table 10.1 Means and standard deviations for the main variables in the two groups

Variable	Reading disability (n = 28)		Normal readers (n = 29)			.
	Mean	SD	Mean	SD	t (55)	Sign
Self-report	34.2	6.9	54.9	6.8	11.4	.000
Rev. spoon.	9.7	4.9	17.7	5.5	5.7	.000
Voc. phon.	13.4	5.6	18.8	4.2	4.1	.000
Phon. choice	15.4	7.5	27.0	9.7	5.0	.000
Work. mem	5.5	5.6	12.1	5.0	4.7	.000
Reading	45.0	19.8	82.6	25.5	6.2	.000

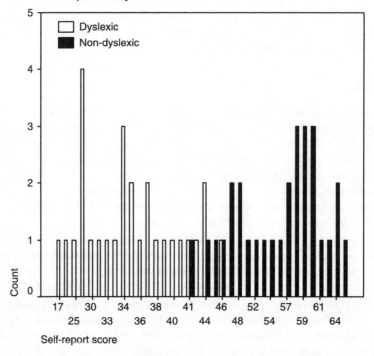

Figure 10.1 Frequency distribution of scores on a self-report questionnaire on dyslexic traits for dyslexic and non-dyslexic participants.

Table 10.2 Hierarchical regression analysis predicting self-report scores of dyslexia symptoms using phonological measures (*N* = 57)

Step	Variable	R	R^2	ΔR^2	F change	p
1.	Gender	.037	.001	.001	0.072	.789
2.	Age	.195	.038	.037	1.99	.164
3.	Voc. phon	.540	.292	.254	18.3	.000
4.	Rev. spoon	.652	.425	.133	11.6	.001
5.	Phon. choice	.669	.448	.023	2.02	.161
6.	Work. mem.	.698	.487	.039	3.67	.061

The multiple correlation with these predictor variables was .70 explaining almost half of the variance in the self-report scale. Gender and age explained together less than 4% of the variance in self-report. When vocabulary (phonologically confusable alternatives) was entered an additional 25% of the variance was explained. Reversed spoonerisms contributed with another 13% and phonological choice had no unique explanatory power. As the last step in the analysis, working memory was introduced. Now an additional 4% was explained over and above the explanation provided by the other factors. However, this modest unique contribution was not really significant ($p = .06$.).

The general conclusion seems to be that phonological factors have rather strong explanatory power. But, although working memory has a respectable and significant zero-order correlation with the self-report score ($r = .55$) it has no significant unique explanatory power.

The phonological choice task as well as the orthographic choice task involves a strong element of word reading. By combining the scores on these variables an index of word recognition ability was obtained. In order to examine the possible impact of working memory on word recognition skill a new hierarchical regression analysis was carried out with the composite score on word reading as the dependent variable. As in the earlier analysis, working memory was entered as the last step to determine whether this factor had a unique contribution over and above the other phonological tasks. The results are presented in Table 10.3.

The simple correlation between working memory and word reading was .56. In the hierarchical analysis with age, gender, vocabulary (phonologically confusable), reversed spoonerism, and working memory the multiple correlation amounted to .83; almost 70% of the total variance in reading scores was explained. However, as in the earlier analysis, working memory had no unique contribution to offer. This lack of explanatory power might imply that only the phonological part of the working memory function is responsible for the relationship with word-reading ability. The processing demand aspect of working memory, with the central executive involved, has no unique explanatory power as far as the rather resource-cheap word-recognition process is concerned. Only a complex set of reading comprehension tests might have revealed the influence of the central executive. It might also be the case that deficits in working memory only characterize a subgroup of dyslexic adults (Pennington, Van Orden, Smith, Green, & Haith, 1990) and affect reading comprehension rather than decoding. Samuelsson and Lundberg (2004) found no correlation between ADHD and word recognition among

Table 10.3 Hierarchical multiple regression analysis with a composite word-reading score as dependent variable and gender, age, and phonological factors as predictor variables.

Step	Variable	R	R^2	ΔR^2	F change	p
1.	Gender	.214	.046	.046	2.55	.116
2.	Age	.244	.059	.013	0.743	.393
3.	Voc. phon	.768	.590	.531	66.1	.000
4.	Rev. spoon	.822	.675	.085	13.0	.001
5.	Work. mem.	.826	.683	.008	1.19	.281

adults. However, the association of ADHD with reading comprehension was strong. This result was interpreted in a similar vein as the present findings (see also Roodenrys, Koloski, & Grainger, 2001). ADHD was seen as a disturbance in executive control functions, which are clearly more involved in reading comprehension than in word recognition. Thus, a two-component model of reading may bring clarity to our findings.

In order to disentangle the influence of various components of working memory on reading disability the present study must be extended to include span measures as well as more complex comprehension assessment. Two of the other phonological tasks should also be supplemented. The vocabulary task should have a base task not involving delicate phonological discriminations. Thus a traditional vocabulary test should be used for setting the base level against which the vocabulary test with confusable alternatives could be evaluated. The difference would then reflect the phonological impairment without the confounding of general word knowledge.

The reversed-spoonerism task was designed to minimize working memory load, the prime requirement being to indicate recognition. In a more conventional spoonerism task a word pair is presented and the subject has to make the substitution of the initial phonemes and produce the spoonerism. Obviously this task involves a working-memory load of some significance. By comparing the degree of association with a reading comprehension task the role of the processing aspect could be estimated.

Although the assessment of individual differences in working memory and phonological processing has clear practical as well as theoretical implications, the issue of causal direction is not easy to deal with. Longitudinal studies starting with preliterate children are needed.

Lundberg, Olofsson, and Wall (1980) followed children from kindergarten to grade 2 and demonstrated that phonological skills among pre-readers were powerfully predictive of the development of reading and spelling skills two years later in school. An even more convincing demonstration of the causal direction was provided by a training study (Lundberg, Frost, & Petersen, 1988), where preschool children, who had enjoyed the benefit of phonological training over a period of eight months in kindergarten, clearly outperformed a non-trained control group on a number of reading and spelling tasks later in school. Obviously, phonological awareness and related abilities are important enabling skills causally related to reading and not a consequence of reading acquisition. Similar longitudinal training studies including short-term memory span and working memory would certainly clarify the nature of the clear association between reading and memory.

Although a clear association between working memory and reading disability has been demonstrated in the present study, the most critical memory aspect of literacy has not been examined. The most important memory in literacy activities is related to the use of the enormously expanded memory bank provided by media, especially printed texts and documents. The skill of getting access to these sources is not only a question of decoding the printed words. Navigating in this sea of information requires complex procedural memories and advanced cognitive strategies for locating items, for finding the right entries, using the right keywords, knowing the conventions of tabular packing of information, searching manuals, recipes and diagrams, remembering passwords, pin codes and efficient search procedures, etc. These skills are certainly vulnerable to memory loss due to disuse, accidents or ageing. In contrast to episodic memory and long-term memory, literacy-skills memory used to access external memory systems has not been studied extensively but it certainly deserves closer examination as the demands increase dramatically in post-modern society.

References

Baddeley, A. D. (1986). *Working memory*. Oxford: Oxford University Press.

Baddeley, A. D. (2000). Short-term and working memory. In E. Tulving & F. I. M. Craik (Eds.), *The Oxford handbook of memory* (pp. 77–92). New York: Oxford University Press.

Baddeley, A. D., & Hitch, G. J. (1974). Working memory. In G. Bower (Ed.), *Recent advances in learning and motivation* (Vol. 8, pp. 47–89). New York: Academic Press.

Cabeza, R., & Nyberg, L. (2000). Imaging cognition II: An empirical review of 275 PET and fMRI studies. *Journal of Cognitive Neuroscience, 12*, 1–47.

Castro-Caldas, A., Petersson, K. M., Reis, A., Stone-Elander, S., & Ingvar, M. (1998). The illiterate brain: Learning to read and write during childhood influences the functional organization of the adult brain. *Brain, 121*, 1053–1063.

Chafe, W. L. (1985). Linguistic differences produced by differences between speaking and writing. In D. R. Olson, N. Torrance, & A. Hildyard (Eds.), *Literacy, language, and learning. The nature and consequences of reading and writing* (pp. 105–123). Cambridge: Cambridge University Press.

Conrad, R. (1964). Acoustic confusions in immediate memory. *British Journal of Psychology, 55*, 75–84.

Daneman, M., & Carpenter, P. A. (1983). Individual differences in integrating information between and within sentences. *Memory and Cognition, 9*, 561–584.

Desmond, J. E. (2001). Cerebellar involvement in cognitive function: Evidence from neuroimaging. *International Review of Psychiatry, 13*, 283–294.

Donald, M. (1991). *Origins of the human mind*. Cambridge, MA: Harvard University Press.

Grigorenko, E. (2001). Developmental dyslexia: An update on genes, brains, and environments. *Journal of Child Psychology and Psychiatry, 42*, 91–125.

Hoien, T., & Lundberg, I. (2000). *Dyslexia. From theory to intervention*. Dordrecht, NL: Kluwer Academic Publishers.

Kail, R., & Hall, L. K. (2001). Distinguishing short-term memory from working memory. *Memory and Cognition, 29*, 1–9.

Liberman, A. M., Cooper, F. S., Shankweiler, D., & Studdert-Kennedy, M. (1967). Perception and the speech code. *Psychological Review, 74*, 431–461.

Longoni, A. M., Richardson, J. T., & Aiello, A. (1993). Articulatory rehearsal and phonological storage in working memory. *Memory and Cognition, 21*, 11–22.

Lundberg, I. (1999). Towards a sharper definition of dyslexia. In I. Lundberg, F. E. Tonnessen, & I. Austad (Eds.), *Dyslexia. Advances in theory and practice* (pp. 9–29). Dordrecht, NL: Kluwer Academic Publishers

Lundberg, I., Olofsson, S., & Wall, S. (1980). Reading and spelling skills in the first school years predicted from phonemic awareness skills in kindergarten. *Scandinavian Journal of Psychology, 21*, 159–173.

Lundberg, I., Frost, J., & Petersen, O.-P. (1988). Effects of an extensive program for stimulating phonological awareness in pre-school children. *Reading Research Quarterly, 33*, 263–284.

Merzenich, M. M., Jenkins, W. M., Johnston, P., Schreiner, C., Miller, S. L., & Tallal, P. (1996). Temporal processing deficits of language impaired children ameliorated by training. *Science, 271*, 77–81.

Newport, E. L., & Meier, R. P. (1985). The acquisition of American sign language. In D. J. Slobin (Ed.), *The crosss-linguistic study of language acquisition. Vol 1. The data* (pp. 881–938). Hillsdale, NJ: Lawrence Erlbaum Associates, Inc.

Nicolson, R. I., Fawcett, A. J., & Dean, P. (2001). Developmental dyslexia: The cerebellar deficit hypothesis. *Trends in Neuroscience, 24*, 508–511.

Oakhill, J., & Cain, K. (1998). Problems in text comprehension: Current perspectives and recent research. In P. Reitsma & L. Verhoeven (Eds.), *Problems and interventions in literacy development* (pp. 177–192). Dordrecht, NL: Kluwer Academic Publishers.

Olson, R. K. (1999). Genes, environment, and reading disabilities. In R. J. Sternberg & L. Spear-Swerling (Eds.), *Perspectives on learning disabilities* (pp. 3–21). Boulder, CO: Westview Press.

Olson, R. K., Forsberg, H., Wise, B., & Rack, J. (1994). Measurement of word recognition, orthographic, and phonological skills. In G. R. Lyon (Ed.), *Frames of reference for the assessment of learning disabilities* (pp. 243–277). Baltimore, MD: Brookes.

Paulesu, E., Frith, C. D., & Frackowiak, R. S. (1993). The neural correlates of the verbal component of working memory. *Nature, 362*, 342–345.

Pennington, B. F., Van Orden, G. C., Smith, S. D., Green, P. A., & Haith, M. M. (1990). Phonological processing skills and deficits in adult dyslexia. *Child Development, 61*, 1753–1778.

Plato (1961). Phaedrus. In E. Hamilton & H. Cairns (Eds.), *The collected dialogues*. Princeton, NJ: Princeton University Press.

Pugh, K. R., Mencl, E. W., Shaywitz, B. A., Shaywitz, S. E., Fulbright, R. K., Constable, R. T., Skudlarski, P., Marchione, K. E., Jenner, A. R., Fletcher, J. M., Liberman, A. M., Shankweiler, D. P., Katz, I., Lacadie, V., & Gore, J. C. (2000). The angular gyrus in developmental dyslexia: Task-specific differences in functional connectivity within posterior cortex. *Psychological Science, 11*, 51–60.

Repp, B. H., & Liberman, A. M. (1984). Phonetic categories are flexible. *Haskins: Status Report on Speech Research*, SR-77/78, 31–53. Haskins Laboratories, New Haven, CT.

Roodenrys, S., Koloski, N., & Grainger, J. (2001). Working memory function in attention deficit hyperactivity disordered and reading disabled children. *British Journal of Development Psychology, 19*, 325–337.

Samuelsson, S., Lundberg, I., & Herkner, B. (2004). ADHD and reading disability in male adults: Is there a connection? *Journal of Learning Disabilities, 37*, 155–168.

Stein, J., Talcott, J., & Witton, C. (2001). The sensorimotor basis of developmental dyslexia. In A. Fawcett (Ed.), *Dyslexia. Theory and good practice* (pp. 65–88). London: Whurr.

Wolff, U., & Lundberg, I. (2002). The prevalence of dyslexia among art students. *Dyslexia. An International Journal of Research and Practice, 8*, 34–42.

11 A workspace for memory in healthy and damaged cognition

Robert H. Logie and Sergio Della Sala

Human beings have the capacity for retaining information on a temporary basis, and for manipulating, transforming, and reinterpreting that information during the performance of a wide range of everyday tasks. For around three decades, this range of abilities has been referred to as working memory. During that time a large literature has been established with continued growth at an accelerated pace, offering evidence that working memory has a role in holding partial solutions during problem solving, reasoning, and mental arithmetic, supporting the acquisition of vocabulary and the comprehension of language both written and spoken, and in aiding mental discovery and creativity. Working memory also offers temporary memory for words and numbers, for the visual appearance of objects and scenes, for the location of objects, and for routes through unfamiliar environments.

The concept of a limited-capacity processing and temporary storage device that is distinct from the store of knowledge and past experiences has a long pedigree, with roots in the writings of the philosopher John Locke (1690/ 1959). The contemporary view of working memory has its origins in a seminal paper by Baddeley and Hitch (1974). Their ideas grew out of a dissatisfaction with the literature at the time on short-term verbal memory and verbal learning that seemed to be focused on a narrow range of verbal memory tasks devised in the laboratory, with no clear reference to how such a mental capacity might have evolved or might be used in everyday life. Locke's (1690) original suggestion was of a single device used in daily life for ". . . keeping the idea which is brought into it, for some time actually in view . . .". Baddeley and Hitch examined a range of tasks involving visual as well as verbal temporary memory and some aspects of higher cognition, such as logical reasoning and language comprehension. It became clear from their work that what used to be referred to as short-term memory was better considered as a working memory, or a mental workspace that could undertake processing as well as temporary storage, and was best viewed as comprising multiple, domain-specific components.

The multiple-component model of working memory (for a review see Baddeley & Logie, 1999) has been particularly successful in accounting for many aspects of everyday cognition, such as immediate verbal and visual memory, through acquisition of vocabulary to mental arithmetic, reasoning and creative thinking. It provides not only an understanding of healthy adult cognition, but also offers insight into the cognitive impairments that arise from some forms of focal brain damage, as well as from brain diseases. In this chapter we will discuss some current theoretical arguments regarding working memory, and will then report the results of two lines of experimental research that illustrate how the multiple task working memory model has been particularly fruitful in the study of (a) mental imagery in healthy adults and brain-damaged individuals and (b) dual-task performance impairments that arise in the early stages of Alzheimer's disease.

Results offer insight into: (1) some of the processes of mental discovery and creative thinking; (2) the possibility that perception and mental imagery are rather more distinct than has been assumed hitherto; (3) some of the cognitive difficulties that brain-damaged individuals might encounter in daily life with advice for carers; (4) non-invasive methods for detecting and monitoring the impact of some forms of brain damage; and (5) further theoretical development in the area of on-line cognition.

Working memory: Variations on a theme

Although the original concept of working memory was of a multiple-component system, several different theoretical frameworks have now been developed. A full discussion of these alternative views is beyond the scope of this chapter and is given elsewhere (Miyake & Shah, 1999). However, one key difference between current conceptions is whether working memory comprises multiple components as did the original concept, or consists of a single, general-purpose mental resource that can be used as a temporary memory store, for directing attention, as the recipient of activated prior knowledge, and for manipulation of the information it holds. This approach has been common in the investigation of working memory in reading comprehension and in the investigation of individual differences in working memory capacity (e.g., Just & Carpenter, 1992). One implication of this single-resource framework, is that as more of the working memory resource is required for memory storage, then less is available for directing attention or for manipulating information and vice versa.

However, there is a significant body of evidence to suggest that the single, flexible resource framework is rather limited and may be misleading. This conclusion arises from a wide range of experimental studies showing clear patterns of dissociation among domain-specific cognitive resources. Dissociations have been demonstrated clearly between verbal, visual and spatial tasks, in differential patterns of development of domain-specific cognitive performance in children, in patterns of domain-specific cognitive deficits following brain damage, and in domain-specific patterns of brain activation detected by brain-imaging techniques such as PET or fMRI (for reviews see Baddeley & Logie, 1999; Logie & Della Sala, 2003). One view of this "multiple-component" working memory is illustrated in Figure 11.1. Two components, the visual cache and the inner scribe, are thought to support, respectively, temporary memory for the visual appearance and layout of a scene together with pathways or movements through the scene. A second pair of components, the phonological store and "inner speech", offer, respectively, temporary memory for the acoustic and phonological properties of words, letters and numbers together with serial ordered, subvocal (mental) rehearsal of those items. The component labelled "executive functions" comprises a

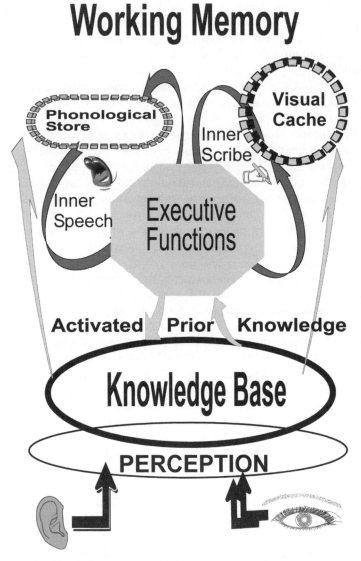

Figure 11.1 Working memory as a multiple-component workspace.

range of such functions, which include the coordination of the memory and rehearsal systems, for manipulation of information that is held in the temporary memory systems or is generated from the knowledge base of skills and information acquired from past experience (Logie, 1995; Baddeley & Logie, 1999). More recent conceptions of working memory based on the individual differences approach also now recognize the need for separate, domain-specific temporary memory stores in addition to a general-purpose executive capacity (e.g., Kane & Engle, 2002)

Although presented as a set of identifiably separate components in Figure 11.1, it is clear that in the healthy brain and for most everyday cognitive tasks, the systems within working memory act in cooperation. For example, if we are trying to imagine how our furniture will fit into the house that we are planning to buy, then we would hold in mind the names of the items of furniture, their shape and potential location in each of the new rooms, but would also have some idea from our past experience of how heavy these items are, how easily they could be moved, and some information about the costs of buying new furniture or the possible difficulties of locating the piano in an upstairs room. Therefore, what appears to be primarily a task that requires visual imagery and the resources of visuo-spatial working memory, also draws on a great deal of prior knowledge about the meaning of the shapes that we are manipulating and about the environment in which they are to be placed, as well as on aspects of verbal working memory. It also allows us to generate a mental image of the new layouts – that is to generate new knowledge derived from mental manipulation of knowledge that we have already, and which is represented in the material being manipulated in working memory.

The suggestion that the material in working memory is meaningful, raises an additional important feature of Figure 11.1, namely that the contents of working memory incorporate some form of interpretation based on prior knowledge. It does not handle raw sensory patterns of edges, contours, shades and textures directly from the environment. Rather, it deals with objects and shapes that have been identified by the processes of perception and that draw on our knowledge base of past experience. This also suggests that there is no direct link between working memory, and the processes involved in perception of the current environment, but that our store of knowledge somehow "sits between" perception and working memory. This is in complete contrast to the traditional view that continues to appear in introductory textbooks suggesting that working memory acts as some form of temporary buffer for material that is on its way between perceptual input and the long-term memory system.

This alternative to the traditional view of working memory can be illustrated readily. In looking at the desk that we are using for the writing of this chapter, the contents of our visuo-spatial working memory comprise a desk lamp, a computer screen, a keyboard and mouse, a coffee mug, a telephone, a pyramid paperweight, a model of a brain, a globe of the earth, and a small

Egyptian figure named "The Sitting Scribe". The identification of these objects is possible only if the patterns of light and shade, edges, textures and contours in the visual field have been successfully perceived as specific objects, and successful identification relies on our previous experience of these objects and objects of this kind. This process of identification could not be so readily accomplished by a new-born baby. Identification of the objects also would present something of a challenge to people who had never experienced computer technology or electrical light sources, such as the ancient Egyptian character on whom "The Sitting Scribe" figure is modelled. So too, as people unfamiliar with Japanese and with ancient Egyptian writings, we have trouble making sense of Japanese characters or the hieroglyphic symbols that accompany the Sitting Scribe figure. In sum, perception involves the activation of previously stored knowledge in response to a particular configuration of stimuli from the environment. Much of perception, including object identification, is automatic and requires no direct involvement of working memory. Even when we encounter a novel stimulus, we have available some idea of the category of the materials, e.g., Japanese characters, or hieroglyphics, even if we do not know their precise meaning. As healthy adults, what we deal with in working memory is the product of what has been activated from our knowledge base, not the direct input from perception.

This more distant, and indirect, link between perception and working memory is somewhat controversial, since a great deal of research in cognitive psychology is predicated on the assumption that there is a fairly intimate relationship between perception and mental representations, such as mental images (e.g., Kosslyn, 1994; Denis & Kosslyn, 1999). The next two sections of this chapter focus on some of the evidence for the divorce between imagery and perception as well as for the semantic content of our images, addressing, first, how the semantic content of working memory might constrain or support mental discovery and, second, the characteristics of brain-damaged individuals with impairments of imagery but not of perception and vice versa.

Visuo-spatial working memory and mental discovery

Some important aspects of creative thinking can be captured by the concept of mental discovery, offering a means to generate new knowledge from old. When attempting to come up with a new idea, we might do so by recombining or reinterpreting some aspects of our existing knowledge. If indeed the contents of working memory are interpreted at some level, this could act to inhibit our ability to shed the current interpretation and generate new ones. This might be one possible reason why creative thinking is difficult for many people, and why few individuals are recognized as being highly creative.

Some insight into the involvement of working memory in creative thinking comes from studies of mental synthesis tasks. In these tasks, participants might be given the names of familiar, canonical shapes, such as a circle, a square and the figure 8, and then be asked to generate a mental image of these items and to combine the shapes mentally such that they form a recognizable object (e.g., Barquero & Logie, 1999; Finke & Slayton, 1988; Helstrup & Anderson, 1991, 1996). One crucial feature of the Barquero and Logie experiments was that volunteers were asked to generate a name for the mental image that they formed before they drew their image. After drawing the image, they were then asked if they wished to change the name that they had generated. The drawings, together with their names were then shown to independent judges who were asked to rate the degree of correspondence between each name and the drawing given. The judges rated the second name (produced after drawing) as having a greater degree of correspondence with the drawing than did the first name given. In other words, the volunteers were better able to interpret their newly generated object forms when they could inspect their own drawing of the mental image than they could when they had to rely on the mental image alone.

Barquero and Logie (1999) also asked volunteers mentally to combine shapes of real objects, such as a cigar, a glass and a banana. Again, they were given the names of the shapes and were asked to combine these shapes to form a recognizable object that was different from the component parts. Many volunteers had difficulty performing this task, and when productions were judged independently, the ratings given were significantly poorer than those that had been allocated to the drawings and names derived from the canonical shapes. Apparently, volunteers had difficulty in separating the object identities from their shape, and this made it difficult to use the object shapes in a way in which they could be combined to form different objects.

One possible interpretation is that mental manipulation is simply a demanding cognitive task, and the problems arose from simply holding relatively complex shapes while they were transformed and combined. However, this interpretation might predict that the participants would forget to include some of the objects or miss out object details, and this was no more likely with the real object shapes than with the canonical shapes. With a larger number of shapes, participants did forget to include some of the shapes, but the number of shapes to be combined had no impact on the judged quality of the drawings and names that were produced; correspondence ratings were no different for successful combinations of five shapes than they were for combinations of three shapes (see also Pearson, Logie, & Gilhooly, 1999). In other words, number of shapes places a load on the storage capacity of working memory, but it does not appear to enhance or to inhibit the process of mental discovery. What does affect mental synthesis performance is the extent to which the images have associated meaning, and it is the associated meaning that inhibits mental synthesis, not the overall storage demand.

Working memory as a vehicle for creative thinking

So far, we have argued that the characteristics of working memory appear to constrain some aspects of mental discovery, but also to serve as the cognitive vehicle within which mental discoveries take place. If working memory deals with interpreted representations, then some of the findings described above suggest that reinterpretation might require active inhibition of the current interpretation. It is also likely to require the activation of other knowledge from prior experience that is not immediately available from perception of the object. If, as described above, we see a set of hieroglyphics, then our initial perception might interpret this as a random collection of lines and shapes. To reinterpret them as anything else we have to have some way of activating other knowledge from our previous experience of objects and symbols that we have encountered. We could do this by looking again at the shapes, realising that they are associated with what looks like an ancient Egyptian figure, turning around the picture, moving it closer or further away. Mentally, we might generate hypotheses as to what they might be – a series of children's drawings perhaps, or objects shown from unusual views, and we might focus our visual perceptual system on the top or bottom row of characters. Eventually, through a combination of changing the external experience, generating hypotheses, and a mental search process, we can reconfigure and reinterpret the characters, realizing that they are not just random drawings of shapes and objects, but comprise some form of written communication that we suspect might be hieroglyphics. In some cases, this process of hypothesis generation, manipulation, and mental search might occur successfully without looking back at the external stimulus and, indeed, the external stimulus may interfere with the mental processes. In other cases the external stimulus may be essential.

The argument then is that working memory offers the mental workspace for hypothesis generation, inhibition, mental manipulation, and mental search (Logie, 2003; Logie & Della Sala, 2003). In this sense, working memory cannot act as a temporary waiting room for information in-between perception and long-term memory. It must deal with the product of activated representations in long-term memory (Logie, 1995, 1996). Nor could working memory simply be the sum total of activated traces in long-term memory (e.g., Ruchkin, Grafman, Cameron, & Berndt, 2003) otherwise how could the processes of mental manipulation, transformation and mental discovery be performed? Where the activated information is incomplete or has to be reinterpreted, working memory acts as the workspace to manipulate the information and seek some means to resolve ambiguities or generate new knowledge. This points to one possible reason why we have evolved with a working memory. If we can make sense of a sensation, scenario, or experience from our current knowledge, this can happen effortlessly by activating the relevant knowledge that allows us to act appropriately for the current context. However, if we are confronted by ambiguity, by implication this means that the knowledge activated by perception from the long-term store is insufficient. What knowledge is activated can be manipulated and transformed within working memory to help resolve the ambiguity. That is, working memory can generate new knowledge from old and as such would have a significant evolutionary value.

Disorders of visuo-spatial working memory: Unilateral spatial neglect

A second area in which the concept of visuo-spatial working memory has been useful is in understanding the disorders of mental imagery suffered by some brain-damaged individuals. For this we will focus on a pattern of impairment referred to as unilateral spatial neglect. The best known early cases with this disorder were reported by Bisiach and Luzzatti (1978) whose patients, with right-hemisphere brain damage, showed impairments in reporting details of their immediate environment and also in reporting details of familiar scenes from memory. Their general visual abilities were intact, and they could describe elements of the scene in the centre and to their right, but they appeared unaware of features of the scene on their left, suggesting a unilateral deficit of visual attention. However, Bisiach and Luzzatti also asked their patients to describe from memory a scene very familiar to them, namely the Cathedral Square in Milan, Italy. When describing the scene as if they were facing the Cathedral, they mentioned a range of buildings and landmarks that would have been on their right from that viewpoint, but reported few details from the left of the square. Later, when asked to imagine themselves in the same square, but facing in the opposite direction, with their backs to the Cathedral, they now reported details that they had previously omitted, but that were now on their imagined right, but left out details now on their imagined left that they had previously reported. In other words, this was a problem associated with the use of a mental image or mental representation of the square, and not a general problem of memory for the crucial details. Although the participants in this study were impaired in both perception of scenes and in reporting scenes from memory, the representational problem could not have been due to perceptual difficulties; the information about Milan Cathedral Square was acquired long before these individuals suffered from their brain damage and the associated cognitive deficits. One interpretation (Bisiach, 1993) is that the representational neglect might arise from an impaired visuo-spatial working memory, using the metaphor of a mental screen that is torn or distorted on the left side. Alternatively, the representational neglect might be the signature of a failure in the ability to direct covert attention to the left half of the mental image that is held in an intact visuo-spatial working-memory system.

One possible interpretation of the patterns of impairment found in individuals with this form of brain damage might be to suggest that the cognitive systems responsible for perception overlap with those that support mental imagery. This would account for the fact that they showed impairments of both perception and of imagery. However, if this were the case, presumably these individuals would have had great difficulty discriminating between real scenes and those that they imagined, yet there was no evidence that they had any difficulty of this kind. Moreover, there have now been many more patients reported who have the characteristic unilateral bias to their visuo-spatial deficit, but who show this only in perception, only in representation, or only when dealing with space close to their body or only for space that is distant from their body. In other words, there are several different forms of neglect, not all of which are accompanied by disorders of both perception and imagery within the same individuals (e.g., Bartolomeo, D'Erme, & Gainotti, 1994; Beschin, Cocchini, Della Sala, & Logie, 1997; Coslett, 1997; Denis, Beschin, Logie, & Della Sala, 2002; Guariglia, Padovani, Pantano, & Pizzamiglio, 1993). Indeed, there is one patient reported by Beschin, Basso, and Della Sala (2000) who showed a perceptual neglect for the right area of space, but showed representational neglect for details on the left of imagined space. This rare dissociation arose from separate lesions in the left and in the right hemisphere of the brain, respectively.

More recently (Denis et al., 2002), we have shown that representational neglect can appear not only for familiar scenes, but also for novel arrays of objects that are verbally described to the patients. For example, the patient might be told to imagine a table top with an orange placed to their right and close to them, that there is an apple behind the orange, a banana to the left of the orange, and a pear in front of the banana. They are then asked to recall each of the objects and their location. Because the task involves auditory presentation of a description of the object layout, there is no problem here of any visual perceptual neglect affecting recall performance. Also, all of the patients showed normal verbal memory. Despite this, there was clear evidence that the patients were attempting to generate visual images of the layout of the objects rather than rely on their intact verbal memory system to perform the task. Some of these data from 11 control participants and 14 patients with representational neglect are shown in Figure 11.2 (standard conditions). As is clear from the figure, the patients showed poorer recall of items that were described as being on the left, neglected side, than those described as being on the right. One of the patients reported by Denis et al. (2002) was a case of pure representational neglect who showed this clear pattern of poorer recall of items that were on his imagined left, but who showed no difficulty whatsoever in describing a scene that he could see. In other words, representational neglect does not arise just from tasks that require access to information held in long-term memory. It also appears when the patients are required to form a mental image of completely novel object layouts. Other patients in our study showed pure perceptual neglect. That is, they showed no difficulty in reporting all of the details of the novel arrays that they heard described, but had difficulty in describing scenes that were presented to them visually.

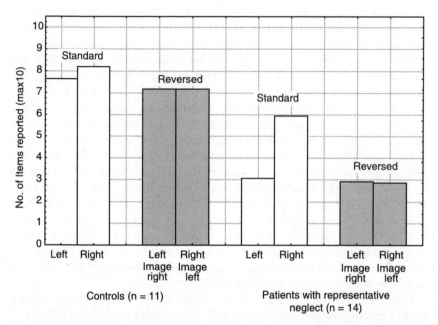

Figure 11.2 Mean number of items correctly reported in the correct location by healthy participants and by patients with representational neglect from the left (max = 10), or right (max = 10) of five arrays of four objects, both as described (standard), and after mental rotation by 180 degrees (reversed).

The fact that a dissociation between representational neglect and perceptual neglect has been shown both across patients and even within the same patient, for both familiar scenes and for novel arrays points to a clearer understanding of the range of particular cognitive difficulties that might be termed neglect. As such, we gain greater practical clinical insight, and the basis for additional diagnostic techniques to detect the presence of representational neglect, a syndrome that hitherto has rarely been reported in the scientific literature, and that would not be apparent from standard neuropsychological test batteries. The dissociation also offers a theoretical contribution in that it points to the clear separation between the perceptual system and the representational system in the healthy brain.

In a further set of studies (Logie, Beschin, Della Sala, & Denis, 2005; Della Sala, Logie, Beschin, & Denis, 2004), we again presented patients with representational neglect with novel arrays that they either saw or heard described. However, in these studies, the patients were asked mentally to rotate the arrays by 180 degrees, and to recall the objects from the locations that they would be in if they were viewed from the other side of the table. Results from 11 healthy controls and 14 patients with representational neglect are shown in Figure 11.2 (reversed conditions). Results for the patients with representational neglect showed that mentally rotating items from the presented (described) left to the imagined right resulted in no further loss of information – performance is the same as if the items had been described on the left and reported from the left. However, items that were presented on the right, but then after mental rotation had to be imagined on the left showed a dramatic drop in performance. If the patients had a difficulty with directing covert attention we might expect that a requirement to direct attention to the left and then mentally rotate whatever objects are available would result in a substantial loss of information. However, the process of mental rotation appeared to be intact. What mattered was whether the items had to be imagined as being on the left or on the right, with any information imagined on the left resulting in very poor recall. This pattern of results is not consistent with the suggestion that representational neglect reflects an impairment in directing covert attention. However, the data are consistent with the idea that representational neglect arises from damage to the component of visuospatial working memory that generates or maintains an image of a familiar or of a novel scene. Again, this adds to a practical, clinical understanding of the problems and retained abilities in these patients, as well as contributing to a theoretical understanding of representational neglect.

These results suggest that the compelling notion that our mental visual and spatial world is intimately and directly linked with the external visual and spatial world begins to seem illusory. The mental workspace allows us to represent visual, spatial and other aspects of the world that we perceive, but that representation incorporates our interpretations, the results of mental manipulations and additional knowledge from our past experience. In this sense it is very different from perception, and our mental workspace is due for an upgrade from a holding area for recently perceived information to a hub that draws on the products of activating knowledge.

Dual-task coordination as an executive function

Thus far, we have argued that the contents of the mental workspace are interpreted and that perception and imagery might not cohabit areas of cognition. The findings from studies of mental discovery point to a system that can draw on both prior knowledge and experiences and can operate on the resulting contents. This leaves open a range of questions as to how we might identify and explore experimentally the range of operations that might be available. In this last section of the chapter, we shall discuss one possible operation that could have an impact on many of the ways in which we use the mental workspace in our daily lives, namely in tackling the challenges of performing two tasks concurrently. For some tasks, most healthy adults can do more than one task at a time, and do so with consummate ease, such as walking and talking. For other tasks, such as reading while holding a conversation, or driving while speaking on a mobile phone, the cognitive challenges are very much greater, and can even be dangerous. However, one group of individuals appears to be greatly challenged by performing two activities concurrently, almost regardless of what those activities or their cognitive demands might be. These are individuals who suffer from a progressive form of brain disease known as Alzheimer-type dementia, or Alzheimer's disease, which we shall refer to by the abbreviation AD.

AD is linked with a range of cognitive impairments resulting from diffuse brain damage. In its very early stages, the individual begins to suffer failures of memory for events or episodic memory (e.g., Perry, Watson & Hodges, 2000), and for intentions or prospective memory (e.g., Maylor, Smith, Della Sala, & Logie, 2002; Smith, Della Sala, Logie, & Maylor, 2000), coupled with other specific deficits such as reading difficulties, or problems in comprehension (e.g., Luzzatti, 1999). Some of these difficulties, notably the episodic and prospective memory failures, also appear to accompany the processes of normal ageing (e.g., Perfect & Maylor, 2000). However, as AD progresses, so the cognitive problems worsen much more rapidly than occurs in normal ageing, and when the diagnosis of AD has been made on standard clinical criteria but is yet thought to be in the early stages of the disease, additional cognitive difficulties become apparent, most notably a difficulty in dual-task performance.

Although there are formal means to assess AD, the range of tools available to detect its onset and monitor its progression or response to treatment remain somewhat limited. There would, therefore, be some advantage to providing enhanced tools for aiding assessment and management of the disease that are both non-invasive and relatively simple to administer. From a theoretical point of view, the development of such tools can allow greater understanding of the impact of AD on aspects of healthy cognition, which, in turn, may offer some further insight into the functioning of cognition in the healthy brain.

The differential sensitivity to dual-task requirements of individuals with AD in its relatively early stages following formal diagnosis was first reported by Baddeley, Logie, Bressi, Della Sala, and Spinnler (1986). In these experiments, healthy young individuals were compared with individuals in the early stages of AD and with healthy elderly people who were matched with the AD group on age and educational background. Each participant was tested on their immediate memory span for serially ordered digit sequences. The sequences were presented aurally for immediate, serial ordered, oral recall. Normal ageing can result in a lower memory span for the elderly than for the young, and AD also results in lowering of span. Even if performance is well above floor for all groups, these differences in memory span, when it is performed as a single task, could make it difficult to interpret the impact of performing a second task at the same time. However, by assessing the memory span for each individual, we could then present digit sequences whose lengths were determined by the individual span, thereby equating cognitive demand and performance levels across groups.

Our second task involved following a moving target around a computer screen. For this, the participant had to place a light sensitive pen on a small square that appeared in the centre of the screen. As soon as they touched the square it began to move in a random fashion around the screen, and the participant was required to keep the light pen on the square as best they could. The speed at which the square moved, gradually increased until the participant was no longer able to maintain contact for more than 40% of the time. This was then taken as the "tracking span" for each individual, and the associated target speed was then employed for that individual for the rest of the experiment.

All participants were then asked to perform both the tracking task and the digit recall task concurrently. Results indicated that the young and the healthy elderly both showed impairments of around 15–20% under dual-task conditions. However, the AD group were very much more severely impaired by performing two tasks simultaneously than were the other two groups. This large dual-task impairment appears then to be specific to AD and is not characteristic of healthy ageing. If this specific impairment can be shown to be robust, it might offer a means to help with diagnosis of the disease and to track its progression. At a theoretical level the result also raises questions as to precisely what kind of cognitive function is impaired in the individuals with AD. These individuals appeared to have only a modest impairment in their performance on each of the tasks performed singly. It was only when the tasks were performed together that the AD group showed the dramatic impairment, suggesting impairment of a cognitive system responsible for coordinating the performance of two concurrent tasks. If there is a function for dual-task coordination that is damaged in AD, then this in turn indicates that such a system might be an identifiable component of cognition in the healthy brain.

A number of questions remain, however. One possible alternative account could be that the AD group have difficulty with any demanding task, and that the performance pattern simply reflects what can be achieved by a damaged brain when confronted by a heavy cognitive demand. This notion of difficulty does not offer a very useful account, because difficulty is often defined by the task performance, making the concept wholly circular. Moreover, difficulty may arise for a wide range of reasons, reflecting, for example, divided attention, limitations of memory capacity, limitations on speed of processing, impoverished stimuli or an impaired sensory system, fatigue across experimental trials, lack of familiarity with the materials or task, presence of environmental or social stresses, the impact of physical disability or illness, or a lack of motivation in the participant. Nevertheless, we might offer an operational definition of difficulty that is independent of task performance. Specifically, a task could be defined as difficult because its demands exceed those associated with previously determined capacity, such as memory span.

In order to assess the potential impact of difficulty as defined by individual span or measured capacity, some more recent experiments have explored the impact of varying the demands of a single task (Logie, Cocchini, Della Sala,

& Baddeley, 2004). In one of these experiments, we asked groups of healthy young and elderly people, and a group of individuals in the early stages of AD to perform digit recall on its own, or tracking on its own. However, for digit recall, we assessed their recall performance below their span, at their span and above their span. For tracking, we assessed performance at tracking speeds well below the individually measured tracking ability level, at that level and above that level. If task difficulty *per se* is the determinant of differential impairments in AD, then we would expect that increasing task demand, for a single task, beyond the measured capacity limits for each individual would lead to a very rapid drop in performance for the AD group compared with the other participants. Results showed that the decrease in performance with increasing demand completely overlapped for the three groups, and this was true both for digit recall and for tracking. In other words, there was no evidence to suggest that simply increasing the demand of a single task had any differential effect on the AD group.

The results of the last experiment described led us back to considering whether it was indeed something specific about performing two tasks at once that presents a peculiar challenge to individuals with AD. In order to test this further, we again asked young, elderly, and AD participants to perform digit recall and tracking. However, in this experiment, they were asked to perform very low-demand versions of the two tasks and to perform them concurrently. That is, digit recall involved sequence lengths well below each participant's digit span, and tracking involved a slow-moving target that, as a single task, could readily be followed with high accuracy by individuals in all three groups. Under dual-task conditions, neither the young nor the healthy elderly participants showed any drop in performance of either task. However, the AD patients showed a reliable reduction in performance on the tracking task when it was combined with concurrent digit recall. Therefore, even when two very low-demand tasks are performed together, AD leads to a drop in performance that is not characteristic of healthy ageing. The pattern of specific deficit that appears in AD patients is not restricted to a combination of digit recall with a perceptual-motor task such as tracking. Even when digit recall is combined with another memory task, involving retention of visually presented matrix patterns, some as yet unpublished data from our laboratory again indicate that AD patients show a very dramatic drop in performance compared with single-task conditions, and this dual-task decrement is not apparent in the healthy elderly group. Moreover, young healthy individuals also show virtually no loss of performance even when performing these two demanding memory tasks concurrently (Cocchini, Logie, Della Sala, & MacPherson, 2002).

A number of other studies have reported dual-task impairments in healthy ageing that, on the whole, we have not found in our studies. However, a major difference in the methodology is that many of the studies showing such effects have based their conclusions on the raw test scores without equating initial levels of single-task performance. Combining two tasks, both of which are showing an effect of healthy ageing, will inevitably demonstrate an age effect on dual-task performance. Even when the combined performance levels show a greater decrement than would be predicted from the age-related decline on the individual tasks, (Fernandez & Moscovitch, 2000; Naveh-Benjamin, Craik, Perretta, & Tonev, 2000), the interpretation remains problematic (Perfect & Maylor, 2000). This means that the dual-task impairments observed in the elderly group could have resulted from the initial differential levels of single-task performance rather than be the result specifically of dual-task requirements. However, the very large and differential dual-task impairment in the early stages of AD does appear to be robust, and specific to dual-task performance rather than reflecting a more general cognitive impairment. Given that individuals with AD appear to have a specific deficit in dual-task coordination, this points to the possibility that healthy adults also have a cognitive function that is responsible for dual-task coordination, possibly required for encoding and retrieving information from domain-specific stores.

The theoretical conclusions from this work are complemented by a range of implications of clinical and societal value. In particular, the identification of a specific dual-task deficit indicates that individuals with AD might have difficulty in dealing with a range of everyday activities that rely on the ability to coordinate concurrent tasks or deal with more than one information source. Alberoni, Baddeley, Della Sala, Logie, and Spinnler (1992) have shown that AD patients have difficulty in keeping track of "who said what" if there is a conversation taking place among several people. This then offers advice to carers of individuals with AD, suggesting that conversations involving several people should be avoided, and that they should not assume that the individuals in their care will be able to cope with even simple tasks that have several elements, such as making a meal or even walking while talking (Cocchini, Della Sala, Logie, Pagani, Sacco, & Spinnler, 2004). Moreover, the development of tasks that are sensitive to the early stages of AD, and to the progression of the disease, but that are insensitive to the effects of normal ageing, have the potential to act as non-invasive behavioural tests to aid initial diagnosis, to monitor progression, and to assess the effectiveness of treatment. They would also be more directly related than physiological indicators of the disease to the abilities of the individual in coping with daily life.

Using working memory in the healthy and damaged brain

Throughout this chapter, we have referred to working memory as a mental workspace, so as to convey the idea of both a temporary memory system, and a means to manipulate information and to derive new knowledge, thereby acting to support both our interactions with the environment and learning from both new experiences and from reinterpreting previous experiences. There is now a growing body of evidence to suggest that perception and working memory are rather less closely linked than has commonly been assumed, with perception activating prior knowledge, and the products of that activation comprising the contents of our mental workspace. Moreover, the concept of working memory offers a means to account for a range of memory disorders linked with specific forms of brain damage, together with enhancement of advice to carers. This reinforces a general argument that working memory offers a framework that is theoretically and empirically fruitful while providing a strong basis for tackling some of the practical problems of everyday cognition for both the healthy and the damaged brain.

References

Alberoni, M., Baddeley, A., Della Sala, S., Logie, R., & Spinnler, H. (1992). Keeping track of a conversation: Impairments in Alzheimer's disease. *International Journal of Geriatric Psychiatry, 7*, 639–646.

Baddeley, A. D., & Hitch, G. J. (1974). Working memory. In G. Bower (Ed.), *The psychology of learning and motivation* (Vol. VIII, pp. 47–90). New York: Academic Press.

Baddeley, A. D., & Logie, R. H. (1999). Working memory: The multiple component model. In A. Miyake & P. Shah (Eds.), *Models of working memory* (pp. 28–61). New York: Cambridge University Press.

Baddeley, A., Logie, R., Bressi, S., Della Sala, S., & Spinnler, H. (1986). Senile dementia and working memory. *Quarterly Journal of Experimental Psychology, 38A*, 603–618.

Barquero, B., & Logie, R. H. (1999). Imagery constraints on quantitative and qualitative aspects of mental synthesis. *European Journal of Cognitive Psychology, 11*, 315–333.

Bartolomeo, P., D'Erme, P., & Gainotti, G. (1994). The relationship between visuospatial and representational neglect. *Neurology, 44*, 1710–1714.

Beschin, N., Basso, A., & Della Sala, S. (2000). Perceiving left and imagining right: Dissociation in neglect. *Cortex, 36*, 401–414.

Beschin, N., Cocchini, G., Della Sala, S., & Logie, R. H. (1997). What the eyes perceive, the brain ignores: A case of pure unilateral representational neglect. *Cortex, 33*, 3–26.

Bisiach, E. (1993). Mental representation in unilateral neglect and related disorders: The twentieth Bartlett memorial lecture. *Quarterly Journal of Experimental Psychology, 46A*, 435–461.

Bisiach, E., & Luzzatti, C. (1978). Unilateral neglect of representational space. *Cortex, 14*, 129–133.

Cocchini, G., Della Sala, S., Logie, R. H., Pagani, R., Sacco, L., & Spinnler, H. (2004). Dual task effects of walking while talking in Alzheimer disease. *La Revue Neurologique, 160*, 74–80.

Cocchini, G., Logie, R. H., Della Sala, S., & MacPherson, S. (2002). Concurrent performance of two memory tasks: Evidence for domain specific working memory systems. *Memory and Cognition, 30*, 1086–1095.

Coslett, B. (1997). Neglect in vision and visual imagery: A double dissociation. *Brain, 120*, 1163–1171.

Della Sala, S., Logie, R. H., Beschin, N., & Denis, M. (2004). Preserved visuo-spatial transformations in representational neglect. *Neuropsychologia, 42*, 1358–1364.

Denis, M., Beschin, N., Logie, R. H., & Della Sala, S. (2002). Visual perception and verbal descriptions as sources for generating mental representations: Evidence from representational neglect. *Cognitive Neuropsychology, 19(2)*, 97–112.

Denis, M., & Kosslyn, S. M. (1999). Scanning visual mental images: A window on the mind. *Cahiers de Psychologie Cognitive, 18*, 409–465.

Fernandez, M. A., & Moscovitch, M. (2000). Divided attention and memory: Evidence of substantial interference effects at retrieval and encoding. *Journal of Experimental Psychology: General, 129*, 155–176.

Finke, R., & Slayton, K. (1988). Explorations of creative visual synthesis in mental imagery. *Memory and Cognition, 16*, 252–257.

Guariglia, C., Padovani, A., Pantano, P., & Pizzamiglio, L. (1993). Unilateral neglect restricted to visual imagery. *Nature, 364*, 235–237.

Helstrup, T., & Anderson, R. E. (1991). Imagery in mental construction and decomposition tasks. In R. H. Logie & M. Denis (Eds.), *Mental images in human cognition* (pp. 229–240). Amsterdam: North Holland.

Helstrup, T., & Anderson, R. E. (1996). On the generality of mental construction in imagery: When bananas become smiles. *European Journal of Cognitive Psychology, 8*, 275–293.

Just, M., & Carpenter, P. (1992). A capacity theory of comprehension: Individual differences in working memory. *Psychological Review, 99*, 122–149.

Kane, M. J., & Engle, R. W. (2002). The role of prefrontal cortex in working memory capacity, executive attention, and general fluid intelligence: An individual differences perspective. *Psychonomic Bulletin and Review, 9*, 637–671.

Kosslyn, S. M. (1994). *Image and brain: The resolution of the imagery debate.* Cambridge, MA: MIT Press.

Locke, J. (1959). *An essay concerning human understanding.* Book II, Chapter X, 1–2. A. Campbell Fraser (Ed.). New York: Dover (original work published 1690).

Logie, R. H. (1995). *Visuo-spatial working memory.* Hove, UK: Lawrence Erlbaum Associates, Ltd.

Logie, R. H. (1996). The seven ages of working memory. In J. T. E. Richardson, R. W. Engle, L. Hasher, R. H. Logie, E. R. Stoltzfus, & R. T. Zacks (Eds.), *Working memory and human cognition.* New York: Oxford University Press.

Logie, R. H. (2003). Spatial and visual working memory: A mental workspace. In D. Irwin & B. Ross (Eds.), *Cognitive vision: The psychology of learning and motivation* (Vol. 42, pp. 37–78). New York: Elsevier.

Logie, R. H., Cocchini, G., Della Sala, S., & Baddeley, A. D. (2004). Is there a specific executive capacity for dual task co-ordination? Evidence from Alzheimer's disease. *Neuropsychology, 18*, 504–513.

Logie, R. H., & Della Sala, S. (2003). Working memory as a mental workspace: Why activated long-term memory is not enough. *Behavioral and Brain Sciences, 26*, 745–746.

Logie, R. H., Beschin, N., Della Sala, S., & Denis, M. (2005). Dissociating mental transformations and visuo-spatial storage in working memory: Evidence from representational neglect. *Memory, 13*, 430–434.

Luzzatti, C. (1999). Language disorders in dementia. In G. Denes & L. Pizzamiglio (Eds.), *Handbook of clinical and experimental neuropsychology* (pp. 809–846). Hove, UK: Psychology Press.

Maylor, E. A., Smith, G., Della Sala, S., & Logie, R. H. (2002). Prospective and retrospective memory in normal aging and dementia: An experimental study. *Memory and Cognition, 30*, 871–884.

Miyake, A., & Shah, P. (Eds.). (1999). *Models of working memory*. New York: Cambridge University Press.

Naveh-Benjamin, M., Craik, F. I. M, Perretta, J. G., & Tonev, S. T. (2000). The effects of divided attention on encoding and retrieval processes: The resiliency of retrieval processes. *Quarterly Journal of Experimental Psychology, 53A*, 609–625.

Pearson, D. G., Logie, R. H., & Gilhooly, K. J. (1999). Verbal representation and spatial manipulation during mental synthesis. *European Journal of Cognitive Psychology, 11*, 295–314.

Perfect, T., & Maylor, E. A. (Eds.). (2000). *Models of cognitive aging.* Oxford: Oxford University Press.

Perry, R. J., Watson, P., & Hodges, J. R. (2000). The nature and staging of attentional dysfunction in early (minimal and mild) Alzheimer's disease: Relationship to episodic and semantic memory impairment. *Neuropsychologia, 38*, 252–271.

Ruchkin, D. S., Grafman, J., Cameron, K., & Berndt, R. S. (2003). Working memory retention systems: A state of activated long-term memory. *Behavioral and Brain Sciences, 26*, 709–777.

Smith, G., Della Sala, S., Logie, R. H., & Maylor, E. A. (2000). Prospective and retrospective memory in normal aging and dementia: A questionnaire study. *Memory, 8*, 311–321.

12 Executive functions and prognoses of patients with memory disorders

Masaru Mimura

From the perspective of the clinical management of patients with memory disorders, one of the most important questions concerning memory and society is the social prognosis of amnesic patients. It is always a matter of great interest to clinicians whether amnesic patients return to society, their job and a normal level of functioning. In this chapter I focus on the social prognosis of two different alcohol-related populations, i.e., those presenting with alcoholism and alcoholic Korsakoff syndrome. It is well recognized that alcoholism per se causes various psychosocial problems and executive dysfunction has been reported to predict the outcome of alcoholics (Morgenstern & Bates, 1999). Alcoholics' functional outcome can be divided into two aspects: alcohol-specific (drinking) and alcohol-non-specific (occupation). Study 1 investigated whether the executive function of alcoholics predicts alcohol-specific outcome, non-specific outcome, both, or neither. Study 2 examined the long-term social prognosis of alcoholic Korsakoff syndrome. Alcoholic Korsakoff syndrome is a well-documented amnesic syndrome, which usually follows Wernicke's encephalopathy and/or delirium tremens (Victor, Adams, & Collins, 1989). Anterograde and retrograde amnesia is prominent in contrast with preserved attention and intelligence (Kopelman, 1995). Patients with alcoholic Korsakoff syndrome are known to show a poorer outcome than other amnesic populations (Mimura, 2000). Study 2 investigated whether there are any neurocognitive factors that determine the future social prognosis of Korsakoff amnesics. Additionally, a characteristic patient with Korsakoff syndrome who remained hospitalized for a prolonged period, is presented in Study 3. By reviewing the clinical problems of this particular patient, I will discuss the role of executive function in the social recovery of patients with Korsakoff syndrome, one of the most difficult memory disorders to treat.

Study 1: Social prognosis of chronic alcoholics and executive dysfunction

The first study concerns neuropsychological predictors for social prognosis of patients with alcoholism. In this study we investigated what neuro-psychological tests predict alcoholic patients' future outcome. Details of Study 1, including statistical analyses, have been published elsewhere (Moriyama et al., 2002).

Method

Subjects

This study included 22 male alcoholics (mean age 51.6 ± 3.7 years; mean length of education 12.5 ± 2.6 years) and 15 non-alcoholic, age- and educa-tion-matched cohorts as controls. All patients underwent a 70-day alcoholism rehabilitation programme between April 1998 and March 1999 at the Alcohol Treatment Unit of Komagino Hospital, Tokyo, Japan. The structured clinical interview for DSM-III-R (Spitzer, Williams, Gibbon, & First, 1990) was used to diagnose alcohol dependence. All patients were given twelve neuro-psychological tests approximately 7 weeks after detoxification (mean 51.4 ± 3.8 days after admission).

Neuropsychological tests

Twelve neuropsychological tests were administered to both the alcoholic sub-jects and the non-alcoholic controls to investigate the relationship between alcoholics' neuropsychological performance and functional outcome. The tests included tasks of:

1 Reaction time;
2 Symbol digit modalities;
3 Digit span;
4 Figure position;
5 Block design;
6 Trail making, and six subtests of the Behavioural Assessment of the Dysexecutive Syndrome (BADS) (Wilson et al., 1996). The BADS included;
7 Rule shift card;
8 Action programme;
9 Key search;
10 Temporal judgement;
11 Zoo map; and
12 Modified six elements.

A total profile score (0–24) was obtained from summation of each subtest (0–4). Detailed descriptions can be found in Wilson, Alderman, Burgers, Emslie, and Evans (1996), Evans, Chua, McKenna, and Wilson (1997), and Ihara, Berrios, and London (2000).

Except for the digit span and the six subtests of the BADS, the remaining tests were taken via a computerized test battery (computer-aided test system, CD-ROM) devised by the Japan Society of Hepatology (Kato et al., 2004). Instruction and stimulus presentation were given by a computer. Subjects' responses were made on a touch-panel monitor. Following are brief descriptions of each test:

1 Reaction time The subject was requested to press a button as soon as a red circle appeared on the touch-panel monitor. The test included three versions: (1) consecutive brief presentation of red circles only; (2) random presentation of red, yellow and blue circles – press a button when a red circle appears; and (3) random presentation of red, yellow and blue circles – press a button only when a red circle followed a yellow circle. Each version lasted for 60 s, and the average time of correct reactions was computed. The reaction times in this test may reflect information-processing speed.

2 Symbol digit modalities (Smith, 1973) The subject was requested to match a symbol to a digit. The number of correct responses achieved within 60 s (instead of 90 s as in the original version) was calculated. This task could be interpreted in several ways, but may reflect visual-motor processing and divided attention.

3 Digit span (Wechsler, 1981) This task was taken from the Wechsler Adult Intelligence Scale–Revised (WAIS-R) subtest. The task in this test reflects auditory verbal short-term memory.

4 Figure position The subject was requested to memorize two to four figures (e.g., a triangle and a square) together with their positions among six possible arrangements. The subject was instructed to recall the figures and their positions after 15 s intervals. The total number of correct responses (maximum = 9) and the summed time for completion was calculated. This task may reflect non-verbal short-term memory or spatial working memory.

5 Block design (Wechsler, 1981) This task was identical to the WAIS-R subtest except for the computerized presentation. The subject was requested to copy a model with four red/white cards. The number of correct responses (maximum = 5, instead of 10 in the original version) and the summed time for completion were computed. This task may reflect visuoconstructional ability.

6.1 Trail making A (Reitan, 1956) The subject was requested to draw lines to connect 25 consecutively numbered circles, which were randomly distributed on the screen. Time of completion was computed. Trail making tests may reflect visuomotor and attentional processing.

6.2 Trail making B (Reitan, 1956)　The subject was requested to draw lines to connect 25 consecutively numbered and lettered circles by alternating between the two sequences. Time of completion was computed. As stated earlier, trail making tests may reflect visuomotor and attentional processing. Trail making B, in particular, requires executive functioning with alternating or dividing attention (Trannel, Anderson, & Benton, 1994).

The following tests were introduced from the BADS. The BADS consists of six subtests. A total profile score (0–24) was obtained from summation of each subtest.

7 Rule shift cards　In trial 1 of this subtest, the subject was instructed to respond "yes" to a red card and "no" to a black card when a pile of 20 playing cards was turned over one at a time. In trial 2, the subject was instructed to respond "yes" if the card was the same colour as the previous one, and "no" if the card was not the same colour. This subtest is believed to reflect cognitive flexibility.

8 Action programme　The subject was presented with a rectangular stand on which a beaker and a tube were placed. The beaker was full of water with a removable lid that had a small hole in the top. The tube had a small piece of cork at its bottom. The subject was instructed to get the cork out of the tube by using either a metal L-shaped rod that was too short to reach the cork or a small screw-top container and its unscrewed top. The subject was required to remove the cork from the tube, making use of the items provided and without touching the main assembly manually. The wire was used to remove the lid from the large container while the top was attached to the small cylindrical tube and this was used to transfer water from the large container into the tall tube to float the cork to the top. This subtest examines the ability to solve a close-ended, sequential problem.

9 Key search　The subject was provided with a piece of paper with a 100 mm square drawn on it and was asked to imagine that the square was a large field and that somewhere in this field he/she had lost a key. The subject was instructed then to draw a line to show how to search this field in order to find the lost key. This subtest examines the ability to solve an open-ended problem.

10 Temporal judgements　This test consisted of four questions in which the subject was asked to estimate the time needed for an activity. This subtest examines the ability of cognitive estimation.

11 Zoo map　The subject was asked to map out a route to visit predetermined places in a zoo according to a designated rule. In the first part, the subject must plan the order of locations to visit. In the second part, the order of visiting locations was given by the examiner as an aid to problem solving. This subtest examines the ability to plan and use feedback in problem solving.

12 Modified six elements The subject was given 10 minutes during which he had to do at least some of six subtests (three different tasks). The tasks were dictation, arithmetic calculation, and picture naming. Each task had two parts. The subject was not allowed to do both parts of the same task right after one another. This subtest is believed to test the ability to plan and divide attention.

Outcome assessment

All patients participated in the follow-up assessment performed approximately 18 months following the initial assessment (mean 534.0 ± 98.7 days after admission). Each patient was questioned regarding the status of his drinking and occupational situation. In cases where a patient was unavailable for the questionnaire (e.g., discontinuation of out-patient clinic), the information was obtained from his family informant. Drinking outcome was determined by the diagnostic criteria of DSM-III-R, as was done in a previous study (Yoshino & Kato, 1996) that used the DSM-III-R's 19 alcohol-related items in a questionnaire. If the patient resumed drinking during the last 6 months, he was classified as drinking (+); if not, he was classified as drinking (−). Occupation outcome was defined as follows according to Donovan, Kivlahan, and Walker (1984). Full-time employment was used to refer to subjects who worked 40 or more hours a week and continued that work schedule for a 6-month period. Full-time employment was regarded as occupation (+). Part-time employment was used to refer to subjects who worked less than 40 hours a week or who continued that work schedule for less than 6 months or to subjects who were disabled. Part-time employment was regarded as occupation (−).

Results

Performance on the neuropsychological tests

Results of alcoholic subjects and control subjects regarding the neuropsychological tests are shown in Table 12.1. Performance of 15 non-alcoholic control subjects on the computerized test battery was identical to that obtained from a larger sample of age-matched normal database. The alcoholic subjects were more impaired on the symbol digit modalities, the trail making B, and three subscores (rule shift card, zoo map, and modified six elements) and the total profile score of the BADS than the non-alcoholic control subjects. The scores of the two groups were comparable on the other tests.

Table 12.1 Results of alcoholic patients and normal controls on the neuro-psychological tests (Moriyama et al., 2002).

		Alcoholics	Controls	Larger sample of normal control data base†
1	Reaction time A (s)	0.46 ± 0.18	0.37 ± 0.05	0.36 ± 0.09
	B (s)	0.41 ± 0.12	0.37 ± 0.04	0.38 ± 0.08
	C (s)	0.45 ± 0.11	0.44 ± 0.04	0.44 ± 0.06
2	Symbol digit modalities (number)	20.5 ± 6.1*	26.2 ± 4.8	26.1 ± 5.6
3	Digit span (number)	6.2 ± 2.5	6.6 ± 2.1	
4	Figure position (s) (correct number)	16.1 ± 6.6 7.8 ± 1.4	14.2 ± 4.7 7.6 ± 2.3	14.7 ± 6.4 8.1 ± 1.8
5	Block design (s) (correct number)	66.9 ± 19.3 4.8 ± 0.5	55.5 ± 16.7 5.0 ± 0.2	60.4 ± 19.4 4.9 ± 0.4
6.1	Trail making A (s)	32.9 ± 11.6	30.2 ± 6.8	27.8 ± 8.3
6.2	Trail making B (s)	62.4 ± 31.7*	42.7 ± 11.9	45.2 ± 20.0
BADS (subtests and total profile score)				
7	Rule shift card	2.8 ± 0.9**	3.9 ± 0.3	
8	Action programme	3.6 ± 0.6	3.7 ± 0.8	
9	Key search	2.2 ± 1.2	2.8 ± 0.9	
10	Temporal judgement	1.4 ± 0.8	1.5 ± 0.7	
11	Zoo map	2.0 ± 1.1**	3.6 ± 0.8	
12	Modified six elements	3.3 ± 0.7*	3.9 ± 0.4	
Total profile score		15.3 ± 2.8**	19.3 ± 1.8	

Data are given as the mean ± *SD*.
* $p < .01$; ** $p < .001$, significantly worse than normal controls.
† Performance of a larger sample of age-matched normal data on the computerized neuro-psychological tests ($n = 204$; mean age 52.1 ± 4.1). There were no significant differences between the performance of this larger sample and that of 15 normal controls.

Relationship between neuropsychological performance, and the variables of drinking and social outcome in alcoholics

Drinking and occupation outcomes are shown in Table 12.2. Three patients discontinued out-patient clinic, so the information on these patients was obtained from their family informants. At follow-up approximately 18 months following the initial assessment, 12 out of 22 patients had returned to drinking, 11 were working full-time, 6 were working part-time or intermit-tently, and the remaining 5 were disabled. The main effect of drinking was not significant for any neuropsychological performance, indicating that both the patients who resumed drinking and those who did not

Table 12.2 Relations between neuropsychological tests, and variables of drinking and social outcome in alcoholic patients (Moriyama et al., 2002).

			Drinking		*Occupation*	
			(−) n = 10	(+) n = 12	(+) n = 11	(−) n = 11
1	Reaction time	A (s)	0.49 ± 0.21	0.43 ± 0.15	0.46 ± 0.17	0.46 ± 0.20
		B (s)	0.43 ± 0.14	0.40 ± 0.10	0.41 ± 0.13	0.41 ± 0.11
		C (s)	0.45 ± 0.11	0.45 ± 0.11	0.43 ± 0.11	0.46 ± 0.11
2	Symbol digit modalities (number)		21.7 ± 4.7	19.6 ± 7.1	22.8 ± 5.0	18.3 ± 6.4
3	Digit span (number)		6.3 ± 2.1	6.2 ± 2.0	6.3 ± 2.3	6.2 ± 2.4
4	Figure position (s) (correct number)		16.2 ± 7.8 8.1 ± 1.0	16.1 ± 5.9 7.6 ± 1.6	16.2 ± 8.1 8.3 ± 1.1	16.1 ± 5.2 7.4 ± 1.5
5	Block design (s) (correct number)		69.1 ± 18.8 4.9 ± 0.3	65.1 ± 20.3 4.7 ± 0.7	60.3 ± 14.2 4.9 ± 0.3	73.6 ± 22.0 4.6 ± 0.7
6.1	Trail making A (s)		34.5 ± 13.2	31.6 ± 10.5	28.6 ± 9.5	37.2 ± 12.2
6.2	Trail making B (s)		53.4 ± 22.9	69.9 ± 36.8	45.6 ± 12.7	79.2 ± 36.4
BADS subtests						
7	Rule shift card		3.1 ± 0.6	2.5 ± 1.1	3.2 ± 0.4	2.4 ± 1.1
8	Action programme		3.7 ± 0.7	3.5 ± 0.5	3.8 ± 0.6	3.4 ± 0.5
9	Key search		2.1 ± 1.2	2.3 ± 1.3	2.7 ± 1.0	1.6 ± 1.2
10	Temporal judgement		1.3 ± 0.9	1.4 ± 0.8	1.8 ± 0.8	0.9 ± 0.7*
11	Zoo map		2.2 ± 1.0	1.8 ± 1.2	2.6 ± 1.0	1.4 ± 0.8*
12	Modified six elements		3.5 ± 0.7	3.2 ± 0.7	3.5 ± 0.5	3.2 ± 0.9
Total profile score			15.9 ± 2.4	14.8 ± 3.1	17.6 ± 1.4	13.0 ± 1.7**

Data are given as the mean ± *SD*.
* $p < .01$; **$p < .0001$.

performed equally on all the indices of the BADS and on all the other neuropsychological tests.

In contrast, the main effect of occupation had statistically significant differences between patients who were working full time at follow-up, occupation (+), and those who were not on the two subtests of BADS (temporal judgement and zoo map), and the BADS total profile score. Occupation (+) and (−) groups did not show significant differences on the other neuropsychological tests.

Discussion

Executive dysfunction in alcoholics

Executive functions in the Japanese alcoholics in this study were impaired as demonstrated by the depressed BADS scores. Previous studies have demonstrated various types of frontal lobe or executive dysfunction in chronic alcoholics, which included deficits in abstract reasoning, set shifting and set persistence (Tarter, 1973), word fluency (Hewett, Nixon, Glenn, & Parsons, 1991), allocating attentional resources for information processing (Smith & Oscar-Berman, 1992), capacity to temporally organize, sequence, and sustain goal-directed behaviour (Alterman, Tarter, Petrarulo, & Baughman, 1984; Cynn, 1992), problem solving (Beatty, Katzung, Nixon, & Moreland, 1993), working memory (Zhang et al., 1997), and decision making (Bechara et al., 2001). These cognitive functions are very related to the executive function (Trannel et al., 1994; Giancola & Moss, 1998). The results of this study are in concord with these previous findings.

More specifically, the results in this study were suggestive of deficits in cognitive flexibility (rule shift cards), planning (zoo map and modified six elements), sequential behaviour and ability to use feedback (zoo map), and the ability to divide attention (modified six elements). These results are consistent with findings reported in English patients by Ihara et al. (2000).

The BADS has been reported to be useful in detecting executive dysfunction in various types of diseases, such as focal frontal damage, closed head injury, and schizophrenia (Evans et al., 1997). Our results together with those of Ihara et al. (2000) suggest further usefulness in detecting executive dysfunction in alcoholics.

In this study, alcoholics were also impaired in the trail making B and the symbol digit modalities. These tasks have also been reported as being sensitive in detecting chronic alcoholics' cognitive dysfunction (Beatty, Tivis, Stott, Nixon, & Parsons, 2000). Impairment in these tasks may also suggest executive dysfunction of alcoholics.

Relationship between executive dysfunction and functional outcome

A major question addressed by the present study was whether executive dysfunction, as evidenced by low BADS scores, relates to functional outcomes in alcoholics. The results of this study suggest that executive dysfunction predicts alcohol-non-specific social functioning (occupation) but not alcohol-specific drinking outcome. Regarding the result of alcohol-specific outcome, Giancola and Moss (1998) suggested a heuristic alcohol addiction model and hypothesized that impaired executive function (higher-level cognitive ability) may result in stereotypic and overlearned, alcohol-taking behaviours. In the present study, however, scores on the BADS didn't predict alcoholics' drinking outcome. One possible explanation is that drinking reflects relatively simple and fundamental functions, such as risk avoidance or motivation, rather than the learning of complicated problem-solving or coping skills (Morgenstern & Bates, 1999).

In contrast, alcohol-non-specific outcome (occupation) was related to executive function. Hanks, Rapport, Millis, and Deshpande (1999) reported that executive function in patients with traumatic brain injury predicts functional outcome. They emphasized that higher-level cognitive abilities, such as cognitive flexibility, appear to be important for successful social behaviours, including return to work. This suggestion can also apply to an alcoholic's occupational outcome. Two subtests of BADS, i.e., the temporal judgement and the zoo map were most effective in discriminating job status of alcoholics. One may argue that among multiple components of executive functioning, sensible judgement with reasonable estimation and appropriate use of feedback may contribute to successful employment. However, we should be cautious about concluding that the other four subtests are insensitive since the sample size of the patients was small.

The BADS total profile score had more significant, discriminative power in predicting occupational outcome than a similar executive task, such as trail making B. An advantage of BADS in predicting social outcome may be accounted for by Cripe's (1996) argument that multicomponent neuropsychological impairment indices, rather than performance decrements on any one test, are more predictive. Alternatively, the BADS may have ecological validity, which contributes to predicting alcoholics' occupational outcome.

Limitations of this study include the little attention paid to economic status. Recently, Japan has experienced a severe depression of economic status, and the unemployment rate has been increasing. We cannot neglect these economic and social situations, because they could have an influence on occupational outcomes in alcoholics although we did not notice any patients whose occupation was directly affected by this socioeconomic problem. We should also note that other factors that have been known to affect outcome in alcoholism, include typology, motivation for abstinence, the complications of depression or physical illness, and general psychosocial dysfunction (Abbott & Gregson, 1981; Morgenstern & Bates, 1999). Another weakness is that the present study regarded part-time employment as occupation (–). It will be interesting to compare full-time and part-time workers in further research. Future studies are warranted to better define the interrelationship between the factors mentioned above.

In conclusion, executive dysfunction in alcoholics evaluated by the BADS was indicative of alcohol-non-specific outcome (occupation). However, executive dysfunction was not indicative of alcohol-specific outcome, such as drinking behaviour. In addition, the BADS total profile score predicts future functional recovery better than other neuropsychological tasks.

Study 2: Social prognosis of alcoholic Korsakoff amnesics and executive dysfunction

Study 2 focused on the relation between long-term social outcome and neuropsychological performance of alcoholic Korsakoff amnesics. In the course of the development of alcoholic Korsakoff syndrome three main stages emerge. Usually patients manifest abrupt initial symptoms of Wernicke's encephalopathy or delirium tremens at the acute phase. In the subsequent subacute phase patients still present with mild attentional deficits and impaired intelligence together with dense amnesia. Confabulations remain prominent. At the chronic stage approximately 6 to 12 months from onset, Korsakoff patients' attention and general intelligence are relatively well recovered while their dense amnesia persists and becomes stabilized. However, only a little is known about the further prognosis of Korsakoff amnesic syndrome. Specifically, it is not clear whether their cognitive functions subsequently deteriorate, remain unchanged or gradually show improvement but not perfect recovery (Figure 12.1). Kato and Yoshino (1994) divided alcoholic dementia into two types of clinically diagnosed subgroups; acute onset (> 3 months) and chronic onset (≤ 3 months). They believed that patients with acute onset Korsakoff syndrome have a prognosis that is poorer than those with chronic onset. Amnesia and frontal dysfunction of the acute onset subgroup appear to remain unchanged for a long period whereas such cognitive impairment in the chronic subgroup may gradually show improvement.

From the neuropsychological and social point of view, an important question concerns the effect of cognitive dysfunction upon social prognosis. Blansjaar, Takens, and Zwinderman (1992) performed a follow-up investigation on the intellectual functions of Korsakoff amnesics 3 years after discharge. They reported that patients who entered a nursing home showed deterioration of intelligence whereas those who were transferred to a small-scale shelter showed some improvement. Their findings suggest that social and environmental factors influence future cognitive functions. Alternatively,

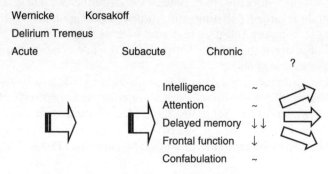

Figure 12.1 Time course of alcoholic Korsakoff amnesics.

Korsakoff amnesics may consist of heterogeneous subgroups of different social functioning and cognitive potentials.

What kind of cognitive impairment, then, determines Korsakoff patients' social prognosis? In other words, is it possible to predict their social prognosis from an initial neuropsychological profile? In this context, we studied social functions of 26 patients with Korsakoff syndrome at a mean of 81.9 months from onset (Mimura, 2000). Social prognosis of Korsakoff patients as indexed by place of abode and job status appeared poorer than our amnesic patients with other aetiologies (including herpetic and non-herpetic encephalitis, ruptured aneurysm of the anterior communicating artery, head injury, and cerebral infarction) and amnesic patients reported by Wilson (1991). Compared to amnesic subjects with other aetiologies, Korsakoff patients showed a far less promising social outcome (Table 12.3). The combination of amnesia and frontal dysfunction may account for their poor prognoses. As noted above, Korsakoff patients may have variable future social prognoses. Study 2 attempted to further clarify cognitive factors that may predict future social prognosis of Korsakoff amnesics. This is of great importance when we consider cognitive rehabilitation to ameliorate their quality of life. Details of Study 2 have been published elsewhere (Mimura & Moriyama, 2002).

Methods

Subjects

Fifteen Korsakoff amnesic patients (mean age = 54.2 ± 9.1 years; mean length of education = 12.6 ± 2.7 years) who had been hospitalized in the Alcohol Treatment Unit at Komagino Hospital, Tokyo, Japan, were included

Table 12.3 Social prognosis of alcoholic Korsakoff syndrome, amnesics with other aetiologies and amnesic patients reported by Wilson (1991) (Mimura, 2000, with modification)

	Korsakoff		Other aetiologies		Wilson (1991)	
	n = 26	(%)	*n* = 20	(%)	*n* = 51	(%)
Place of abode						
Living alone	2	7.7	2	10.0	10	19.6
Living with others	10	38.5	13	65.0	25	49.0
Institutionalized	2	7.7	2	10.0	9	17.6
Open ward	4	15.4	1	5.0	0	0
Closed ward	5	19.2	2	10.0	0	0
Dead	3	11.5	0	0	7	13.7
Job						
(+)	3	13.0	5	25.0	15	34.1
(−)	20	87.0	15	75.0	29	65.9

in this study. All the patients initially had Wernicke's encephalopathy or delirium tremens and were in a chronic and stable condition at the time of the study. They showed severe anterograde amnesia with a variable degree of retrograde amnesia. Those who had a history of liver cirrhosis, diabetes mellitus, coronary artery disease, cerebrovascular disease, or head injury were excluded from the study. Patients with a history of other drug dependence or major psychiatric illness were also excluded. In addition, subjects whose full-scale IQ scored less than 80 were excluded in order to rule out dementia.

Neuropsychological tests and outcome assessment

Neuropsychological assessment was performed at a mean of 16.3 months from the onset of Wernicke's encephalopathy or delirium tremens. The patients underwent the WAIS-R, Wechsler Memory Scale – Revised (WMS-R; Wechsler, 1987), modified version of the Wisconsin Card Sorting Test (WCST; Kato, 1988), modified Stroop test (Kato, 1988) and word fluency.

The follow-up assessment on outcome was performed at approximately 7 years (mean = 86.8 months) after the onset. All the patients were interviewed at the out-patient clinic or by telephone about their place of abode and vocational status. Based on this outcome assessment, 8 patients were assigned to a poor prognosis group (5 patients remained hospitalized, 1 had transferred to another institution, 2 had died) whereas 7 patients who had been discharged home were assigned to a good prognosis group. None of the participants returned to an active (full-time) job.

Performances of the good and poor prognosis groups on the neuropsychological tests were compared. Statistical analyses were conducted using unpaired *t*-tests.

Results

The results of neuropsychological performance of the good and poor prognosis groups are shown in Table 12.4. There were no differences observed in intelligence scores. Verbal and visual memory scores were also equivalent in the two groups. In terms of frontal functions, there were no group differences in word fluency and modified Stroop tests, but the performance of WCST was lower in the poor prognosis group as compared to the good prognosis group.

Discussion

Overall social prognosis of Korsakoff patients was extremely poor as indexed by the place of abode and job status. The results were in line with our previous findings (Mimura, 2000). Most of the Korsakoff patients remained hospitalized or institutionalized and none of the patients in the present study returned to an active job.

Neuropsychological examination disclosed that general intelligence and

Table 12.4 Results of neuropsychological tests of good prognosis and poor prognosis patients with Korsakoff syndrome (Mimura & Moriyama, 2002)

		Prognosis	
		Good	*Poor*
WAIS-R	VIQ	96.1 ± 10.1	92.3 ± 13.8
	PIQ	86.0 ± 11.1	93.9 ± 13.2
	TIQ	92.8 ± 14.3	93.3 ± 14.1
WMS-R	Verbal	60.8 ± 60.8	63.4 ± 6.4
	Visual	78.5 ± 12.5	81.4 ± 9.7
	General	57.5 ± 8.5	66.1 ± 9.6
	Attention/ concentration	90.6 ± 15.2	88.7 ± 10.6
	Delayed recall	59.5 ± 8.3	63.3 ± 10.0
WCST	Categories	3.1 ± 1.6	1.6 ± 1.1*
	Perseveration	8.3 ± 6.0	10.3 ± 8.2
Word fluency	3 Initials	18.5 ± 6.1	18.6 ± 4.2
	3 Categories	21.5 ± 5.1	25.3 ± 6.0
Stroop (s)	Part III–Part I	15.8 ± 6.8	20.4 ± 11.8

* $p < .05$.

attention were equivalently well preserved for both good and poor prognosis groups. Dense amnesia was also a common feature for both groups. Differences between the good and poor prognosis groups emerged in frontal and executive functions. The results of Study 2 suggest that frontal function as indexed by WCST relates to social prognosis. Wilson et al. (1996) studied the long-term prognosis of memory-impaired individuals and found that the absence of executive dysfunction was one of the factors indicating good prognosis. Our results are consistent with the proposal by Wilson et al. (1996). Specifically, Hanks et al. (1999) and Leblanc, Hayden, and Paulman (2000) indicated that WCST scores in the subacute phase may predict future social prognosis. Our results appear to support their findings.

Two reasons could be postulated for frontal impairment by Korsakoff syndrome leading to poor social prognosis. First, frontal impairment per se may relate to poor social functioning. Second, frontal impairment may interfere with compensating activities for memory problems. From the perspective of memory rehabilitation, frontal and executive dysfunction frequently interrupt the utilization of external memory aids such as a notebook or an alarm. Other frontal-related memory activities include prospective memory. Prospective memory refers to timely recall of predetermined and intended actions (e.g., taking medication, feeding a pet) and is well known to play a crucial role in daily activities of healthy populations and amnesic subjects as well. We demonstrated that Korsakoff amnesics and patients with Alzheimer's disease have qualitatively dissociable patterns of impairment in prospective memory (Umeda, Kato, Mimura, Kashima, & Koyazu, 2000). Severe amnesic patients including Korsakoff amnesics rarely benefit from internal mnemonic techniques. Accordingly, from the perspective of daily activities, it is of great importance for Korsakoff patients to ensure the success of future plans and actions by actively using external memory aids (Figure 12.2).

Study 3: Case presentation of Korsakoff amnesic patient

Study 2 clarified that a considerable number of patients with Korsakoff syndrome remain hospitalized even after a long period. In Study 3, I briefly describe a typical patient with poor prognosis. Clinical manifestations in this particular patient demonstrated difficulties of intervention strategies regarding social recovery in severely amnesic populations.

Case report

KI was a 68-year-old medical practitioner who had been healthy until 1995 except for extensive alcohol abuse. He had an abrupt onset of conscious disturbance on 19 January 1995. Subsequent symptoms of Wernicke's encephalopathy included disorientation and ataxia together with marked spontaneous confabulation. His extraordinary spontaneous confabulation persisted throughout the initial and subacute stage and was characterized by its fantastic and grandiose features. He claimed that he was currently working as a ship's doctor. He also considered that he was a professional baseball player. Although he was hospitalized on a mountainside in the greater Tokyo area, he believed that he was on a southern island. He said, "I now stay in this island as a doctor. You see a port over there. My ship came here from Taiwan and will move to Southeast Asia soon." "I am also a professional baseball

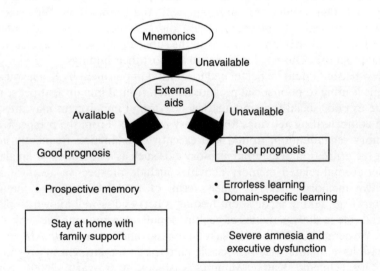

Figure 12.2 Framework of cognitive rehabilitation for patients with Korsakoff syndrome.

player. When I stop at a port, I play baseball." "The last time I played base-ball was last summer. Ichiro is my teammate." Although he had worked as a medical practitioner, he had never worked as a ship's doctor. He was very fond of watching baseball games and was a fan of Osaka Hankyu Braves, a professional baseball team in the Kansai district. The Hankyu Braves were later renamed Orix Blue Wave, which is where Ichiro played before he moved to the Seattle Mariners. KI's spontaneous and fantastic confabulation grad-ually lessened and ceased in a year.

Neuropsychological evaluation was performed twice: T1 approximately one year after the onset; and T2 at approximately 7 years post onset. Table 12.5 shows longitudinal changes in his neuropsychological perform-ances. His cognitive status appeared to be quite stabilized and there were no remarkable changes observed. Intelligence and attention were well preserved from the beginning. In contrast, neuropsychological examination demon-strated severe anterograde memory loss together with frontal impairment, which did not show any improvement. Although he granted that he had memory problems, he did not take it seriously. Retrograde memory loss was also prominent. Figure 12.3 indicates KI's performance on a standard remote memory questionnaire devised by Kopelman, Wilson, and Baddeley (1989) and Yoshimasu et al. (1998).

KI had been an enthusiastic fan of Takarazuka Revue since he was a teenager. Takarazuka Revue was founded in 1913 and the company became popular enough to get its own theatre by 1924. Takarazuka is famous for presenting song-and-dance shows featuring female actresses only. The com-pany had four troupes until recently: Hana; Tsuki; Hoshi; and Yuki (Flower, Moon, Star, and Snow) and each troupe had its top star actresses who played

Table 12.5 Neuropsychological performance of case KI

		T1	T2
WAIS-R	VIQ	108	111
	PIQ	98	100
WMS-R	Verbal	67	70
	Visual	85	83
	General	74	72
	Attention/concentration	101	104
	Delayed recall	62	71
RAVLT	Immediate recall	4–5–4–4–4	5–6–6–7–4
ROCFT	Copy	36/36	36/36
ROCFT	Delayed recall	7/36	9/36
WCST	Categories	0	1
	Perseveration	17	13
Word fluency	3 Initials	15	13
	3 Categories	15	20
Stroop (s)	Part III–Part I	33	25

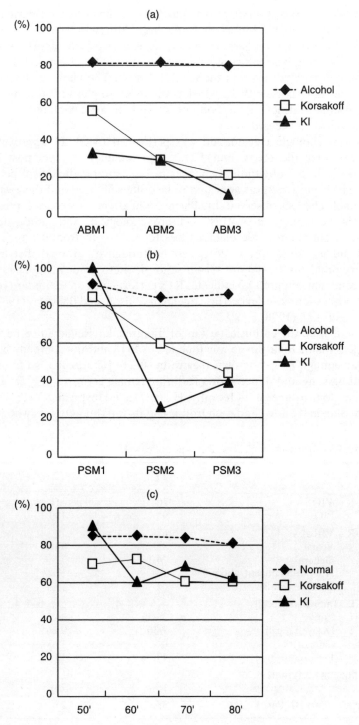

Figure 12.3 Retrograde amnesia of KI (a) autobiographical memory, (b) personal semantic memory, and (c) memory of public events.

the male parts (otokoyaku) and female parts (musumeyaku). Although KI enjoyed watching Takarazuka performances until the onset of Wernicke's encephalopathy, he was unable to recall the names of any top stars from the 1990s. When he was presented with a picture of recent top stars (Figure 12.4) he could not recall anyone's name. Interestingly enough, when KI was presented with a picture of top stars from the 1950s, he correctly named all of the stars in the picture (Figure 12.5). This suggests that he had severe

Figure 12.4 Takarazuka top stars in the 1990s.

Figure 12.5 Takarazuka top stars in the 1950s.

retrograde amnesia with a temporal gradient even in domain-specific know-ledge. To confirm this hypothesis, KI was systematically questioned about names, works and episodes concerning Takarazuka actresses from three different generations (1918–1945, 1946–1970, 1971–1995). The results demonstrated a steep temporal gradient in that semantic knowledge was completely extinguished regarding recent top actresses (1970 and thereafter) in contrast to highly intact knowledge regarding actresses appearing before 1945 (Figure 12.6). Such a temporal gradient in specific semantic knowledge has been reported by Verfaellie, Reiss, and Roth (1995). Although KI was willing to answer questions about old stars by looking at old bromides, he admitted that he was not interested in Takarazuka any more. Accordingly, it was natural that he was unable to answer any questions concerning top stars in the post-morbid decade.

Although KI required intensive daily health care and support, he lived happily and had no serious medical problems or complaints. He was unaware of his memory problems and was not motivated by any rehabilitation pro-grammes for his amnesia. He remained hospitalized even 7 years after onset and was unable to use any memory compensation techniques. Since he lived under limited and protected circumstances he did not need to use any form of memory compensation.

Discussion

As demonstrated by Study 2, those patients who remained hospitalized many years after onset had a relatively homogeneous profile from the perspective of neuropsychological performances. Although attention and intelligence were well preserved even after 7 years, memory and frontal executive functions

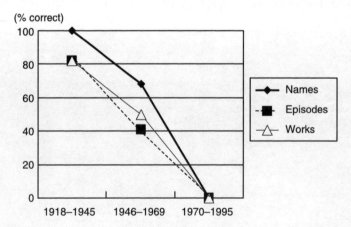

Figure 12.6 A steep temporal gradient observed in KI's semantic knowledge. Extin-guished information regarding recent top actresses (1970 and thereafter) in contract to highly intact information regarding actresses appearing before 1945.

were severely impaired and did not show any change over time. The clinical manifestations of KI depict several pathological features of chronic Korsakoff syndrome. Only rehabilitation approaches for severe memory deficits may benefit such treatment-resistant patients.

Cognitive intervention techniques for densely amnesic patients include domain-specific learning (Schacter & Glisky, 1986) and errorless learning technique (Baddeley & Wilson, 1994). Domain-specific learning implies that even amnesic subjects can learn some restricted knowledge by repetitive training and that acquisition of such necessary information may lessen their cognitive and behavioural disturbances. Along this line, we reported the effectiveness of acquiring domain-specific knowledge in Korsakoff amnesics by teaching them face–name associations of the ward staff (Yoshimasu et al., 1996). Errorless learning implies that eliminating errors optimizes memory rehabilitation since densely amnesic patients are unable to learn from trial and error situations. Errorless learning is not a specific single procedure. Rather, it should be viewed as a guiding principle that includes various different possible techniques. We confirmed the effectiveness of errorless learning in Korsakoff amnesics and also indicated that not only errorless but also effortful processes may optimize memory rehabilitation (Komatsu, Mimura, Kato, Wakamatsu, & Kashima 2000).

In the Alcohol Treatment Unit at Komagino Hospital, Tokyo, we have a weekly session of the Korsakoff Rehabilitation Program in which various approaches have been pursued. These approaches include utilization of preserved action memory (Mimura et al., 1998), utilization of preserved implicit memory (Komatsu, Mimura, Kato, & Kashima 2003), effective errorless learning (Komatsu et al., 2000), and effective domain-specific learning (Yoshimasu et al., 1996). Although memory rehabilitation has been established as effective and recommended for mildly amnesic patients after head injury (Cinerone et al., 2000), the use of this approach for severe amnesic patients is far from evidence-based. However, clinical researchers on memory disorders should keep in mind that patients in the most severe conditions, i.e., dense amnesia with executive dysfunction and severe metamemory problems, are those who need appropriate intervention the most. Further research is warranted to ameliorate deficits in the most severely impaired populations.

General conclusions

Prognoses of alcoholics and alcoholic Korsakoff amnesics were examined, focusing on different aspects of memory and executive function. Study 1 demonstrated that alcoholics' performance on BADS predicted alcohol-non-specific (occupation) outcomes but not alcohol-specific (drinking) outcomes. Study 2 suggested that patients with Korsakoff syndrome in general have poor social outcomes. Cognitive functions in domains including memory, intelligence and attention were equivalent in the poor prognosis and good prognosis groups. In contrast, frontal and executive impairment as indexed by WCST performance showed slight differences. Initial WCST scores in the poor prognosis group were lower than those in the good prognosis group. Korsakoff patients remaining hospitalized for long periods only infrequently use memory compensation and are rarely motivated to improve their memory. The patient KI described in Study 3 depicted such a treatment-resistant case. Executive dysfunctions play a crucial role in the prognoses of patients with alcohol-related problems.

References

Abbott, M. W., & Gregson, R. A. W. (1981). Cognitive dysfunction in the prediction of relapse in alcoholics. *Journal of Studies on Alcohol, 42*, 230–243.

Alterman, A. I., Tarter, R. E., Petrarulo, E. W., & Baughman, T. G. (1984). Evidence for impersistence in young male alcoholics. *Alcoholism: Clinical and Experimental Research, 8*, 448–450.

Baddeley, A., & Wilson, B. A. (1994). When implicit learning fails: Amnesia and the problem of error elimination. *Neuropsychologia, 32*, 53–68.

Beatty, W. W., Katzung, V. M., Nixon, S. J., & Moreland, V. J. (1993). Problem-solving deficits in alcoholics: Evidence from the California card sorting test. *Journal of Studies on Alcohol, 54*, 687–692.

Beatty, W. W., Tivis, R., Stott, H. D., Nixon, S. J., & Parsons, O. A. (2000). Neuro-psychological deficits in sober alcoholics: Influences of chronicity and recent alcohol consumption. *Alcoholism: Clinical and Experimental Research, 24*, 149–154.

Bechara, A., Dolan, S., Denburg, N., Hindes, A., Anderson, S. W., & Nathan, P. E. (2001). Decision-making deficits, linked to a dysfunctional ventromedial prefrontal cortex, revealed in alcohol and stimulant abusers. *Neuropsychologia, 39*, 379–389.

Blansjaar, B. A., Takens, H., & Zwinderman, A. H. (1992). The course of alcohol amnesic disorder: A three-year follow-up study of clinical signs and social disabilities. *Acta Psychiatrica Scandinavica, 86*, 240–246.

Cicerone, K. D., Dahlberg, C., Kalmar, K., Lanenbahn, D. M., Malec, J. F., Bergquist, T. F., Felicetti, T., Giacino, J. T., Harley, J. P., Harrington, D. E., Herzog, J., Kneipp, S., Laatsch, L., & Morse, P. A. (2000). Evidence-based cognitive rehabilitation: Recommendations for clinical practice. *Archives of Physical Medicine and Rehabilitation, 81*, 1596–1615.

Cripe, L. I. (1996). The ecological validity of executive function testing. In R. J. Sbordone & C. J. Long (Eds.), *Ecologically Validity of Neuropsychological Testing* (pp. 171–202). New York: St Lucie Press.

Cynn, V. (1992). Persistence and problem-solving skills in young male alcoholics. *Journal of Studies on Alcohol, 53*, 57–62.

Donovan, D. M., Kivlahan, D. R., & Walker, R. D. (1984). Clinical limitations of neuropsychological testing in predicting treatment outcome among alcoholics. *Alcoholism: Clinical and Experimental Research, 8*, 470–475.

Evans, J. J., Chua, S. E., McKenna, P. J., & Wilson, B. A. (1997). Assessment of the dysexecutive syndrome in schizophrenia. *Psychological Medicine, 27*, 635–646.

Giancola, P. R., & Moss, H. B. (1998). Executive cognitive functioning in alcohol use disorders. *Recent Developments in Alcoholism, 14*, 227–251.

Hanks, R. A., Rapport, L. J., Millis, S. R., & Deshpande, R. A. (1999). Measures of executive functioning as predictors of functional ability and social integration in a rehabilitation sample. *Archives of Physical Medicine and Rehabilitation, 80,* 1030–1037.

Hewett, L. J., Nixon, S. J., Glenn, S. W., & Parsons, O. A. (1991). Verbal fluency deficits in female alcoholics. *Journal of Clinical Psychology, 47,* 716–719.

Ihara, H., Berrios, G. E., & London, M. (2000). Group and case study of the dysexecutive syndrome in alcoholism without amnesia. *Journal of Neurology Neurosurgery and Psychiatry, 68,* 731–737.

Kato, M. (1988). A study on the concept formation and shift of the patients with frontal lesions: A neuropsychological investigation by the new modified Wisconsin card sorting test. *Keio Journal of Medicine, 65,* 861–885. (in Japanese)

Kato, A., Kato, M., Ishii, H., Ichimiya, Y., Suzuki, K., Kawasaki, H., Yamamoto, S. I., Kumashiro, R., Yamamoto, K., Kawamura, N., Hayashi, N., Matsuzaki, S., Terano, A., Okita, K., & Watanabe, A. (2004). Development of quantitative neuropsychological tests for diagnosis of subclinical hepatic encephalopathy in liver cirrhosis patients and establishment of diagnostic criteria – multicentre collaborative study. *Hepatology Research, 30,* 71–78. (in Japanese)

Kato, M., & Yoshino, A. (1994). Effect of clinical typology and neuropsychological deficits on prognosis of chronic alcoholism. *Research Reports on Pathogenesis and Treatment of Alcohol Dependence* (pp. 45–56). Tokyo: Ministry of Health and Welfare. (in Japanese)

Komatsu, S., Mimura, M., Kato, M., & Kashima, H. (2003). Cross-script and within-script priming in alcoholic Korsakoff patients. *Perceptual and Motor Skills, 96,* 495–509.

Komatsu, S., Mimura, M., Kato, M., Wakamatsu, N., & Kashima, H. (2000). Errorless and effortful processes involved in the learning of face–name associations by patients with alcoholic Korsakoff's syndrome. *Neuropsychological Rehabilitation, 10,* 113–132.

Kopelman, M. D. (1995). The Korsakoff syndrome. *British Journal of Psychiatry, 166,* 154–173.

Kopelman, M. D., Wilson, B. A., & Baddeley, A. D. (1989). The autobiographical memory interview: A new assessment of autobiographical and personal semantic memory in amnesic patients. *Journal of Clinical and Experimental Neuropsychology, 11,* 724–744.

Leblanc, J. M., Hayden, M. E., & Paulman, R. G. (2000). A comparison of neuropsychological and situational assessment for predicting employability after closed head injury. *Journal of Head and Trauma Rehabilitation, 15,* 1022–1040.

Mimura, M. (2000). Rehabilitation for memory impairment and long-term prognosis. *Japanese Journal of Rehabilitation Medicine, 37,* 154–158. (in Japanese)

Mimura, M., Komatsu, S., Kato, M., Yoshimasu, H., Wakamatsu, N., & Kashima, H. (1998). Memory for subject performed tasks in patients with Korsakoff syndrome. *Cortex, 34,* 297–303.

Mimura, M., & Moriyama, Y. (2002). Chronic state of Wernicke–Korsakoff syndrome and strategy for its treatment. *Japanese Journal of Psychiatric Research on Alcohol, 9,* 25–31.

Morgenstern, J., & Bates, M. E. (1999). Effects of executive function impairment on change processes and substance use outcomes in 12-step treatment. *Journal of Studies on Alcohol, 59,* 846–855.

Moriyama, Y., Mimura, M., Kato, M., Yoshino, A., Hara, T., Kashima, H., Kato, A.,

& Watanabe, A. (2002). Executive dysfunction and clinical outcome in chronic alcoholics. *Alcoholism: Clinical and Experimental Research, 26*, 1239–1244.

Reitan, R. (1956). *Trail making test: Manual for administration, scoring, and interpretation*. Bloomington, IN: Indiana University.

Schacter, D. L., & Glisky, E. L. (1986). Memory remediation: Restoration, alleviation, and acquisition of domain-specific knowledge. In B. Uzzell & Y. Gross (Eds.), *Clinical neuropsychology of intervention* (pp. 257–282). Boston, MA: Martinus Nijhoff.

Smith, A. (1973). *Symbol digit modalities test. Manual*. Los Angeles, CA: Western Psychological Services.

Smith, M. E., & Oscar-Berman, M. (1992). Resource-limited information processing in alcoholism. *Journal of Studies on Alcohol, 53*, 514–518.

Spitzer, R. L., Williams, J. B. W., Gibbon, M., & First, M. B. (1990). *Structured clinical interview for DSM-III-R (SCID): User's guide*. Washington, DC: American Psychiatric Press, Inc.

Tarter, R. E. (1973). An analysis of cognitive deficits in chronic alcoholics. *Journal of Nervous and Mental Disease, 157*, 138–147.

Trannel, D., Anderson, S. W., & Benton, A. (1994). Development of the concept of executive function and its relationship to the frontal lobes. In F. Boller & J. Grafman (eds.), *Handbook of neuropsychology*, (Vol. 9, pp. 125–148). New York: Elsevier.

Umeda, S., Kato, M., Mimura, M., Kashima, H., & Koyazu, T. (2000). Prospective memory in patients with Korsakoff syndrome. *Japanese Journal of Neuropsychology, 16*, 193–199. (in Japanese)

Verfaellie, M., Reiss, L., & Roth, H. L. (1995). Knowledge of new English vocabulary in amnesia: An examination of premorbidly acquired semantic memory. *Journal of International Neuropsychological Society, 1*, 443–453.

Victor, M., Adams, R. D., & Collins, G. H. (1989). *The Wernicke–Korsakoff syndrome and related neurologic disorders due to alcoholism and malnutrition* (2nd ed.). Philadelphia, PA: FA Davis.

Wechsler, D. (1981). *WAIS-R manual: Wechsler adult intelligence scale–revised*. New York: Harcourt Brace and Jovanovich.

Wechsler, D. (1987). *Wechsler memory scale–revised manual*. San Antonio, TX: Psychological Corporation.

Wilson, B. A. (1991). Long-term prognosis of patients with severe memory disorders. *Neuropsychological Rehabilitation, 1*, 117–134.

Wilson, B. A., Alderman, N., Burgess, P. W., Emslie, H., & Evans, J. J. (1996). *Behavioural assessment of the dysexecutive syndrome*. Bury St Edmunds, UK: Thames Valley Test Company.

Yoshimasu, H., Kato, M., Mimura, M., Wakamatsu, N., Saito, F., Kashima, H., & Asai, M. (1998). Neuropsychological assessment of remote memory. *Higher Brain Function Research, 18*, 205–214. (in Japanese)

Yoshimasu, H., Kato, M., Mimura, M., Wakamatsu, N., Yoshino, A., Tatsuzawa, Y., Hara, T., Kashima, H., & Asai, M. (1996). Cognitive rehabilitation for Korsakoff's syndrome: Acquisition of domain-specific knowledge through face–name association. *Japanese Journal of Psychiatric Treatment, 11*, 833–838. (in Japanese)

Yoshino, A., & Kato, M. (1996). Prediction of 3-year outcome of treated alcoholics by an empirically derived multivariate typology. *American Journal of Psychiatry, 153*, 829–830.

Zhang, X. L., Begleiter, H., & Porjesz, B. (1997). Is working memory intact in alcoholics? An ERP study. *Psychiatry Research, 75*, 75–89.

13 Memory failures and their causes in everyday life

Douglas Herrmann, Michael M. Gruneberg, Steve Fiore, Jonathan W. Schooler and Rebecca Torres

Basic memory research has extensively investigated memory failures in the laboratory. This research has shown that memory failures may be attributed to: the difficulty of the memory task; the environmental causes that dispose a person to fail while performing the task; individual differences in approaches to memory tasks; and individual differences in processing tasks and causes. Nevertheless, memory tasks in everyday life often differ from the tasks used in basic research, making it necessary to find ways to extend basic theory to the performance of such tasks (Davies & Logie, 1993).

Causes of memory phenomena are best established experimentally. However, experiments in the field often change the phenomena being measured, requiring the use of a non-experimental procedure to investigate memory failure and their causes. Thus, we investigated memory failures and their causes in everyday life by asking people to recall some of their memory failures and to indicate what they thought were the causes of those failures. This paradigm was first reported by Colgrove (1899). When participants perform this task, they typically describe a failure in one to several sentences and report the causes in a few short sentences or words (Brown, 2002; Herrmann & Gruneberg, 1999; Terry, 1984; Williams & Gruneberg, 2002). The *failure/cause recall* paradigm allows researchers to identify the causes of memory failure much in the same way that investigators determine the causes of automobile, airplane, and industrial accidents (Perrow, 1984).

It is important to note that the failure/cause recall paradigm differs from memory questionnaires, which have generally shown poor memory for memory performance (Cavanaugh, Feldman, & Hertzog, 1998; Herrmann, 1982, 1984, 1990; Hertzog, Park, Morrell, & Martin, 2000). The failure/cause recall procedure asks a participant to recall a particular memory failure that comes to mind, generally without any restriction on the nature of the memory failure. In contrast, the memory questionnaire asks a participant about the frequency or proportion of failures out of many or all attempts at a certain kind of memory task. Thus, the failure/cause recall paradigm evaluates whether people may know a lot about certain memory failures in their past regardless of having poor recollection of memory failures in general as assessed by memory questionnaires. Table 13.1 presents some examples of the memory failure and causes reported by participants in our research.

Purpose

The present research sought to identify the causes of everyday memory failure through an investigation of memory failure/cause recall. First, the frequency of memory failures was investigated as a function of the orientation of the failed memory task, i.e., prospective or retrospective (Andrzejewski, Moore, Corvette, & Herrmann, 1991; Baddeley, 1990; Brandimonte, Einstein, & McDaniel, 1995; Harris, 1984). Orientation of a failed task, retrospective or prospective, might be expected to influence the likelihood of memory failure for a number of reasons. People may recall more retrospective errors than prospective errors because a person presumably retains more retrospective memories than prospective memories. Retrospective memories are held for a long time, sometimes a lifetime, whereas prospective intentions are usually held in memory until the intended task is carried out. Alternatively, people might be expected to recall more prospective memories than retrospective memories because prospective memories are more recent and closer to consciousness than retrospective memories. Also many prospective memory failures may be regarded as more embarrassing, and therefore better encoded, than memories of events past.

Second, the research examined how often a memory failure was

Table 13.1 Examples of memory failures and cause recall in everyday life

---

Forgot his departure day
Description of the memory failure – "My wife and I arrived at the airport a day early."
Causes of this memory failure – "My wife was confident of the date and I thought she knew. I did not ask her to check or I did not check myself." [Prospective, Commission]

Forgot his coat
Description of the memory failure. – "I gave a lecture on memory improvement. When I left to go home, I forgot to take my coat."
Causes of this memory failure – "I hung my coat behind a door; later door was pushed back so coat was out of view; the weather became unseasonably warm by midday so I did not need my coat." [Prospective, Omission]

Misrecognized one person as another
Description of the memory failure – "I passed a person in the hall who looked very similar to another person and I called her by the wrong name."
Causes of this memory failure – "I became inclined to call this person by the wrong name because of the similarity in appearance and because I was thinking of the other person at the time." [Retrospective, Commission]

Failed to recognize his mother on the train
Description of the memory failure – "I understood that my mother would not be within 200 miles of my train ride."
Causes of this memory failure – "I did not expect my mother to be on that train. Also the train was crowded." [Retrospective, Omission]

---

characterized by one of two types of error, i.e., an error of omission (failing to remember) or commission (remembering incorrectly). One error type (either an error of omission or an error of commission) might be expected to produce more memory failures than the other error type for various reasons (Reason, 1988). For example, it might be expected that errors of commission would be reported more than errors of omission because errors of commission – overt acts – would be remembered better than errors of omission. People may not remember errors of omission because they may not know that they made an error whereas people know when they make an error of commission because it captures attention as a response is initiated. Alternatively, errors of omission might be reported more often than errors of commission because people avoid errors of commission so that others will not know their fallibility. Table 13.1 presents the orientation and error type of the four memory failures mentioned above.

Cause characteristics

The present research examines several aspects of the possible causes of memory failure as reported by participants. First, the research assessed whether participants report that an everyday memory failure is produced by just a few causes or many causes. Second, the research examined whether different kinds of memory failures are produced by the same causes or different causes. Third, the research evaluated the relative influence on memory failure of causes that act either directly or indirectly on the memory system (Bendiksen & Bendiksen, 1992, 1996; Herrmann & Plude, 1996; Herrmann, Plude, Yoder, & Mullin, 1999; Herrmann & Parente, 1994; Johnson, 1983; Parente & Herrmann, 2003; see also Broadbent, Broadbent, & Jones, 1986; Broadbent, Cooper, Fitzgerald, & Parkes, 1982). For example, direct causes include: insufficient encoding procedures, long retention interval, misguided retrieval attempts with poor cues, doing too many things at once, being preoccupied during input or output. Causes that act indirectly on the memory system affect either a person's physical or emotional state, such as stress, fatigue, or lack of sleep (Reason, 1984, 1988, 1990).

Two investigations are reported in this chapter. They addressed the proportion of memory failures according to task orientation, the type of error made, and various aspects of the causes as reported by participants. Because the procedure and measures were the same in both investigations, the results can be compared across investigations in order to determine the reliability of memory failures and causes. In addition, the results of the second investigation are broken down according to individual differences in order to determine whether a person's knowledge of memory research affects the causes that he or she recalls for memory failures.

Table 13.2 Investigations 1 and 2. Percentage of failures made to prospective and retrospective tasks, error type, directness of cause sets, and cause set size

	P	R	Om	Com	i	m	d	1	2	3	4	5	6
Investigation 1	57.8*	42.2	84.4*	15.6	17.8	46.7	35.5	20.0	31.1	22.2	17.7	11.1	4.4
Investigation 2	59.3*	40.7	88.0	12.0	15.3*	23.5	61.2	49.8*	34.9	12.9	1.9.	0.5	–
Analysis of Investigation 2 by groups													
N	60.8*	39.2	86.6*	13.4	19.3*	26.2	54.6	59.4*	27.5	5.1	4.3	3.6	6
E	52.6*	47.4	86.6*	13.3	7.5*	12.5	80.0	33.3*	40.0	22.2	4.5	–	–
C	63.3*	36.7	96.7*	3.3	29.0*	25.8	45.2*	60.0	20.0	20.0	–	–	–

Note: P, prospective; R, retrospective. Error type: Om, Omission; Com, Commission. Directness: d, direct; m, mix of direct and indirect; i, indirect. Cause set size: from 1 to 6 causes. Investigation 1 (*n* = 4); Investigation 2 (*n* = 209). Groups: N, novices (*n* = 128); E, experts (*n* = 49); C, controls (*n* = 32). *Significant comparisons (*p* < .05); Chi squared > 3.84.

Investigation 1: Influences on the frequency of everyday memory failures

Forty-five undergraduates served in Investigation 1. Each participant recalled one failure and its causes. Table 13.2 presents the results for Investigation 1 in the top row of data in the table. These results include the percentage of failures of prospective and retrospective tasks, error type, directness of causes reported for the failures, and the number of causes reported per failure (called here the cause set size).[1]

The participants in this investigation reported more prospective failures than retrospective failures, although this difference was not significant. Far more failures were reported to involve an error of omission than an error of commission. More failures were also reported for cause sets that impair memory functioning directly or directly and indirectly than for cause sets that impair memory functioning indirectly only. Most failures were reported by participants to be due to one or two causes, but a few participants reported that their failures were due to as many as six causes.

Across the forty-five participants, twenty-five causes were reported as responsible for memory failure. Table 13.3 shows the proportion of failures for the eight most common causes as a function of failures of prospective or retrospective tasks and of errors of omission and commission. Inspection of the table shows that some causes led to the same proportion of prospective errors as retrospective errors. However, other causes were clearly associated more with a prospective errors (e.g., "vanished cue") or with a retrospective task (e.g., "insufficient encoding"). Similarly, some causes were implicated primarily in errors of omission (e.g., "preoccupied") whereas other causes were implicated in an error of commission (e.g., "change of context"). The table also suggests that indirect causes and direct causes were also associated with errors of commission and omission. Finally, the indirect causes shown in Table 13.3 were involved more with retrospective failures than prospective failures.

Investigation 2: An attempt to replicate the results of Investigation 1

Two-hundred nine participants, comprising a more heterogeneous group, served in Investigation 2 (Fiore, Shooler, Whiteside, & Herrmann, 1997). This

---

1 Investigation 1 and 2 each employed five independent variables. We conducted a complete analysis, which included nine two-way tables, six three-way tables, five four-way tables, and one five-way table. Analyses that included error type, ranging from the three-way tables to the five-way table, did not permit a strong test of the interaction with error type in these tables because so few participants made errors of commission. Similarly, analyses that included directness and cause set size, including the four-way and five-way tables did not provide a strong test of interactions with directness because there were so few failures to indirect causes alone or because there were so few sets with sizes four, five, and six. Nevertheless, the first-, second-, and third-order tables presented here provide a good sense of how reports of everyday memory failures and their causes varied with the independent variables.

Table 13.3 Investigation 1: Proportion of failures per cause as a function of task characteristics and the top eight causes

Causes	P $n = 26$	R $n = 19$	O $n = 36$	C $n = 9$
Doing too many things at once (d)	73.1	73.6	80.6	44.4
Preoccupied (d)	34.6	26.3	36.1	11.1
Stress (i)	23.1	15.7	25.0	0
Vanished cue (d)	26.9	5.3	16.7	22.2
Insufficient encoding (d)	7.6	26.3	16.7	11.1
Fatigue (i)	11.5	21.0	11.1	33.3
Change in context (d)	11.5	15.8	8.3	33.3
Lack of sleep (i)	11.5	10.5	11.1	11.1

Note: P, prospective task; R, retrospective task. O, error of omission; C, error of commission. In parentheses: d, direct cause; i, indirect cause.

group included three subgroups, which differed in the amount of knowledge that they possessed about memory research. The analysis first addressed the responses of all the participants in order that the results of Investigation 1, based on a heterogeneous group, might be compared to another heterogeneous group. Later in the chapter we compare the responses of each of the three groups to one another.

Each participant reported a memory failure and the causes for it. As in Investigation 1, the analysis first examined whether the frequency of failure differed between retrospective and prospective tasks, errors of omission and commission, directness of causes, and the cause set size for the failures. These results are presented in the second row of data in Table 13.2.

This study obtained significantly more reports of prospective failures than retrospective failures. Significantly more failures were reported to have involved an error of omission than an error of commission. Direct causes were again regarded as responsible for a larger proportion of failures than mixed or indirect causes. Most failures were again reported to be due to one or two causes but a few failures were reportedly due to as many as six causes.

The causes were further analysed with regard to their nature and effect on memory failure. Over 100 causes were reported across the 209 failure reports in Investigation 2. To simplify the analysis of the cause reports, they were coded by two judges into eight cause categories (with 86% agreement on the classification of causes into cause categories). Table 13.4 presents the names of these categories. As with Investigation 1, the analysis in Investigation 2 found that the cause categories varied in the number of memory failures that the cause categories were reported to have caused. The cause categories that were implicated in the most memory failures may be presumed to disrupt memory processing more than the causes implicated in the least number of memory failures.

Table 13.4 Investigation 2: Proportion of failures per cause category as a function of task orientation, error type, and the directness of the causes

Causes	P *n* = 117	R *n* = 92	O *n* = 193	C *n* = 16
Inadequate cues (d)	12.8	11.1	17.5	0
Deviated from routine (d)	8.5	3.3	8.8	0
Poor rehearsal (d)	1.7	6.7	8.3	6.3
Interference (d)	0	10.0	5.2	12.5
Distraction (d)	40.2	24.4	32.2	43.8
Physical state (i)	7.7	14.4	10.4	6.3
Poor emotional state (i)	11.1	14.4	7.8	12.5
Motivational state (i)	19.7	15.6	13.0	18.8

Note: P, prospective task; R, retrospective task. O, error of omission; C, error of commission. In parentheses: d, direct cause; i, indirect cause.

The cause category that was reported to have disrupted memory the most was "distraction", which was the most common for both prospective and retrospective tasks. "Deviation from a routine" appears to have impaired prospective memory more than retrospective memory. Conversely, "interference" led to retrospective memory failure but not to prospective memory failure. Poor physical and emotional states appear to have affected retrospective memory performance more than prospective memory performance but the latter performance appears to be affected the most by motivational states.

Cause-specific reports were also evident in errors of omission and commission. For example, "inadequate cues" and "deviation from a routine" were reported to affect errors of omission only. The cause categories of "poor emotional state" and "poor motivational state" were more often reported to apply to errors of commission.

Comparison of results for Investigations 1 and 2

The results for task orientation, error type, directness of cause sets, and cause set sizes for Investigation 2 (Tables 13.2 and 13.4) closely resembled the results for these measures in Investigation 1 (Tables 13.2 and 13.3). Clearly the participants' reports in both investigations indicated that some causes exerted a somewhat different effect on different tasks (defined as prospective and retrospective). The different causes in both investigations tended to be associated with either errors of omission or commission. Both investigations found that direct causes led to more memory failures than indirect or mixed causes and both investigations found that most of the failures were attributed to one or two causes.

At first glance, the causes in Table 13.3 and the cause categories in Table 13.4 may seem to suggest that the causes in Investigation 1 differed from the those reported in Investigation 2. However, the causes shown for Investigation 1 may be seen to be subsumed by the cause categories of Investigation 2. For example, the cause of "doing too many things at once" in Investigation 1 belongs to the cause category of "distraction" in Investigation 2. The causes of "preoccupation, stress, fatigue, and lack of sleep" in Investigation 1 represent the cause category of "poor physical states" in Investigation 2. Also, the cause category of "inadequate cues" addresses the cause of "vanished cues" – as well as other cue problems. The cause category of "poor rehearsal" includes the cause of "insufficient encoding". Similarly, the cause category of "deviation from a routine" is consistent with the cause of "a change in context". Only the cause category of "interference" was not evident in the causes in Investigation 1.

Investigation 2 continued: An analysis of individual differences in cause reports

The third investigation consisted of an additional analysis of the data from Investigation 2 according to the differences in failure/cause recall of the three groups of participants that made up the sample in the second investigation. This analysis focused on whether reports of memory failure and their causes varied with individual differences in the amount of knowledge that a person had about memory: no knowledge (novices, i.e., undergraduates); extensive knowledge (memory experts); and no knowledge but same age as experts (controls). Recent research has indicated that memory expertise disposes experts to perform memory tasks differently from novices (Ericsson & Simon, 1980; Park, Smith, & Cavanaugh, 1986), providing a precedent for expecting expertise to be related to everyday memory failure. If memory knowledge affects a person's memory performance, it might be expected that novices and controls would report experiencing failure with smaller cause categories than reported by experts. Alternatively, if knowledge just disposes a person to notice more causes of failure, experts might be expected to focus their reports on causes consistent with memory theory. In addition, if novices report the same causes for their memory failures as are reported by experts and controls, then it could be concluded that scientific knowledge about memory is irrelevant to memory failures.

The number of participants in the three groups were as follows. The "novice" group consisted of undergraduates at the University of Pittsburgh ($n = 128$). The "expert" group consisted of memory experts (attendees at the 1994 Practical Aspects of Memory Conference; $n = 49$). A third group served as non-memory controls; the members of this group were comparable in age to the experts ($n = 32$). The data of these three groups originated from Investigation 2 wherein the data from the three groups were combined.

Differences in orientation, error type, directness and cause set size as a
function of knowledge of memory science

The third, fourth, and fifth data rows in Table 13.2 show that the failures of
all three groups involved more prospective than retrospective tasks, although
experts recalled somewhat fewer prospective failures and more retrospective
failures than the other two groups. The failures recalled by all three groups
involved more errors of omission than errors of commission. The novices
and control participants recalled more failures involving indirect causes than
did the experts. They also recalled more cause sets with just one cause than
did the experts.

Cause categories and the memory failures of novices, experts,
and controls

The first three columns of Table 13.5 show how the three groups differed
from each other in the proportion that they attributed their memory failures
to the eight cause categories. Novices reported "inadequate cues" as causes
less often than experts and novices. Experts reported being affected by "interference" more than novices or controls. Novices attributed their failures more
to indirect causes, "physical, emotional, and motivational states", than did
experts and controls. Comparison of the proportion in the first three columns
shows that experts and controls attributed the eight cause categories to their
failures similarly ($r = .989$, $df = 7$, $p < .01$). The proportions of the novices
and the experts, as well as the novices and the controls, did not agree as
strongly ($.715 < r < .752$, $df = 7$, $p < .01$).

The proportions of cause category attributions for the three groups were
fairly similar across prospective memory tasks and retrospective memory
tasks. Experts reported failing at retrospective tasks because of deviating
from a routine more than did novices and controls. The controls indicated
that the states affected failure the same way as novices for retrospective tasks
but more like experts in the prospective tasks. (A table comparable to
Table 13.5 was not developed for error types because there were too many
empty cells as a function of errors of commission.)

Discussion

Although experts attributed a substantial number of their failures to interference whereas novices and controls did not, it seems unlikely that experts are
confronted with more memory tasks susceptible to interference than are novices. Instead, it appears that expertise prepared experts to recognize the presence of interference when experiencing a memory failure more easily than
novices. Conversely, in comparison to the older experts and controls (who
were similar in age), the novices (who were younger than both groups) were
more likely to attribute their failures to taking poorer care of their physical,

Table 13.5 Investigation 2: Percentage of causes for prospective and retrospective memory failures by groups

Causes	Overall			Retrospective			Prospective		
	Nov $n = 128$	Exp $n = 49$	Con $n = 32$	Nov $n = 77$	Exp $n = 22$	Con $n = 19$	Nov $n = 51$	Exp $n = 27$	Con $n = 13$
Inadequate cues	7*	22	23	10	18	6	6	25	30
Deviated from routine	7	9	3	0	11	0	9	7	4
Poor rehearsal	4	3	6	7	4	13	2	0	0
Interference	2*	13	4	4	28	6	0	0	0
Distraction	33	33	37	25	21	31	36	44	46
Poor physical state	13*	4	10	17	4	18	11	7	4
Poor emotional state	16*	7	7	17	7	13	13	7	4
Poor motivational state	17*	9	10	20	7	13	23	10	12

Note: Direct cause categories include: inadequate cues; deviated from a routine; poor rehearsal; interference; and distraction. Indirect causes include: poor physical state; poor emotional state; and poor motivational state.
Nov, novices ($n = 128$); Exp, experts ($n = 49$); Con, controls ($n = 32$).
* Represents significant differences among the frequencies for Nov., Exp. and Con. Participants in the overall sample.

emotional, and motivational states than the older experts and controls. This difference is consistent with known differences in lifestyles of younger people versus older people (Petro, Herrmann, Burrows, & Moore, 1991).

General discussion

Summary

Setting aside the issue of differences in understanding memory, the present results indicate aspects of causation of memory failure that deserve consideration in the development of a theory of everyday memory.

Memory task orientation

As shown in Investigations 1 and 2, more failures were recalled that were prospective than retrospective. This result appears robust but its origin remains for future research. It is not clear whether prospective memory failures occur more often than retrospective memory failures or whether prospective memory failures are simply remembered better than retrospective memory failures because people find prospective memory failures more embarrassing or upsetting than retrospective memory failures.

Error types

As shown in Investigations 1 and 2, more failures involved errors of omission than errors of commission. Signal detection theory holds that the frequency of errors of omission and commission depends on both the strength of a memory and the pressures that motivate a person to report in a particular way (Gruneberg & Sykes, 1993). Another explanation of the frequency of error types is provided by the "Zeigarnik (1927) effect" in which uncompleted acts are registered better in memory than completed acts. Thus, errors of omission may be remembered better than errors of commission because errors of omission constitute uncompleted acts and errors of commission constitute completed acts.

Directness of causes

More memory failures in the present investigations involved direct causes than indirect causes. The report that memory performance is affected by indirect processes is consistent with previous findings (Herrmann & Parente, 1994; Herrmann & Plude, 1996; Herrmann, Plude, Yoder, & Mullin, 1999; Herrmann & Searleman, 1990; Mullin, Herrmann, & Searleman, 1993; Parente & Herrmann, 2003). Nevertheless, direct causes are usually more destructive (lead to failure more reliably) than indirect causes (Searleman & Herrmann, 1994).

Size of cause sets

The number of memory failures decreased as the size of cause sets increased. This result indicates that most memory failures are produced by just a few causes. More research is needed to determine how people derived their causes, although content analyses of the causes reported indicate that people report largely what they remember but sometimes infer that the failure must have been produced by a certain cause (Herrmann & Gruneberg, in press; Herrmann, Sheets, Gruneberg, & Torres, in press).

Relative destructiveness of causes

Investigation 1 found that the majority of memory failures were reportedly caused by being too busy, i.e., doing too many things at once. Being busy led to twice as many or more memory failures than any other cause. The least destructive cause was lack of sleep.

In Investigation 2, more memory failures were attributed to the cause category of "distraction", which was also reported to produce twice as many failures as any other cause category. "Poor rehearsal" was reported to be a cause of memory failure less often than any other cause category.

Accuracy of memory failure and cause reports

The preceding investigations demonstrated that, overall, several aspects of memory failure and their causes appeared reliable across Investigations 1 and 2, and across the three groups in Investigation 2. However, are these reports accurate?

A substantial literature indicates that people may be unable to generate accurate causes for their memory failures because they are poor at introspecting about cognitive processes in a variety of tasks (Nisbett & Wilson, 1977). Alternatively, there are several reasons for concluding that cause reports for particular failures may, nevertheless, be valid.

First, considerable research has shown that people are able to introspect accurately about cognitive processes under certain conditions (Schooler & Fiore, 1997; Smith & Miller, 1978). For example, cause reports are expected to be accurate if elicited while the behaviour occurs or shortly thereafter (Bowers, 1981; Ericsson & Simon, 1980; Smith & Miller, 1978; White, 1980). Certain processes are more likely to be consciously observed (Schooler & Fiore, 1997), such as when failing at a cognitive task in a way that is embarrassing or upsetting.

Second, recent investigations of ours have shown that selected memory failures of some people can be corroborated by another observer. For example, husbands and wives remember the details (e.g., where it occurred, time of day, others present) and the causes of their partner's memory failures with remarkable agreement, about 73% of details and causes reported by the husband or wife (Torres, Herrmann, Adams-Price, & Gruneberg, 2002; Herrmann et al., in press). Another study asked husbands and wives whether they and their spouse ever experienced each of ten common memory failures (e.g., forgetting chores, forgetting an appointment with the spouse). The agreement in these reports was substantial as well (about 70% which was well above chance; Herrmann, Sheets, Gruneberg, & Torres, 2002).

Similarly, room-mates reported on each other's memory failures over a four-day period. Each room-mate recorded his or her memory failures that occurred in a day; in the evening, the room-mates assessed whether they agreed with the perception of their memory failures. Ninety-nine per cent of self-reported failures were detected by the room-mate (Roesner, McCandless, Gruneberg, & Herrmann, 2000), confirming that the self-reported failure occurred. No doubt people do not watch each other for memory failures as the room-mates did in this study. Normally, many memory failures go unobserved by others but under some conditions the failures are observed and the reports made about them are sometimes extremely accurate.

Third, it should not be surprising that memory for memory failures is sometimes fairly accurate because memory for autobiographical memory in general tends to have good validity (McAdams, 2001; Pillimer, 1998, 2001; Rubin, 1986; Schacter, 1999; Schwarz & Sudman, 1994). In that everyday memory failures constitute autobiographical events, it seems reasonable that reports of memory failure should be relatively accurate.

Finally, even if people are unable to introspect on how they derive the causes of a memory failure, they still may be able to correctly identify some of the causes of the failure (Nisbett & Wilson, 1977). For example, a person may know that they were distracted from performing a memory task without being aware of the cognitive processes that enabled them to recognize the distraction. Distractions can be so salient that labelling them need not require a conscious process. Similarly, a person may realize that a memory failure was due to fatigue without being aware of the cognitive process that enabled them to attribute the failure to fatigue. Fatigue is sufficiently common that it is associated with impaired performance at many tasks, allowing the identification of fatigue as a cause of memory failure without a conscious memory process.

Of course, not all memory failure reports can be trusted. No one can be expected to remember every detail and every cause of even well-remembered failures. Some errors are to be expected in the recall of individual memory failures. Indeed, a person may not remember some memory failures at all. Nevertheless, if a person attempts to remember a memory failure that they already know occurred, the failure and cause report might understandably be fairly accurate.

As noted earlier in this chapter, reports about memory failures in general (such as are required by memory questionnaires) have generally been found to have poor validity (Cavanaugh et al., 1998; Herrmann, 1982, 1984, 1990; Hertzog et al., 2000; Zelinski, 1990). However, reports about memory failures in general are more difficult to make than to recall a particular memory failure and its causes. Reports about memory failures in general are difficult because they must be based on a person's memory for an indefinitely large number of attempts at a memory task. The recall of a particular memory failure is much easier than trying to estimate failure across a lifetime of memory failures. Thus, it may be the case that people can remember particular memory failures while being poor at recalling or judging their memory performance in general.

Accident investigation

The present results suggest that memory failure and cause reports may contribute to our understanding of memory failure in everyday life. The conclusion that memory failure reports are valid is also consistent with human factors psychology and standard procedures for accident investigation. Investigation of automobile accidents (Johns, 1976) and airplane accidents (Dekker, 2002; Jentsch, Barnett & Bowers, 1999; O'Hare, Wiggins, Batt, & Morrison, 1994; Perrow, 1984; Senders & Moray, 1991) routinely rely on a person's memory for an accident, including his or her own mistakes that led to the accident. Reports are not taken at face value; an accident investigator seeks corroboration with the operator's account of the accident, what other witnesses say occurred, and with physical evidence. Similarly, memory failure and cause reports should be interpreted in the light of the context of the failure and theories of memory.

Thus, the conclusion that people have little or no memory of their memory failures contradicts the wisdom and procedures of accident investigators. The present findings eliminate this conflict. It is possible that people accurately remember specific memory failures while not necessarily remembering their overall memory failures.

Memory improvement

In order to improve memory, people need first to determine what aspect of their typical memory performance they need to improve. Without such meta-cognitive knowledge, people would not be able to figure out what aspects of their memory needed improvement. The present results indicate that people can recognize what causes their memory difficulty, suggesting thereby how their memory might be improved (Parente & Herrmann, 2003; Searleman & Herrmann, 1994).

In addition, the present results suggest how people in general may avoid memory failure. Based on the present findings, people can avoid memory failures if society slows down and members of society take better care of themselves. Investigations 1 and 2 demonstrated that the most damaging things that a person can do to memory performance is to rush, to try to do two things at the same time, to not take good care of their physical and emotional health, and/or to not be motivated to perform a particular memory task. Thus, when you observe a person moving fast, in a hurry, looking fatigued or hassled, then stop that person and advise him or her to slow down and to take care of themselves, lest they forget something that is important. If that person is you, a psychologist who specializes in memory and cognition, it should be clearer yet what you have to do – and what you have to do to help others – to avoid memory failure.

Acknowledgement

The authors are grateful to many colleagues who provided suggestions about how to do this research and how to interpret the results, especially Adam Hoffman, Angel Torrez, Nicki Roesner, Steve McCandless, Virgil Sheets, and Carol Yoder.

References

Andrzejewski, S. J., Moore, C. M., Corvette, M., & Herrmann, D. (1991). Prospective-memory skill, *Bulletin of the Psychonomic Society, 29*, 304–306.

Baddeley, A. D. (1990). *Human memory: Theory and practice*. Boston, MA: Allyn & Bacon.

Bendiksen, M., & Bendiksen, I. (1992). A multidimensional intervention program for a solvent injured population. *Cognitive Rehabilitation, 10*, 20–27.

Bendiksen, M., & Bendiksen, I. (1996). Multi-modal memory rehabilitation for the toxic solvent injured population. In D. Herrmann, M. Johnson, C. McEvoy, C. Hertzog, & P. Hertel (Eds.), *Basic and applied memory research: New findings*. Hillsdale, NJ: Lawrence Erlbaum Associates, Inc.

Bowers, K. S. (1981). Knowing more than we can say leads to saying more than we can know: On being implicitly informed. In P. Magnusson (Ed.), *Toward a psychology of situations: An interactional perspective*. Hillsdale, NJ: Lawrence Erlbaum Associates, Inc.

Brandimonte, M. A., Einstein, G. O., & McDaniel, M. A. (Eds.) (1995). *Prospective memory: Theory and application*. Mahwah, NJ: Lawrence Erlbaum Associates, Inc.

Broadbent, D. E., Broadbent, H. P., & Jones, H. P. (1986). Performance correlates of self-reported cognitive failures and of obsessionality. *British Journal of Clinical Psychology, 25*, 285–299.

Broadbent, D. E., Cooper, P. E., Fitzgerald, P., & Parkes, K. R. (1982). Cognitive failures questionnaire (CFQ) and its correlates. *British Journal of Clinical Psychology, 21*, 1–16.

Brown, A. (2002). Mending your memory: [a review of] How to cure your memory failures by D. J. Herrmann & M. M. Gruneberg. *Applied Cognitive Psychology, 16*, 118–119.

Cavanaugh, J. C., Feldman, J. M., & Hertzog, C. (1998). Memory beliefs as social cognition: A reconceptualization of what memory questionnaires assess. *Review of General Psychology, 2*, 48–65.

Colgrove, F. W. (1899). Individual memories. *American Journal of Psychology, 10*, 228.

Davies, G. M., & Logie, R. (1993). *Memory in everyday life*. New York: North Holland.

Dekker, S. (2002). *The field guide to human error investigations*. Mahwah, NJ: Lawrence Erlbaum Associates, Inc.

Ericsson, K. A., & Simon, H. A. (1980). Verbal reports as data. *Psychological Review*, *87*, 215–251.

Fiore, S., Shooler, J., Whiteside, D., & Herrmann, D. (1997). *Perceived contribution of cues and mental states to prospective and retrospective memory failures*. Presented at the meeting for the Society for Research on Memory and Cognition, Toronto, July.

Gruneberg, M. M., & Sykes, R. N. (1993). The generalizability of confidence-accuracy studies in eyewitnessing. *Memory*, *1*, 185–190.

Harris, J. E. (1984). Remembering to do things: A forgotten topic. In J. E. Harris & P. E. Morris (Eds.), *Everyday memory, actions, and absent-mindedness* (pp. 71–92). London: Academic Press.

Herrmann, D. J. (1982). Know thy memory: The use of questionnaires to study and assess memory. *Psychological Bulletin*, *92*, 434–452.

Herrmann, D. J. (1984). Questionnaires about memory. In J. E. Harris & P. E. Morris (Eds.), *Everyday memory, actions and absent-mindedness* (pp. 133–152). London: Academic Press.

Herrmann, D. J. (1990). Self perceptions of memory performance. In W. K. Schaie, J. Rodin, & C. Schooler (Eds.), *Self-directedness and efficacy: Causes and effects throughout the life course*. Hillsdale, NJ: Lawrence Erlbaum Associates, Inc.

Herrmann, D., & Gruneberg, M. (1999). *How to cure your memory failures*. London: Cassell.

Herrmann, D., & Gruneberg, M. (in press). The causes and consequences of memory failures in the workplace and in everyday life. In W. Karwowski (Ed.) *International Encyclopedia of Ergonomics and Human Factors* (2nd ed.). Boca Raton, FL: CRC Press.

Herrmann, D., & Parente, R. (1994). A multi-modal approach to cognitive rehabilitation. *NeuroRehabilitation*, *4*, 133–142.

Herrmann, D., & Plude, D. (1996). Museum memory. In J. Falk & L. Dierking (Eds.), *Public institutions for personal learning: The long-term impact of museums*. Washington, DC: American Association of Museums.

Herrmann, D., Plude, D., Yoder, C., & Mullin, P. (1999). Cognitive processing and extrinsic psychological systems: A holistic model of cognition. *Zeitschrift für Psychologie*, *207*, 123–147.

Herrmann, D. J., & Searleman, A. (1990). The new multimodal approach to memory improvement. In G.H. Bower (Ed.), *The psychology of learning and motivation* (Vol. 26, pp. 175–205). San Diego, CA. Academic Press.

Herrmann, D., Sheets, V., Gruneberg, M., & Torres, R. (2002). *Accuracy of remembering memory failures*. Kansas City, KS: Psychonomic Society.

Herrmann, D., Sheets, V., Gruneberg, M., & Torres, R. (in press). Are self reports of memory failure accurate? *Applied Cognitive Psychology*.

Hertzog, C., Park, D. C., Morrell, R. W., & Martin, M. (2000). Ask and ye shall receive: Behavioural specificity in the accuracy of subjective memory complaints, *Applied Cognitive Psychology*, *14*, 257–275.

Jentsch, F., Barnett, J., & Bowers, C. A. (1999). Who is flying this plane anyway? What mishaps tell us about crew member role assignment and air crew situation awareness. *Human Factors*, *41*, 1–14.

Johns, C. T. (1976). *Taking statements*. Cincinnati, OH: National Underwriter Company.

Johnson, M. H. (1983). A multiple-entry, modular memory system. In G. H. Bower (Ed.), *The psychology of learning and and motivation* (Vol. 17, (pp. 81–123)). New York: Academic Press.

McAdams, D. P. (2001). The psychologies of life stories. *General Psychology, 5*, 100–122.

Mullin, P., Herrmann, D., & Searleman, A. (1993). Forgotten variables. *Memory, 1*, 43–64.

Nisbett, R. E., & Wilson, T. D. (1977). Telling more than we can know: Verbal reports on mental processes. *Psychological Review, 84*, 231–259.

O'Hare, D., Wiggins, M., Batt, R. & Morrison, D. (1994). Cognitive failure analysis for aircraft accident investigation. *Ergonomics, 7*, 1855–1869.

Parente, R., & Herrmann, D. (2003). *Retraining cognition*. Austin, TX: Pro-Ed.

Park, D., Smith, A., & Cavanaugh, J. (1986). Metamemories of memory researchers. *Memory and Cognition, 18*, 321–327.

Perrow, C. (1984). *Normal accidents: Living with high-risk technologies*. New York: Basic Books.

Petro, S., Herrmann, D., Burrows, D., & Moore, C. (1991). Usefulness of commercial memory aids as a function of age. *International Journal of Aging and Human Development, 33*, 295–309.

Pillimer, D. B. (1998). *Momentous events, vivid memories*. Cambridge, MA: Harvard University Press.

Pillimer, D. B. (2001). Momentous events and life story. *General Psychology, 5*, 123–134.

Reason, J. T. (1984). Absent-mindedness and cognitive control. In J. Harris & P. Morris (Eds.), *Everyday memory, actions and absent-mindedness* (pp. 113–132). London: Academic Press.

Reason, J. T. (1988). Stress and cognitive failure. In S. Fisher & J. Reason (Eds.), *Handbook of life stress, cognition and health*. Chichester, UK: Wiley.

Reason, J. T. (1990). *Human error*. Cambridge: Cambridge University Press.

Roesner, N., McCandless, S., Gruneberg, M., & Herrmann, D. (2000) *Assessment of the frequency of everyday memory failures*. Indiana Academy of Sciences, Anderson, Indiana, April.

Rubin, D. (1986). *Autobiographical memory*. Cambridge, MA: Cambridge University Press.

Schacter, D. L. (1999). The seven sins of memory: Insights from psychology and cognitive neuroscience. *American Psychologist, 54*, 182–203.

Schooler, J. W., & Fiore, S. M. (1997). Consciousness and the limits of language: You can't always say what you think or think what you say. In J. D. Cohen & J. Schooler, (Eds.), *Scientific approaches to consciousness*. Mahwah, NJ: Lawrence Erlbaum Associates, Inc.

Schwarz, N., & Sudman, S. (1994). *Autobiographical memory and the validity of retrospective reports*. New York: Springer Verlag.

Searleman, A., & Herrmann, D. J. (1994). *Memory from a broader perspective*. New York: McGraw-Hill.

Senders, J., & Moray, N. (1991). *Human error: Cause prediction and reduction*. Hillsdale, NJ: Lawrence Erlbaum Associates, Inc.

Smith, E. R., & Miller, F. D. (1978). Limits on perception of cognitive processes: A reply to Nisbett and Wilson. *Psychological Review, 85*, 355–362.

Terry, W. S. (1984). A "forgetting journal" for memory courses. *Teaching of Psychology, 11*, 111–112.

Torres, R., Herrmann, D., Adams-Price, C., & Gruneberg, M. (2002). *Accuracy of remembering memory failures: Spouse agreement.* Chicago, IL: Midwestern Psychological Association.

White, P. (1980). Limitations on verbal reports of internal events: A refutation of Nisbett and Wilson and Bem. *Psychological Review, 87*, 105–112.

Williams, S., & Gruneberg, M. (2002). Memory failures in supermarket shoppers: Evidence for age and gender differences. *Cognitive Technology, 7*, 34–38.

Zeigarnik, B. (1927). Uber das Behalten von erledigten und unnerledigten Handlungen. *Psychologische Forschung, 9*, 1–85.

Zelinski, E. M. (1990). Memory functioning questionnaire: Concurrent validity with memory performance and self-reported memory failures. *Psychology & Aging, 5*, 388–399.

14   Rehabilitation of memory for everyday life

Barbara A. Wilson

Introduction

The main goal of rehabilitation is to enable people disabled by injury or disease to return to their own most appropriate environment. Memory rehabilitation should also follow this principle and focus on real-life problems rather than experimental material. Although people with memory impairments and their families should not be led to believe that significant improvement in memory can occur once the period of natural recovery is over, they can, nevertheless, be helped to manage, cope with or bypass problems arising from such impairment.

Successful memory rehabilitation will go beyond the understanding, assessment and treatment of the memory difficulties to cover a range of associated problems and individual needs. People with organic memory deficits will come to rehabilitation with: (a) a pre-morbid lifestyle; (b) a social network; (c) hopes and expectations; and (d) possible additional problems such as further cognitive problems, emotional difficulties and psychosocial problems. All these need to be addressed as part of the rehabilitation programme. Consequently, rehabilitation providers need to be aware of a number of theoretical and methodological influences that impact on the design of treatment to reduce everyday memory difficulties.

Imagine that a brain-injured person has been referred to you (and your team) for help with memory problems. Where does one start and what does one do?

Planning a memory rehabilitation programme

When first seeing someone who requires memory therapy, it is probably best to start by formally interviewing the person and one or more of their relatives. It may also be helpful to interview therapists or others who know and have worked with the memory-impaired person. In addition to information about the precipitating illness or accident and resultant problems as manifested in real life, it is useful to find out about pre-morbid lifestyle, likes and dislikes, and what the patient and family hope to achieve as a result of

memory rehabilitation. The Brain Injury Community Rehabilitation Outcomes (Powell, Beckers, & Greenwood, 1998) and the European Brain Injury
Questionnaire (Teasdale et al., 1997) both attempt to identify pre- and
post-morbid characteristics of people with brain injury – so these tests can be
administered during the first or second interviews to provide additional
information.

Following the initial interview, it may be necessary to explain to the patient
and the family that although we are unable to restore or retrain lost memory
functioning, there may well be actions that we can take to help them manage
their everyday problems more successfully. What actions we take will depend
on a number of factors including the nature, extent and severity of the brain
damage, the presence or absence of additional cognitive and emotional
impairments, the current social and vocational situation and the environmental demands of the patient's lifestyle. Each of these factors will need to be
assessed.

The nature, extent and severity of brain damage may be available from
hospital notes and referral forms. Neurological investigations and results
from imaging studies may be available or it may be possible to request further
investigations.

Neuropsychological investigations can identify the pattern of cognitive
strengths and weaknesses (see Wilson, 2004), for a more detailed discussion of
assessment of memory and other cognitive functions). It is also important to
assess emotional well-being and identify any psychosocial and behavioural or
conduct difficulties. One should also bear in mind whether or not further
recovery is likely to take place as this may confound any changes seen in
rehabilitation. This is particularly likely when people are seen in the early
days, weeks or months after an insult. The cause of the brain damage is also
relevant as, for example, people with encephalitis may reach their maximum
level of recovery well before someone with a traumatic brain injury.

In addition to this background information one needs to identify the current everyday problems as these are the ones that will become the focus of the
rehabilitation efforts. Not only do we need to draw on different models
(models of cognitive functioning, emotion, behavioural and psychosocial
functioning), we also need to carry out a more direct assessment of everyday
problems through observations, rating scales, checklists and other measures.
This information can be combined with information from standardized tests
to help delineate the real-life practical problems to be tackled.

Implementing a memory rehabilitation programme

By the time all the previous investigations have been carried out, one may
have some idea of which particular goals to consider for the individual
patient and his or her family. Goals should be negotiated between patient,
family and staff members. Goal planning is increasingly used in rehabilitation
centres and would appear to be a sensitive and sensible way to carry out

cognitive rehabilitation. It is simple, focuses on practical, everyday problems, is tailored to the needs of individuals and includes a measure of outcome that avoids the artificial distinction between many outcome measures and real-life functioning.

Goal planning has been used in rehabilitation for many years with a number of diagnostic groups including people with brain injury, learning difficulties, spinal injuries and cerebral palsy (McMillan & Sparkes, 1999).

Houts and Scott (1975) stated five principles of goal planning, namely: (1) involve the patient; (2) set reasonable goals; (3) describe the patient's behaviour when a goal is reached; (4) set a deadline; and (5) spell out the method so that anyone reading it would know what to do. McMillan and Sparkes (1999) expand on this. They suggest that there should be long-term and short-term goals. Long-term goals usually refer to disabilities and handicaps as rehabilitation should improve day-to-day functioning and these goals should be achievable by the time of discharge from the centre. Short-term goals are the steps required to achieve the long-term goals. McMillan and Sparkes add to the principles of Houts and Scott (1975) by saying that goals should: (a) be client centred; (b) be realistic and potentially attainable during admission; (c) be clear and specific; (d) have a definite time deadline; and (e) be measurable.

The process of a goal-planning approach involves allocation of a chairperson, formulation of a plan of assessment, goal-planning meetings, drawing up of a problem list, and plans of action recording whether or not goals are achieved, and if not, why not. Wilson, Evans and Keohane (2002) describe a successful goal-planning approach for a man with both a head injury and a stroke.

Specific goals for a brain-injured person with significant memory difficulties might include the following:

1 Develop an awareness of strengths and weaknesses in a written form consistent with the neuropsychological profile (the written account to be rated by a relative and members of the staff team).
2 Use an electronic organizer and a voice organizer to plan activities and record telephone conversations.
3 Describe how the memory problems would impact on social, domestic and work situations (again the description would be rated for accuracy by a relative and members of the staff team).
4 Be able to manage own financial affairs independently.
5 Demonstrate competence in work skills (as rated by a work colleague).
6 Develop a range of leisure interests.
7 Learn breathing and relaxation exercises to reduce anxiety.

Each long-term goal would be achieved by a series of weekly (or fortnightly) short-term goals. For example, a patient described by Wilson, Evans and Williams, (in press) was helped to achieve goal number 5 by first shadowing colleagues at work. He then discussed work problems with these colleagues before carrying out "minimal risk" tasks. He gradually undertook more demanding tasks at work with his manager checking each decision. Finally, the man was given full responsibility and returned to the company's pay roll. At each stage, the memory strategies learned in goal 2 were implemented. Goal 1, developing an awareness of his strengths and weaknesses, was achieved by education about the nature of memory and the problems that may exist after brain injury. The young man attended groups about "understanding brain injury" and "memory" with handouts and summaries for him to keep. He was given feedback about his assessments and asked to keep a diary of his memory errors. If necessary he was prompted to record these errors. Seven months after starting the rehabilitation programme, the young man was back on the pay roll and has remained in employment for over two years.

Strategies for reducing everyday memory problems

There are numerous strategies that one can employ to achieve the rehabilitation goals. Before discussing some specific strategies if might be helpful to discuss some general guidelines.

General guidelines for use in memory rehabilitation

In 1991, Berg, Koning-Haanstra, and Deelman (1991) described a memory group in the Netherlands. The participants were told, "Try to accept that a deficient memory cannot be cured: make a more efficient use of your remaining capacities; use external aids when possible; pay more attention; spend more time; repeat; make associations; organise; link input and retrieval situations" (p. 101). These general guidelines were given to brain-injured people in the form of a textbook illustrated with examples. In addition, participants tackled real-life problems in their sessions and were given homework to enable them to practice and rehearse the strategies that they were taught. For each participant about three real-life problems were selected and worked on in an 18-session therapy programme. In the short term, participants in the memory rehabilitation group did better than those in the control group although a follow-up four years later showed that the control group had caught up (Milders, Berg, & Deelman, 1995)

The advantage of general strategy training is that it enables memory-impaired people to deal with whatever difficulties come their way. Ideally, of course, this is what all of us in memory rehabilitation would like. In practice, we may need to set our sights a little lower particularly for those clients who have more widespread cognitive difficulties (say memory, attention, planning and organizational problems) or who are so severely impaired that it is difficult to teach them to remember to apply a strategy.

There are general guidelines that psychologists, therapists, family members and others can apply to help memory-impaired people take in, store and retrieve information more successfully. While these guidelines will not solve memory problems, they may improve or ease situations for those with impaired memory functioning. These guidelines are the result of theoretical experiments to determine whether the amnesic syndrome is due to a deficit of (a) encoding, or (b) storage, or (c) retrieval. Although accounts that explain amnesia as a failure in only one of these processes are insufficient in themselves, experiments trying to prove or disprove these views have provided us with a number of useful pointers.

People are more likely to encode (i.e., take in) information efficiently if:

- The information is simplified (it is easier to remember short words than long words and jargon should be avoided).
- They are required to remember one thing at a time (do not present three or four names/instructions/words at once).
- The information is understood (ask the memory-impaired person to repeat the information back in his or her own words to check for understanding).
- The information is linked or associated with something already known (for example, when trying to remember my name – Barbara – I check if they have an Aunt Barbara, or it they know the song "Barbara Allen" or the film star Barbra Streisand).
- The little and often or distributed practice rule is followed (present the new information frequently but with breaks in-between each presentation).
- The information is processed or manipulated in some way (don't let your memory-impaired clients be passive recipients of the information, instead ask them to think about it, question it, do something with it, to ensure that they process the information).

Once the information is encoded, it has to be stored. Rehearsal, practice and testing can all be used to try to ensure that the information remains in storage. The method known as "spaced retrieval" (also called "expanding rehearsal") is a good testing procedure to follow. Present the information, test immediately, test again after a very brief delay and so forth. The retention interval is gradually increased.

Another problem, faced at times by all of us, is retrieving the information from memory when it is required. Some memory-impaired people seem to have particular problems with retrieval. If we can provide a hook in the form of a cue or prompt, they may be able to retrieve the information more readily. The first letter of a word or name to be recalled, can be a powerful retrieval cue. The problem here, of course, is that someone needs to be available to provide the first letter. Some people, including some memory-impaired people, can systematically go through the alphabet to try to find their own first letter cue. Even for these people, however, the system is haphazard and unreliable.

Perhaps the best way to improve retrieval is to avoid context specificity, i.e., if material is learned in one situation, it is recalled better in the same situation (Godden & Baddeley, 1975; Watkins, Ho, & Tulving, 1976). Most of us will have experienced this phenomenon. You may, for example, know a work colleague very well and be able to greet him or her by name at work without a second thought. However, if you meet that colleague at a swimming pool or theatre the name may become inaccessible because of the change of context. In rehabilitation it is not uncommon to find clients who use a memory aid in occupational therapy but do not use it elsewhere, or who can tell you the name of their speech therapist in the language sessions but not elsewhere. The answer here is to avoid such context-specific learning by teaching the use of the memory aid not only in occupational therapy but in a number of other situations too. Similarly, the speech therapist will need to be met and interacted with in other settings.

Another general guideline when working with severely memory-impaired people is to avoid trial-and-error learning. As errorless learning is such a large part of current memory rehabilitation, it deserves a section to itself and will be discussed at some length later.

Specific strategies in memory rehabilitation

Environmental adaptations

One of the simplest ways to help people with memory impairment is to arrange the environment so that they rely less on memory. Examples include using written labels or drawings for cupboards in the kitchen or bedroom as reminders of where things are kept; positioning objects so that they cannot be missed or forgotten (for instance taping a timetable to a wheelchair or painting the toilet door a distinctive colour so that it is easier to find). Sometimes changing the wording of our questions or comments can reduce problems. For example, CW, a former musician, became densely amnesic following encephalitis. He frequently thinks he has just woken up and says, "This is the first time I've been awake. I don't remember you coming into this room but now I'm awake" (or words to that effect). Sympathizing with him, or offering explanations, seems to increase his agitation and causes escalation of the number of repetitions he makes about awakening. One partial solution is to distract him by introducing another topic of conversation or asking him a question about music. Such a ploy can also be viewed as an environmental adaptation, although in this case it is the verbal rather than the physical environment that is being modified.

For people with severe intellectual deficits, or progressive deterioration, or extremely dense amnesia, environmental adaptations may be the best we can offer to enable them and their families or carers to cope, and to reduce some of the frustration and confusion associated with their conditions.

Improving learning in memory-impaired people

One of the greatest handicaps for memory-impaired people is their inability to learn new information. In recent years a number of studies have been carried out to investigate errorless learning in memory rehabilitation. Error-less learning is a teaching strategy whereby people are prevented, as far as possible, from making mistakes while they are learning a new skill or acquiring new information. Instead of teaching by demonstration, which may involve the learner in trial and error, the experimenter or teacher presents the correct information or procedure in ways that minimize the possibility of erroneous responses.

There are two theoretical backgrounds influencing errorless learning work with cognitively impaired people. The first is errorless discrimination learning from behavioural psychology, developed by Terrace (1963, 1966) in his work with pigeons, and later used with people with severe learning difficulties (Sidman & Stoddard, 1967). The second influence is from studies of implicit learning in amnesic subjects, (Brooks & Baddeley, 1976), showing that people with amnesia can learn some information normally although they may have no conscious recollection (explicit recall) that they have previously engaged in the task.

Building on these two strands of research we posed the question, "Do amnesic subjects learn better when prevented from making errors during the learning process?" In one group study and several single-case studies (Baddeley & Wilson, 1994; Wilson, Baddeley, Evans, & Shiel, 1994) it was demonstrated that people with severe memory disorders learn more success-fully with an errorless learning strategy. Others have adapted this strategy for people with non-progressive brain injury (Squires, Hunkin, & Parkin, 1997) and recently we have used errorless learning procedures with patients who have Alzheimer's disease (Clare, Wilson, Carter, Breen, Gosses, & Hodges, 2000; Wilson, Carter, Hodges, & Adams, 2001). All patients benefited to a greater or lesser degree and were able to learn some useful everyday information.

Compensating for memory loss

Much of the work in memory rehabilitation involves teaching people to compensate for their impairments by employing aids such as diaries, tape recorders, organizers, computers, and other similar items. These external memory aids are probably the most useful devices for helping memory-impaired people and they are likely to be used more by them in the long run (Wilson & Watson, 1996). Despite their value, it is not always easy to persuade patients to use compensatory strategies. Some feel that it is cheating and believe that they should not rely on such aids; others feel that such devices will reduce the chances of natural recovery occurring; and others simply forget to use them or may use them in a disorganized manner. After all, remembering to use a compensation is in itself a memory task. Despite these difficulties, some memory-impaired people use compensatory aids and strategies very efficiently. Kime, Lamb, and Wilson (1996) describe a young amnesic woman who was able to get back to paid employment once she had been taught to use a comprehensive system of external aids. Wilson, C., & Hughes (1997a) describe the 10-year natural history of a compensatory memory system devised by a young man who became amnesic following the rupture of a posterior cerebral artery aneurysm. Using results from a long-term follow-up study, Wilson and Watson (1996) made some predictions as to which people were more likely to use compensatory aids effectively and which were not. Age, absence of additional cognitive deficits, and scoring above floor level on a test of everyday memory were all predictors of independence and the use of aids.

Other work looking at how to help memory-impaired people compensate involves the use or modification of new technology (Kapur, Thompson, Cook, Lang, & Brice, 1996). One fairly recent development that appears to help people with a wide range of conditions and degrees of memory impairment is NeuroPage® (Hersh & Treadgold, 1994), which is a simple and portable paging system with a screen that can be attached to a belt. It utilizes an arrangement of microcomputers linked to a conventional computer memory and, by telephone, to a paging company to produce a programmable messaging system. The scheduling of reminders or cues for each individual is entered into the computer and from then on no further human interfacing is required. On the appropriate date and time NeuroPage® accesses the user's data files and transmits the appropriate information by modem to a terminal where the reminder is converted and transmitted to the receiver corresponding to the particular user. The reminder is graphically displayed on the screen of the receiver. NeuroPage® is easy to use and avoids many of the problems inherent in other external aids. It is highly portable, has an audible alarm that can be adapted to vibrate if required, together with an accompanying explanatory message, and rather than being embarrassing to use, it is more likely to be seen as conveying prestige. In a pilot study (Wilson, Evans, Emslie, & Malinek, 1997b) the average number of target behaviours achieved by 15 people during a 2- to 6-week baseline was 37%. Once the pager was provided (for a 12-week period) the average number of targets achieved rose to over 85%. A later randomized control study with 143 people confirmed that NeuroPage® significantly reduces the everyday memory and planning problems of people with organic impairment (Wilson, Emslie, Quirk, & Evans, 2001). Other electronic aids may also be of considerable help for memory impaired people (Wright et al., 2001; Wright et al., 2001).

*Managing anxiety and other emotional sequelae resulting from
impaired cognition*

Anxiety and depression are frequently seen in memory-impaired people. Kopelman and Crawford (1996) found depression in over 40% of 200 consecutive referrals to a memory clinic. Evans and Wilson (1992) found anxiety to be common in attenders of a weekly memory group. Dealing with these emotional problems should be an integral part of memory rehabilitation. Obviously, listening, trying to understand, and providing information are key factors in encouraging families to cope with their difficulties. Wearing (1992) provides a helpful reference on the problems faced by families of memory-impaired people, and makes suggestions as to what can be done to help. Providing information or explanations is one very simple and therapeutic strategy that can help reduce the fear and anxiety accompanying memory impairment. Written information is best, as most people, whether memory impaired or not, are unlikely to have good recall of information at times of stress. *Memory problems after head injury* (Wilson, 1989) written for the National Head Injuries Association; *Managing your memory* (Kapur, 1991); and *Coping with memory problems* (Clare & Wilson, 1997), are all useful publications to have available for patients and their relatives.

In addition to providing information, it may be necessary to offer therapy for anxiety and depression. Relaxation therapy can be helpful in reducing anxiety, even if memory problems are severe enough to prevent a participant from remembering the actual therapy sessions. Depression, too, may exacerbate difficulties in people with organic memory impairment. It is possible that cognitive behavioural therapy approaches such as those employed by Beck (1976), might be appropriate for those with depression associated with organic memory impairment, although no studies appear to have been reported. Psychotherapy, on the other hand, is a well-established intervention for patients with neurological damage. Prigatano (1999), firmly believes in group and individual psychotherapy with brain-injured clients. Jackson and Gouvier (1992), provide descriptions and guidelines for group psychotherapy with brain-injured adults and their families.

Other groups for memory-impaired people can be useful in reducing social isolation, which is also common in people with memory problems (Wearing, 1992). Wilson and Moffat (1992) describe several kinds of groups for patients. Moffat (1989) reports on a relatives' memory group for people with dementia, and Wearing (1992) offers suggestions for setting up self-help groups. Evans and Wilson (1992) point out the social value of memory groups as well as their effect in reducing anxiety.

Summary and conclusions

This chapter has been concerned with the rehabilitation of people with memory difficulties. Rehabilitation is taken to mean enabling people to achieve their optimum level of functioning and return to their most appropriate environment. It does not have, as a major concern, the improvement of scores on tests.

If recovery is taken to include partial resolution of cognitive deficits then some recovery is to be expected after non-progressive brain injury. Most memory-impaired people show relatively little recovery once the early stages are passed, although most learn to adapt to and compensate for their problems – at least to some extent.

There are some general strategies that can be taught to memory-impaired people and their families or carers. These include guidelines to enable people to encode, store and retrieve information more effectively. In addition to these general guidelines, more-specific techniques are considered, particularly environmental adaptions, ways to improve learning such as "errorless learning" and compensations for memory impairment including electronic memory aids.

The final section addresses the emotional consequences of memory impairment. Anxiety, depression and social isolation are common in people with memory difficulties, they may be as handicapping as the cognitive deficits themselves and should be part of any memory rehabilitation programme.

Although we probably cannot restore memory functioning to the level present before the neurological insult, we can reduce the effects of impaired memory on everyday life and can improve quality of life for clients and their families.

References

Baddeley, A. D., & Wilson, B. A. (1994). When implicit learning fails: Amnesia and the problem of error elimination. *Neuropsychologia, 32*, 53–68.

Beck, A. T. (1976). *Cognitive therapy and emotional disorders.* New York: International Universities Press.

Berg, I. J., Koning-Haanstra, M., & Deelman, B. G. (1991). Long term effects of memory rehabilitation: A controlled study. *Neuropsychological Rehabilitation, 1*, 97–111.

Brooks, D. N., & Baddeley, A. D. (1976). What can amnesic patients learn? *Neuropsychologia, 14*, 111–122.

Clare, L., & Wilson, B. A. (1997). *Coping with memory problems: A practical guide for people with memory impairments, relatives, friends and carers.* Bury St Edmunds, UK: Thames Valley Test Company.

Clare, L., Wilson, B. A., Carter, G., Breen, E. K., Gosses, A., & Hodges, J. R. (2000). Intervening with everyday memory problems in dementia of Alzheimer type: An errorless learning approach. *Journal of Clinical and Experimental Neuropsychology, 22*, 132–146.

Clare, L., Wilson, B. A., Carter, G., Hodges, J. R., & Adams, M. (2001). Long-term maintenance of treatment gains following a cognitive rehabilitation intervention in early dementia of Alzheimer type: A single case study. *Neuropsychological Rehabilitation, 11*, 477–494.

Evans, J. J., & Wilson, B. A. (1992). A memory group for individuals with brain injury. *Clinical Rehabilitation*, *6*, 75–81.

Godden, D., & Baddeley, A. D. (1975). Context-dependent memory in two natural environments: On land and under water. *British Journal of Psychology*, *66*, 325–331.

Hersh, N., & Treadgold, L. (1994). NeuroPage: The rehabilitation of memory dysfunction by prosthetic memory and cueing. *NeuroRehabilitation*, *4*, 187–197.

Houts, P. S., & Scott, R. A. (1975). *Goal planning with developmentally disabled persons: Procedures for developing an individualized client plan.* Hershey, PA: Department of Behavioral Science, Pennsylvania State University College of Medicine.

Jackson, W. T., & Gouvier, W. D. (1992). Group psychotherapy with brain-damaged adults and their families. In C. J. Long & L. K. Ross (Eds.), *Handbook of head trauma: Acute care to recovery* (pp. 309–327). New York: Plenum Press.

Kapur, N. (1991). *Managing your memory: A self help memory manual for improving everyday memory skills.* Available from the author at the Wessex Neurological Centre, Southampton General Hospital, Southampton, UK.

Kapur, N., Thompson, S., Cook, P., Lang, D., & Brice, J. (1996). Anterograde but not retrograde memory loss following combined mammillary body and medial thalamic lesions. *Neuropsychologia*, *34*, 1–8.

Kime, S. K., Lamb, D. G., & Wilson, B. A. (1996). Use of a comprehensive program of external cuing to enhance procedural memory in a patient with dense amnesia. *Brain Injury*, *10*, 17–25.

Kopelman, M., & Crawford, S. (1996). Not all memory clinics are dementia clinics. *Neuropsychological Rehabilitation*, *6*, 187–202.

McMillan, T., & Sparkes, C. (1999). Goal planning and neurorehabilitation: The Wolfson Neurorehabilitation Centre approach. *Neuropsychological Rehabilitation*, *9*, 241–251.

Milders, M. V., Berg, I. J., & Deelman, B. G. (1995). Four-year follow-up of a controlled memory training study in closed head injured patients. *Neuropsychological Rehabilitation*, *5*, 223–238.

Moffat, N. (1989). Home based cognitive rehabilitation with the elderly. In L. W. Poon, D. C. Rubin, & B. A. Wilson (Eds.), *Everyday cognition in adulthood and late life* (pp. 659–680). Cambridge: Cambridge University Press.

Powell, J. H., Beckers, K., & Greenwood, R. (1998). The measurement of progress and outcome in community rehabilitation after brain injury: Towards improved outcome. *Archives of Physical Medicine and Rehabilitation*, *79*, 1213–1225.

Prigatano, G. P. (1999). *Principles of neuropsychological rehabilitation.* New York: Oxford University Press.

Sidman, M., & Stoddard, L. T. (1967). The effectiveness of fading in programming simultaneous form discrimination for retarded children. *Journal of Experimental Analysis of Behavior*, *10*, 3–15.

Squires, E. J., Hunkin, N. M., & Parkin, A. J. (1997). Errorless learning of novel associations in amnesia. *Neuropsychologia*, *35*, 1103–1111.

Teasdale, T. W., Christensen, A.-L., Wilmes, K., Deloche, G., Braga, L., Stachowiak, F., Vendrell, J. M., Castro-Caldas, A., Laaksonen, R. K., & Leclercq, M. (1997). Subjective experience in brain-injured patients and their close relatives: A European Brain Injury Questionnaire study. *Brain Injury*, *11*, 543–563.

Terrace, H. S. (1963). Discrimination learning with and without "errors". *Journal of Experimental Analysis of Behavior*, *6*, 1–27.

Terrace, H. S. (1966). Stimulus control. In W. K. Honig (Ed.), *Operant behavior: Areas of research and application* (pp. 271–344). New York: Appleton-Century-Crofts.

Watkins, M. J., Ho, E., & Tulving, E. (1976). Context effects in recognition memory for faces. *Journal of Verbal Learning and Verbal Behavior*, *15*, 505–517.

Wearing, D. (1992). Self help groups. In B. A. Wilson & N. Moffat (Eds.), *Clinical management of memory problems* (2nd ed., pp. 271–301). London: Chapman & Hall.

Wilson, B. A. (1989). *Memory problems after head injury*. Nottingham, UK: National Head Injuries Association.

Wilson, B. A. (2004). Assessment of memory disorders. In A. D. Baddeley, M. D. Kopelman, & B. A. Wilson (Eds.), *The essential handbook of memory disorders for clinicians* (pp. 159–178). Chichester, UK: Wiley.

Wilson, B. A., Baddeley, A. D., Evans, J. J., & Shiel, A. (1994). Errorless learning in the rehabilitation of memory impaired people. *Neuropsychological Rehabilitation*, *4*, 307–326.

Wilson, B. A., C., J., & Hughes, E. (1997a). Coping with amnesia: The natural history of a compensatory memory system. In A. J. Parkin (Ed.), *Case studies in the neuropsychology of memory* (pp. 179–190). Hove, UK: Psychology Press.

Wilson, B. A., Emslie, H. C., Quirk, K., & Evans, J. J. (2001). Reducing everyday memory and planning problems by means of a paging system: A randomised control crossover study. *Journal of Neurology, Neurosurgery and Psychiatry*, *70*, 477–482.

Wilson, B. A., Evans, J. J., Emslie, H., & Malinek, V. (1997b). Evaluation of NeuroPage: A new memory aid. *Journal of Neurology, Neurosurgery and Psychiatry*, *63*, 113–115.

Wilson, B. A., Evans, J. J., & Keohane, C. (2002). Cognitive rehabilitation: A goal-planning approach. *Journal of Head Trauma Rehabilitation*, *17*(6), 542–555.

Wilson, B. A., Evans, J. J., & Williams, H. (in press). Memory problems. In A. D. Tyerman (Ed.), *Rehabilitation after traumatic brain injury: A psychological approach*. Leicester, UK: The British Psychological Society.

Wilson, B. A., & Moffat, N. (1992). The development of group memory therapy. In B. A. Wilson & N. Moffat (Eds.), *Clinical management of memory problems* (2nd ed., pp. 243–273). London: Chapman & Hall.

Wilson, B. A., & Watson, P. C. (1996). A practical framework for understanding compensatory behaviour in people with organic memory impairment. *Memory*, *4*, 465–486.

Wright, P., Rogers, N., Hall, C., Wilson, B., Evans, J., & Emslie, H. (2001). Enhancing an appointment diary on a pocket computer for use by people after brain injury. *International Journal of Rehabilitation Research*, *24*, 299–308.

Wright, P., Rogers, N., Hall, C., Wilson, B. A., Evans, J. J., Emslie, H., & Bartram, C. (2001). Comparison of pocket-computer aids for people with brain injury. *Brain Injury*, *15*, 787–800.

Author index

Subject index